FINANCIAL ANALYSIS AND DECISION MAKING

FINANCIAL ANALYSIS AND DECISION MAKING

Tools and Techniques to Solve Financial Problems and Make Effective Business Decisions

DAVID E. VANCE, MBA, CPA, JD

McGraw-Hill

New York   Chicago   San Francisco   Lisbon   London   Madrid
Mexico City   Milan   New Delhi   San Juan   Seoul
Singapore   Sydney   Toronto

1 2 3 4 5 6 7 8 9 0   AGM/AGM   0 9 8 7 6 5 4 3 2

ISBN 0-07-140665-4

This publication is designed to provide accurate and authoritative information in regard
to the subject matter covered. It is sold with the understanding that neither the author
nor the publisher is engaged in rendering legal, accounting, futures/securities trading, or
other professional service. If legal advice or other expert assistance is required, the
services of a competent professional person should be sought.
—From a Declaration of Principles jointly adopted by a Committee
of the American Bar Association and a Committee of Publishers

McGraw-Hill books are available at special quantity discounts to use as premiums and
sales promotions, or for use in corporate training programs. For more information, please
write to the Director of Special Sales, Professional Publishing, McGraw-Hill, Two Penn
Plaza, New York, NY 10121-2298. Or contact your local bookstore.

 This book is printed on recycled, acid-free paper containing a
minimum of 50% recycled, de-inked fiber.

Library of Congress Cataloging-in-Publication Data

Vance, David E.
    Financial analysis and decision making : tools and techniques to solve
financial problems and make effective business decisions / David E.
Vance.
        p. cm.
    ISBN 0-07-140665-4 (hardcover : alk. paper)
    1. Corporations—Finance.   2. Financial statements.   3. Cash flow.
    I. Title: Financial analysis and decision making.   II. Title.
    HG4026 .V364 2002
    658.15'1—dc21
                                                            2002011405

CONTENTS

PREFACE   xi

ACKNOWLEDGMENTS   xv

Chapter 1

Financial Statements and Accounting Concepts   1

Income Statement   1

Balance Sheet   5

Statement of Cash Flows   10

Accounting Definitions   13

Generally Accepted Accounting Principles   14

Summary   17

Chapter 2

Financial Ratios and Other Measures of Performance   19

Measurement of Operating Performance   19

Measures of Financial Performance   30

Risk Measurement   38

Cautions on Ratios   47

Summary   48

Chapter 3

Factors Determining Interest Rates and Required Debt Yields   51

Components of Interest: Risk-Free Rate of Return, Default, Liquidity, and Maturity Risk Premiums   52

Effect of Supply and Demand on Interest Rates   56

Summary   65

Chapter 4

Forecasting Yield and Risk   67

Forecasting with A Priori Probabilities   68

Forecasting with Historical Data   75
Using Expected Values and Standard Deviations to Make Decisions   77
Portfolio Theory   81
How to Use Required Rate of Return   85
Summary   85

Chapter 5

Time Value of Money   87

Four Classes of Time Value Problems   87
Future Value   88
Future Value: Annual Growth Rates   90
Future Value Formula   90
Present Value Theory and Mathematical Formula   91
Present Value Using Tables   92
Present Value of an Annuity   94
Loan Payments   94
Loan Amortization Schedules   96
Mathematical Formula for Present Value of an Annuity   98
Future Value of an Annuity   98
Mathematical Formula for Future Value of an Annuity   99
Summary   100

Chapter 6

Bond Valuation   101

Bond Valuation   101
Callable Bonds   104
Convertible Bonds   106
Bond Yield   107
Yield to Call   112
Interpolation Theory   114
Summary   116

Chapter 7

Leases   119

Operating Versus Capital Leases   119
Imputed Interest Rates   120

Effect of Deposits and Prepayments on the Imputed Interest Rate   122
Capitalizing Leases   125
Summary   128

Chapter 8

Stock Valuation   129

Stock Valuation   129
Computing Stock Value   132
Stock Yield   136
Stock Valuation Based on Cash Flow   136
Stock Valuation Based on Earnings   138
Stock Valuation Based on Sales   140
Summary   142

Chapter 9

Cost of Capital   143

Cost of Debt Capital   143
Cost of Preferred Stock Capital   144
Cost of Common Equity   145
Cost of New Common Equity Capital   148
Cost-Free Capital   151
Weighted Average Cost of Capital (WACC)   151
When Should New Common Stock Be Issued?   154
Cost of Leased Capital   158
Marginal Cost of Capital   158
Decision Rules for the Optimal Capital Budget   160
Summary   162

Chapter 10

Capital Budgeting   165

Methods for Evaluating Capital Projects   166
Payback Method   166
Discounted Payback Method   168
Net Present Value   170
Internal Rate of Return   171

Modified Rate of Return   175
Comparison of Capital Budgeting Methods   178
Summary   178

Chapter 11

Cash Flow Estimation for Capital Budgeting   181

Capital Budgeting Ground Rules   181
Capital Budgeting Format   183
Replacement Equipment   185
Inflation and Price Pressure   185
Spreadsheet Modeling   185
Summary   187

Chapter 12

Product Costing   189

Cost Versus Expense   189
Financial Accounting Versus Managerial Accounting   190
Unallocated Manufacturing Overhead   193
Expenses Versus Inventory   197
Full Absorption Cost of Purchased Merchandise   197
Make or Buy Decisions   198
Managerial Accounting   199
Gross Profit Versus Contribution   201
Summary   203

Chapter 13

Break-Even Analysis and Modeling   205

Break-Even Analysis   205
Modeling Profit   208
Sales Volume Break-Even   210
Relevant Range   212
Reality Testing   212
Break-Even and Risk   213
Summary   216

Chapter 14

Working Capital and Cash Budgeting   217

Working Capital   217
Cash Budgeting   218
Opening a New Facility   221
Line of Credit   226
Seasonal Cash Demand   228
Managing Working Capital   230
Summary   248

Chapter 15

Master Budgets and Variance Analysis   251

Basic Budgets   252
Master Budgets   253
Master Budgets Versus Financial Statements   259
Supplemental Budgets   261
Summary   261

Chapter 16

Pricing Theory   263

Cost-Centered Pricing   263
Market-Centered Pricing   265
Engineered Cost   269
Price Elasticity   270
Product Life Cycle   272
Transfer Pricing   273
Opportunistic Pricing   275
Microeconomics Pricing   277
Summary   286

Chapter 17

Advanced Cost Concepts and Allocation of Resources   289

Cost Drivers   289
Activity-Based Costing   291

Job Costing   293
Cost Drivers as a Method for Overhead Allocation   297
Traditional Overhead Allocation   298
Joint Products: Two Product Problem   299
Theory of Constraints   300
Profit Ladder   303
New Product Selection   307
Summary   310

Chapter 18

Labor Costs   313

Overtime   313
Turnover Costs   315
Workers' Compensation   316
Unemployment Compensation Taxes   319
Summary   321

APPENDIXES   323

Appendix A: Future Value Interest Factor: FVIF(i, n)   324
Appendix B: Future Value Interest Factor for an Annuity:
              FVIFA(i, n)   326
Appendix C: Present Value Interest Factor: PVIF(i, n)   328
Appendix D: Present Value Interest Factor for an Annuity:
              PVIFA(i, n)   330
Appendix E: Chapter Exercises   332
Appendix F: Exercise Answers   383

INDEX   399

PREFACE

Financial analysis is about shaping the future. It provides the tools management needs to make sophisticated judgments about complex and challenging business issues. As a corporate controller, chief financial officer, and retired CPA, I found that outside auditors, purchasing managers, accountants, and corporate executives were making bad decisions because they didn't understand how to apply financial analysis to real-world situations. One example was a company president who was signing leases with a 24% imputed interest rate because neither he nor his auditors understood how to analyze leases.

Three principles guide this book: (1) it should get to the point without forcing the reader to wade through a lot of text, (2) there should be plenty of examples, and (3) the rationale for each analytical technique should be plainly stated.

In this book, we provide an overview of the three main financial statements: income statement, balance sheet, and statement of cash flows, and we discuss the major landmarks in each. We discuss financial ratios and other measures of performance that management can use to detect problems and isolate their root cause.

Interest rates are a factor in a number of decisions, including the required rate of return on a project, expansion, refinancing, lease versus buy decisions, and others. We discuss the factors that cause interest rates to rise or fall and what can be done about them.

The world is complicated, and things never unfold exactly according to plan. We discuss measures of risk in terms of yield or output and ways to manage that risk.

In the chapter on the time value of money, we discuss the accumulation of future wealth in terms of both a single investment and periodic investments. We also find the present value of investments, that is, the value in today's dollars of cash that will not be received until some future date. The principles discussed can be applied to savings, loans, mortgages, leases, annuities, and capital budgeting decisions. This chapter also provides the formulas needed to create computer programs or spreadsheets tailored to the needs of individual businesses.

The chapter on bond valuation demonstrates how the value of bonds rises as interest drops, and how the value of bonds drops as interest rates rise. This has implications for both investments and issuance of bonds. We also discuss bond yield to maturity and yield to call.

The chapter on leases builds on the time value of money principles and integrates the effect of deposits, prepayments, and application fees to find the real cost of leasing in such a way as to make leases with different terms comparable to each other and to other financing sources.

A number of methods to value stocks are discussed along with the strengths and weaknesses of each. Stock valuation is important for investing, deciding on convertible bond terms, and initial public offerings.

The cost of capital is the composite cost of all sources of capital used by a company. It is used as a benchmark for determining whether management is creating or destroying wealth, and in making decisions about investments in new projects or acquisitions. The marginal cost of capital is the cost of incremental blocks of capital, which can be compared to the return on projects to determine the optimum capital budget.

In the chapter on capital budgeting, we discuss five methods for analyzing capital projects, that is, projects for which the payback is stretched out over several years. These methods include (1) payback, (2) discounted payback, (3) net present value, (4) internal rate of return, and (5) modified internal rate of return. We also discuss decision rules for ranking projects for each method of analysis. There is also a chapter on estimating cash flow for capital budgeting.

Correct product costing is critical to decisions about pricing, make versus buy, and production volumes. We discuss full absorption costing, which is used for valuing inventory, and the cost of goods sold, and we discuss variable costing. Each approach to costing is used to make a different class of decision.

We discuss break-even analysis, a technique that can be expanded to address issues of production volume, target profits, and overhead targets. It can also be used to model strategic decision options and test the reasonableness of each.

Cash is oxygen to a company, and cash budgeting and working capital management are important keys to assure that a company has enough cash. We discuss the cash demand of opening a new facility, cash required for accounts receivable and inventory to support sales growth, and working capital as a source of cash.

Operating budgets are an important tool for management to guide a company's progress, but traditional budgets often fail to account for changes in sales volume. Master budgets, on the other hand, are designed to be flexible as sales volume changes. This flexibility improves variance analysis and helps improve placement of responsibility.

Most finance books concentrate on costs, but few discuss pricing in any depth even though correct pricing decisions are crucial to a company's financial health. We discuss a number of price setting techniques as well as the effects and strategic implications of supply and demand, market segmentation, product differentiation, and product life cycle.

We also discuss a number of financial analysis and decision-making techniques that don't fit neatly into any of the foregoing categories. These include cost drivers, activity-based costing, and job costing. We discuss two approaches to resource allocation: the theory of constraints and the profit ladder. We also discuss issues arising when discontinuing old products and selecting new products for introduction.

Finally, we discuss labor costs. Labor is one of the largest costs of any company, but it can be significantly reduced without layoffs by managing overtime, turnover, workers' compensation, and unemployment costs. We discuss techniques for better management of these areas and quantify the impact of improvements.

In sum, this book embraces a broad range of financial analyses and can be used as a primer by finance, accounting, and general management on the tools and techniques to solve financial problems and make effective business decisions.

Dave Vance

ACKNOWLEDGMENTS

I would like to thank the more than 300 corporate managers and graduate and undergraduate students who have used, commented on, and vetted various versions of this text. Their comments, questions, and criticisms have helped sharpen explanations and make sample problems more realistic. Their relentless probing of why things work as they do has shifted the focus of the book from the theoretical to the practical. Anything good about this book I owe to them. The faults are my own.

CHAPTER 1

Financial Statements and Accounting Concepts

How does a company make money? A company can succeed only if it identifies and meets its customers' needs. It must also make a profit, but is that enough? Not quite. A company can make a profit every year and still run out of cash.

This chapter discusses three financial statements that provide a good understanding of company performance: (1) the income statement, (2) the balance sheet, and (3) the statement of cash flows. We will also define some of the terms accountants use and the philosophy underlying why accountants do what they do.

If you have a strong accounting background, you may want to skip this chapter. However, if you have no accounting background, or if it has been a long time since your last accounting course, take a few minutes to review this chapter. It will provide an overview of the accounting concepts that support financial decision making.

INCOME STATEMENT

Consider the income statement of the Gladstone Book Store (Figure 1–1). Last year it had revenue of $1,000,000. Revenue is another name for sales. The books they sold cost them $500,000. This is called the cost of goods sold (COGS). The difference between revenue and COGS is called gross profit. Gross profit is the amount

FIGURE 1–1

Gladstone Book Store Income Statement

GLADSTONE BOOK STORE
Income Statement
For the year ended 12/31/2002

Revenue	1,000,000
Cost of goods sold	500,000
Gross profit	500,000
Advertising, sales, and marketing	50,000
Store operations	350,000
Depreciation	10,000
Total operating expense	410,000
Operating profit	90,000
Interest	25,000
Earnings before tax	65,000
Taxes	15,000
Net income	50,000

generated from the sale of books before operating expenses are subtracted. Gladstone has a gross profit of $500,000.

Expenses are separated into cost of goods and operating expenses because they have different characteristics. Cost of goods sold tends to increase in rough proportion to sales, whereas operating expenses should not increase in proportion to sales.

Gross profit allows us to compute gross margin, which is gross profit divided by revenue. The relationship between revenue, COGS, gross profit, and gross margin is given in Eq. 1–1.

$$\text{Gross margin} = \frac{\text{Revenue} - \text{COGS}}{\text{Revenue}} = \frac{\text{Gross profit}}{\text{Revenue}} \qquad \text{(Eq. 1–1)}$$

Gross margin represents the percentage of each dollar available for operating expenses, financing costs, taxes, and profit after COGS are subtracted from revenue. Gross margin is important because it can be used to help forecast gross profit as revenue rises or falls. The gross margin for Gladstone Books is

$$\text{Gross margin} = \frac{\$1,000,000 - \$500,000}{\$1,000,000} = \frac{\$500,000}{\$1,000,000} = 50\%$$

Operating expenses are sometimes called overhead. It includes things like advertising, sales, and marketing costs; salaries and rent for store operations; and depreciation. Gladstone's operating expenses were $410,000.

Operating profit is gross margin less operating expenses. Operating profit is a measure of the fundamental performance of a company, independent of a company's financing or tax structure. It is also called earnings before interest and taxes (EBIT). Gladstone's operating profit was $90,000.

Since interest is tax deductible, it is subtracted from operating profit before taxes are computed. Gladstone's earnings before taxes (EBT) were $65,000. On an income statement, taxes mean taxes on income. Real estate, franchise, or other taxes not related to income are included in either the cost of goods sold, if they are related to the purchase or manufacture of a product, or the operating expenses, if they are not. Gladstone's income taxes were $15,000.

Net income is income after all expenses, including interest and taxes, are subtracted. It is the amount available for distribution of profits or to increase retained earnings. Gladstone's net income is $50,000.

The Gladstone Book Store example uses a number of important terms. Having crisp definitions for these terms will be important as we discuss decision making in this and other chapters. The terms are as follows:

Cost of goods sold   Cost of goods sold are all the costs necessary to make a product or to deliver a service. It also includes the cost to make an item ready for sale. In Gladstone, the cost of goods sold (COGS) includes the cost of books, the cost of transportation if Gladstone paid for it, and any other work that had to be performed to prepare the goods for sale. Suppose, for example, books had to be uncrated by store employees; the labor for uncrating would become part of the COGS. Other names for cost of goods sold are cost of products sold (COPS) or cost of services (COS).

Gross profit   Gross profit is the amount of revenue left over after the cost of goods sold is subtracted. Gross profit increases more or less linearly with increases in revenue. Conversely, as revenue drops, the gross profit available to cover operating expenses, interest, taxes, and profit drops as well.

Gross margin   Gross margin is simply the ratio of gross profit to revenue. In Gladstone, gross margin is 50%, that is, gross profit of $500,000 divided by revenue of $1,000,000. Gross margin is important because it can be used as a performance measure. It is also important because it can be used as an estimator for break-even analysis, budgets, and other analytical techniques.

Overhead   Overhead, also called operating expenses, is all expenses not included in the cost of goods sold except interest and taxes.

Earnings before tax   Earnings before tax (EBT) is revenue less all expenses except income taxes.

Taxes   Only taxes assessed on income are included in this income statement line.

Net income   Net income is the amount of income available to the owners or shareholders of the business.

Performance Standards

Suppose a company has a 50% cost of goods sold and a 50% overhead cost. How do we know whether 50% cost of goods sold is good or bad? How do we know whether overhead costs are out of control or as good as can be expected?

Ratios for other companies are summarized and published by Robert Morris Associates (RMA) and by Dun & Bradstreet. Ratios are provided by industry, as determined by SIC (standard industrial classification) code, and by the size of business in terms of revenue. RMA and D&B reports are available in most libraries. A U.S. Department of Commerce manual, available in most libraries, cross-references industries and SIC codes.

Another way to determine whether a company's cost of goods sold, overhead, or gross margin is appropriate is through benchmarking. Benchmarking is the process of gathering the financial statements of *the best* companies in an industry, and computing their financial ratios.

Closing the Books and the Income Statement

At the end of each accounting period, say, a year, sales and expense transactions are summarized into categories like revenue, cost of good sold, and overhead. Certain period-end adjustments, for example, depreciation, are added or subtracted as appropriate, and the result of these transactions for a period are then formatted into an income statement.

After the income statement is formatted, revenue and expense accounts are zeroed out by transferring their balances to a profit account. Profits are then transferred (added to) retained earnings, as are losses, if any.

BALANCE SHEET

A balance sheet has three major sections: assets, liabilities, and equity. Assets are all the things a business has to make money with. Liabilities are the money it owes to others, and equity is what would be left over if all assets were sold at their stated value and all debts were paid off. Another way to think about a balance sheet is that assets are the resources a company has, and liabilities and equity are the means for financing those resources. These have a critical relationship because assets *must always* equal liabilities plus equity.

$$\text{Assets} = \text{Liabilities} + \text{Equity} \qquad \text{(Eq. 1–2)}$$

Figure 1–2, the Balance Sheet for Gladstone Books, shows that it has assets of \$181,000 at the end of 2002. It also had liabilities of \$88,200, and equity of \$92,800.

Assets   At its simplest, assets are everything a company has at its disposal to use: real estate (whether or not financed), furniture,

FIGURE 1-2

Balance Sheet for Gladstone Books

GLADSTONE BOOK STORE
Balance Sheet
For the year ended of 12/31/2002

	2002	2001
Cash	29,600	2,400
Accounts receivable	9,400	7,400
Inventory	120,000	90,000
Current assets	159,000	99,800
Plant and equipment	22,000	7,000
Total assets	181,000	106,800
Accounts payable	9,800	7,500
Accrued payroll	800	6,100
Bank Loan—current portion	21,000	15,000
Leases—current portion	3,600	3,600
Current liabilities	35,200	32,200
Bank Loan—long term	45,000	48,000
Leases—long term	8,000	8,800
Total liabilities	88,200	89,000
Paid in capital at par	1,000	1,000
Retained earnings	91,800	16,800
Total equity	92,800	17,800
Liabilities and equity	181,000	106,800

fixtures, machinery, cash, securities, accounts receivable, and inventory.

Liabilities   Liabilities are money owed to others. Examples of liabilities include mortgage balances, bank loans, accounts payable, accrued payroll (wages earned by employees at the financial statement date, but have not yet been paid to them), and lease capital balances (the present value of lease payment obligations).

Equity   Equity is the amount that would be left over if all assets were sold at book value, and all liabilities were paid off. Equity includes invested capital and retained earnings. Retained earnings is the sum of all the profits and losses from the time the business was formed to the present, less dividends paid. Net income increases retained earnings; losses reduce retained earnings.

Note that the income statement is a summary of revenue and expenses in a year. In contrast, a balance sheet is a snapshot at a point in time.

Current Assets, Current Liabilities, and Working Capital

Assets and liabilities are divided into current and noncurrent accounts. Current assets include cash and anything expected to be converted to cash within a year. Examples include accounts receivable, inventory, and securities held for investment purposes.

Current liabilities are debts that will come due within a year. Examples include accounts payable, accrued payroll, lines of credit, and the principal portion of bank and lease payments that must be paid within a year.

The reason for segregating assets and liabilities into current and noncurrent accounts is to help determine whether a company has the capacity to pay its bills. If more bills come due in a year than a company can pay, serious consequences could follow, including bankruptcy.

We will see that most transactions in the course of normal business affect current assets and current liabilities. Therefore, these accounts are often called working capital accounts. Net working capital is current assets less current liabilities, as shown in Eq. 1–3.

Net working capital = Current assets − Current liabilities

(Eq. 1–3)

The amount of net working capital is a measure of whether a company can pay its bills as they become due. If it is zero or negative, the company is in trouble. If the company has a lot of net working capital, it means they should have no trouble paying their bills.

Gladstone's net working capital can be computed as follows:

Net working capital = $159,000 − $88,200 = $70,800

One of the problems with using net working capital is that we know zero or negative amounts are always bad, but we can't tell from this one calculation whether $70,800 is good. It might be terrific for a million-dollar bookstore, but dangerously close to zero for a billion-dollar company. In the next chapter, we will discuss ratios and other techniques to determine whether a company is at risk.

Relationship Between Income Statement and Balance Sheet

What is the relationship between the income statement and the balance sheet? Suppose Gladstone bought a book for $11 and sold it for $20. This activity would cause a series of transactions to be generated in the accounting system. If the book were purchased on credit, we would have to reflect the fact that Gladstone created a liability. On the other hand, it also acquired an asset, the book, which would become part of its inventory.

Accounting transactions are often represented by journal entries. A journal entry identifies the accounts that are affected by a transaction and the amount of the effect. Transactions are debits, which mean the left side, and credits, which mean the right side. Think of the accounting equation (Eq. 1–2): assets are on the left, or debit side of the equal sign, and liabilities and equity are on the right side of the equal sign. So purchase of an $11 book on credit can be represented by the following journal entry:

	Debit	Credit
Inventory	$11	
Accounts payable		$11

We have increased our assets, and we financed that increase in assets by increasing a liability, accounts payable.

Suppose we sell the book for $20 cash. This triggers two transactions in the accounting system. First, let's consider the effect of receiving cash. We increase (debit) cash, an asset, by $20, and since we have to maintain the balance demanded by Eq. 1–2, we have to increase something on the credit side of the equation.

As it turns out, there are temporary accounts inside equity that can be used. These temporary accounts are revenue and expense accounts. We call them temporary because we know that they are closed out to the profit account each year, which returns their balance to zero. Sometimes these temporary accounts are called nominal accounts. We can now rewrite Eq. 1–2 as Eq. 1–4 to reflect these nominal accounts.

$$\text{Assets} = \text{Liabilities} + \text{Equity} + \text{Revenue} - \text{Expenses} \quad \text{(Eq. 1–4)}$$

The expansion of Eq. 1–2 to Eq. 1–4 should make sense on an intuitive level because during year-end closing procedures the balances in revenue and expense accounts are ultimately folded into the retained earnings account, which is an equity account. So the credit side of the equation for the book sale is revenue. The debit is to cash. The journal entry to record the sale is:

	Debit	Credit
Cash	$20	
Revenue		$20

Here, for the first time, we see how transactions cross over from the balance sheet to the income statement. The crossover is required to keep Eq. 1–4 in balance.

There are two more transactions to complete this cycle. Since we sold the book, we no longer have it in inventory. Ordinarily, we increase things on the left-hand side of the equal sign, assets, with debits, and decrease them with credits. We usually increase things on the right-hand side of the equal sign—like liabilities, equity, and revenue—with credits, and decrease them with debits. But there is always an exception. The exception is expenses; the way to remember this it that expenses always work against revenue. If revenue is increased with a credit, then expenses must be increased with a debit.

Let us reduce inventory to reflect the sale of the book, and that reduction will have to be a credit. Then what is the debit? Logically, it should be something that offsets revenue, some kind of expense. Actually, it is a specific expense called cost of goods sold.

	Debit	Credit
Cost of goods sold	$11	
Inventory		$11

The final transaction to complete this cycle involves paying the publisher for the book. We know that we will have to reduce cash, an asset, by $11, which means we will have to credit cash. But what do we debit? We have already accounted for the expense, so it can't be an expense account. The answer is to debit accounts payable, which offsets the liability created when Gladstone purchased the book. Credits are used to increase liabilities like accounts payable, so to reduce accounts payable, we will have to use a debit. The journal entry to do this is

	Debit	Credit
Accounts payable	$11	
Cash		$11

Generally accepted accounting principles (GAAP) require a double entry accounting system. The equation assets = liabilities + equity is one of the double entry rules. Another double entry rule is that debits must always equal credits. Double entry bookkeeping rules are designed to determine whether a mistake has been made in data entry. Income statement and balance sheet accounts have been carefully arranged so that double entry bookkeeping rules can always be followed *and* the final result makes sense.

STATEMENT OF CASH FLOWS

What in the world is a statement of cash flows? Isn't it enough to know whether a company is profitable by looking at the income statement? Isn't it enough to know a company's assets and liabilities? What else could anybody want to know?

Actually, for a long time, most businesses did very well without a statement of cash flows. However, as businesses got bigger and more complex, investors, banks, and managers wanted more information to tie the income statement to the balance sheet, to see where money was coming from and how it was being used.

Before actually looking at a statement of cash flows (at one time called a sources and uses of funds statement), let's think about some of the concepts involved.

All businesses hope that a big source of cash is profits. In addition, there are several other sources of cash. Depreciation is a source of cash. Why? Depreciation is one of the expenses subtracted from revenue to get net income. But depreciation, unlike rent, is not a cash expense. It is just a bookkeeping entry.

Suppose a company purchased a $3,000 computer in 2001 that had a three-year life. It would be depreciated over three years. That is, some of the cost of the computer would be allocated to each year it contributes to company operations.

So as we see, some deductions from revenue represent cash payments, and some do not. To get cash generated by operations, we must add noncash deductions back to net income. Therefore, a good estimate of a company's cash flow is given by Eq. 1–5.

$$\text{Cash flow} = \text{Net income} + \text{Depreciation} \qquad \text{(Eq. 1–5)}$$

If net income for 2002 were $20,000 in Eq. 1–5, a good estimate of cash flow would be $21,000 ($20,000 profit plus $1,000 noncash deduction for depreciation expense on the computer).

Accounts payable can also affect cash. Suppose at the end of 2001, and at the end of 2002, accounts payable were exactly $9,800. This would neither increase nor decrease cash. But suppose your bookkeeper wanted to start the new year clean, so on December 31, 2002, he paid off all outstanding accounts. Accounts payable would decrease from $9,800 in 2001 to $0 in 2002. This would be a *use of cash.*

Likewise, if accounts payable increased (that is, the company used its vendors to finance more of their operation), that would be a *source of cash.*

Changes in accounts receivable work the same way. If accounts receivable were $13,200 at the end of 2001, and through diligent collection efforts they were reduced to $8,200 in 2002, that reduction in accounts receivable would represent a *source of cash.*

FIGURE 1-3

Statement of Cash Flows for Gladstone Books

GLADSTONE BOOK STORE
Statement of Cash Flows
For the period ending 12/31/2002

Cash from operations	
Net income	50,000
Depreciation	10,000
Total from operations	60,000
Changes in working capital	
Decrease (increase) in A/R	−2,000
Decrease (increase) in inventory	−30,000
Increase (decrease) in payables	2,300
Increase (decrease) accrued payroll	−5,300
Total from working capital	−35,000
Acquisitions and divestitures	
Plant and equipment acquired	0
Plant and equipment sold	0
Total from acquisitions and divestitures	0
Financing activities	
Company stock sold (purchased)	0
Loans received (paid) net	3,000
Leases received (paid) net	−800
Total financing activity	2,200
Change in cash position	27,200

Likewise, if accounts receivable increased (that is, the business financed more of its customer's purchases), that would be a *use of cash*.

A statement of cash flows sums all the sources and uses of cash and ties them back to the changes in the amount of cash on a balance sheet from year to year. Figure 1–3 is a statement of cash flows for Gladstone Books.

Gladstone generated $50,000 in cash from net income and another $10,000 in depreciation for a total of $60,000 from operations. We can also see that cash was used by Gladstone's working capital accounts. For example, accounts receivable increased by $2,000 from 2001 to 2002, which means that the company lent out $2,000 more to customers than it collected. This was a use of cash. More inventory was purchased than sold using another $30,000 of cash.

On the other hand, accounts payable increased, which means that Gladstone borrowed more from its suppliers than it paid back, a source of cash. Looking at financing activity, we increase the current portion of our bank loan by $6,000 and paid off $3,000 of the long-term portion of the bank loan. So the bank provided $3,000 in cash net.

So the statement of cash flows starts with net income and depreciation, and adds or subtracts changes in balance sheet accounts to get a change in cash position. This change in cash position must exactly equal the year-to-year change in the cash account on the balance sheet. If it does, we have successfully tied the income statement to balance sheet changes, which means we have substantially reduced the likelihood of errors in all three statements.

There is one more thing to consider before examining a statement of cash flows. The other obvious source or use of cash is from financing activity. Selling stock or borrowing money provides cash in the same way that repurchasing stock or repaying loans uses cash. Acquiring equipment on a capital lease is like borrowing money to finance an equipment purchase, and borrowing money is a source of cash. Making lease payments has the opposite effect and uses cash.

ACCOUNTING DEFINITIONS

To communicate effectively with accountants, a manager should know a few more definitions.

General ledger   Accountants talk about the general ledger and general ledger entries a lot, but what are they? A general ledger is just a database containing accounting entries. Journal entries of one sort or another are the primary input to this database. Financial statements, and other reports are the output from the database. One unique feature of a general ledger database is that the accounting equation is always maintained in the data such that if all the debits were added up and all the credits were added up, they would always equal one another.

Journal entry   A journal entry is simply a set of related debits and credits. Recall how Gladstone recorded the purchase of a book? The debit to inventory and related credit to accounts payable were a journal entry. Debits must always equal credits in a journal entry.

Trial balance   A trial balance is just a listing of all the debits and all the credits in a general ledger, subtotaled by account number, with a grand total at the end. It is called a trial balance because its purpose is to make sure that the total credits in the general ledger equals the total debits.

Chart of accounts   A chart of accounts is just a list of all general ledger account numbers and titles. The number of accounts is a function of how summarized or detailed management wants their information. For example, some companies prefer to book all revenue in one revenue account; others prefer one revenue account per product, or even per client.

EBIT   Earnings before interest and taxes (EBIT) is often called operating income. It is a measure of the capacity of a company to generate *income independent of the method by which assets are financed* and *independent of tax strategies used.*

EBT   Different companies use different tax strategies, and earnings before taxes (EBT) is useful in evaluating a company independent of tax strategy.

GENERALLY ACCEPTED ACCOUNTING PRINCIPLES

What else? Financial statements can't be that simple. True enough. We have not discussed the role of taxes, different forms of financing, or the extensive footnotes that accompany most financial statements. On the other hand, this is meant to be an overview of financial statements. It is not meant to turn you into an accountant. There are, however, a few rules of the road called Generally Accepted Accounting Principles (GAAP) that provide a philosophical framework for accounting transactions. A few of the more common principles follow:

Entity principle   The entity principle states that it is important to draw a boundary around the entity being reported on so that it is clearly defined. It is common for small businesspeople to co-mingle their financial affairs with those of the "company," making it difficult or impossible to determine a business's true financial condition. Co-mingling of assets also increases the risk of audits and excessive tax assessments.

Suppose, for example, an entrepreneur were constantly putting his or her own funds into a business, or paying a business's bills from his or her own checking account. Such a business might look very profitable to a banker or investor because expenses were underreported. Another type of problem is co-mingling the sales of one company with another one. In such a case, the IRS might allocate sales in such a way as to maximize taxes.

Objectivity   Revenue and expenses are reported on the basis of their historical transaction data rather than market value. The rational is that historical data are objective, verifiable, and not subject to judgment. Although there are some exceptions to this rule (for example, inventory is reported at the lower of cost or market value), historical data are usually considered the gold standard for reliability.

Conservatism   Financial statements are often used by, and relied upon, by strangers to the enterprise. Examples include bankers, investors, vendors extending credit to the company, regulators, and taxing authorities. To avoid overstating, and thereby misleading these outsiders, financial statements are presented in the most conservative light possible. The principle of recording inventory at the lower of cost or market is one example of conservatism. Creating an allowance for doubtful accounts (which is a way of estimating how much of a company's accounts receivable are uncollectible) is another example of conservatism.

Matching principle   Financial statements attempt to match revenues to the costs that produced them. For example, if a builder buys 600 tons of sand and uses half of that sand this year to build houses that it sells, and uses half of the sand next year, the matching principle allocates half the cost to the first year and half the cost to the next year. Depreciation is another example of the matching principle. An asset, for example, a truck, may be bought in one year, but it may help generate revenue for five years. The allocation of cost to each year is called a depreciation expense.

Specific time periods   We have seen that the income statement and statement of cash flows report the cumulative effect of transactions over a period of time. It is therefore extremely important to properly classify transactions into their relevant time period. For example, if Gladstone buys and uses 50 pounds of coffee in December 2002, but does not get invoiced until February 2003, should the coffee be a 2002 or 2003 expense? The answer is that it should be a 2002 expense because Gladstone used the coffee to generate revenue in 2002.

Comparability   Financial statements should be comparable from year to year. That means, among other things, that the format of statements should be the same, the accounting rules and their application should be the same, and accounting assumptions should be the same. For example, if Gladstone was very profitable in 2002, but not so profitable in 2003, they could not elect to depreciate their building over 5 years in 2002 to reduce profits, and then depreciate the same building over 50 years in 2003 to reduce expenses.

Materiality   Materiality means that financial statements should be substantially correct, not perfect. The cost of perfection is high, and often outweighs the incremental benefit to users of financial statements. Something is material if it would change a person's decision to lend money to the company, invest in it, or extend credit. This is a very difficult theoretical test to administer. However, over time, a 3% rule has developed. If revenue is within 3% of the "perfect" revenue number, the difference is not considered material; likewise, with expenses.

However, there has been some controversy in applying 3% as a standard of materiality. Some companies have been accused of accurately determining their expenses, but reporting only 97% of them on the theory that the 3% difference is not material. This is a dangerous practice. Use of the materiality rule should be strictly limited to situations in which the cost of achieving greater accuracy is prohibitive, or where it is impossible to get more precise data.

SUMMARY

The income statement, also called the profit and loss statement, summarizes revenue and expenses for a period of time. A balance sheet lists a company's assets, liabilities, and equity at a point in time. A statement of cash flows ties the income statement and balance sheet together by showing where the cash to operate the business came from, and how it was spent.

A balance sheet is a representation of the accounting equation: assets = liabilities + owner's equity. The equity section can be expanded to include the revenue and expense accounts that make up the income statement.

Double entry bookkeeping is based on the accounting equation, which means that every transaction affects at least two accounts. Journal entries debiting and crediting accounts are a formal way of expressing this equality. Journal entries are recorded on a database called a general ledger. The general ledger provides the information used to create financial statements.

Generally accepted accounting principles (GAAP) provide philosophical guidance for compiling and using accounting statements. The purpose of this guidance is to make financial statements comparable from year to year and from company to company.

CHAPTER 2

Financial Ratios and Other Measures of Performance

It is often difficult to determine how well a company is doing simply by looking at financial statements. So over the years, managers and financial analysts have developed a number of techniques for looking "inside" financial data to find clues to past, current, and, most important, future performance. In this chapter, we will explore uses of financial ratios and several related techniques to address a number of investment and management issues.

The types of questions financial ratios are designed to answer include

- Are assets productively employed?
- Is there enough inventory to service customers? Or is there too much?
- What are reasonable expectations for profit margin? And is the company meeting those expectations?
- Is leverage being used appropriately?
- Is the company at risk of running out of cash?
- Are the shareholders getting value for their investment?

MEASUREMENT OF OPERATING PERFORMANCE

One group of ratios is designed to address operating performance and is a measure of a company's efficiency in managing sales, costs, collections, and inventory. Operating ratios can be distinguished from ratios that measure a company's financial performance, which involves use of equity. Operating performance can be distinguished from measures of financial risk used by banks and other creditors to determine whether a company has sufficient liquidity to pay its bills as they become due.

Return on Assets

Return on assets (ROA) is a key concept in financial analysis. It is used to measure whether assets are being productively employed. Why is it important that assets be productively employed? Idle assets tie up capital that could be used to invest in new product development, start or upgrade a marketing campaign, buy out a competitor, pay down debt, or issue a cash dividend. Idle assets may also deteriorate over time resulting in foreseen losses. Return on assets computations are also used to help make decisions to close plants or divest subsidiaries. It is also a measure of management efficiency.

Return on assets (ROA) =   (Eq. 2–1)

$$\frac{\text{Net income} + \text{Interest (net of income tax savings)}}{\text{Average assets}}$$

Why add back interest? The reason is that ROA is designed to measure how well assets are being used, not how they were financed. By "scrubbing out" the effect of financing, results become more comparable year to year for a given company, and more comparable among companies in the same industry.

Why add back interest "net of taxes"? Taxes reduce the effect of interest. Some say that taxes subsidize interest. This seems counterintuitive to a lot of people until they consider their own taxes. If someone wrote a $100 check to charity, they would claim it on their tax return. Why? The donation is tax deductible. If they were in the 20% bracket, the $100 deduction would save them $20 in taxes. The net cost of the donation would only be $80 ($100 donation less $20 tax savings). Interest deductions work the same way. The cost of interest net of taxes equals the interest paid less the amount of taxes saved by paying interest.

Example

Alpha Corporation has net income of $100,000; interest expense of $10,000; and it is in the 30% bracket. At year-end 2, its assets were $1,200,000, and at year-end 1, its assets were $800,000.

The real cost of that interest is not going to be $10,000, but $10,000 less the amount of taxes saved because interest is tax deductible. The amount of tax savings is

$$\$10,000 \times 30\% \text{ tax rate} = \$3,000$$
$$\text{Interest net of taxes} = \$10,000 - \$3,000 = \$7,000$$

Therefore,

$$\text{Net income} + \text{Interest (net of taxes)} = \$100,000 + \$7,000 = \$107,000$$

Interest net of taxes can be rewritten as

$$\text{Interest net of taxes} = \text{Interest} \times (1 - \text{Tax rate}) \quad \text{(Eq. 2-2)}$$

In most cases, it can be assumed that assets were acquired gradually over the period in question, usually a year. Therefore, a good estimate of average assets is given by the equation

$$\text{Average assets} = (\text{Assets at end of year 1} \quad \text{(Eq. 2-3)}$$
$$+ \text{ Assets at end of year 2}) / 2$$

$$\text{Average assets} = (\$800,000 + \$1,200,000) / 2$$
$$= \$2,000,000 / 2 = \$1,000,000$$

The return on assets of Alpha Corporation is

$$\text{ROA} = \frac{\text{Net income} + \text{Interest} \times (1 - \text{Tax rate})}{(\text{Assets at year 1} + \text{Assets at year 2}) / 2}$$
$$= \frac{\$107,000}{\$1,000,000} = 10.7\%$$

How does a company know whether its ROA is good or bad? A retailer might compare the ROA of one of their stores to their other stores, or they might compare the same store's ROA year to year to determine whether productivity is increasing or decreasing. Nonretailing companies might compare their year-to-year performance as well. But both of these provide only relative measures of ROA. An increasing ROA may only indicate a business has gone from terrible to simply bad. A broader standard of performance is needed.

This need for performance standards, or targets, has long been recognized, and several exist. These include ratios published by Robert Morris Associates (RMA), Dun & Bradstreet, (D&B), and the U.S. Department of Commerce. These data, organized by industry, are available in most good libraries.

Another, and perhaps better, standard or target can be developed through *benchmarking*. Whereas RMA and D&B represent average ratios across all companies in an industry, benchmarking focuses on the *best* companies in an industry. To perform a benchmark study, a manager or financial analyst would get the annual reports of the top five to ten companies in their industry and compute their ROA and other ratios. These would provide an objective benchmark for measurement of a company's results.

This raises another question. Suppose the company being analyzed compares unfavorably to other companies, then what? In that case, the manager or financial analyst should look deeper by analyzing other ratios. If the problem can be traced to its source, corrective action can be taken.

Thinking about ratios generally, if a measure of performance is unsatisfactory, it can usually be broken down into simpler components, each of which can be analyzed until the cause(s) of the unsatisfactory performance are identified and corrective action can be taken.

Return on assets is a very high-level analysis, but it can be broken down into two components.

$$\text{ROA} = \text{Profit margin} \times \text{Asset turnover ratio} \quad \text{(Eq. 2–4)}$$

Profit Margin

Profit margin examines the relationship between revenue and expenses. Throughout this chapter, we use sales and revenue interchangeably. If expenses are high relative to sales, profits will be thin or nonexistent. When there is a loss, this ratio has no real meaning. When expenses are low relative to sales, profit margins will be high. The equation is

$$\text{Profit margin} = \frac{\text{Net income} + \text{Interest (net of taxes)}}{\text{Sales}} \quad \text{(Eq. 2–5)}$$

Example

Alpha Inc. has net income of $100,000, on sales of $1,200,000. Interest is $10,000, and it is in the 30% tax bracket. What is its profit margin?

$$\text{Profit margin} = \frac{\$100,000 + \$10,000 \times (1 - 30\%)}{\$1,200,000}$$

$$= \frac{\$107,000}{\$1,200,000} = 8.9\%$$

Note that we add back interest net of taxes because we don't want the means of financing operations (debt versus equity) to distort the profit margin. By eliminating the effects of financing, it is easier to make profit margins comparable year to year and company to company.

What if the profit margin were unsatisfactory? Then a manager or analyst would (1) work with marketing to determine whether their product pricing was appropriate, (2) work with sales to determine whether volume could be increased, (3) work with purchasing and manufacturing to determine whether the cost of goods sold could be reduced, and (4) analyze overhead to determine whether any expenses could be reduced or eliminated.

Asset Turnover Ratio

The asset turnover ratio asks how many dollars of sales the company generates for each dollar of assets it employs. This isn't a trivial issue. It helps analyze the efficiency with which the company is reaching its customers. It also helps inform decisions about the number of stores, size and distribution of warehouses, equipment placed at point of sale, and other decisions.

$$\text{Asset turnover} = \frac{\text{Sales}}{\text{Average assets}} \qquad \text{(Eq. 2–6)}$$

Note that interest is not added back here. Why? Because the method a company uses to finance operations is independent of the efficiency with which it reaches its customers.

Example

Alpha Inc. has sales of $1,200,000. In year 1, it had assets of $800,000, and in year 2, it had assets of $1,200,000. What is its asset turnover?

$$\text{Asset turnover} = \frac{\$1,200,000}{(\$800,000 + \$1,200,000) \ / \ 2}$$

$$= \frac{\$1,200,000}{\$1,000,000} = 1.2$$

Suppose it is determined that the amount of assets it takes to generate a dollar of sales is excessive. Stated another way, suppose it is determined that the sales per dollar of assets is too low. What would be the next step in the analysis? The next step would be to analyze the performance of major assets: accounts receivable, inventory and plant, property and equipment, and determine whether they were being properly utilized. However, before analyzing assets, there is one more ratio that should be considered, and that is revenue per employee.

Revenue per Employee

Revenue per employee (as compared to sales per dollar of assets) is used as a gross measure of whether a company is overstaffed. Unproductive employees tie up assets in terms of plant, property, office and production equipment, computers, and vehicles. Unproductive employees also increase expenses unnecessarily.

The appropriate level of revenue per employee will vary from industry to industry. In telemarketing, revenue per employee averages around $35,000 per year. In capital-intensive, high-tech industries, a revenue above $200,000 is not uncommon, and in law firms, revenue of $200,000 per lawyer is usually a minimum.

$$\text{Revenue per employee} = \frac{\text{Revenue}}{\text{Number of employees}} \qquad \text{(Eq. 2–7)}$$

Suppose Alpha were the best company in the cement industry and generated revenue of $100 million with 400 employees. Suppose Beta were a cement company you just took over, and it was generating $23 million in revenue with 120 employees. Is your company overstaffed or understaffed compared to the best in the industry?

$$\frac{\text{Alpha revenue}}{\text{per employee}} = \frac{\$100,000,000}{400} = \$250,000/\text{employee}$$

$$\frac{\text{Beta revenue}}{\text{per employee}} = \frac{\$23,000,000}{120} = \$191,667/\text{employee}$$

Clearly, Alpha employees are more productive than Beta employees. So this ratio serves as a diagnostic test of employment efficiency. Suppose you set a target for your management team to cut the gap in half between the best in the industry and yourselves assuming constant sales. Revenue per employee would be

$$\text{Target revenue per employee} = \frac{\$250,000 + \$191,667}{2} = \$220,834$$

How would that translate into a target number of employees? We can determine that by plugging the target revenue per employee into Eq. 2–7.

$$\frac{\$220,834 \text{ Target revenue}}{\text{per employee}} = \frac{\$23,000,000}{\text{Target number of employees}}$$

$$\text{Target number of employees} = \frac{\$23,000,000}{\$220,834} = 104$$

Accounts Receivable Turnover

Accounts receivable turnover is a measure of how quickly credit sales are collected. The formula is

$$\text{Accounts receivable turnover} = \frac{\text{Net sales on account}}{\text{Average accounts receivable}}$$

$$\text{(Eq. 2–8)}$$

Example

Alpha Inc. had credit sales of $1,200,000. In year 1, accounts receivable were $300,000, and in year 2, accounts receivable were $500,000. What is its accounts receivable turnover?

$$\text{Accounts receivable turnover} = \frac{\$1,200,000}{(\$300,000 + \$500,000) / 2}$$

$$= \frac{\$1,200,000}{\$400,000} = 3.0$$

The higher the turnover, the better. A more intuitive way to look at this data is to convert accounts receivable turnover ratio to days sales outstanding (DSO). The DSO formula is

$$\text{Days sales outstanding} = \frac{365 \text{ days/year}}{\text{Accounts receivable turnover}} \quad \text{(Eq. 2–9)}$$

$$\text{DSO} = \frac{365 \text{ days}}{3.0} = 121.7 \text{ days}$$

What does DSO represent? Selling on credit is like lending money. So in this example, Alpha is lending $1,200,000 to its customers for an average of 121.7 days. A DSO of 121.7 days is a long, average collection period regardless of the industry. An excessive collection period could indicate (1) the collection department is not working hard or smart enough; (2) customers might be having severe financial problems, and that is why they are paying slowly; (3) the credit department is not screening customers closely enough for their ability and willingness to pay; (4) the marketing department is granting payment terms that are too liberal; or (5) there may be an accumulation of uncollectible accounts receivable on the books that should be written off.

Accounts Payable Turnover and Days to Pay

Management of accounts receivable begins before the first item is sold on credit, which raises the question should you extend credit to everyone who wants to buy from you? Sales and marketing will want to extend credit to everyone, but is this prudent? Remember, the objective isn't to make a sale; the objective is to get paid!

One way to evaluate the creditworthiness of potential customers is to compute their accounts payable turnover and use that to compute the average number of days it takes for them to pay their bills.

Financial statements for publicly traded companies are available from the SEC's Edgar database, Yahoo, and elsewhere. If a company isn't publicly traded, your company's credit application should capture the information you need to compute accounts payable turnover. The formula is

$$\text{Accounts payable turnover} = \frac{\text{Purchases}}{\text{Average accounts payable}}$$

$$\text{(Eq. 2–10)}$$

Recall that absent any extenuating circumstances, average account balances, in this case average accounts payable, can be computed by taking the beginning and ending account balance, adding them together and dividing by 2.

This formula is a little more difficult than some others because purchases, per se, are not usually broken out on financial statements, so we will have to compute purchases using the following formula:

$$\text{Purchases} = \text{Cost of goods sold} \qquad \text{(Eq. 2–11)}$$
$$+ \text{Ending inventory} - \text{Beginning inventory}$$

Cost of goods sold is on a company's income statement, and beginning and ending inventory, as well as beginning and ending accounts payable, can be found on a company's balance sheet for the prior year and current year, respectively.

The average number of days it takes customers to pay their bills may be estimated using the following formula:

$$\text{Days to pay} = \frac{365 \text{ days / year}}{\text{Accounts payable turns}} \qquad \text{(Eq. 2–12)}$$

Example
Slick-Ko Construction wants to buy 20 million board feet of lumber at an average sales price of $0.15 per board foot. You pull their financial statements and find the following: beginning inventory

$3 million, ending inventory $5 million, cost of goods sold $16 million, beginning accounts payable $2 million, ending accounts payable $3 million.

Purchases = Cost of goods sold   (Eq. 2–13)
                + Ending inventory − Beginning inventory
                    = $16 M + $5 M − $3 M = $18 M

$$\text{Accounts payable turnover} = \frac{\text{Purchases}}{\text{Average accounts payable}}$$

$$= \frac{\$18\ M}{(\$2\ M + \$3\ M)\ /\ 2} = 7.2$$

(Eq. 2–14)

Days to pay = 365 / Accounts payable turns   (Eq. 2–15)
                = 365 / 7.2 = 50.7 days to pay on average

If your goal is to collect credit sales in 30 days, Slick-Ko Corporation is not the kind of customer you want to extend credit to. Does this mean you decline the sale? No. It means that Slick-Ko Corporation must arrange some alternative means of financing the purchase. Consider asking for payment in advance, COD, or a credit card. Credit cards are a rapidly expanding method of financing business-to-business sales.

Inventory Turnover and Days in Inventory

Inventory is an important asset for all manufacturers, wholesalers, and retailers, but is less important in service industries. The formula for inventory turnover is

$$\text{Inventory turnover} = \frac{\text{Cost of goods sold}}{\text{Average inventory}} \qquad \text{(Eq. 2–16)}$$

Cost of goods sold (COGS) is computed as

COGS = Beginning inventory + Purchases − Ending inventory

(Eq. 2–17)

This formula can be broken down into parts so that it is easy to remember. Beginning inventory plus purchases are all that a company has available to sell over the course of a year. Ending inventory is what is left over at year-end and was not sold. The difference must be the inventory that was sold, or stated another way, the difference is the cost of goods sold.

Example

Alpha Inc. has Beginning inventory of $125,000, purchases of $800,000, and ending inventory of $135,000.

$$\text{Inventory turnover} = \frac{\$125,000 + \$800,000 - \$135,000}{(\$125,000 + \$135,000) / 2}$$

$$= \frac{\$790,000}{\$130,000} = 6.1$$

The higher the turnover the better because it means inventory is being bought, sold, and replaced faster. If inventory turnover is too low, it could indicate (1) too much inventory is being stocked, (2) sales should be increased by investing in more advertising or recruiting more salespeople, (3) some of the inventory is damaged, or (4) some of the inventory is obsolete. Obsolete inventory is an obvious risk for high-technology equipment that evolves rapidly, such as computers. It is also a risk for more ordinary items like cars; no one wants to pay full price for last year's model; clothes, few people want to buy bathing suits in January; and toys whose popularity may be measured in weeks.

A more intuitive feel for inventory turnover can be obtained by computing average days in inventory (DII). This formula is

$$\text{Days in inventory} = \frac{365 \text{ days/year}}{\text{Inventory turnover}} \quad \text{(Eq. 2–18)}$$

$$= \frac{365 \text{ days}}{6.1} = 59.8 \text{ days}$$

This means, on average, inventory is held just under 60 days before being sold. Depending on the industry, this might be good or bad. A 60-day turnover for an airplane manufacturer might be good, but it would be terrible for an egg seller.

Plant Asset Turnover

Plant asset turnover is another component of return on assets. It addresses the issue of how many dollars of sales are generated for each dollar invested in plant. Plant includes real estate, furniture, fixtures, computers, machinery, and manufacturing equipment.

$$\text{Plant asset turnover} = \frac{\text{Sales}}{\text{Average plant assets}} \qquad \text{(Eq. 2–19)}$$

Example
Alpha Corporation has sales of $1,200,000. At year end 2, its plant assets were $250,000, and at year end 1, its assets were $240,000.

$$\text{Plant asset turnover} = \frac{\$1,200,000}{(\$250,000 + \$240,000) / 2}$$

$$= \frac{\$1,200,000}{\$245,000} = 4.9$$

Arguably, the higher the plant asset turnover the better. However, a high plant asset turnover may mean the company is using old, possibly obsolete, machinery and production methods. This adverse condition might show up in other areas, for example, a lower profit margin caused by (1) excess labor utilization to compensate for lack of automation, (2) loss of sales because of production delays, or (3) quality control problems because worn tools and dies are being used beyond their expected life.

Assuming for the moment that plant and equipment are relatively modern, even state of the art, a low plant asset turnover ratio, compared to industry averages, could indicate (1) machinery is not being fully utilized (how many hours or shifts per day is it being used, and how many days per week?); (2) plant property and equipment may be broken, obsolete, or in storage; (3) sold or retired equipment still remains on the books; or (4) the company has excess productive capacity.

MEASURES OF FINANCIAL PERFORMANCE

To this point, the focus has been on the productivity of assets regardless of how those assets were acquired. Now it is time to consider sources of capital, debt and equity, and how ratios can help measure performance of the capital structure. This is just another way of saying measure how well debt and equity are being managed to increase shareholder wealth.

Return on Common Shareholder's Equity

Return on common shareholder's equity (ROCE, also called ROE by many) is a measure of benefit to the common shareholders. Since common shareholders shoulder the largest risk in an enterprise, and have the most to gain if the enterprise performs well, ROE is important to both current and prospective shareholders.

$$\frac{\text{Return on}}{\text{common equity}} = \frac{\text{Net income} - \text{Dividends on preferred stock}}{\text{Average common shareholder equity}}$$

(Eq. 2–20)

Why are preferred dividends being subtracted from net income? Unlike interest, preferred dividends are *not* one of the items subtracted from revenue to get net income. Therefore, it must be subtracted from net income to find the residue available to common shareholders. Since preferred dividends are not tax deductible, there is no tax "subsidy."

Shareholder's equity includes stock at par, paid in capital, and retained earnings. The term *stock at par* is derived from corporate law. When a corporation applies for a charter, it must state the par value of each share of stock. Par value was initially supposed to give creditors and other investors comfort by assuring them the company had a significant amount of capital. For example, if a corporation were incorporated with 1,000 shares of stock issued and outstanding, with a par value of $1,000 per share, the implication would be that the company had $1,000,000 of capital. If an entrepreneur started a company and issued himself 500 shares of such stock, but didn't pay $500,000 to the company, and the company went bankrupt, the entrepreneur would be personally liable for the par value of stock times the amount of shares he held. For that reason, companies began stating the par value of their stock as $0.01. If the entrepreneur were able to sell a share of stock to an investor for $1,000, the corporation would book 1 share sold at par of $0.01 per share, and they would book the remaining $999.99 as paid in capital. Retained earnings is the sum total of all profits and losses a company has made since its inception less dividends paid out.

Example
Alpha Corporation has net income of $100,000 and preferred dividends of $5,000. Total equity at the end of year 1 was $400,000, and $480,000 at the end of year 2.

$$ROE = \frac{\$100,000 - \$5,000}{(\$480,000 + \$400,000) / 2}$$

$$= \frac{\$95,000}{\$440,000} = 21.6\%$$

Is it possible, or reasonable, for a ROE to be 60% or more? If I invest $1 in Girl Scout Cookies, and sell them for $3, I have made 200% on my equity. Of course, it is difficult to sustain such returns over the long haul. However, where gross margins are large, overhead minuscule, and leverage extensively employed, ROE can, for a period of time, be extraordinary.

Relation Between Return on Assets and Return on Common Shareholder's Equity

The rate of return on assets represents the amount of profit generated by all the assets. Return on equity represents that portion of the profits that is to be allocated to common shareholders. It is important to remember that others supply capital in addition to common shareholders, and some portion of the total profits must be allocated to them in return for capital provided. This gives rise to the identity

Return on assets = Return to creditors (interest)   (Eq. 2–21)

+ Return to preferred shareholders

+ Return to common shareholders

Example
Suppose Alpha Corporation and Beta Corporation each had $1,000,000 in assets. The shareholders of Alpha Corporation put up the entire $1,000,000 as common equity. However, the shareholders

of Beta Corporation invest only $500,000 in their company and borrow $500,000 at 12% interest. Both companies earn $100,000 (earnings before interest and taxes). That is, both have an ROA of 10%, and both are in the 40% tax bracket.

Alpha Corporation's earnings before taxes (EBT) is $100,000, whereas Beta Corporation's EBT is only $64,000.

$$\text{EBT Alpha Corporation} = \$100,000 - \$0 \times (1 - 40\% \text{ tax rate})$$
$$= \$100,000$$

$$\text{EBT Beta Corporation} = \$100,000 - \$500,000 \times 12\% \times (1 - 40\%)$$
$$= \$100,000 - \$60,000 \times 60\% = \$64,000$$

In this example, there are no preferred shareholders, but if there were, preferred dividends would be subtracted from income in the same manner as interest although they would not be tax affected.

Alpha Corporation ROE = $100,000 / $1,000,000 = 10.0%

Beta Corporation's ROE = $64,000 / $500,000 = 12.8%

The difference in returns created by use of credit is called leverage.

Consider the ROA identity another way. The assets of each company generate $100,000 of income before taxes and interest. This income must be allocated among those supplying capital, that is, among creditors and shareholders.

The first portion of income is paid to the creditors in the form of interest. But since interest is tax affected (some would say subsidized), the amount of income that must be allocated to the creditors is reduced.

Income generated by assets =
$1,000,000 × 10% return on assets   = $100,000

Less allocation to creditors =
$500,000 borrowed × 12% interest × (1 − 40% tax rate)
                                                            = $36,000
Income available to common shareholders   = $64,000

This is the same as \$500,000 shareholder investment $\times$ 12.8% ROE = \$64,000.

Does use of debt always increase ROE? If so, why not finance a company with 100% debt? The answer is that debt increases ROE only under certain circumstances. The rule is that

If ROA is greater than the after-tax cost of debt, use of debt *increases* ROE.

However,

If the after-tax cost of debt is greater than ROA, use of debt *decreases* ROE.

If ROA is greater than the tax-adjusted cost of debt, can a company increase their use of debt indefinitely? Even though ROE approaches infinity as use of debt increases, there are other constraints on use of debt. One is that banks simply won't lend to companies with little or no equity.

Suppose return on equity does not meet expectations. How would one identify the root cause(s) of the problem? Back up through the elements of the equation and examine each of them one by one. For example, is too much equity being used to finance the company? This question can be answered by looking at norms for the industry. Often, the company is simply not making enough profit from the equity employed, and that takes us back to an analysis of the efficiency of management.

Earnings per Share

Earnings per share (EPS) of common stock is a way to measure profitability from the point of view of the common shareholder. The formula is

$$\frac{\text{Earnings per}}{\text{share}} = \frac{\text{Net income} - \text{Preferred stock dividends}}{\text{Weighted average number of common shares}}$$

(Eq. 2-22)

Preferred stock dividends are excluded (subtracted from net income) because they are not available to common shareholders. The denominator is the *weighted* average shares outstanding because unlike changes in assets, inventory, or accounts receivable, the number of shares outstanding usually does not change continuously. Rather, the number of shares outstanding will remain relatively static until a large block of shares is issued, or repurchased. Therefore, averaging the beginning and ending number of shares will distort the calculation.

The weighted average number of common shares outstanding is computed as follows:

$$\text{Weighted average} = \hspace{4cm} \text{(Eq. 2–23)}$$
$$(N1 \times D1 + N2 \times D2 + N3 \times D3 \ldots)/(D1 + D2 + D3 \ldots)$$

where   N1 is the number of common shares outstanding at the beginning of the period
D1 is the number of days the initial amount of shares is outstanding
N2 is the total number of common shares outstanding in the second interval
D2 is the number of days in the second interval, etc.

Example
Alpha Corporation has 300,000 shares outstanding at January 1. On April 1 (90 days later), Alpha issues 50,000 shares. On December 2, Alpha issues 50,000 more shares. What is the weighted average number of shares?

Weighted average = (300,000 shares × 90 days + 350,000 shares
        × 245 days + 400,000 × 30 days) / (90 + 245 + 30 days)
        = (27 million + 85.75 million + 12 million) / 365 days
        = 124.75 million / 365 days
        = 341,781 shares

If Alpha has net income of $100,000 and preferred dividends of $5,000, its earnings per share are:

$$\text{Earnings per share} = \frac{\$100,000 - \$5,000}{341,781} = \frac{\$95,000}{341,781} = \$0.278/\text{share}$$

Fully Diluted Earnings per Share

Sometimes corporations issue bonds or preferred stock that are convertible to common shares. They may also issue warrants or options that give individuals the right to purchase stock at predetermined prices. Fully diluted earnings per share is a theoretical calculation that spreads income over all potential shares assuming convertible bonds and convertible preferred are converted, and warrants and options are exercised on a rational basis. Suppose for example an individual had an option to purchase a share of stock for $10. If the market value of that stock were $12, it would be rational to purchase stock from the issuing company for $10 and sell it in the marketplace for $12, realizing a $2 profit. However, if the market value of that stock were only $8, it would be irrational to pay the issuing company $10.

This calculation has a number of difficulties. For example, if an investor had a $1,000, 12% bond convertible to 100 shares of common stock, and the market price were $11 per share, he could convert the bond, get 100 shares, and immediately sell them for $1,100, making a $100 profit. But would a rational investor forego a 12% interest stream for a one-time profit of 10%?

Problems also arise calculating the effects of exercising warrants and options. Suppose an investor had an option to purchase a stock for $10 that was selling for $11. In theory, the company could use the proceeds from exercise of options to enter the marketplace and repurchase stock, reducing somewhat the dilution caused by the exercise of options. But is it reasonable to assume companies would use funds in that manner, or would they use them in some other way?

Suppose the price of a stock rises to $11 per share for a month, a day, an hour. Is it reasonable to assume all, some, none of those holding convertible securities or options would exercise their rights?

The number of difficulties in calculating fully diluted earnings per share combined with the number of assumptions required draws the value of this particular ratio into question as a means of either shaping decision making or diagnosing problems. However, if more information is needed, we recommend consulting an intermediate accounting or advanced accounting text.[1]

Price/Earnings Ratio

The price earnings (P/E) ratio is the current market price of a stock divided by its earnings per share. In a sense, it is the market price to buy $1 of earnings in a company. The formula is

Price/earnings ratio = Market price/Earnings per share

(Eq. 2–24)

The market price is the price quoted, for example, in *The Wall Street Journal*, on tickers, and so forth. It is always the current price. This makes the price earnings ratio somewhat volatile since it changes day to day with the market. However, the long-term average price earnings ratio for several thousand individual stocks is quoted in *Value Line*, a publication available in most libraries.

Example
Alpha Corporation's stock was recently quoted at $5.00 per share. Its EPS is $0.278 per share.

Price/earnings ratio = $5.00/$0.278 = 18:1

The theory is that by comparing a stock's long-term P/E ratio to its current P/E ratio, stocks can be identified that are overvalued or undervalued. For example, if Alpha Corporation's stock has historically sold for a multiple (i.e., P/E) of 15, and the stock is currently selling for 18 times earnings, it may be somewhat overbought (overpriced considering its historical earnings, growth, and risk characteristics). On the other hand, if Alpha historically sells for 20 times earnings, and it is currently priced at 15 times earnings, it may be a bargain. Note that P/E ratios only provide a relative measure of the value for a company. Since it is relative, and since the stock market is subject to random price fluctuations, a change in P/E of a few percent is indistinguishable from background noise and may not represent an overbought or undervalued situation.

Example
Alpha Corporation has historically sold for a P/E ratio of 18:1. The stock market rises, and Alpha Corporation's stock rises with it to a P/E of 19:1. Since this change is within about 10% of historical

P/E ratios, it has little significance. The stock market rises further, and Alpha's P/E rises to 25:1. This is almost 40% higher than historical norms, and absent any other information, like a hostile takeover announcement, the stock is probably overbought. A significantly higher than average P/E might indicate a selling opportunity. It is August; the Dow Jones Industrial Average drops 500 points. Alpha Corporation's P/E drops to 12:1. The stock now looks significantly undervalued compared to historical norms. Absent other information, such as a pending bankruptcy filing, this might represent a buying opportunity.

RISK MEASUREMENT

Financial ratios are also used to measure the liquidity risk of a company. That is, they measure whether a company is likely to run out of money in either the short or long term.

Current Ratio

The current ratio is one of the first ratios most banks look at in determining a company's credit risk. The current ratio compares the assets a company can quickly convert to cash to the liabilities it must pay in the near term. Put simply, does the company have enough assets it can turn into cash to cover current obligations as they become due?

Current assets are assets that a company expects to turn into cash within a year. These include cash and cash equivalent securities (U.S. government T-bills, for example), stocks held for investment purposes (as compared to stocks that represent a long-term investment in another company), accounts receivable, notes receivable (except notes from officers and directors that are generally considered noncurrent assets), and inventory (including finished goods, work in process, and raw material).

Current liabilities are all liabilities that must be paid within a year. These include accounts payable, accrued payroll, customer deposits and prepayments, a bank line of credit, the portion of term loans and mortgages that will become due within a year, and the portion of financial or capital lease obligations that will become due within a year.

The formula for the current ratio is

$$\text{Current ratio} = \frac{\text{Current assets}}{\text{Current liabilities}} \qquad \text{(Eq. 2–25)}$$

Consider the balance sheet for Alpha Corporation given in Figure 2–1.

The current assets are cash, accounts receivable, and inventory. Plant and equipment are not included in current assets because they are generally not converted to cash within a year. Prepaid items, for example, insurance paid in advance, and loans to officers are not considered current assets.

FIGURE 2–1

Alpha Corporation Balance Sheet

Assets	
Cash	$ 20,000
Accounts receivable	$ 290,000
Inventory	$ 300,000
Total current assets	$ 610,000
Plant and equipment	$ 590,000
Total assets	$1,200,000
Liabilities	
Accounts payable	$ 310,000
Accrued payroll	$ 40,000
Line of credit	$ 200,000
Term loan current	$ 20,000
Leases current	$ 30,000
Current liabilities	$ 600,000
Loan long term	$ 230,000
Leases long term	$ 120,000
Total liabilities	$ 950,000
Equity	$ 250,000
Total liability and equity	$1,200,000

The current liabilities are accounts payable, accrued payroll, the line of credit, term loans current (that is, due in within one year) and leases current (that is, due within one year).

Note that only the current portion of capital, or financing leases, is included in current liabilities. Lease payments on a building, auto, or copier would not be included *unless* the company has a right to buy the leased item for a nominal value ($100 or less) at the end of the lease period. If a lease has such a bargain purchase option at lease end, the lease is probably a capital lease used as an alternative method of financing. If it were a capital lease, amounts due should be separated into current and long-term portions and booked accordingly.

Current ratio

$$= \frac{\$20,000 + \$290,000 + \$300,000}{\$310,000 + \$40,000 + \$200,000 + \$20,000 + \$30,000}$$

$$= \frac{\$610,000}{\$600,000} = 1.02$$

A current ratio of 1.02 implies that a company has just barely enough current assets to cover current liabilities. Should the current ratio drop below 1.0, banks and many investors would question whether the company has enough liquidity (assets it can convert to cash) to pay ongoing obligations.

Suppose Alpha Corporation had to write off 10% of its accounts receivable because a large customer went bankrupt, or suppose it had to write down 10% of its inventory because of damage or obsolescence? If accounts receivable dropped from $290,000 to $261,000, and inventory dropped from $300,000 to $270,000, its current ratio would then drop to

Current ratio

$$= \frac{\$20,000 + \$261,000 + \$270,000}{\$310,000 + \$40,000 + \$200,000 + \$20,000 + \$30,000}$$

$$= \frac{\$551,000}{\$600,000} = 0.92$$

The implication of a 0.92 current ratio is that the company, as presently structured, will not have enough cash to meet ongoing obligations. Banks and investors therefore like to see some multiple above 1 to protect themselves against unforeseen impairment of current assets. Current ratios vary by industries, but ratios above 2.0 are common.

Aged Accounts Receivable: Risk of Uncollectible Accounts

Another way banks protect themselves from the risk of borrower insolvency is to demand an analysis of aged accounts receivable. There are two ways to age accounts receivable: from the invoice date or from the shipping date (that is, the date on which the goods or services were supplied to the customer). Sophisticated banks demand that accounts receivable be aged from the date service was rendered or products were shipped so that delays in invoicing do not mask old accounts receivable. An aging is simply an analysis of account balances that are (1) zero to 30 days old, (2) 30 to 60 days old, (3) 60 to 90 days old, and (4) over 90 days old. Figure 2–2 is an example of the format of a typical aged accounts receivable.

Banks often treat accounts receivable over 90 days old as uncollectible even though most of these accounts may well be collected. This is significant because most bank loans contain

FIGURE 2-2

Format of Typical Aged Accounts Receivable

Customer Invoice no.	0–30 Days	31–60 Days	61–90 Days	Over 90 Days
Adams Communications				
30315	$ 1,600			
29993			$ 900	
Betatron				
30314	$ 6,000			
30318	$ 7,500			
28043				$ 136
.				
.				
.				
Totals	$2,645,000	$1,085,000	$531,000	$90,000

covenants that certain ratios of assets to liabilities be maintained. Large write-offs of accounts receivable may cause covenant violations that will trigger loan default.

Suppose an aging of Alpha Corporation's accounts receivable disclosed $90,000 was over 90 days old. A bank might reduce Alpha's accounts receivable by $90,000 when making their risk computations.

Most outside accounting firms (CPA firms) insist that reserves be taken against old accounts receivable. The definition of "old" varies from firm to firm, and industry to industry, depending on the totality of the circumstances. Many CPA firms insist on booking an allowance for doubtful accounts when accounts receivable are over 120 days old, and a larger reserve when accounts receivable are more than 180 days old. Almost all CPA firms insist on allowances for, or write-off of, accounts receivable more than a year old.

Allowance for Doubtful Accounts

An allowance for doubtful accounts recognizes the probability that some portion of accounts receivable will eventually become uncollectible.

An allowance for doubtful accounts is a contra account usually listed just below accounts receivable in the general ledger. Whereas accounts receivable have a debit balance, the allowance for doubtful accounts has a credit balance. When financial statements are prepared, the balance in the allowance account is netted against the balance in accounts receivable and reported as accounts receivable net of allowance for doubtful accounts or simply accounts receivable net.

Booking an allowance creates a credit; it must have an offsetting debit. The debit is usually bad debt expense.

Example

The sum of all outstanding balances from the accounts receivable detail ledger is $1,200,000. However, the auditors have analyzed the accounts and found that $300,000 is more than 180 days old. None is over a year old. They recommend a 50% allowance be set up for these accounts.

Amount of the allowance (Eq. 2–26)
    = Amount over 180 days × Allowance percent
    = \$300,000 × 50% = \$150,000

The entry would be

	Debit	Credit
Bad debt expense	\$150,000	
Allowance for doubtful accounts		\$150,000

However, on the balance sheet, this would be reported as follows:

Accounts receivable net of allowance for doubtful accounts	\$1,050,000
(\$1,200,000 less allowance of \$150,000)	

A more sophisticated analysis would look at collection histories for accounts that aged out to the 90 to 180 day bracket, collections for those that aged out to 180 to 365 days, and collections for accounts over 365 days old. Eq. 2–26 would be adapted for each bracket.

Quick Ratio

We have seen how banks protect themselves from impairment of one of the most important current assets, that is accounts receivable, through aging. They find it more difficult to protect themselves from the risk that inventory is damaged, obsolete, or otherwise impaired to the extent that its book value cannot be realized at sale. To remedy this situation, they have developed the quick ratio.

The quick ratio, also known as the acid test ratio, is current assets less inventory divided by current liabilities. This ratio addresses the issue of whether current assets could cover current liabilities if inventory were found to be worthless. The formula is

$$\text{Quick ratio} = \frac{\text{Current assets} - \text{Inventory}}{\text{Current liabilities}} \quad \text{(Eq. 2–27)}$$

Example

Alpha Corporation has current assets of $610,000, of which $300,000 is inventory. Current liabilities are $600,000. What is its quick ratio?

$$\text{Quick ratio} = \frac{\$610,000 - \$300,000}{\$600,000} = \frac{\$310,000}{\$600,000} = 0.52$$

Alpha Corporation would not have enough assets to cover current expenses if it could not sell its inventory for very close to its book value. Depending on how marketable the bank perceives the inventory to be, this could create a strong bias against granting a bank loan. On the other hand, if the inventory were easily liquidated gold bars, oil, or some item for which there is a ready market, an adverse quick ratio would be less important.

Cash Flow from Operations Versus Current Liabilities

Another way to think about the risk of lending to, or investing in, a company is to compare the cash flow from operations to average current liabilities. Obviously, if the company is generating enough cash flow, the impact of an adverse current or quick ratio may be mitigated.

A good estimate of cash flow is income from operations plus depreciation. Here it is important to focus on income from operations rather than looking at the bottom line, which may be inflated from one-time events such as sale of an asset, gains made investing in the stock market, interest, or dividend income.

The formula for comparing cash flow from operations to current liabilities is

$$\frac{\text{Cash flow operations}}{\text{Average current liabilities}} = \qquad \text{(Eq. 2–28)}$$

$$\frac{\text{Net income} - \text{Gains on sale or investing} + \text{Depreciation}}{\text{Average current liabilities}}$$

Example

Alpha Corporation has net income of $100,000, gains on sale of a computer-controlled drill press were $5,000, and gains from investing in the stock market were $3,000. Average current liabilities are $600,000. Depreciation is $50,000.

$$\frac{\text{Cash flow operations}}{\text{Current liabilities}} = \frac{\$100,000 - \$5,000 - \$3,000 + \$50,000}{\$600,000}$$

$$= \frac{\$142,000}{\$600,000} = 0.24$$

The ratio of 0.24 would not be considered good because at their current level of operations, it would take four years to pay off current liabilities (1 / 0.24 = ~4 years) should current assets be impaired. An observant investor, banker, or manager would look closely to determine whether this trend was improving (meaning the ratio was getting larger) or deteriorating (meaning the ratio was getting smaller). According to one study, healthy firms have a ratio of 0.4 or more.[2]

Long-Term Measures of Liquidity Risk

Assuming a company can meet its bills as they become due, how can a company's longer-term prospects be evaluated? Several measures can be considered.

Debt/Equity Ratio
The debt/equity ratio is total liabilities (short and long term) divided by equity. The formula is

$$\text{Debt/equity ratio} = \frac{\text{Total liabilities}}{\text{Equity}} \qquad \text{(Eq. 2–29)}$$

Example
Alpha Corporation has total liabilities of $600,000 and equity of $250,000.

$$\text{Debt/equity ratio} = \frac{\$600,000}{\$250,000} = 2.4$$

This ratio is a relative measure of who is bearing the financial risk of the enterprise: the owners, who are putting up the equity, or the creditors, who are lending the company money. The higher this ratio, the more nervous the creditors, especially banks, become.

At a debt/equity ratio of 3:1, creditors are supplying $3 out of every $4 used in the enterprise. At a debt/equity ratio of 4:1, creditors are supplying $4 out of every $5 used. As the ratio goes up, more risk is shifted from owners to creditors. Experience shows that few banks are willing to lend when the debt/equity ratio rises to 5:1.

Another way to think of this "risk shifting" is by recalling the accounting equation, which states

$$\text{Assets} = \text{Liabilities} + \text{Equity} \qquad \text{(Eq. 2–30)}$$

Liabilities are another name for debt. We can use the format in Figure 2–3 to analyze the burden of risk of the enterprise. For example, suppose a company has a debt/equity ratio of 3.5 to 1. About 78% of the risk is borne by creditors.

Interest Coverage Ratio

The interest coverage ratio, also called times interest earned, attempts to estimate how much "safety" there is in a company's earning power, in terms of making interest payments. It is net income before interest and taxes divided by interest. The formula is

$$\text{Interest coverage ratio} = \frac{\text{Net income} + \text{Interest} + \text{Taxes}}{\text{Interest}}$$

$$\text{(Eq. 2–31)}$$

Interest and taxes are added back to get earnings before interest and taxes. Interest is not added back to net of taxes because the "tax savings" of interest are already reflected in the amount of taxes paid. As an alternative to adding back interest and taxes to net income, EBIT may be used in the numerator.

$$\text{Interest coverage ratio} = \frac{\text{EBIT}}{\text{Interest}} \qquad \text{(Eq. 2–32)}$$

FIGURE 2–3

Format for Analyzing Owner's Risk Versus Creditor's Risk

		Portion of Assets Financed		
Debt	3.5	3.5 / 4.5	77.8%	Risk borne by creditors
Equity	1.0	1.0 / 4.5	22.2%	Risk borne by equity
Assets	4.5		100.0%	

Example

Alpha Corporation has net income of $100,000, interest of $10,000, and taxes of $40,000. What is its interest coverage ratio?

$$\text{Interest coverage ratio} = \frac{\$100,000 + \$10,000 + \$40,000}{\$10,000}$$

$$= \frac{\$150,000}{\$10,000} = 15:1$$

The problem with this ratio is that it fails to address the issue of principal repayment. Term loans and capital leases require both principal and interest to be paid. Otherwise, the loan is in default, or the lease contract is breached. For short-term loans, principal constitutes the bulk of the dollars that must be paid.

This ratio also fails to acknowledge that line of credit loans must be paid down to zero at least once per year. As such, it may give a false sense of security. On the other hand, if the interest coverage ratio is less than 1.0, the company is probably in trouble.

CAUTIONS ON RATIOS

Ratios, alone, are not sufficient to understand a company's past performance or to forecast future performance. They must be used in the context of (1) other companies in the industry, (2) the prior performance of the company, and (3) whether the ratios, taken together, tell a consistent story.

When looking at historical trends, bear in mind that changing conditions can radically alter the outcome of a company's performance. For example, an airline that loses money when jet fuel is $3.00 per gallon may be wildly profitable when jet fuel is $0.90 per gallon. It takes time for even the most nimble management team to adjust to such radical changes in the environment.

When using ratios involving assets, especially plant assets, which tend to change slowly over time, the historical cost basis required by generally accepted accounting principles may make a company with old, worn-out equipment look more profitable than a new state-of-the-art company. Should inflation reappear as an economic force, this type of problem would become more pronounced.

SUMMARY

Financial statements, by themselves, don't provide a lot of insight into how well a company is performing year to year or in comparison to other companies in their industry. One of the reasons it is difficult to make comparisons is that companies rarely have exactly the same revenue; another reason is that companies have varying financing structures.

Ratios and other performance measures have been developed to make financial information comparable from company to company, to establish norms, and to identify areas of under performance. These measures fall into three broad categories: operating performance, financial performance, and financial risk.

Operating performance deals with the efficiency of management. Measures such as return on assets (ROA) measure how well management is using the assets they have been given. Profit margin is a measure of the relationship of revenue to expenses. Other measures of operating efficiency include things like revenue per employee, which helps a company decide whether it is overstaffed, or whether management is simply not effectively employing human resources.

Financial performance deals with issues related to a company's financial structure. Return on equity (ROE), also called return on common equity (ROCE), addresses whether shareholders' equity is being effectively utilized. For example, is debt being appropriately used to leverage shareholder equity? It also deals with issues such as whether earnings per share are growing or deteriorating as a company's financial structure changes.

Analysis of a company's financial risk is important to banks, suppliers, and investors. Short-term measures of financial risk such as the current ratio and quick ratio address whether a company can pay its bills as they come due. Longer-term measures of financial risk such as the debt/equity ratio address who is bearing the financial risk of company operations, creditors or shareholders, and by how much. If companies can't pay their debts on time or too much risk of the enterprise is shifted to creditors, banks will stop lending and vendors will stop extending the company credit.

Ratios by themselves provide little information unless there is a yardstick to measure them against. Several companies publish ratios by industry, and those ratios provide a basis of determining whether a company is underperforming, overperforming, or meeting industry expectations. Benchmarking can also be used as a yardstick. Benchmarking involves analyzing the financial statements of the best companies in an industry and using their financial ratios as a basis for evaluation of a company's performance.

Ratios and other performance measures should be used in the context of (1) other companies in an industry; (2) prior company performance; and (3) whether the ratios, taken together, tell a consistent story. Given these considerations, ratio analysis and the other measures of performance discussed in this chapter can be very useful as a diagnostic tool to probe a company's financial statements provided they are used with the proper professional judgment.

ENDNOTES

1. See an advanced accounting text, such as *Intermediate Accounting*, 6th edition, Mosich, pp. 907 and 919; *Fundamentals of Financial Management*, 8th edition, Brigham p. 791; or *Advanced Accounting*, 3rd edition, Griffin, pp. 205 and 207.
2. Cornellius Casey and Norman Bartzcak, "Using Operating Cash Flow Data to Predict Financial Distress—Some Extensions," *Journal of Accounting Research*, Spring 1985, pp. 384–401.

CHAPTER 3

Factors Determining Interest Rates and Required Debt Yields

Financial analysis is about shaping the future, and one of the key factors used to make decisions about the future is interest rates. Interest rates are a key factor in determining the cost of capital; interest rates also provide benchmarks against which to make investment decisions.

Closely related to interest is the concept of required yield. What yield, or stated another way, what return on investment is required to induce an investment in A versus B? If a "safe" investment, like U.S. T-bills, pays 6%, how much would be required to induce someone to invest in, say, Argentina's bonds? The required yield is the minimum return necessary to induce an investment. As the interest rate on T-bills rises, the yield required to induce an investment in Argentina's bonds will also rise. So required yield and interest are inextricably linked, but the linkage is not necessarily linear.

The other side of investment decisions is fund raising. If a company needs to raise funds for various projects, they need a firm understanding of what the market will demand in terms of yield. If they don't have that understanding before going to capital markets, they will be at the mercy of banks, underwriters, and other firms supplying capital.

In this chapter, we will explore the factors that drive interest rates and, by implication, the factors that drive the yields required to induce investments of various types.

COMPONENTS OF INTEREST: RISK-FREE RATE OF RETURN, DEFAULT, LIQUIDITY, AND MATURITY RISK PREMIUMS

Interest rates are generally influenced by (1) how productively borrowed funds can be deployed, (2) the preference of individuals for saving rather than consuming, (3) inflation, and (4) other risk factors.

Risk-Free Rate of Return

Generally, the preference for saving rather than consuming, and the current inflation rate are represented by Krf, which is known as the risk-free rate of return. Krf can be estimated by the interest rate on a one-year T-bill. Krf is said to be risk free because it is assumed that the federal government will always pay its debts.

Default Risk Premium

The default risk premium (DRP) reflects the risk that a creditor will not pay back its loan. Businesses incurring a loss have a higher DRP than profitable businesses, and businesses sliding headlong toward bankruptcy have a higher DRP. On the other hand, businesses generating a lot of cash relative to their debt service have a low DRP.

Liquidity Premium

The liquidity premium (LP) is a premium to reflect the fact that there may not be a ready buyer for a security. There are always buyers for U.S. government securities or G.E. bonds. However, it may be difficult to find a buyer for bonds issued by the Minsk Brick Works.

Maturity Risk Premium

The maturity risk premium (MRP) is a premium that reflects the likelihood that the risk-free rate of return will rise over time. The maturity risk premium may be relatively small for bonds of short maturity, perhaps 2 to 5 years, but large for 30-year bonds.

Formula for *K*, the Required Rate of Return

The required rate of return on a bond, or any debt instrument, is designated as K. It is the yield it must provide to attract investors. K can be computed as follows:

$$K = \text{Krf} + \text{DRP} + \text{LP} + \text{MRP} \qquad \text{(Eq. 3–1)}$$

Eq. 3–1 shows the required rate of return for U.S. dollar-denominated debt, issued by a U.S. company, institution, or government agency. Were this debt denominated in another currency, or issued by a company or institution in another country, even if dollar denominated, the borrower would, in theory, have to pay an additional premium for exchange rate risk (ERR). Since few finance texts explicitly recognize ERR as a separate type of risk premium, an insufficient amount of research has been done in this area. Institutional investors constantly underestimate this risk and are often surprised by losses they should have anticipated. Therefore, unless stated otherwise, the following discussion is confined to domestic U.S. interest rates.

Estimating Components of Interest

We have already seen that the risk-free rate of return, Krf, can be estimated by the rate on one-year T-bills. The government's risk-free securities also provide insight into a value for the maturity risk premium as well. Why? Government bonds have a zero default risk premium and zero liquidity premium. That means the rate difference between a one-year T-bill and a five-year T-note must be largely due to the risk of future inflation, the maturity risk premium. Since government bonds are continually issued and traded, a wealth of information about bonds and notes of all maturities is widely available. One source is *The Wall Street Journal*, "Money and Investing" section.

Liquidity is a function of the number of buyers and sellers in a marketplace. If, for example, a company issues $10 million of $100,000 bonds, there will only be 100 bonds to trade, hardly enough to make it worthwhile for a broker to make a market in that particular security. On the other hand, $1 billion of $10,000 might be more attractive because there is the potential of 100,000 bonds being in play. Bond brokers make a market for a security by offering to buy a security at a stated price and offering to sell that same security at a stated price. The difference between the purchase price and sales price is the spread, and that is how brokers make their profit. Making a market provides an economic service because it facilitates purchase and sale of bonds and minimizes the liquidity premium.

The default risk premium is correlated with bond ratings provided by Moody's Investor Service, Standard & Poor's, and others. Each service has a slightly different definition of its ratings and the factors that go into its ratings. A bond's rating may start out as, for example, AAA, which means a bond has very little default risk, and decline below investment grade, which means it has a significant default risk. When this happens, a bond's default risk premium rises. As a company's fortune can change over time, so can its bond rating and default risk premium.

Forecasting Interest Rates: Expectation Theory

Expectation theory is a way to forecast the risk-free rate of return a number of years into the future. This is important because many capital projects take a year or more from inception until they require funding. The ability to forecast shifts in future interest rates allows businesses to make more sophisticated project analyses, which means the financial risk of a project can be minimized.

Expectation theory states that all things being equal, the yield on a two-year bond will be the average of the yield on a one-year bond, and the expected yield on a *one-year bond, purchased one year from today*. By looking at T-notes with varying maturity dates, one-year T-bills can be estimated into the future.

To simplify the discussion, we need to standardize our notation. Let $K(i, j)$ represent bonds with a varying number of years to maturity and purchased at different times

where i is the year a bond was purchased. If $i = 0$, the bond is purchased now; if $i = 1$, the bond is purchased one year from now; if $i = 2$, the bond is purchased two years from now; etc.

j is the number of years until a bond matures

For example, a bond $K(0, 2)$ would be a bond purchased now, with a two-year maturity. A bond $K(3, 1)$ would be a bond purchased in three years, with a one-year maturity.

If we know the rate on a two-year bond is 5.5% $K(0, 2)$, when a one-year bond is yielding 5% $K(0, 1)$, can we use that to predict the yield on a one-year bond purchased next year?

$$K(0, 2) = [K(0, 1) + K(1, 1)] / 2 \qquad \text{(Eq. 3–2)}$$

Stated in words, we expect the yield, K, on a two-year bond purchased today to equal the average of the yield on a one-year bond purchased today and a one-year bond purchased in one year.

Substituting into this equation the quantities we know

$$5.5\% = [5\% + K(1, 1)] / 2$$

And multiplying both sides by 2 gives

$$11\% = 5\% + K(1, 1)$$
$$K(1, 1) = 11\% - 5\% = 6\%$$

Using this method, it is possible to deconstruct the yield on three-year bonds to find the expected Krf in year three, deconstruct four-year bonds to find the expected Krf in four years, and so forth.

Yields of bonds of various maturities are published in *The Wall Street Journal* and other financial newspapers. Using expectation theory, we can "look ahead" to what experts believe will be interest rates in the future. This can inform judgment about whether to invest in the long or short term, whether to refinance one's house now or wait for interest rates to drop further, or make any number of other financial decisions.

EFFECT OF SUPPLY AND DEMAND ON INTEREST RATES

To this point, we have discussed interest rates as a function of the risk-free rate of return, default risk, liquidity risk, and maturity risk. But what about supply and demand? Don't they control prices in a free market? Of course they do.

However, the supply of capital to the marketplace by savers, as well as demand for capital by borrowers, does not operate in a vacuum. In part, supply is based on alternative investments, such as short-term U.S. Treasury securities; and in part, supply is based on perceived risks, such as default risk, liquidity risk, or maturity risk.

The demand for business capital is based on the belief that a company can get a greater return on assets (ROA) for new investments than interest net of taxes. Since some projects will have a higher forecast ROA than other projects, the demand for capital will expand when money is cheap (when interest rates are low) and will contract when money becomes expensive (when interest rates rise).

Consumer demand for credit is usually based on other factors, such as lifestyle, the need for (better) transportation, (better) housing, and so on, balanced against a person's personal financial security and outlook.

Capital Supply Curve

The principles of capital supply and demand can be illustrated through an experiment I conducted in a recent finance class. I put the following hypothetical question to the class: Given that banks are paying about 2.75% interest on savings accounts, what rate of interest would induce you to invest $1,000 with Bruno's Credit Corporation for a year? I provided no information about Bruno's.

At 2% interest, there were no takers, nor were there at 3% or 4%. At 5%, two hands went up; at 6%, two more hands went up; and so forth to 15%. At that point, 18 of the 20 students in class had participated. On asking the remaining two students what interest rate would induce them to invest $1,000 with Bruno's, one said 25%, the other said 40%. The results are tabulated in Figure 3–1.

FIGURE 3-1

Capital Supply Table for Bruno's Credit Corporation

Cumulative Number of Students	Minimum Required Interest	Amount of Student Capital Raised	Amount of Capital Raised if Each Student Represented 10 Like Them
2	5%	$ 2,000	$ 20,000
4	6%	$ 4,000	$ 40,000
6	7%	$ 6,000	$ 60,000
8	8%	$ 8,000	$ 80,000
10	9%	$10,000	$100,000
12	10%	$12,000	$120,000
14	12%	$14,000	$140,000
18	15%	$18,000	$180,000
19	25%	$19,000	$190,000
20	40%	$20,000	$200,000

Suppose, for a moment, each of these 20 students had the risk characteristics of 10 other savers. Then the money supply curve for the entire group of savers with respect to Bruno's could be plotted as shown in Figure 3–2.

After asking the class how many were paying 15% to 18% on credit cards, 10% to 12% on car loans, and 8% to 10% on mortgages or second mortgages, I asked the following question: Suppose Bruno's Credit offered to lend you $20,000 for five years, no questions asked. What interest rate would induce you to borrow from Bruno's? In the hypothetical, I made it clear that Bruno's did not care whether they were using the money for a vacation or to refinance credit cards or a home mortgage.

No one was interested in borrowing from Bruno's above 12% interest, and only one student was interested at 12%. Two more people were interested in borrowing money at 10%, and two more at 8%. At 1% interest, 15 out of 20 students were interested in borrowing. The results of this hypothetical are tabulated in Figure 3–3.

Notice that even with a hypothetical 200 students willing to invest in, or deposit money with, Bruno's, the capital demand of just 15 students exceeded the total capital Bruno's could raise.

Plotting demand for capital on top of Bruno's capital supply curve yields Figure 3–4.

FIGURE 3-2

Capital Supply Curve for Bruno's Credit Corporation

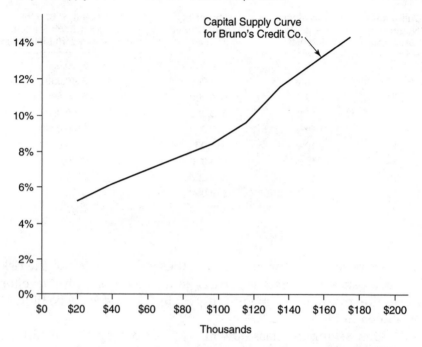

Thousands

FIGURE 3-3

Capital Demand Curve for Bruno's Credit Corporation

Cumulative Number of Students	Maximum Interest Students Willing to Pay	Amount of Student Loan Demand
1	12%	$ 20,000
3	10%	$ 60,000
5	8%	$100,000
6	6%	$120,000
7	5%	$140,000
10	4%	$200,000
12	3%	$240,000
13	2%	$260,000
15	1%	$300,000

FIGURE 3-4

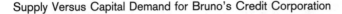

Supply Versus Capital Demand for Bruno's Credit Corporation

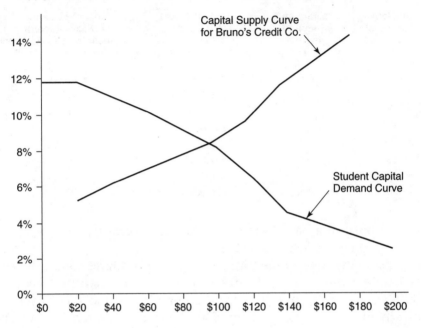

The intersection of Bruno's capital supply curve and the student capital demand curve sets the nominal interest rate students can charge for use of their money, and the maximum rate Bruno's can demand their customers pay in loan interest. While students understandably want higher interest rates, there is no point in Bruno's paying investors or depositors more than about 8% because they cannot lend, at a profit, more than about $97,000.

The experiment was then recast as follows: Suppose rather than investing or making a deposit in Bruno's Credit Corporation, you were given the opportunity to deposit money in a national bank, insured by the FDIC. What interest rate would induce you to make a deposit of $1,000 in the bank for a year? Figure 3–5 is a tabulation of the results.

Plotting the capital supply curve for the national bank against the capital supply curve for Bruno's Credit Corporation, Figure 3–6 reveals some interesting insights into risk. Since the perceived risk

FIGURE 3-5

Capital Supply Curve for a National Bank

Cumulative Number of Students	Minimum Required Interest	Amount of Student Capital Raised	Amount of Capital if Each Student Represented 10 Like Them
0	2%	$ 0	$ 0
2	3%	$ 2,000	$ 20,000
4	4%	$ 4,000	$ 40,000
7	5%	$ 7,000	$ 70,000
11	6%	$11,000	$110,000
15	7%	$15,000	$150,000
17	8%	$17,000	$170,000
19	10%	$19,000	$190,000
20	15%	$20,000	$200,000

of a deposit in a bank was less than with Bruno's, students were willing to accept less interest.

Note that two of the four factors that set interest rates, the alternative investment in risk-free T-bills, and the maturity risk are the same for both investments. The default risk and liquidity risk of a bank are practically zero. Therefore, the difference between the bank's credit supply curves and Bruno's represents students' intuitive estimate of Bruno's default and liquidity risks.

Since people were willing to supply money to the bank at much lower rates than to Bruno's, the supply and demand for capital reach equilibrium at a different point, about 6.25% for the bank, compared to about 8% for Bruno's.

The bank can therefore supply more credit, about $120,000 worth in this hypothetical, at a lower cost, about 6.25%.

When dealing with corporate and government bonds, bond rating agencies assess risk and give bonds different ratings. Bonds of different risk will give rise to different capital supply curves. The amount of capital available, and the price of the capital, in terms of interest, will be a reflection of the risk evaluation, or quality rating, placed on bonds by these services.

Returning to our hypothetical, neither Bruno's nor a national bank would lend money for the same interest rate they paid depositors. They make their money from the difference between the amount they pay to borrow money and the rate at which they can

FIGURE 3-6

Capital Supply Curves for Bruno's and a Bank Versus Student Capital Demand Curve

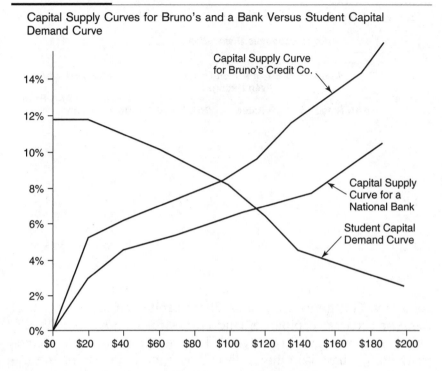

lend it out. This difference is called the spread, and could be from 2% for creditworthy customers to 8% for those with a poor credit history.

Another factor to consider is that in the real world, the equilibrium point, the point at which supply and demand for capital intersect to yield an interest rate, is always being buffeted by market forces and can move from day to day.

Arguably, the capital supply curve will be the same for all companies with the same creditworthiness. If we assume Moody's, Standard & Poor's, and other bond rating services are timely and accurate, then all the companies rated AAA should be one curve, all those rated BBB should be on one curve, and so forth.

Capital Demand Curve

We have seen that the amount and price of capital that the market is willing to supply is a function of the creditworthiness of a

F I G U R E   3–7

Survey of Bond Purchasing Preferences Before and After Economic Dislocation

Prior to Economic Dislocation

Interest Rate	Cumulative Number of Money Managers Who Would Buy a Million-Dollar Bond at Given Ratings			After Dislocation
	AAA Rated	BBB Rated	CCC Rated	Cumulative AAA-Rated Bond Demand (millions)
5%	1	0	0	1 = 1
6%	2	0	0	2 = 2
7%	5	1	0	5 + 1 = 6
8%	9	3	1	9 + 3 + 1 = 13
9%	12	6	3	12 + 6 + 3 = 21
10%	16	9	7	16 + 9 + 7 = 32
11%	21	12	8	21 + 12 + 8 = 41
12%	30	18	13	30 + 18 + 13 = 61

company. This gives rise to a family of capital supply curves. Will there be separate capital demand curves for companies with different credit ratings? Probably not. The credit demand of each company will be based on the projects they have to invest in, and the return on those projects. In Chapter 9, Cost of Capital, we will explore how companies rate and rank projects.

Changes in Supply

Supply can be affected by a number of environmental factors. Suppose the risk-free rate of return, Krf, increases from 4.75% to 6.75%? Since default risk and liquidity risk are added to Krf at each point along the capital supply curve, we would expect it to shift up by about 2% along its entire length provided the maturity risk premium remained unchanged.

Another phenomenon that can affect the capital supply curve is the so-called flight to safety. When there are major dislocations in the domestic or international economy, capital tends to flee from, or not be available to, high-risk investments. Examples of dislocations include the 500-point drop in the Dow Jones Industrial Average in 1987 and again in 1998, the Russian credit default of 1998,

FIGURE 3-8

Graph of Capital Supply Before and After Flight to Safety

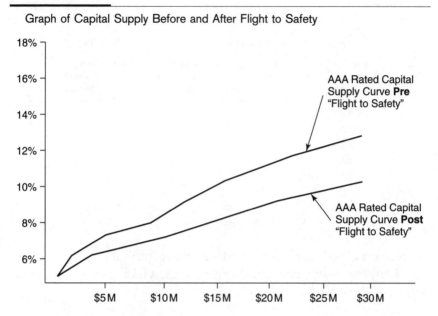

and the Brazilian default threatened in 1999, the collapse of the Internet bubble in 2000, and the Argentine default of 2002.

We can graphically see the effect of this flight to safety through a hypothetical exercise. Suppose those who were willing to purchase BBB-rated bonds now insist on AAA-rated bonds and are willing to forego 1 percentage point of interest for the increased safety. Suppose further, those willing to purchase CCC-rated bonds now only want to purchase AAA-rated bonds and are willing to forego 2 percentage points of interest.

Shifts in bond demand are the same as shifts in capital supply. When investors shift their risk preference toward safety, the safest companies, that is, the ones with the highest credit ratings, will benefit because more capital will become available to them at lower cost. See Figures 3–7 and 3–8.

How can the capital supply be measured in actual practice? One way is to survey brokers and institutional investors to determine the quantity of a bond they would buy given various interest rates. On the other hand, if one wasn't interested in the entire capital supply curve, but simply that region of the curve very near

Table Shift in Capital Demand for Poor Economic Outlook

Original Demand Information		Modified
Project Return on Assets	Cumulative Millions Required for AAA Company Projects	Adjustment for One-Third Cancellations
20%	1	1
18%	2	1
16%	4	3
14%	6	4
12%	10	7
10%	15	10
8%	40	27

the market clearing price (the place where capital supply and demand curves meet), one could examine the yield on bonds of companies with similar credit ratings.

Changes in Demand

The demand for capital can change as well as the supply, thus affecting the amount of capital and the cost of that capital. Suppose, for example, the economic outlook were poor. With little assurance of revenue growth, companies might defer or cancel orders for new plant capacity, plant upgrades, or even replacement of operational but inefficient equipment.

When the demand for capital slackens, the demand curve moves downward and to the left. This reduces both nominal interest rates and the amount of capital companies are willing to borrow.

Suppose the economic outlook turns grim, unemployment is expected to rise, and recession looms on the horizon. What would the capital demand curve look like if companies canceled one third of their projects? Considering only the capital supply and demand of AAA-rated companies, a table of capital demand would be changed as shown in Figure 3-9.

Plotting modified capital demand against the capital supply curves from the preceding problem shows graphically that both

FIGURE 3-10

Capital Supply and Demand Illustrating Both Flight to Safety and Shift in Economic Outlook

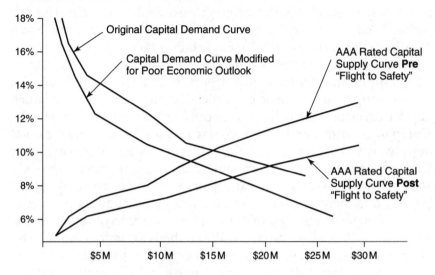

the interest rate and the amount of money companies are willing to borrow decrease, as shown in Figure 3–10.

Plotting the modified capital demand curve graphically illustrates that both borrowing and the nominal interest rate decrease. Interest rates drop from about 10% to 9.25% under normal conditions, that is, when there is no flight to safety, and drop from about 9% to about 8.25% when there is a flight to safety in this hypothetical.

SUMMARY

Interest rates and the yield demanded by investors are inextricably intertwined. Understanding how interest rates move provides insight into investment alternatives and raising capital. The required rate of return on a bond, or any security, is the minimum needed to get investors to invest in it. The required interest rate for a bond can be estimated using the formula $K = Krf + DRP + LP + MRP$, where Krf is the risk-free rate of return that can be estimated by the yield on one-year U.S. T-bills; DRP is the default risk premium; LP is the liquidity premium; and MRP is the maturity risk premium, that is, the risk that interest rates will rise. Bonds issued by non-U.S. corporations are subject to exchange risk as well as the risk associated with foreign government regulation. This additional risk can be represented by an additional term in the equation, exchange rate risk (ERR). Expectation theory provides a technique for estimating the risk-free rate of return for future years.

Supply and demand play a part in shifting interest rates. A capital supply curve can be constructed by determining how much capital investors are willing to supply at any given interest rate. Companies with similar risk characteristics have similar capital supply curves. As a general rule, risky companies must pay higher interest rates than good companies. In times of crisis, there is a flight to safety, which means investors shift funds into better companies; this increases their capital supply and reduces their relative borrowing costs. Capital demand is a function of return on the projects available to companies. When the economic outlook deteriorates and companies cut back on the projects they plan to invest in, capital demand drops, so the point at which supply and demand reach equilibrium drops, lowering interest rates.

CHAPTER 4

Forecasting Yield and Risk

The world is not a machine. Events never unfold exactly as planned. Sophisticated decision makers understand and plan for bumps, bruises, and potholes by using quantitative risk management techniques. Risk is a term for deviations from a plan. But risk has meaning only in the context of the expected outcome of a plan. Since many financial analyses focus on return on investment, or yield, these analytical techniques are often referred to together as forecasting yield and risk. In this chapter, we will examine three techniques for forecasting yield and risk, as well as discuss the application of risk management principles to everyday business problems.

The expected yield is the weighted average yield from a set of investments. Generalizing this a bit, the expected value is a weighted average value of a certain outcome. The expected value might be the expected number of cars sold, units manufactured, or anything else. The expected yield, or expected value, is the forecast result.

The standard deviation is a particularly useful measure of risk. When data are normally distributed, which is almost always the case for a large number of events, the standard deviation can be used to forecast the probability of certain outcomes.

There are two basic ways of forecasting yield and risk. The first uses a priori probabilities, which are probabilities assigned to certain events based on the knowledge and judgment of experts.

This method is problematic because the quality of the data may vary from forecast to forecast. The second method is based on historical data, which, on the surface, seems more objective, but does not give weight to emerging conditions. Since both types of problems are encountered in finance, it is important to know both methods.

FORECASTING WITH A PRIORI PROBABILITIES

A priori probabilities are probabilities determined in advance. The expected yield, Ke, for this class of problem may be computed using Eq. 4–1.

Expected rate of return = $Ke = P1 \times K1 + P2 \times K2 + \ldots Pn \times Kn$

(Eq. 4–1)

where   Ke is the expected yield

P1, P2, . . . Pi is the probability of a certain outcome

K1, K2, . . . Ki are the yields associated with P1, P2, . . . respectively

The standard deviation for this type of problem may be computed using Eq. 4–2

$$\sigma = \sqrt{\Sigma \ (Ki - Ke)^2 \times Pi}$$ (Eq. 4–2)

The coefficient of variation (CoVar) is a method of giving context to the standard deviation by comparing it to the expected value. The coefficient of variation can be computed using Eq. 4–3.

$$CoVar = \sigma \ / \ Ke$$ (Eq. 4–3)

Example

An investor wants to know the expected return, Ke, and the standard deviation, σ, and the coefficient of variation for Sellcomm Telemarketing. During her investigation, she interviewed marketing and accounting department staff, and given that information, constructed Figure 4–1.

Note that most of the computations for expected value and standard deviation have been formatted into a table. If these computations are being made manually, laying them out in a tabular

FIGURE 4-1

Computation of Yield and Risk for Sellcomm Telemarketing

Condition	Yield Ki	Proability Pi	Expected Value Ki × Pi	Ki − Ke	(Ki − Ke)²	(Ki − Ke)² × Pi
1. Major new client	20%	0.1	2.0%	20% − 9.5% = 10.50%	110.25%	11.03%
2. Minor new client	15%	0.2	3.0%	15% − 9.5% = 5.50%	30.25%	6.05%
3. Same clients	10%	0.4	4.0%	10% − 9.5% = 0.50%	0.25%	0.10%
4. Lose minor client	5%	0.2	1.0%	5% − 9.5% = −4.50%	20.25%	4.05%
5. Lose major client	−5%	0.1	−0.5%	−5% − 9.5% = −14.50%	210.25%	21.03%
Expected yield			Ke = 9.5%			42.25%

format improves accuracy and data checking because every part of every computation can be checked for reasonableness at a glance. Formatting the computation as a table also facilitates development of spreadsheets for analysis of yield and risk.

Examining the table, we see that the leftmost column contains all the possible marketing conditions the company could face in the next year. Next to each is the yield associated with each possible condition. For example, if the only change in their client mix is one new minor client, a yield of 15% is expected. On the other hand, if they lose a major client, their yield will be −5%. The third column from the left is the probability of each of the named conditions occurring. There is a 0.2 (20%) probability of getting one minor client, and only a 0.1 (10%) probability of losing a major client.

The expected value of each event, fourth column, is simply the product of the yield of each condition times the probability of each condition. When these partial probabilities are summed, we get the overall expected value, Ke, which is 9.5%.

The standard deviation, σ, is a measure of dispersion from the expected value, so we begin the computation of σ by subtracting the expected value, Ke, from each individual yield to get some sense of how different the outcome of any one condition is from the overall expected value. Some of these differences are positive and some are negative, so if we simply added the differences, they would tend toward zero, minimizing what might be large differences from the expected value. In the fifth column, we square the differences. This has the effect of converting all the differences to a positive number so that negative differences don't offset positive differences.

Notice that some of these measures of dispersions at this point in the computation are large. The conditions Major new client and Lose a major client have the largest measures at 110.25% and 210.25%, respectively. But these are the two lowest probability conditions. Retaining the same clients has a small measure of dispersion at 0.25%, but it has the highest probability. To recognize these facts, each measure of dispersion is multiplied by the probability of its associated condition occurring, giving us the data in the last column.

Adding the last column in Figure 4–1 gives a weighted average measure of dispersion, which is the same as the expression inside the square root sign in Eq. 4–2. Taking the square root of this value, as shown next, gives the standard deviation for this forecast.

$$\sigma = \sqrt{42.25\%}$$
$$\sigma = 6.5\%$$
$$\text{CoVar} = 6.5\% \ / \ 9.5\% = 0.68$$

Having found the expected value, standard deviation, and coefficient of variation of a set of yields and probabilities, the next question is what do they mean?

Expected value is a forecast, an estimate, the quantitative expression of the yield one would expect on Sellcomm. There is no guarantee the expected yield will be realized. This is just a likely outcome based on the information provided.

And what of the standard deviation? The standard deviation is an estimate of the quality of the expected value. When we speak of the quality of an estimate, we mean how far the estimate is likely to diverge from the *actual* yield. Where we can assume there is a normal probability distribution, Eq. 4–4 provides a formula for determining the range of values given: an expected value, a standard deviation, and a confidence level.

$$\text{Ke} - Z \times \sigma \quad \text{to} \quad \text{Ke} + Z \times \sigma \qquad \text{(Eq. 4–4)}$$

where   Ke is the expected value
σ is the standard deviation
Z is a value from normal distribution tables

We will explain the origin of those tables later in the chapter. For now, let's see how they are applied.

If we assume a normal probability distribution, we can say there is about a 68.3% probability that the *actual yield* will be within plus or minus one standard deviation of the expected value. So for a 68.3% confidence, Z = 1.0. When we say we want a 68.3% confidence, we mean we want a 68.3% probability that the actual yield will be in the range

$$\text{Ke} - 1 \times \sigma \quad \text{to} \quad \text{Ke} + 1 \times \sigma$$
$$9.5\% - 1 \times (6.5\%) \quad \text{to} \quad 9.5\% + 1 \times (6.5\%) \text{ or}$$
$$3\% \quad \text{to} \quad 16\%$$

If we wanted a 95% confidence about the range of *actual* yields, we could look at a table of standard deviations and find that a 95% confidence level equates to plus or minus 1.96 standard deviations.

$$K - 1.96 \times \sigma \quad \text{to} \quad K + 1.96 \times \sigma$$
$$9.5\% - 1.96 \times (6.5\%) \quad \text{to} \quad 9.5\% + 1.96 \times (6.5\%) \text{ or}$$
$$-3.24\% \quad \text{to} \quad 22.4\%$$

When making *any* financial computation, ask whether the answer seems reasonable. The best-case scenario is that Sellcomm will yield 20%. The worst-case scenario is that Sellcomm will yield −5%. Based on a 95% confidence level, the range of yields is −3.24% to 22.4%, which is close to the ends of the range of outcomes. Therefore, at a gross level, this is a sensible answer.

Computational errors are very common when dealing with percents. Two things can reduce the likelihood of error. First, state the probability of an event occurring as a decimal number. For example, if a condition has a 20% probability of occurring, state it as a 0.2 probability. Second, think of percents as whole numbers. For example, think of 10% as ten tiles or ten oranges or ten units, not one tenth of a unit. After the expected yield and risk are calculated, you can think of them in terms of percents. Otherwise, your computations will become hopelessly flawed.

The coefficient of variation, in a sense, provides a way to relate the amount of dispersion, represented by σ, to the magnitude of the expected value. For Sellcomm, it is

$$\text{CoVar} = 6.5\% \ / \ 9.5\% = 0.68$$

which means that one standard deviation is equal to a significant fraction of the expected value. Suppose, rather than computing yields, one was computing stock values. Consider two stocks each with a standard deviation of $5.00. If one were IBM, with an expected stock value of $125, and the other were Murray's Sandwich Shop, which had an expected stock value of $3.00, the impact of a $5.00 standard deviation would be quite different. The coefficient of variation, therefore, helps scale, or measure, the relative significance of the variability of the data.

$$\text{Coefficient of variation of IBM} = \$5 \ / \ \$125 = 0.04$$
$$\text{Coefficient of variation of Murray's} = \$5 \ / \ \$3 = 1.67$$

Recommendation: Pay careful attention to the format in which the problem is set up. A good columnar format will facilitate computations by saving time and reducing or eliminating many computational errors.

A venture capitalist might use this sort of analysis in valuing a prerevenue company. They might set out a list of possible outcomes in terms of company revenue, say, five years hence, and the regulatory, competitive, or managerial conditions that might lead to any particular outcome.

Example

VC Ventures is considering an investment in a prerevenue technology company. They want to exit the investment in five years. Historically, they know that this kind of technology company is valued at four times revenue. Therefore, they want to estimate revenue in five years to determine the exit value of their investment. They set up Figure 4–2 to find the expected value of the revenue, Re, and the risk inherent in reaching that revenue.

Based on this model, the target company will have an expected revenue of $40.7 million in five years. This is significantly different from the $50 million in revenue in management's plan. As a result, VC Ventures will demand a larger percentage of the company for the same number of dollars invested so their ultimate payoff on exit will be the same.

Suppose VC Ventures wanted to know the range of revenue for the company they were thinking about investing in, and they wanted to be 90% confident the actual revenue would fall within the specified range. To make this calculation, they would have to compute the standard deviation, which based on the information in Figure 4–2, would be

$$\sigma = \sqrt{86.4}$$
$$= 9.3$$

If the expected value of revenue for the target company is $40.7 million, and the standard deviation is $9.3 million, then all we need is the Z factor from a normal distribution table that corresponds to 90% to compute the range of revenue with 90% confidence. That Z factor is about 1.65. In other words, VC Ventures can be 90%

FIGURE 4-2

VC Ventures Revenue Model

Condition	Revenue Millions R_i	Probability P_i	Expected Value $R_i \times P_i$	$R_i - R_e$	$(R_i - R_e)^2$	$(R_i - R_e)^2 \times P_i$
1. Market demand exceeds expectations	52	0.1	5.2	52 − 40.7 = 11.3	127.7	12.8
2. Management's growth plan met	50	0.3	15.0	50 − 40.7 = 9.3	86.5	25.9
3. Competitors force prices down	40	0.2	8.0	40 − 40.7 = −0.7	0.5	0.1
4. Time to market exceeds plan	40	0.1	4.0	40 − 40.7 −0.7	0.5	0.0
5. Major competition	30	0.2	6.0	30 − 40.7 = −10.7	114.5	22.9
6. Management performs poorly	25	0.1	2.5	25 − 40.7 = −15.7	246.5	24.6
Expected Revenue			$R_e = 40.7$			86.4

84.6 $^{.5}$ = 9.3

confident that the actual revenue will be within plus or minus 1.65 times the standard deviation of the expected value.

$$\text{Re} - 1.65 \times \sigma \quad \text{to} \quad \text{Re} + 1.65 \times \sigma$$
$$\$40.7\text{ M} - 1.65 \times \$9.3\text{ M} \quad \text{to} \quad \$40.7\text{ M} + 1.65 \times \$9.3\text{ M}$$
$$\$25.4\text{ M} \quad \text{to} \quad \$56.0\text{ M}$$

Forecasting with probabilities can become quite complex and sophisticated. Consider the type of forecasting an airline might do. Suppose market research indicates there is a 40% chance travel will increase by 10%, a 50% chance travel will be unchanged, and a 10% chance travel will decline. Suppose further that there is a 30% chance fuel prices will decline by 10%, a 50% probability fuel costs will remain the same, and a 20% chance fuel prices will rise 10%. Just modeling these two variables results in nine different sets of conditions, each with its own outcome. If an analyst then factored in labor unrest, positing a 2% chance of a work stoppage, the number of conditions to model would increase to 18 (3 levels of travel × 3 fuel price levels × 2 possible labor scenarios).

FORECASTING WITH HISTORICAL DATA

Consider the more common case wherein no one is providing probabilities, and all that is available to compute return, standard deviation, and the coefficient of variation is historical data.

The expected return, Ke, is simply the average returns for the periods, as shown in Eq. 4–5.

Expected return = Ke = (K1 + K2 + K3 + . . . Kn) / n   (Eq. 4–5)

Here, K1, K2 . . . Ki are the yield data points, and n is the number of such data points. Unlike forecasting with probabilities where each data point has its own weight (probability) historical data points are assumed to have equal weight.

The standard deviation is equal to the square root of the sum of the differences between each Ki and Ke, the expected value, divided by the number of data points minus 1, as shown in Eq. 4–6.

$$\sigma = \sqrt{\frac{\Sigma\,(Ki - Ke)^2}{n - 1}} \qquad \text{(Eq. 4–6)}$$

FIGURE 4–3

Forecast of Yield and Risk for the Winslow Market

Year	Historical Yield	(Ki − Ke)	(Ki − Ke)²
2002	6.9%	6.9% − 7.0% = −0.1%	0.01
2001	7.8%	7.8% − 7.0% = 0.8%	0.64
2000	6.7%	6.7% − 7.0% = −0.3%	0.09
1999	7.2%	7.2% − 7.0% = 0.2%	0.04
1998	6.5%	6.5% − 7.0% = −0.5%	0.25
	35.1%		Σ = 1.03

Average yield = Ke = 35.1% / 5 = 7.02% ~ 7.0%

The coefficient of variation, or CoVar, is still the standard deviation divided by the expected value and serves the same purpose as when a priori probabilities are used. It scales the standard deviation in relation to the expected value. See Eq. 4–3.

Example

Consider the annual returns for Winslow Market given in Figure 4–3, and how the expected value and standard deviation are computed.

The expected yield, Ke, is the same as the average yield or about 7%. The expected yield is subtracted from each annual yield to get each year's difference from the expected value. Once again, we see that if we simply choose the sum of the differences as a measure of deviation from norms, the positive and negative differences would tend to cancel each other out. Therefore, the differences are squared, which gives a set of positive numbers representing a measure of dispersion from the expected value. These measures are summed and divided by $n − 1$. The square root of this computation is the standard deviation.

The standard deviation is the square root of the result.

$$\sigma = \sqrt{\frac{1.03}{5 - 1}}$$

$$\sigma = \sqrt{0.2575}$$

$$\sigma = 0.51\%$$

Assuming a normal distribution of data points, we can expect the yield on Winslow Markets to be in the following range 68.3% of the time:

$$Ke - 1 \times \sigma \quad \text{to} \quad Ke + 1 \times \sigma$$
$$7.02\% - (1)\,(0.51\%) \quad \text{to} \quad 7.02 + (1)\,(0.51\%)$$
$$6.51\% \quad \text{to} \quad 7.52\%$$

or about 6.5% to 7.5%. To find the range of expected yields to a 95% confidence expands the interval to plus or minus 1.96 standard deviations.

$$Ke - 1.96 \times \sigma \quad \text{to} \quad Ke + 1.96 \times \sigma$$
$$7.02 - (1.96)\,(0.51\%) \quad \text{to} \quad 7.02 + (1.96)\,(0.51\%)$$
$$6.02\% \quad \text{to} \quad 8.02\%$$

or about 6% to 8%.

Coefficient of variation = σ / Ke = 0.51% / 7.02% = 0.073

USING EXPECTED VALUES AND STANDARD DEVIATIONS TO MAKE DECISIONS

Too often the mechanics of computational techniques become separated from their real-world application, so it is important to return to the basic reasons for the computation.

Normal Distribution Curve and Z Table

Most things, for example, height of people, bushels per acre, portfolio yield, or unit sales, follow a normal distribution curve. This curve, centered on the expected value, tails off in either direction as one moves above or below the expected value. Figure 4–4 is what a normal distribution curve looks like.

One way to visualize this curve is to think about it as a count of the number of items at each location along the x axis. The area under the curve from point A to point B represents the probability of finding an item with a value between A and B. Probability is sometimes called the confidence level.

The standard deviation measures how similar the members of a sample are. The standard deviation of heights of women in a

FIGURE 4–4

Normal Distribution Curve

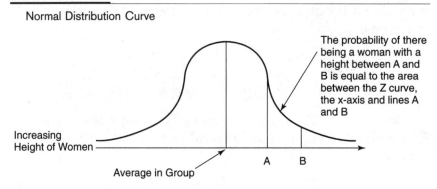

The probability of there being a woman with a height between A and B is equal to the area between the Z curve, the x-axis and lines A and B

Increasing Height of Women

Average in Group

A B

family might be small, it might be a little larger if all American women were considered, and it might be very large if women worldwide were considered.

Standard deviation is related to a normal distribution curve in a very interesting way. While some normal distribution curves are tall and narrow, and some are low and very spread out, the area between $-1.0 \times$ standard deviation (σ) and $+1.0 \times$ standard deviation (σ) is always the same. It is always 68.3%.

Z distribution tables convert areas (probabilities) under a normal distribution curve to numbers of standard deviations. This information can be used to forecast the probability of certain events. Conversely, if we want a certain event to have a given probability of occurring, we can use Z distribution tables to find the number of standard deviations from the mean we need to include to reach the preselected probability. Figure 4–5 is called a Z distribution table. It links areas with Z values.

Suppose a company were designing a sports car and they wanted to make sure 95% of women would be comfortable driving it. For those women taller than average, they want to make sure there is enough leg room; and for those shorter than average, they want to make sure the women can touch the pedals. What parameters should they design to?

Given an expected height, He, of 64″, a standard deviation of 3″, and an objective of fitting 95% of women in their target market, the company should size the cars as follows:

FIGURE 4-5

Z Distribution Table

Area/Probability/Confidence	± Number of Standard Deviations
68.3%	± 1.00 σ
79.9%	± 1.28 σ
90.1%	± 1.65 σ
95.0%	± 1.96 σ
98.0%	± 2.06 σ
99.0%	± 2.58 σ

Shortest drivers = Expected height − 1.96 standard deviations
Tallest drivers = Expected height + 1.96 standard deviations
Height range: 64″ − 1.96 × 3″   to   64″ + 1.96 × 3″
64″ − 5.88″   to   64″ + 5.88″
58.12″   to   69.88″

If all the area under the curve equals 100% of women, and the area between He −1.96 σ and He + 1.96 σ equals 95%, then the area to the left of −1.96 σ plus the area to the right of 1.96 σ must equal 5%. In the absence of any information to the contrary, we can reasonably conclude that each of these areas equals 2.5% (5% / 2). Areas toward the right and left end of a Z curve are called tails. Figure 4–6 illustrates this relationship.

FIGURE 4-6

Z Curve Tails

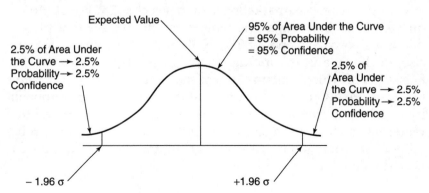

Based on statistical analysis, an auto maker could reasonably expect the probability of a female customer being shorter than 58.12" to be only 2.5%, and the probability of a female customer being taller than 69.88" to be only 2.5%.

Sales Forecasting with Statistics

Companies don't want to order excess product and then be stuck with the burden of storing, insuring, and paying inventory tax. On the other hand, they don't want to under order by too much because they don't want to lose sales unnecessarily. Statistics can be used to minimize inventory overhang by more correctly forecasting sales. How? Data from past sales campaigns could be used with marketing estimates to forecast expected sales and the standard deviation of sales.

If expected sales were 100,000 units, with one standard deviation equal to 6,000 units, how would the company determine the number of units to order if their goal was to have no inventory left after the promotion? To answer that question, we need to know how confident they want to be about the result.

Suppose they wanted to be 90% confident (that is, have a 90% probability) of selling all of their inventory. They could construct a graph of the probability of sales with the expected value of sales, 100,000 units, at the center of the graph. They would then look in the Z distribution tables to find out how many standard deviations they need on either side of the expected value to assure the probability unsold goods would be less than 10%.

In this example, marketing would select a Z value of plus or minus 1.28 σ. Looking at the table carefully, we see that plus or minus 1.28 σ covers about 80% (79.9% to be somewhat more precise) of the area in the middle of the graph. That leaves the two tails, each of which contains 10% of the area (probability). For this problem, we don't care about the tail that represents the probability of selling more than expected. We only care about the tail that represents a shortfall in sales. To find the sales where the probability of shortfall is only 10%, we can subtract 1.28 σ from the expected value.

Forecast sales (90% probability of complete sell out, 10% probability of inventory left over = 100%)

$$= \text{Expected sales} - 1.28\ \sigma$$
$$= 100{,}000 - 1.28 \times 6{,}000$$
$$= 100{,}000 - 7{,}680 = 92{,}320$$

Based on this analysis, if the company orders 92,320 units, they could be 90% confident of selling all the inventory they order.

PORTFOLIO THEORY

Another approach to managing risk and yield is called portfolio theory. Portfolio theory is usually applied to the stock market and is based on the idea that there are two basic kinds of risk: (1) diversifiable or relevant risk and (2) nondiversifiable or market risk. Diversifiable risk is associated with events occurring in individual companies such as strikes, new marketing programs, lawsuits, and new inventions. Nondiversifiable or market risk is associated with factors that affect all companies such as inflation, war, and recession. By carefully constructing a portfolio of securities, diversifiable risk can be minimized, theoretically to zero. Market risk, however, cannot be eliminated.

Beta as a Measure of Risk

Beta is a measure of relative risk. The benchmark against which the risk of any one stock is measured is the risk inherent in the stock market as a whole, that is, the nondiversifable risk.

If, for example, Fred Inc. goes up 10% when the stock market goes up 10%, and Fred Inc. goes down 10% when the stock market goes down 10%, Fred Inc. will have a beta of 1.0, meaning its moves, on average, match those of the stock market.

Suppose, however, a stock goes up 13% when the market goes up 10%, and goes down 13% when the market goes down 10%. In that case, movement in Fred Inc.'s stock price would be exaggerated by swings in the market. Such a stock would have a beta of 1.3, meaning we could expect any change in the market to be exaggerated by 130%. Suppose the market went up 15%? Then we could expect a stock with a beta of 1.3 to go up by about 19.5% (15% rise in the market × 130%, which is what a beta of 1.3 means). Likewise, if the market dropped 15%, we would expect a stock with a beta of 1.3 to drop by about 19.5%.

Some stocks are less volatile than the market, and therefore have a beta of less than 1. For example, a stock with a beta of 0.6 would fluctuate about 60% as much as the market as a whole. For such a stock, if the market rose 10%, we would expect this stock to rise by 6% (10% market rise × 60%, which is equal to a beta of 0.6). However, if the market dropped 10%, we would expect a stock with a beta of 0.6 to drop by only 6%, not the full 10% the market dropped.

A simplified formula for beta is given in Eq. 4–7.

$$\text{Beta} = \frac{\Delta S}{\Delta M} \qquad \text{(Eq. 4–7)}$$

where ΔS is the change in the stock value, and ΔM is the change in the market value.

Example

Alpha Corporation's value rises by 13% when the stock market rises by 10%, and it declines by 13% when the market declines by 10%. What is Alpha Corporation's beta?

$$\text{Beta} = \frac{\Delta S}{\Delta M} = \frac{13\%}{10\%} = 1.3$$

While the simplified formula beta = ΔS / ΔM is useful in helping conceptualize the relation between a particular stock and the marketplace, it has some theoretical flaws. In actual practice, the market fluctuates day to day, as does the value of any particular stock. Further, changes in the market and in a particular stock are never correlated 100%. As a result, regression analysis must be used to determine the "average" beta over a period of time. Since data gathering and regression analysis are tedious, beta values have been computed for many stocks. *Value Line,* available at most libraries, provides beta for several thousand stocks.

Portfolio Risk

In practice, it is very difficult to structure a portfolio in which all diversifiable risk is eliminated. Nevertheless, a prudent investor may want to limit the risk of investing in high-risk, high-yield securities by purchasing stocks with a lower beta. The beta of a portfolio of stocks is given in Eq. 4–8.

$$Bp = W1 \times B1 + W2 \times B2 + \ldots Wi \times Bi \qquad \text{(Eq. 4–8)}$$

where   Bp is the beta of the portfolio
          Wi is the weighted average of the investment in a
          particular stock
          Bi is the beta of that stock

The weighted average Wi is the dollar amount invested in a particular stock divided by the total invested in all stocks in a portfolio.

Figure 4–7 shows an example of the procedure for computing the beta of a portfolio and a format for the computation.

Portfolio Yield

Knowing the risk of a portfolio, alone, provides little decision-making guidance. An investor may be willing to tolerate a 30% risk on an investment expected to yield 50%, but be intolerant of a 10%

FIGURE 4-7

Example of Computing the Beta of a Portfolio

Stock	Amount Invested	Beta	Weight
Microsoft	$ 50,000	1.2	$50,000 / $120,000 = 41.6%
PECO Energy	$ 20,000	0.5	$20,000 / $120,000 = 16.7%
Wild West Wranglers	$ 50,000	3.0	$50,000 / $120,000 = 41.6%
	$120,000		100.0%

Portfolio beta = Bp = 41.6% × 1.2 + 16.7% × 0.5 + 41.6% × 3.0
            Bp = 0.4992 + 0.0835 + 1.248
            Bp = 1.8307

risk on an investment expected to yield 5%. Therefore, risk and reward, or risk and return, must be considered together.

A portfolio's yield is simply the weighted average of the yields on each asset in the portfolio, as shown in Eq. 4–9.

$$Kp = W1 \times K1 + W2 \times K2 + \ldots Wi \times Ki \quad \text{(Eq. 4–9)}$$

where   Kp is the portfolio yield
W1, W2, Wi are the weighted average of the dollars invested in each asset
K1, K2, Ki are the expected yields on each asset in the portfolio

The example given in Figure 4–8 demonstrates that the weightings factors are the same for the yield computation as they are for the beta of a portfolio. Therefore a professional would probably arrange her spreadsheet so the weighting computation were made once and used to compute both risk and yield.

Capital Asset Pricing Model

The capital asset pricing model (CAPM) is a method for computing a stock's required rate of return based on its beta. Assume the equity risk premium (ERP) is the premium that must be paid to induce an individual to invest in the stock market rather than accepting the risk-free rate of return, Krf.

The equity risk premium can be found by subtracting Krf from the yield on the market *overall*. The overall market yield is

FIGURE 4–8

Computation of Expected Portfolio Yield

Stock	Amount Invested	Expected Yield	Weight
Microsoft	$ 50,000	20%	$50,000 / $120,000 = 41.6%
PECO Energy	$ 20,000	10%	$20,000 / $120,000 = 16.7%
Wild West Wranglers	$ 50,000	40%	$50,000 / $120,000 = 41.6%
	$120,000		100.0%

Portfolio yield = Kp = 41.6% × 20% + 16.7% × 10% + 41.6% × 40%

Kp = 8.32% + 1.67% + 16.64% = 26.63%

denoted as Km. Equation 4–10 gives the formula for the equity risk premium.

$$\text{Equity risk premium} = ERP = Km - Krf \quad \text{(Eq. 4–10)}$$

The risk premium for individual stocks is the ERP × beta. The required rate for a particular stock is given by Eq. 4–11.

$$Kr = Krf + ERP \times Beta \quad \text{(Eq. 4–11)}$$

Suppose equity risk premium for the market as a whole is 6%; Krf is 4.5%, and a stock's beta is 1.2. What return will the market demand for an investment in that stock?

$$Kr = 4.5\% + 6\% \times 1.2 = 4.5\% + 7.2\% = 11.7\%$$

Example

Pet Food Wholesalers has a beta of 0.8; Km = 12%, and Krf = 5%. What is Pet Food's required rate of return, Kr? Using Eqs. 4–10 and 4–11 gives Eq. 4–12.

$$K = Krf + (Km - Krf) \times Beta \quad \text{(Eq. 4–12)}$$
$$= 5.0\% + (12\% - 5\%) \times 0.8 = 5\% + 7\% \times 0.8 = 10.6\%$$

HOW TO USE REQUIRED RATE OF RETURN

How can we use information on the required rate of return, Kr? Since Kr is the *minimum* we should accept to induce us to purchase an asset, we should simply not invest in anything with a return lower than *its* Kr. On the other hand, if assets, stocks or other investments, yield more than *their* Kr, that additional yield makes the asset relatively inexpensive, and it may represent a bargain-priced asset.

In Chapter 5 on the time value of money, we discuss discounting as a method for valuing money to be received in the future. The required rate of return is one method of estimating the appropriate discount rate.

SUMMARY

In this chapter, we have discussed three ways to forecast yield and risk. The forecast yield of an investment provides little guidance without its associated risk. For that reason, yield and risk are often computed at the same time. One method of forecasting yield and risk is to list a number of outcomes for a project, and then specify the probability that each outcome will occur and estimate the yield from each outcome. Another method of forecasting yield and risk is to use historical yield data, and assume that each historical data point has an equal weight.

Techniques used to forecast with probabilities and with historical data can be to forecast variables other than yield. These techniques can be used to forecast sales and a number of other probabilities. Expected value is a term used to generalize the idea of yield to problems other than investment returns. Standard deviation is a specific measure of risk that can be used when data are normally distributed to forecast the probability of events occurring or not occurring.

Portfolio theory is a technique for forecasting yield and risk as a function of the stock market. This theory says that everyone demands at least Krf, the risk-free rate of return, on investments. If the investment is a stock, an equity risk premium will be demanded in return for accepting greater risk. The equity risk premium for the market as a whole is the difference between the market yield Km and Krf. Beta is a measure of whether a stock is riskier than the market or less risky than the market. The yield required on any particular stock is equal to Krf plus ERP times a stock's beta. This required yield is used in the capital asset pricing model and provides the discount rate for investments in a particular stock. The yield, or required rate of return, on a portfolio as well as the portfolio beta may be found by taking the weighted average investment in each security. The weighting factor is equal to the amount invested in each stock divided by the total invested in the portfolio.

CHAPTER 5

Time Value of Money

Finance is about shaping the future. The time value of money is a technique for comparing investments made in today's dollars with payoffs in future dollars. The time value of money has applications to compound interest, mortgage and auto loans, leases, and investments. In this chapter, we will learn the four classes of time value problems and how to solve each using lookup tables. We will also explore mathematical solutions for problems that don't fit neatly into lookup tables.

FOUR CLASSES OF TIME VALUE PROBLEMS

The four basic equations that can solve virtually all problems dealing with the time value of money are

1. Future value $\quad\quad$ FV = PV $\times$ FVIF(i, n) $\quad\quad$ (Eq. 5–1)
2. Present value $\quad\quad$ PV = FV $\times$ PVIF(K, n) $\quad\quad$ (Eq. 5–2)
3. Present value $\quad\quad$ PVA = PMT $\times$ PVIFA(K, n) $\quad\quad$ (Eq. 5–3)
   of an annuity
4. Future value $\quad\quad$ FVA = PMT $\times$ FVIFA(i, n) $\quad\quad$ (Eq. 5–4)
   of an annuity

$\quad$ FVIF, PVIF, PVIFA, and FVIFA are functions of the variables i, K, and n, where i is the period interest rate, K is the period discount rate, and n is the number of periods. PV is a value in present dollars, and FV is a value in future dollars. PMT is a payment amount. PVA and FVA are the present value of an annuity and future value of an annuity, respectively. These functions have already been computed for selected values of i, K, and n, and are published in tables in all finance, and most accounting books, including this one. However, the tables in Appendixes A through D provide more precision than virtually all books on the market and provide more relevant values of i and n than are found in most books.

Reading Tables

These tables are generally formatted with numbers of periods down the left side, and interest rates across the top. If, for example, you want to find the future value interest factor, FVIF(i, n), for a given problem, read down the leftmost column in the table, which is usually labeled "Periods" or simply "n," and then read across to the column for interest i. At the intersection of row n, and column i, there will be a number that is equal to FVIF(i, n). Tables for present value, PVIF(K, n), and the other equations listed are read the same way.

Find the factors used in the sample problems in each section. As you do, you will become familiar with the tables, and in a short time, using them will become second nature.

FUTURE VALUE

The future value equation is used to project the growth of an initial sum of money over time at a given interest rate. Equation 5–1 uses a future value interest factor (FVIF) table, Appendix A, to simplify this computation.

$$FV = PV \times FVIF(i, n)$$

where   PV is the present value of the initial investment
FV is the future value of the sum after a period of time
FVIF(i, n) is a factor from the future value table, where i is the interest rate *per period*
n is the number of periods for compounding

Example

Suppose $5,000 is invested in a CD that yields 4% per year for ten years. We can use Eq. 5–1 and compute the solution.

$$FV = \$5,000 \times FVIF(4\%, 10) = \$5,000 \times 1.48024 = \$7,401.20$$

Find FVIF in Appendix A, read down the left column to ten periods, then across to the column underneath the heading 4% to find 1.48024.

Suppose interest is compounded more than once per year. In that case, the annual percentage rate (APR) is divided by the number of periods per year. If interest is compounded quarterly, the APR would be divided by 4. If compounding were monthly, the APR would be divided by 12.

The number of periods of compounding would also be increased. For example, a ten-year CD with quarterly compounding would have an n of 40 (4 quarters/year $\times$ 10 years).

Example

Suppose $5,000 is invested in a ten-year CD with an APR of 4% compounded quarterly. What would be its value at maturity?

$$FV = \$5,000 \times FVIF(4\% \ / \ 4, \ 4 \ quarters/year \times 10 \ years)$$
$$= \$5,000 \times FVIF(1\%, 40)$$
$$= \$5,000 \times 1.48886 = \$7,444.30$$

In this example, changing the compounding period from annual to quarterly changed the outcome only by $43.10, or about 1.8% of the accrued interest ($43.10 / $2,401.20). However, as compounding becomes more frequent, and the number of years and interest rate increase, the difference becomes more pronounced. Suppose, for example, the interest rate were compounded daily.

$$FV = \$5,000 \times FVIF(4\% \ / \ 365, \ 365 \ days/year \times 10 \ years)$$
$$= \$5,000 \times 1.49179 = \$7,458.96$$

Now the difference is $57.76 ($7,458.96 − $7,401.20), or about 2.4% of accrued interest ($57.76 / $2,401.20). These differences also become more significant as the dollar value of transactions increases. Were we computing interest on a $5 million bond, verses a $5,000 CD, the difference would have been $57,760!

FUTURE VALUE: ANNUAL GROWTH RATES

The future value formula can be used to compute growth rates. Suppose, for example, a company has $5 million in sales this year, but only had $240,000 in sales ten years ago. What is its compound annual growth rate? We can use Eq. 5–1 as the basis of analysis.

$$FV = PV \times FVIF(i, n)$$

What do we know? We know the starting point for sales. Call that the PV. We know where sales ended up. Call that the FV. What we don't know is FVIF(i, n). However, we do know n is ten years. By convention, growth rate is compounded annually, so we don't have to adjust i or n. Plugging what we know into the future value formula, we get

$$\$5,000,000 = \$240,000 \times FVIF(i, 10)$$

Dividing both sides by $240,000 yields

$$\$5,000,000 \, / \, \$240,000 = 20.8333 = FVIF(i, 10)$$

In the future value table, Appendix A, read down the number of periods column on the left side of the table to the ten-year row, then read across until you reach the closest number to 20.8333. In this case, the closest number is 21.6466. Reading up this column, the interest rate is 36%. This is the approximate "growth rate" of sales for the company. (To get a more precise rate, we would interpolate between the two table numbers that bracket 20.8333. Interpolation is explained in a later chapter.)

This same technique can be used to estimate the rate of earnings growth, cash flow growth, or any other compound growth rate.

FUTURE VALUE FORMULA

Another way to compute the future value of an investment is by using the formula given in Eq. 5–5.

$$FV = PV \times (1 + i)^n \qquad \text{(Eq. 5–5)}$$

where   FV is the future value to be computed
PV is the present value of the investment
i is the interest rate
n is the number of periods of compounding

As before, if there is more than one compounding period per year, the APR is divided by the number of periods per year, and n is the number of compounding periods per year multiplied by the number of years.

Example

Suppose $1,000 is invested at 6% compounded semiannually for two years. The period interest is 3% (6% / 2 periods/year). The number of periods for compounding n is 4 (two years compounded twice per year).

$$FV = \$1,000 \times (1 + 3\%)^4 = \$1,000 \times 1.1255 = \$1,125.50$$

PRESENT VALUE THEORY AND MATHEMATICAL FORMULA

Present value addresses the issue of what a future sum of money is worth today. When present value is being computed, we use the term *discount rate*, and the symbol K instead of interest. Interest represents what is being paid to the investor, bondholder, or CD holder. The discount rate, on the other hand, represents a reduction in the value of a financial asset due to such risk factors as inflation, default risk, or liquidity risk.

Consider whether you would rather have $1,000 today or $1,000 a year from today. If they had exactly the same value, you would be indifferent to which you got. However, there is a difference. If you had $1,000 today, you could put it in a bank and earn interest so that in a year you would have more than $1,000. Suppose your bank paid 4% interest on a one-year CD; $1,000 invested today would become $1,040 in a year. But what is $1,000 to be delivered to you in a year worth today? Stated differently, what amount would you have to invest today to get $1,000 in a year? We can find a mathematical solution to this problem by rewriting Eq. 5–5 as Eq. 5–6. Assume annual compounding to simplify the example.

$$FV = PV \times (1 + i)^n$$

Dividing both sides of Eq. 5–5 by $(1 + i)^n$ gives

$$PV = \frac{FV}{(1 + i)^n} \qquad \text{(Eq. 5–6)}$$

Filling in the parameters we get

$$PV = \frac{\$1,000}{(1 + 4\%)^1} = \frac{\$1,000}{1.04} = \$961.54$$

So in theory, we would be indifferent to $961.54 today or $1,000 from our bank in one year. In reality, we make this type of decision every time we make a deposit or buy a CD. But suppose the hypothetical changed. Suppose you had to choose between a sum of money today or $1,000 a year from now from Bruno's Credit Corporation. The only thing we know about Bruno's is they aren't FDIC insured. Would you demand more interest to compensate you for the additional perceived risk? Stated another way, would you accept less money today rather than waiting a year for Bruno's to pay off? Suppose you would be willing to wait a year to get $1,000 from Bruno's if they were paying 8% interest. The additional 4% interest over and above what a bank would pay represents your estimate of the risk of dealing with Bruno's. Applying the facts in this hypothetical, we say we are discounting a $1,000 payoff from Bruno's to find its present value. Using Eq. 5–6, we find

$$PV = \frac{\$1,000}{(1 + 8\%)^1} = \frac{\$1,000}{(1.08)} = \$925.93$$

We are indifferent to accepting $925.93 today, or $1,000 from Bruno's in one year. Suppose we needed to know the present value of a $1,000 Bruno's bond that would mature ten years from now. We would still use Eq. 5–6, but n would be 10.

$$PV = \frac{\$1,000}{(1 + 8\%)^{10}} = \frac{\$1,000}{2.15892} = \$463.19$$

PRESENT VALUE USING TABLES

Use of the present value interest factor (PVIF) table, Appendix C, can simplify analysis because compounding for specified periods and interest rates have already been computed.

Suppose your stockbroker offers you a Wild West Wrangler note that will pay $20,000 in four years. What is that note worth today? Assume for the moment a note of comparable riskiness yields 15%. We can use Eq. 5–2 to get a solution.

$$PV = FV \times PVIF(K, n)$$

where   FV is the future value, in this case, $20,000
          K is the discount rate, 15%
          n is the number of years, 4

Using the present value tables, we find

PV = $20,000 × PVIF(15%, 4) = $20,000 × 0.57175 = $11,435

If there is more than one period per year, the discount rate must be divided by the number of periods per year to get the discount rate per period before using the present value formula. Likewise, the number of periods, n, used in the present value equation is equal to the number of years multiplied by the number of times per year an amount is discounted. Most corporate bonds pay interest twice per year, and so they would be discounted twice per year. However, in the absence of any other information, assume discounting is annual.

Example
Compute the present value of a five-year, $1,000, noninterest-bearing note. Notes of similar risk yield 10%. Because this particular note is going to be compared to the performance of a corporate bond, discount it semiannually.

The interest for the present value formula would be 5% (10% per year / 2 periods), and the number of compounding periods, n, would be 10 (5 years × 2 discounting periods per year).

PV = $1,000 × PVIF(5%, 10) = $1,000 × 0.61391 = $693.91

After computing an answer, always do a reasonableness check. When computing future value, the answer should always be more than the amount invested. On the other hand, when computing a present value, the answer should always be less than the amount of the eventual payoff.

Think of the present value formula like sandpaper, wearing away the value of the payoff. If the discount is high, that is like course sandpaper that will wear away value quickly. If the discount is low, a payoff's value will erode more slowly. When thinking about reasonableness checks also think about the amount of time the sandpaper is reducing the value of the payoff. Fine sandpaper, applied over a very long period of time, will eventually erode the payoff to nothing. On the other hand, course sandpaper, applied even briefly, will greatly reduce the present value of the payoff.

PRESENT VALUE OF AN ANNUITY

A series of even payments over time is called an annuity. Annuities appear in a variety of contexts. From the point of view of a mortgage company, the monthly mortgage payment you make to them is an annuity. So how can we find the present value of an annuity? In theory, we could discount each payment to the present and sum the present values of all the payments, but that would be extremely tedious for a 30-year mortgage with monthly payments. Are there any alternatives? Yes. Because annuities are a common class of problem, tables have been developed to simplify computations. The present value interest factor for an annuity (PVIFA) table, is in Appendix D. Consider Eq. 5–3.

$$PVA = PMT \times PVIFA(K, n)$$

where   PMT is the payment
         PVA is the present value of an annuity
         K (or i) and n have the usual meanings

Example
What is the present value of ten annual, $100 payments, assuming a discount rate of 6%? Reading down the leftmost column of Appendix D, find ten periods. Then read across the table to the column for 6% to find PVIFA(6%, 10).

$$PVA = \$100 \times PVIFA(6\%, 10) = \$100 \times 7.36009 = \$736.01$$

Reasonableness check: We know that future money is always worth less than present money, so the present value of an annuity will always be less than the payment amount times the number of payments!

LOAN PAYMENTS

How can the present value of an annuity be used to compute loan payments? Return to Eq. 5–3.

$$PVA = PMT \times PVIFA(i, n)$$

Divide both sides of the equation by PVIFA(i, n).

$$PMT = \frac{PVA}{PVIFA(i, n)} \qquad \text{(Eq. 5–7)}$$

PVA is the amount of the loan. We are usually given an annual interest rate and number of years for a loan. Since most loans require monthly payments, we would divide the annual APR by 12 to get i, and multiply the length of the loan in years times 12 to get n. We can than use the present value interest factor for an annuity (PVIFA) tables in Appendix D to find the value of the function PVIFA(i, n).

Example

What are the payments on a ten-year-old Porsche 911 with a cost of $30,000 at 12% interest over five years? Since there are 12 payments per year on car loans, the interest rate must be divided by 12 before the PVIFA tables are used. Likewise, the number of periods must be computed by multiplying the number of years by 12 payments per year.

$$PMT = \frac{\$30,000}{PVIFA(1\%, 60)} = \frac{\$30,000}{44.955} = \$667.33$$

How sensitive are annuity payments to changes in interest rates? This is easy to test by changing our hypothetical to assume the Porsche can be financed at 9% versus 12%. That would make the period interest 0.75%.

$$PMT = \frac{\$30,000}{PVIFA(0.75\%, 60)} = \frac{\$30,000}{48.1734} = \$622.75$$

How sensitive are annuity payments to changes in their number of years? Suppose, rather than getting a lower interest rate, the Porsche was financed over six years rather than five years. Period interest would remain 1%; however, the number of periods would increase to 72 (12 payments/year × 6 years).

$$PMT = \frac{\$30,000}{PVIFA(1.0\%, 72)} = \frac{\$30,000}{51.1504} = \$586.51$$

When we first discussed present value, we spoke in terms of discount rate K; however, in this example, we are talking about interest rate i. What accounts for the discrepancy? Whether we talk about i or K is a function of whether we are "lending" money to a bank, or Bruno's, or whether we are "borrowing" money to buy a car or build a factory. By convention, when we are "lenders," we use the discount rate to find the value in today's dollars of some future payoff. When we are "borrowers," we think of the value paid for use of money as interest. Mathematically, the equations are the same. What changes is our point of view about the transaction.

LOAN AMORTIZATION SCHEDULES

A loan amortization schedule is an analysis of how each loan payment is allocated between principal and interest, and how this allocation affects the loan balance.

Loan amortization schedules are used to find payoff balances for auto and home mortgage loans, and to determine how to allocate lease payments between interest expense and reduction of leases payable.

Given a loan amount, interest rate, and number of payments, the amount of each payment can be computed. Each payment is allocated by multiplying the outstanding loan balance times the period interest rate to get the period interest amount. Subtracting the period interest from the loan payment gives the amount of principal reduction.

This process is repeated every month until the loan principal is reduced to zero.

Example
What is the loan amortization schedule for a $12,000, 12% car loan paid monthly for two years? First, compute the monthly payment, the formula for which can be derived from Eq. 5–3.

$$PVA = PMT \times PVIFA(i, n)$$

Or Eq. 5–7 may be used directly.

$$PMT = \frac{PVA}{PVIFA(i, n)}$$

$$= \frac{\$12,000}{PVIFA(12\% \, / \, 12, \, 2 \times 12)} = \frac{\$12,000}{21.2434} = \$564.88$$

Second, compute the monthly interest rate.

12% / 2 months/year = 1%

The balance starts as $12,000. However, after one payment, this balance is reduced. How much is it reduced? That depends on how much of the payment was allocated to interest. Equations 5–8 to 5–10 take us through the allocation process step by step.

Payment interest = Loan balance × Monthly interest rate
$120 = $12,000 × 1%   (Eq. 5–8)

Principal payment = Monthly payment − Interest payment
Principal payment = $564.88 − $120.00 = $444.88   (Eq. 5–9)

New balance = Prior balance − Principal payment
New balance = $12,000 − $444.88 = $11,555.12   (Eq. 5–10)

This process may seem tedious. However, it can be done very efficiently using a spreadsheet or computer program. Amortization schedules can also be prepared fairly quickly with a calculator and little practice.

The most efficient way to prepare such a schedule is to use the format shown in Figure 5–1.

This table can be continued for all 24 monthly payments. Notice that the amount allocated to interest drops every month. By the 23rd month, practically the entire payment is principal, and little is allocated to interest.

FIGURE 5-1

Format for Loan Amortization Schedule

Payment Number	Payment	Interest	Principal	Balance
				$12,000.00
1	$564.88	$120.00	$444.88	$11,555.12
2	$564.88	$115.55	$449.33	$11,105.79
3	$564.88	$111.06	$453.82	$10,651.97
4	$564.88	$106.52	$458.36	$10,193.61

MATHEMATICAL FORMULA FOR PRESENT VALUE OF AN ANNUITY

There will be circumstances when the present value interest factor for an annuity (PVIFA) tables will not provide the information that is needed. This could occur because the number of periods is not in the table, the interest is not in the table, or more precision is needed. In those circumstances, it may be necessary to fall back to the formula that underlies the PVIFA tables. That formula is given in Eq. 5–11.

$$\text{PVIFA}(i, n) = \left[\frac{1}{i} - \frac{1}{i \times (1 + i)^n} \right] \qquad \text{(Eq. 5–11)}$$

Example

What is the present value of ten annual, $100 payments, assuming an interest rate of 6%?

$$\text{PVA} = \text{PMT} \times \text{PVIFA}(6\%, 10)$$

which may be rewritten using Eq. 5–11 as

$$= 100 \times \left[\frac{1}{i} - \frac{1}{i \times (1 + 6\%)^{10}} \right]$$

$$= 100 \times \left[16.66667 - \left(16.6667 \times \frac{1}{1.79085} \right) \right]$$

$$= \$100 \times (16.66667 - 9.30658)$$

$$= \$100 \times 7.3601 = \$736.01$$

FUTURE VALUE OF AN ANNUITY

The future value of an annuity addresses the question of how much will accumulate if a set amount is paid into a fund for a number of years. Think of this as a "saving for retirement," "saving for a boat," "saving for the children's college," kind of problem. As with other time value of money problems, tables have been constructed to ease the computational burden. The future value interest factor for an annuity (FVIFA) table is provided in Appendix B. The formula is given as Eq. 5–4.

Future value of an annuity = FVA = PMT × FVIFA(i, n)

where   PMT is the amount deposited at the end of each
         period
         FV is the amount at the end of the payment stream
         i and n have their usual meanings

Example

Suppose you deposit $1,500 each year into a money market that yields 7%. You plan to make ten annual deposits to get a down payment on the sailboat you always wanted. How much will you have in ten years?

$$FVA = \$1,500 \times FVIFA(7\%, 10) = \$1,500 \times 13.8164 = \$20,724.60$$

Note that if payments are made more than once a year, the APR will have to be divided by the number of payments per year to get i for purposes of this formula. In addition, n will have to be computed by multiplying the number of payments per year by the number of years that deposits are made.

Reasonableness check: Since each payment is going to grow due to the power of compounding, the future value of an annuity will always be greater than the number of payments times the payment amount!

MATHEMATICAL FORMULA FOR FUTURE VALUE OF AN ANNUITY

The formula for computing the future value interest factor for an annuity at i interest per period, and n periods is

$$FVA = PMT \times FVIFA(i, n) = PMT \times \frac{(1 + i)^n - 1}{i} \qquad \text{(Eq. 5–12)}$$

Example

Suppose you deposit $1,500 each year into a money market that yields 7%. You plan to make ten annual deposits to get a down payment on a sailboat. How much will you have in ten years?

$$FV = \$1,500 \times FVIFA(7\%, 10) = \$1,500 \times \frac{(1 + 7\%)^{10} - 1}{7\%}$$

$$= \$1,500 \times \frac{(1.96715 - 1)}{7\%} = \$1,500 \times 13.81643 = \$20,724.65$$

This is $0.05 more than the value computed using the FVIFA table. Tables have only a limited precision. Where extreme precision is required, use the formulas.

SUMMARY

The time value of money is a group of analytical techniques for comparing values in today's dollars with values in future dollars. Future value calculations can be used to find the dollar value in the future of investments made today. Future value techniques can also be used to estimate a company's sales, earnings, or dividend growth rate.

Present value analysis uses a discount factor to estimate the present worth of some future payoff. The discount factor is a function of several risk factors, including default risk, liquidity risk, and the risk of inflation.

Payment streams, also known as annuities, present special computational problems. Mortgage payments and car payments are examples of annuities. The present value of an annuity is the value of all the future payments discounted back to the present. From the lender's point of view, payments are discounted to the present to get the present value of the annuity. To a lender, the present value of an annuity is the amount lent. The rate the lender calls a discount rate is, from the borrower's point of view, interest. Techniques for computing the present value of a payment stream can also be used to compute payment amount given the loan balance, interest rate, and length of the loan. The future value of annuities can be used to determine how much will accumulate in investment accounts if even payments are invested over a period of time.

Tables have been developed to ease the computational burden of time value calculations. See Appendixes A, B, C, and D. However, there are circumstances that are not covered by the tables. The mathematical formulas underlying each of the four tables can be used under such circumstances.

CHAPTER 6

Bond Valuation

Cash flow is the fuel of corporate growth and personal wealth, but all cash is not the same. As we have seen, cash in hand today it better than cash in the future. Discounted cash flow is a better measure of opportunity than cash promised some time in the future. In this chapter, we will discuss cash flow as related to bonds. We will also see how changes in interest and discount rates affect bond valuation. We will also push beyond the bounds of most texts and discuss bond yield problems that cannot be solved using tables.

BOND VALUATION

When someone purchases a bond, he usually purchases two things: (1) a stream of interest payments and (2) a payment at the maturity of the bond equal to its par, or face value. The value of a bond should then be equal to the present value of the interest payments *plus* the present value of the par value.

Bond value = $VB = PMT \times PVIFA(K, n) + FV \times PVIF(K, n)$

(Eq. 6–1)

where   PMT is the regular interest payment
                 K is the discount rate
                 n is the number of periods for discounting
                 FV is the future value of the bond at maturity

The par or face value of the bond is the future value under most circumstances. The face value plus the call premium is the future value when computing value to call.

Interest Rate Versus Discount Rate

In the context of bond valuation, the interest rate is the stated rate on the bond at the time of issue. This "stated" or "coupon rate" is used to compute the dollar amount of each interest payment, PMT. This interest rate never changes over the life of the bond.

The discount rate, K, on the other hand, is used in present value functions. It is used to adjust for the amount of risk in an investment and may change over time based on the financial condition of the company issuing the bond, the state of the economy, and other factors.

Since there is virtually no risk in a U.S. government T-note, the discount rate used for these bonds is very close to the risk-free rate of return, Krf, plus some maturity risk premium, MRP. General Electric bonds are also safe, but not quite as safe is U.S. government bonds, so we might use a somewhat higher rate when discounting them. Contrast this to the risk inherent in purchasing a bond issued by a Russian company. To buy such a bond, one might demand a discount rate of 25%, 30%, perhaps even 40%.

How does the discount rate relate to the yield on a bond? The discount rate is the yield demanded by investors to take on various levels of risk. The higher the risk, the greater the discount rate (yield) demanded.

For most of the problems in this chapter, the discount rate, K, is also called the required rate of return. This required rate of return is often discussed in terms of the risk on similar bonds. "Bonds (or stocks) of similar risk yield . . ." or "The required rate of return on bonds (stocks) of similar risk is. . . ."

An alternative way to write the bond valuation Eq. 6–1 is to substitute the mathematical functions underlying the table entries PVIFA and PV, giving Eq. 6–2.

$$VB = PMT \times \left[\frac{1}{K} - \frac{1}{K \times (1 + K)^n} \right] + \frac{FV}{(1 + K)^n} \quad \text{(Eq. 6–2)}$$

Why might we need to compute the value of a bond without using tables or a financial calculator? There are several reasons: (1) there might be a situation in which tables are not available; (2) the tables may not cover the range of values of K and n that are of interest; (3) the formulas underlying tables may be necessary to write a computer program or to supervise someone writing a bond valuation program; (4) to write a "proof" to verify calculated values for K or n; or (5) if more precision was needed than can be obtained using the tables (which usually have only four decimal places).

Example

What is the value of a ten-year, $100,000 corporate bond that returns $5,600 interest once per year? Assume bonds of similar quality, that is, risk, yield 8%.

$$VB = PMT \times PVIFA(8\%, 10) + FV \times PVIF(8\%, 10)$$
$$= \$5,600 \times 6.71008 + \$100,000 \times 0.46319$$
$$= \$37,576.45 + \$46,319.00 = \$83,895.41$$

When solving bond valuation problems, be sure to use the interest rate i only to compute the payment amount. The risk inherent in the bond, represented by the discount rate K, is used in the present value formula. The interest rate and the discount rate will almost always be different *after* the bond is issued.

Just as with other time value of money problems, if there is more than one compounding or payment period in a year, the annual interest must be divided by the number of periods in the year to get the period interest rate, i, to compute the interest payment amount. Likewise, the discount rate, K, must be divided to determine the discount rate to use in each period. Also remember to adjust the number of periods so that it equals the number of periods per year times the number of years.

In the preceding example, the market value of the bond, $83,895.45, is less than the face value of the bond. It is possible for a bond to have a higher market value than its face value? Yes. This will occur when the required rate of return, K, is less than the stated interest rate.

If a bond is selling at 103, that means it is selling for 103% of its face value. A $100,000 face value bond selling for 103 is priced

FIGURE 6-1

Required Rate of Return: Bond Value Seesaw

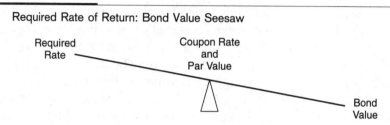

at $103,000. Such bonds are said to sell for a premium. Similarly, a bond selling for 98 is selling for 98% of its face value. A $100,000 bond selling for 98 is priced at $98,000. Such bonds are said to sell at a discount.

Required Rate: Bond Value Seesaw

Bonds with a required rate of return less than their coupon rate sell at a premium. The theory is that if a bond pays more in interest than its required rate of return, it should command a higher price. A bond with a required rate of return higher than its coupon rate usually sells at a discount.

One way to visualize this relationship between bond value and yield is to think of a seesaw. The market value of a bond is on one end of the seesaw. The *required* rate of return is on the other end. In the middle is both the coupon rate and the par value. As the required rate of return rises above the center, the bond value goes down. As the bond value goes up, the required rate of return drops (see Fig. 6–1).

It is important to understand this relationship for a number of reasons. The first reason is to do reasonableness checks on computations. If a computed answer violates the seesaw principle, that is an indication that the mathematics should be rechecked. Second, it helps visualize the yield impact of bonds selling at a premium or a discount.

CALLABLE BONDS

A bond is just a contract to pay principal and interest at fixed times and in fixed amounts. A callable bond is one in which the contract provides that an issuer can *buy back* their bond before maturity. Issuers usually pay a call premium for this privilege although not every callable bond pays a premium. Companies call bonds and pay the call premium, if any, when they can refinance their debt at lower rates. However, from the investor's point of view, a call option may make the bond less attractive than it would otherwise be.

Example

Suppose a broker offers your company a $500,000, 30-year, G.E. bond, with a coupon rate of 10%, interest payable annually. The bond was issued 15 years ago. The call provision says the bond may be called in its 20th year at a call premium of 10% of par value. The yield on bonds of this quality is 6%. What is the value of the bond?

In either case, the annual interest payment, PMT, will be the coupon interest rate, 10%, times the face value of the bond, $500,000.

$$PMT = 10\% \times \$500,000 = \$50,000$$

To be fair, one should compute the value to maturity, V_m, and compare that to the value to its call date, V_c. Value to maturity is

$$V_m = PMT \times PVIFA(6\%, 15) + FV \times PVIF(6\%, 15)$$
$$= \$50,000 \times 9.71225 + \$500,000 \times 0.41727$$
$$= \$485,612.50 + \$208,635.00 = \$694,247.50$$

Value to call, V_c, is

$$V_c = PMT \times PVIFA(6\%, 5) + FV \times PVIF(6\%, 5)$$
$$= \$50,000 \times 4.21236 + \$550,000 \times 0.74726$$
$$= \$210,618.00 + \$410,993.00 = \$621,611$$

There are two major differences between the computation of value to maturity and the value to call. The first is that the terminal or final value of the bond to call is $550,000, the face value of the bond plus the 10% call premium. The second is that the number of periods to call is 5, whereas the number of periods to maturity is 15.

Note also that the difference between the bond's value to maturity and its value to call is $72,636.50. If you, or one of your co-workers, recommended buying the bond at the "to maturity" price because you forgot to check for call provisions, it would be very hard to explain to your boss if the bond were called! The prudent person would compute both bond values and offer to pay only the lower of the two values.

CONVERTIBLE BONDS

Convertible bonds are bonds that may be exchanged for company stock, usually common stock. Convertibility is a feature used to increase the appeal of a bond. Some investors are reluctant to invest in common stock either because they believe stock prices are volatile and they don't want to take the risk of losing their investment or because they don't think a company pays enough dividends to justify the investment.

On the other hand, some individuals are reluctant to purchase bonds because they want to participate in a company's growth through the appreciation of share value. Convertible bonds provide the best of both types of security.

Convertible bonds usually pay interest twice per year, so the investor gains current income. Usually the interest is greater than the dividends an investor could have gotten if he or she purchased common shares. In addition, if a stock's value increases dramatically, the convertibility feature allows the investor to participate in stock appreciation.

Convertible bonds offer some attractive features for issuing companies as well. First, bonds are easier to sell, which means they can offer a lower coupon rate than they would have to if there were no convertibility feature. Interest on bonds is tax deductible, whereas if a company sold common stock and had to pay dividends to attract investors, the dividends would not be tax deductible. If the bonds are converted, the company will not have to pay them off, although, depending on how the transaction is structured, it may have to purchase shares in the marketplace.

Clearly, there are two ways to value a convertible bond: as a bond, or as the equivalent number of shares of stock. Recall that in valuing callable bonds, we computed their value to maturity and value to call, and valued the bond at the lower of the two. In this case, we value the bond at the greater of its value as a debt instrument or its market value if converted.

Example

Tokamak Energy Corporation issued ten-year, $1,000 convertible bonds with an 8% coupon rate, interest payable annually. Bonds of similar risk yield 12%. Each bond is convertible into 50 shares of common stock. Their stock is now selling for $6 per share. What is the value of their bonds?

$$VB = PMT \times PVIFA(12\%, 10) + FV \times PVIF(12\%, 10)$$
$$= (8\% \times \$1,000) \times 5.65022 + \$1,000 \times 0.32197$$
$$= \$452.02 + \$321.97 = \$773.99$$

What is the bond's value if converted? It is simply the number of shares times the market price of the shares, or $300 (50 × $6) in this case. Clearly, this bond has much more value unconverted than converted.

Suppose Tokamak made some notable scientific breakthrough, and the price of their shares was bid up to $18 per share. What is its value then?

With the market value of shares at $900 (50 × $18), higher than its market value as a debt ($773.99), its value would be $900. On the other hand, common stock is inherently risky, and a bond valued on its conversion feature today, while the stock is up, might be worth far less if the stock drops. Therefore, this valuation is contingent on the value of the common shares at an instant in time.

BOND YIELD

Suppose we have bond value, as reflected in its market price, its term, par value, and coupon rate. Can we compute its yield? This is a class of problem that cannot be solved using preprinted tables. One way to find the yield is by trial and error. But that is very time consuming and intellectually unfulfilling. This class of problem can, however, be solved using an algorithm.

The algorithm uses a system of approximations. In the real world, only the simplest problems can be solved by multiplying a handful of numbers together to get a solution. Far more than half of real-world problems require an algorithm, that is, a series of steps, to get the first approximation of an answer. Depending on the robustness of the algorithm, and the accuracy needed, the first approximation of an answer is often sufficient.

An algorithm for finding bond yield is

a. Determine whether the market value of the bond is greater or lower than the par value of the bond.

b. Determine whether the current yield is greater or less than the coupon rate. This can be done by considering Figure 6–1, the Required Rate Bond Value Seesaw. Remember, if the current bond price is *greater than* the par value of the bond, its yield is lower than the coupon rate, and vice versa.

c. We are now going to make something out of nothing. Select k1 and k2 discount rates based on your best judgment. Use k1 and k2 to compute test bond values test1 and test2.

d. If your k1 produces a test1 lower than the market value of the bond, then you picked a k1 that was too large. That is, it discounted the payment stream too much.

Think of the discount rate as sandpaper. If the sandpaper is course, it will wear down the value of the bond's interest payments and its face value more than if it were light sandpaper. So if your test1 is lower than Vm (the market value of the bond), your k1 was too high. Select a lower k2 and proceed. On the other hand, if test1 is higher than Vm, then your k1 is not discounting the payment stream hard enough. Select a higher k2 and proceed.

e. Once you have a k1, k2, test1, test2, and Vm, the market value of the bond, you can use interpolation to find bond yield. Interpolation is based on a calculus trick involving derivatives (slopes of lines). Interpolation theory will be explained later. For now, it is sufficient that you understand the mechanics of interpolation.

Example
Suppose a ten-year, $100,000, 7.5%, G.E. bond, with interest payable annually, is selling for $104,500. What is its yield? (To simplify calculations, we may round to whole dollars.)

The market value of the bond, Vm, is greater than the par value, which implies the yield is lower than the coupon rate. Select a k1 and compute a test1. Let k1 = 7%.

$$\begin{aligned}
\text{test1} &= \text{PMT} \times \text{PVIFA}(7\%, 10) + \text{FV} \times \text{PVIF}(7\%, 10) \\
&= (7.5\% \times \$100{,}000) \times \text{PVIFA}(7\%, 10) \\
&\quad + \$100{,}000 \times \text{PVIF}(7\%, 10) \\
&= \$7{,}500 \times 7.02358 + \$100{,}000 \times 0.50835 \\
&= \$52{,}677.05 + \$50{,}835.00 = \$103{,}512.85
\end{aligned}$$

Since test1, $103,512.80, is less the market value of the bond, $104,500, k1 is too high. Let k2 = 6%.

$$\begin{aligned}
\text{test2} &= (7.5\% \times \$100{,}000) \times \text{PVIFA}(6\%, 10) \\
&\quad + \$100{,}000 \times \text{PVIF}(6\%, 10) \\
&= \$7{,}500 \times 7.36009 + \$100{,}000 \times 0.55839 \\
&= \$55{,}200.68 + \$55{,}839.00 = \$111{,}039.68
\end{aligned}$$

Since test1 and test2 have bracketed Vm, we can conclude that k1 and k2 have bracketed the yield we could get if we purchased the bond for its market price, Vm. We can use this data in the interpolation formula given by Eq. 6–3.

$$\frac{\text{test2} - \text{test1}}{\text{k2} - \text{k1}} = \frac{\text{Vm} - \text{test1}}{K - \text{k1}} \qquad \text{(Eq. 6–3)}$$

where   Vm is the market value of the bond
K is the yield we are trying to compute
k1 and k2 are the estimated yields we selected
test1 and test2 are test bond values we computed

Since the only unknown in the equation is K, the bond yield, we should be able to solve for K using simple algebra.

$$\frac{\$111{,}039.68 - \$103{,}512.85}{6\% - 7\%} = \frac{\$104{,}500.00 - \$103{,}512.85}{K - 7\%}$$

$$\frac{\$7{,}526.83}{-1\%} = \frac{\$987.15}{K - 7\%}$$

Multiplying both sides by $(K - 7\%)$, gives

$$\frac{(K - 7\%) \times \$7{,}526.83}{-1\%} = \$987.15$$

Dividing both sides by \$7,526.83, and multiplying both sides by -1%, respectively, yields

$$K - 7\% = \frac{\$987.20}{\$7,526.83} \times (-1\%)$$

$$K = 7\% - 0.13116 \times 1\%$$

$$= 6.86885\%$$

Reasonableness check: Does a yield of 6.86885% seem reasonable in this problem? We know that the market value of the bond, \$104,500, is greater than test1, the estimated value of the bond, \$103,512.80, which implies that the market yield of the bond is less than our estimate of 7%.

How do we "prove" 6.86885% is a "good" estimate of yield? We can do that by substituting 6.86885% into the bond valuation equations to see whether it returns the market price of the bond. Since there is no table entry for 6.86885%, we must use the formulas for present value and present value of an annuity found in Eq. 6–2.

$$VB = PMT \times \left[\frac{1}{K} - \frac{1}{K \times (1 + K)^n} \right] + FV \times \left[\frac{1}{(1 + K)^n} \right]$$

$$= \$7,500 \times \left[\frac{1}{6.86885\%} - \frac{1}{6.86885\% \times (1.0686885)^{10}} \right]$$

$$+ \$100,000 \times \left[\frac{1}{(1.0686885)^{10}} \right]$$

$$= \$7,500 \times \left[14.5585 - \frac{14.5585}{1.94317} \right] + \left[\frac{\$100,000}{1.94317} \right]$$

$$= \$7,500 \times 7.0664 + \$100,000 / 1.94317$$

$$= \$52,998.00 + \$51,462.30$$

$$= \$104,460.30$$

Wait! Wait! The bond value computed differs from the market value of the bond by \$39.70! True enough, by using tables to compute test1 and test2, we introduced some error because the tables only go to four decimal places. Were we to compute test1 and test2 using Eq. 6–2, we could have added precision that would have made the interpolation somewhat more accurate.

We can quantify the magnitude of the error in the estimate by dividing the error, \$39.70, by the market value of the bond,

$104,500. The relative error in the estimate is about three hundredths of a percent (0.034% = $39.70/$104,500).

Another potential source of error involves selection of k1 and k2. If these estimates are too far from the actual yield K, the estimated K will be less accurate. Accuracy can be improved if the k1 or k2 furthest from estimated K is discarded and a new k1 or k2, as appropriate, is selected to compute a new test value for use in the interpolation formula.

Example
Suppose a broker offers your company a $100,000, 20-year Verizon bond with a coupon rate of 8.0%, interest payable semiannually. The bond was issued eight years ago. It will mature in twelve years. Its current price is $107,200. What is its yield?

a. Is the value of the bond greater than par? Yes. That implies the yield is less than the coupon rate.

b. Using (informed) judgment, select a k1 of 6%.

c. Compute the value of the bond, test1, using the estimated yield k1.

test1 = PMT × PVIFA(6%/2 payments/year, 12 years
$\qquad$ × 2 periods/year) + FV × PVIF(6%/2, 12 × 2)
$\qquad$ = 4% × $100,000 × PVIFA(3%, 24)
$\qquad$ + $100,000 × PVIF(3%, 24)

Remember, the rate used to compute interest payments is the *coupon rate*! And since interest is paid twice per year, half the annual rate is used to compute the semiannual interest.

$\qquad$ = $4,000 × 16.9355 + $100,000 × 0.49193
$\qquad$ = $67,742 + $49,193 = $116,935

d. Is the value test1 higher or lower than the market value of the bond? Higher. This implies the discount rate is not "wearing down" the value of the payment stream fast enough (think of the discount rate as sandpaper). Select a k2 that is higher than k1.

We could select k2 = 7%, but with semiannual compounding we would get a period interest rate of 3.5%, a value not in the table. For simplicity, we will select 8% as a k2.

test2 = INT × PVIFA(8%/2 payments/year, 12 years
        × 2 periods/year) + FV × PVIF(8%/2, 12 × 2)
     = 4% × $100,000 × PVIFA(4%, 24)
        + $100,000 × PVIF(4%, 24)
     = $4,000 × 15.247 + $100,000 × 0.39012
     = $60,988 + $39,012 = $100,000

Interpolate using Eq. 6–3.

$$\frac{test2 - test1}{k2 - k1} = \frac{Vm - test1}{K - k1}$$

$$\frac{\$100,000 - \$116,935}{8\% - 6\%} = \frac{\$107,200 - \$116,935}{K - 6\%}$$

$$\frac{-\$16,935}{2\%} = \frac{-\$9,735}{K - 6\%}$$

Cross-multiplying the denominators,

$$(K - 6\%) \times \$16,935 = \$9,735 \times 2\%$$

Dividing both sides by $16,935,

$$K - 6\% = (\$9,735/\$16,935) \times 2\%$$
$$K = 6\% + 1.15\% = 7.15\%$$

Reasonableness check: Does the computed bond yield seem reasonable compared to the coupon rate? Did you expect the yield to be higher or lower than the coupon rate? We expected the yield to be lower than the coupon rate because the market value of the bond was higher than the face value of the bond. Therefore, the computed yield, K, seems reasonable.

YIELD TO CALL

Yield to call is computed in a similar manner. The number of periods to the call date must be used for discounting. In addition, FV is not just the face value. Rather, it is the face value plus any call premium.

Value to call = PMT × PVIFA(K, n to call)   (Eq. 6–4)
              + Call value × PVIF(K, n to call)

Example

Suppose a $10,000 G.M. bond with a maturity of ten years and a coupon rate of 8%, interest payable annually, is callable in four years. The call premium is 4%. The bond is selling for $11,200. What is its yield to call?

The bond's value on the day it is called is $10,000 × 104% = $10,400.

The bond is selling for more than its call value, which implies its yield is less than its coupon rate. Therefore, let's pick an estimated yield, k1 of 6%. Remember, interest payments are based on coupon rates, not our estimated yield rates, and this interest is multiplied by the par, or face, value of the bond, not the face value plus call premium.

Solving for test1,

$$\text{test1} = 8\% \times \$10,000 \times PVIFA(6\%, 4) + \$10,400 \times PVIF(6\%, 4)$$
$$= \$800 \times 3.4651 + \$10,400 \times 0.7921$$
$$= \$2,772.08 + \$8,237.84 = \$11,009.92$$

We know that k1 discounted the value of the payment stream too much because test1 is less than Vm. Let us select k2 = 4%.

Using a k2 of 4% gives an estimated bond value, test2, of

$$\text{test2} = PMT \times PVIFA(4\%, 4) + \text{Call value} \times PVIF(4\%, 4)$$
$$= \$800 \times 3.6299 + \$10,400 \times 0.8548$$
$$= \$2,903.92 + \$8,889.92 = \$11,793.84$$

With k1, k2, test1, test2, and Vm, we can use interpolation to solve for K.

$$\frac{\text{test2} - \text{test1}}{k2 - k1} = \frac{Vm - \text{test1}}{K - k1} \qquad \text{(Eq. 6-5)}$$

$$\frac{\$11,793.84 - \$11,009.92}{4\% - 6\%} = \frac{\$11,200.00 - 11,009.62}{K - 6\%}$$

$$\frac{\$783.92}{-2\%} = \frac{\$190.38}{K - 6\%}$$

$$(K - 6\%) \times \$783.92 = \$190.38 \times -2\%$$

$$K - 6\% = -(\$190.38/\$783.92) \times 2\%$$

$$K = 6\% - 0.49\% = 5.51\%$$

INTERPOLATION THEORY

How does interpolation work? Why does interpolation work? Interpolation is a technique, an algorithm if you like, that can be used to calculate bond yield, internal rate of return, and a variety of other problems. It is based on a calculus trick involving a derivative, which is a fancy word for the slope of a line near a specified point.

A bond's yield is the discount rate that will make a bond's income stream exactly equal to its market value Vm. Consider the equation for bond valuation, Eq. 6–1.

$$VB = PMT \times PVIFA(K, n) + FV \times PVIF(K, n)$$

where   PMT is the period interest payment
         n is the number of periods
         FV is the value of the bond at redemption. When
         computing yield to maturity, this is the par, or face,
         value of the bond. When computing yield to call, this
         is the bond's par value plus the call premium.
         K is the discount rate

If we let K = 1%, 2%, 3%, and so forth, we could generate a whole range of bond values, VB. If we plotted the K values on the x axis, and the VB values they generated on the y axis, we could create the graph of bond values shown in Figure 6–2.

FIGURE 6-2

Graph of Bond Values Versus All Possible K Values

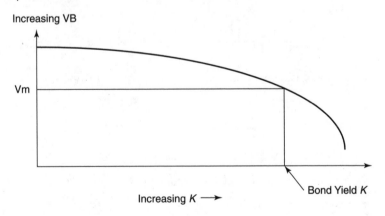

FIGURE 6-3

Graph of Test Yields, Test Bond Values, and Actual Yield and Bond Values

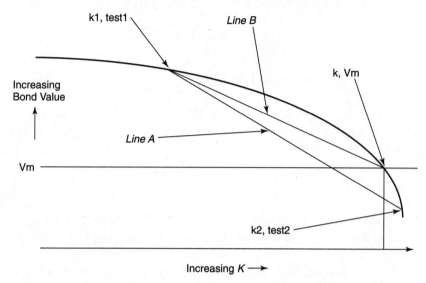

Drawing a horizontal line from the market value of the bond, Vm, to where it intersects the curve, we could read down and find bond yield, K. But graphing is tedious and has inherent precision limitations. Is there a more analytical way to find the yield? Yes. But to do that we must make something out of nothing.

Using our best professional judgment, we select estimated bond yields k1 and k2. Put them into our bond equation and generate test1 and test2, which represent hypothetical bond values assuming discount rates k1 and k2.

We can plot the point defined by (k1, test1) on the curve as well as the point (k2, test2). We can also draw a line, A, between (k1, test1) and (k2, test2). We can also draw a line B between (k1, test1) and (K, VB), as shown in Figure 6–3.

Recall that slope is rise over run. The change in y is the rise. Rise = y2 − y1. The change in x is the run. Run = x2 − x1. The equation for the slope of a line is given by equation Eq. 6–5.

$$\text{Slope} = \frac{y2 - y1}{x2 - x1}$$

Conceptually, we can compute the slope of lines A and B using Eqs. 6–6 and 6–7, respectively. In this case, test1, test2, and VB are the relevant y values; k1, k2, and K are the relevant x values.

$$\text{Slope of line A} = \frac{\text{test2} - \text{test1}}{\text{k2} - \text{k1}} \qquad \text{(Eq. 6–6)}$$

$$\text{Slope of line B} = \frac{\text{Vm} - \text{test1}}{K - \text{k1}} \qquad \text{(Eq. 6–7)}$$

Since the slope of the lines is almost the same, we can set the slope of line A equal to the slope of line B, giving us Eq. 6–3, which we use to find yield.

$$\frac{\text{test2} - \text{test1}}{\text{k2} - \text{k1}} = \frac{\text{Vm} - \text{test1}}{K - \text{k1}}$$

We know k1, k2, test1, test2, and Vm. The only thing we don't know is K. Therefore, we can use algebra to solve for K from this point.

This interpolation algorithm can be used on a number of classes of problems that meet a few conditions: the function used to generate test1 and test2 must be continuous, and the variables k1 and k2 that generate test1 and test2 must be reasonably close to the value being sought, in this case, K. The quality of the selection of k1 and k2, or the closeness, if you will, can be confirmed by inputting K back into the function to see whether the market value, Vm, is returned. The difference between the function output given the estimated K and Vm is a measure of the error in the selection of k1 and k2. The number of decimal places in the computations can also affect precision.

SUMMARY

Bond value is a function of the coupon interest rate, par value or face value, the time to maturity or call, and the discount rate for bonds of similar risk. The discount rate is also called the required rate of return, and it represents the minimum yield necessary to induce investors to purchase the bond. Coupon interest rates remain constant over the life of a bond, whereas the discount rate can change based on the perceived risk of the issuer and general economic factors. If the required rate of return is greater than the coupon rate, a bond will sell at a discount. If the required rate of return is less than the coupon rate, a bond will sell at a premium. Bonds quoted at 103 sell for 103% of their face value, and bonds quoted at 98 sell for 98% of their face value.

Yield to maturity or yield to call may be computed by selecting estimated discount rates k1 and k2, and computing a test bond value using each. The resulting test values can be used in an interpolation formula to get a reasonably close estimate of the bond's actual yield. Interpolation is based on a calculus trick involving derivatives. The closeness of the approximation, or error if you will, can be estimated by plugging the estimated yield back into the bond valuation equation and comparing the result to the market price of the bond. The difference between the computed value and the market value divided by the market value gives an estimate of the error. There are several techniques for improving the precision of the estimated yield.

CHAPTER 7

Leases

Leases are an important source of financing for several reasons, the most important of which is their convenience compared to bank loans. The downside of leasing is that lease calculations are sufficiently difficult that most businesses have a hard time comparing leases to one another and to alternative sources of financing. In the marketplace, when sellers have knowledge and buyers don't, prices tend to rise. That is why lease financing is often much more expensive than necessary. In this chapter, we will examine leases and demonstrate ways to compute true and comparative lease costs. This knowledge will give lessees a much better bargaining position.

OPERATING VERSUS CAPITAL LEASES

There are two basic types of leases: operating leases and capital leases. Operating leases are contracts for rent. At the end of the contract period, title to the equipment being rented remains with the rental company. Operating lease payments are expensed as they are made. Since title will never vest in the renter, equipment under an operating lease is not booked as an asset, and payments due under the lease contract are not booked as liabilities.

Capital leases, also called financial leases, are an alternative to bank financing. At the end of the lease contract, title to the leased equipment is transferred to the lessee for a nominal amount, such as $1. Capital leases are used to acquire equipment because the application process is simpler and quicker than applying for a bank loan. Typically, a company will find and price the equipment they need, then contact a leasing company to arrange financing. Legal title remains with the leasing company until lease termination, at which time title is transferred to the lessee for a bargain price. In this chapter, we deal only with capital leases.

IMPUTED INTEREST RATES

Given the cost of equipment to be purchased (leased) and the length of the lease, the leasing company will quote a monthly payment. Lease companies rarely quote interest rates, which makes it difficult to compare financing alternatives

Example

Rib Rack Restaurants wants to finance purchase of three, 30-foot-tall, lighted signs for their three area restaurants. The total cost is $30,000. Leaszet, the leasing company, quotes $1,025.38 per month for a 36-month lease. What is the imputed rate of interest?

A lease is a stream of payments over time, and sounds like an annuity. Consider Eq. 7–1, which we previously used for loan payments.

$$PVA = PMT \times PVIFA(i, n) \qquad \text{(Eq. 7–1)}$$

We know PV, the purchase price of the signs, is $30,000. We know PMT, the monthly payment of $1,025.38. We also know the number of periods, 36. Dividing both sides of the equation by PMT gives

$$\frac{PVA}{PMT} = PVIFA(i, n) \qquad \text{(Eq. 7–2)}$$

$$\frac{\$30,000}{\$1,025.38} = 29.25745 = PVIFA(i, 36)$$

What we don't know is the imputed interest i. Using the present value interest factor for an annuity table, Appendix D, read down the number of periods column on the left side to find 36.

Read across to the number nearest to 29.25745. Then read up to get an estimate of the interest rate the leasing company is charging. In this case, the imputed interest rate is a little less than 1.25% per month or a little less than 15% per year (12 months $\times$ 1.25% per month).

Suppose, the present value annuity table doesn't have an entry for the number of periods in the lease, or more precision is needed. How can the imputed interest rate be determined?

The technique is somewhat like a bond yield problem in which test values can be computed using selected interest rates k1 and k2, and interpolating the imputed interest rate.

Let the first test interest rate, k1, equal 12%, which is reasonable based on what we found in the PVIFA table. As with all present value problems, it is important to use the *period interest rate* in the formula, when there is more than one period per year, and not the annual interest rate.

$$\text{test1} = PMT \times PVIFA(12\%/12 \text{ months per year, } 36)$$

$$= \$1,025.38 \times \left[\frac{1}{1\%} - \frac{1}{1\% \times (1 + 1\%)^{36}} \right]$$

$$= \$1,025.38 \times \left[100 - \frac{100}{1.43077} \right]$$

$$= \$1,025.38 \times 30.1076$$

$$= \$30,871.73$$

This is somewhat more than the purchase price of the assets being leased, which implies that the selected discount rate, 12% is not high enough (to reduce the payment stream to $30,000). Try k2 = 15%. The period interest rate then becomes 15%/12 months/ year = 1.25%.

$$\text{test2} = \$1,025.38 \times \left[\frac{1}{1.25\%} - \frac{1}{1.25\% \times (1.0125)^{36}} \right]$$

$$= \$1,025.38 \times \left[80 - \frac{80}{1.563944} \right]$$

$$= \$1,025.38 \times 28.8473$$

$$= \$29,578.58$$

Since test1 and test2 bracket the purchase price, we can be confident that interpolation will enable us to converge on the imputed interest rate, K.

$$\frac{test2 - test1}{k2 - k1} = \frac{\$30,000 - test1}{K - k1}$$

$$\frac{\$30,871.73 - \$29,578.58}{15\% - 12\%} = \frac{\$30,000 - \$30,871.73}{K - 12\%}$$

$$\frac{\$1,293.15}{3\%} = \frac{-\$871.73}{K - 12\%}$$

Cross-multiplying the denominators,

$$(K - 12\%) \times \$1,293.15 = -\$871.73 \times 3\%$$

Dividing by $1,293.15,

$$K - 12\% = -(\$871.73/\$1,293.15) \times 3\%$$
$$K = 2.02\% + 12\% = 14\%$$

Reasonableness check: Fourteen percent interest is high, but not outrageous. We generally expect lease rates to be greater than bank rates, but less than credit card rates. Therefore, under the circumstances, the rate seems reasonable.

EFFECT OF DEPOSITS AND PREPAYMENTS ON THE IMPUTED INTEREST RATE

Reading the fine print in the lease contract, Rib Rack Restaurants finds that the leasing company wants a $2,000, non-interest-bearing security deposit at the outset of the lease, plus the first and last month's lease payments in advance. Does this change anything?

Consider the purpose of a capital lease. It is to finance equipment. But just how much financing is the leasing company really providing? Leaszet wants payments on the entire $30,000, but they are only extending financing on $25,949.24 ($30,000 price less $2,000 security deposit and less $2,050.76 in prepayments). Arguably, the $2,000 deposit will be returned at the end of the lease, but $2,000 in 36 months is worth far less than $2,000 today. Failure to analyze the actual amount being financed is a common mistake, and can be very expensive.

The amount being financed, $25,949.24, is equal to the present value of a stream of 34 monthly payments of $1,025.38 less the present value of the $2,000 deposit that will be returned in 36 months.

Why is the present value of the deposit being subtracted? The 34 monthly lease payments are cash outflows. The return of the deposit is a cash inflow. The interest rate that makes the present value of the inflows and outflows balance to the amount financed is the imputed interest rate for the lease. The formula is

Amount actually financed = Present value of the lease payments

$$- \text{ Present value of the deposit}$$

$$\$25,949.24 = \$1,025.38 \times \text{PVIFA}(K, 34) - \$2,000 \times \text{PV}(K, 36)$$

Why is the deposit being discounted over 36 periods? Because deposits are not usually returnable until after a lease is complete. In contrast, the lease payments are discounted over 34 months since two have already been paid.

The imputed interest rate, K, can be closely estimated using an algorithm similar to the one used to compute bond yield. The algorithm involves using informed judgment to select two interest rates, k1 and k2, in the region of the imputed interest, and computing two test values using the preceding equation. The results of these test calculations together with known problem data are used to interpolate to find the imputed interest rate.

Let k1 = 15%, which means that

Period interest rate $k = (\text{k1}/12) = 15\%/12 = 1.25\%$

test1 $= \$1,025.38 \times \text{PVIFA}(1.25\%, 34) - \$2,000 \times \text{PV}(1.25\%, 36)$

$$= \$1,025.38 \times \left[\frac{1}{1.25\%} - \frac{1}{1.25\%} \times \frac{1}{(1 + 1.25\%)^{34}} \right]$$

$$- \$2,000 \times \left[\frac{1}{(1 + 1.25\%)^{36}} \right]$$

$$= \$1,025.38 \times \left[80 - \frac{80}{1.5256} \right] - \$2,000 \times \left[\frac{1}{1.5639} \right]$$

$$= \$1,025.38 \times 27.5616 - \$2,000/1.5639$$

$$= \$28,261.11 - \$1,278.85$$

$$= \$26,982.26$$

Since this is more than the amount financed, $25,949.49, the test discount rate, k1, is too low. That is to say, we have not discounted the payment stream "hard enough." Think of the discount rate as sandpaper, wearing away the value of the dollars over time. Let k2 = 18%, then

$$k = (k2/12) = (18\%/12) = 1.5\%$$

$$\text{test2} = \$1,025.38 \times \text{PVIFA}(1.5\%, 34) - \$2,000 \times \text{PV}(1.5\%, 36)$$

$$= \$1,025.38 \times \left[\frac{1}{1.5\%} - \frac{1}{1.5\% \times (1 + 1.5\%)^{34}} \right]$$

$$- \$2,000 \times \left[\frac{1}{(1 + 1.5\%)^{36}} \right]$$

$$= \$1,025.38 \times \left[66.6667 - \frac{66.6667}{1.6590} \right] - \$2,000 \times \left[\frac{1}{1.7091} \right]$$

$$= \$1,025.38 \times 26.4818 - \$2,000/1.7091$$

$$= \$27,153.91 - \$1,170.21$$

$$= \$25,983.70$$

This is still more than the amount financed of $25,949.24, but only slightly. The question is whether we should select an even higher k2, say 24%, and compute a new test2. Recall that accuracy improves as k1 and k2 approach K, and deteriorates as k1 and k2 move away from K. In this instance we will use our judgment and stay with our original k2 because test2 seems very close to the amount financed.

Interpolating,

$$\frac{\text{test2} - \text{test1}}{k2 - k1} = \frac{\text{Amount financed} - \text{test1}}{K - 15\%} \quad \text{(Eq. 7–3)}$$

$$\frac{\$25,983.70 - \$26,982.26}{18\% - 15\%} = \frac{\$25,949.24 - \$26,982.26}{K - 15\%}$$

$$\frac{-\$998.56}{3\%} = \frac{-\$1,033.02}{K - 15\%}$$

$$K - 15\% = (\$1,033.02/\$998.56) \times 3\%$$

$$K = 15\% + 3.1\% = 18.1\%$$

FIGURE 7-1

Analysis of Imputed Interest Rates for a $100,000 Five-Year Lease Using
Varying Lease Terms, Assuming Monthly Payments of $2,285.56

Case	Origination Fee	Deposit	No. of Prepayments	Prepayment Amount	Amount Actually Financed	Inputed Interest Rate
I	$ 0	$ 0	0	$ 0.00	$100,000	13.2%
II	$2,000	$ 0	0	$ 0.00	$ 98,000	14.1%
III	$ 0	$5,000	0	$ 0.00	$ 95,000	14.4%
IV	$ 0	$ 0	1	$2,285.56	$ 97,714	13.9%
V	$ 0	$ 0	2	$4,571.12	$ 95,429	14.2%
VI	$2,000	$ 0	2	$4,571.12	$ 93,429	16.4%
VII	$2,000	$5,000	2	$4,571.12	$ 88,429	16.7%

This is almost 30% higher than the interest rate Rib Rack inferred from the monthly lease payments alone. Is a lease rate of 18.1% reasonable? The reality is that it is a tough world out there, and if a leasing company can get a client to pay an effective 18.1% or 25% or even 30%, they are going to do it. The best defense against such overcharging is to read the fine print in lease agreements and do your own computations. If your computations show the actual interest rate is too high, and the leasing company refuses to negotiate, go to another leasing company.

Other factors besides deposits and prepayments can affect the imputed interest rate. Leasing companies often charge processing, origination, or application fees. Figure 7–1 analyzes the effect of various prepayment, deposit, and origination fee clauses on imputed interest rates for a $100,000 five-year lease.

CAPITALIZING LEASES

Generally accepted accounting principles require that assets financed with capital leases be treated as though they were purchased assets. This means debiting an asset account for the purchase price of the acquired equipment and crediting a lease payable account for the amount financed.

As each lease payment is made, some portion of it must be allocated to imputed interest, which is a subdivision of interest expense. The balance of the payment reduces leases payable.

The monthly allocation is made through an amortization table. The important thing to note is that the interest rate used to generate the amortization table, as well as the number of periods, must be adjusted based on the whole effect of the lease agreement, including provision for prepayments, fees, and deposits.

Example

Rib Rack Restaurants discovers too late that the effective interest rate on their lease is 18.1%. They book the acquisition and then create an amortization table for 34 payments (Fig. 7–2). Notice that while the asset is still valued at $30,000, the liability is much less be-cause of the security deposit and prepayment. The liability is just the amount they are financing ($25,949.24 = $30,000 − $2,000 deposit − $2,050.76 prepayments).

	Debit	Credit
Asset signs	$30,000.00	
Cash		$ 4,050.76
(security and prepayments)		
Leases payable		$25,949.24

Recall the monthly interest is the outstanding lease balance times the monthly interest rate. Here the monthly interest rate is 18.1%/12 months per year = 1.508%. The principal is the payment

FIGURE 7–2

Lease Amortization Table

Payment No.	Amount	Interest	Principal	Balance
				$25,949.24
1	$1,025.38	$391.31	$634.07	$25,315.17
2	$1,025.38	$381.75	$643.63	$24,671.54
3	$1,025.38	$372.05	$653.33	$24,018.21
.	.	$362.19	$663.19	$23,355.03
.	.	.	.	.
34				

less each month's interest, and the balance is reduced by each month's principal.

In the first month, the payment entry, based on the amortization schedule is

	Debit	Credit
Leases payable	$634.07	
Imputed interest expense	$391.31	
Cash		$1,025.38

In the second month, the payment entry would be

	Debit	Credit
Leases payable	$643.63	
Imputed interest expense	$381.75	
Cash		$1,025.38

Each month the amount of imputed interest declines, and the portion of the payment that reduces lease payable increases. Of course, depreciation would be booked as with any other asset, and it would be based on the full purchase price of $30,000.

The accounting becomes somewhat sticky at the end of the lease term. Payments 33 and 34 will result in a negative lease payable. Then there is the problem of how to book the cash received when the deposit is returned. Fortunately, there is a solution. If one debits cash for the amount of the return deposit received, and credits leases payable, the balance in the leases payable account returns to zero, as it should.

No doubt some accountant will argue that the $2,000 deposit should be booked as an asset rather than a down payment. However, that would ignore the time value of money. It would also violate the accounting principle that assets must be booked at their present value. Were the deposit booked at its present value, then every month it would have to be *increased* by some interest amount so that when the lease was over, the deposit amount would equal $2,000. I would argue that approach is needlessly complicated, and misleads readers of the report into thinking the company has a current asset with a present value of $2,000, which is just not the case.

There is one more consideration when booking capital leases. At year-end (perhaps even quarterly), liabilities must be segregated into current, that is, those due in a year or less, and long-term liabilities. To find the current portion of leases payable, sum (add up) the principal amounts due in the 12 months after the financial statement date. This becomes leases payable current, obviously a current liability. Any lease payments due more than 12 months from the balance sheet date are treated as a long-term liability. Usually the allocation of current lease payments is made via a period-end journal entry, which is reversed at the beginning of the next period.

Publicly traded companies are usually required to analyze lease obligations by year in a footnote. Lease amortization schedules will facilitate this analysis.

SUMMARY

Capital leases are an important source of financing and provide an alternative to bank loans. As a general rule, the imputed interest on leases is higher than the interest on bank loans. On the other hand, leases can be finalized more timely and with less paperwork than bank loans.

One of the major drawbacks with leases is that the imputed interest is rarely stated, and that makes it difficult to compare lease, bank, or other financing alternatives. Imputed interest rates can be computed using present value and interpolation methods.

To get the true interest rate, it is important to know how much is actually being financed. When deposits, fees, and prepayments are considered, the amount financed is often much less than originally planned. For this reason, simply comparing lease payment amounts offered by lessors is no guarantee that one lease is more cost effective than another.

Assets acquired through capital leases are booked the same as other assets. Offsetting assets are credits to lease payable and cash. The amount booked as lease payable should be the amount actually financed, which is often much less than the value of the asset acquired with a lease. Leases payable must be amortized just like a bank loan. Each lease payment must be allocated between imputed interest, which is an expense, and reduction of the balance of lease payable.

Stock Valuation

Do stock valuations fluctuate randomly? Or is there a rational method of valuing a stock? The answer is both. In theory, if the fair value of a stock is determined, no matter how many random forces act on it, it should return to its fair value. The investment strategy that flows from this theory is that a stock should be purchased when below its fair value, and sold when it rises above its fair value.

This is not a chapter on investing. Rather, it is designed to help financial managers understand how their company's stock may be perceived based on some standard measures of stock valuation. In this chapter, we shall explore several valuation techniques as well the limitations of each.

STOCK VALUATION

Classical stock valuation is based on a number of simplifying assumptions. These are that stocks pay dividends (not true in the real world); growth rates are constant (again a simplification); and growth rates are less than Kr, the required rate of return for a stock (not always true in the real world). However, even with these assumptions and limitations, classical methods of computing stock value and yield can add insight into investment decision making.

Definitions

Throughout this chapter, we will use the following symbols and definitions to facilitate discussion.

Po = Actual market price.

Pt = Actual market price at some future time, where $t = 1$, 2, 3 . . . are 1, 2, or 3 years in the future.

Do = Last dividend paid.

Dt = Dividends to be paid in the future. D1 is the next dividend; D2, the dividend in 2 years; and so on.

Pet = Expected, or intrinsic, value of a stock at time t. It may or may not be equal to Pt. This is usually referred to as the expected price at time t, or Pet.

g = Growth rate. The classical model implicitly assumes the growth rate for dividends, stock price, earnings, and cash flow are the same. For most stocks, this will not be true. Dividends are set by a resolution of the board of directors and subject to certain legal constraints. Earnings growth is a function of revenue and expenses, and stock price is set by the marketplace.

Dividend Yield

There are two different ways of looking at dividend yield; one is based on historical yield, the other projects yield into the future.

Historical Dividend Yield

Historical dividend yield measures the historical performance of a stock and is reported in *The Wall Street Journal* and other major newspapers. It is the dividends for the last 12 months divided by the current stock price. The historical dividend yield can be computed using Eq. 8–1.

$$\text{Historical dividend yield} = \frac{\text{Do}}{\text{Po}} \qquad \text{(Eq. 8–1)}$$

Example
In the last 12 months, a stock has paid dividends of $1.10 per share. Its current price is $40 per share.

$$\text{Historical dividend yield} = \frac{\$1.10}{\$40} = 2.75\%$$

The advantages of this performance measure are that it is objective and comparable to the historical dividend yields of other stocks and interest bearing instruments like CDs and bonds.

Projected Dividend Yield
Projected dividend yield is the next expected dividend divided by the current price. Why the next expected dividend? Finance is about evaluating and shaping the future. If a person purchases a stock today, he or she wants to know what the return will be in the future, not the past. The assumption is that if a company has a positive growth rate, the dividend will grow as well. The projected dividend yield can be computed using Eq. 8–2.

$$\text{Projected dividend yield} = \frac{D0 \times (1 + g)}{P0} \qquad \text{(Eq. 8–2)}$$

Example
In the last 12 months, a stock has paid a dividend of $1.10 per share. Its current price is $40 per share, and its growth rate is 12%.

$$\text{Projected dividend yield} = \frac{\$1.10 \times (1 + 12\%)}{\$40}$$

$$= \frac{\$1.232}{40} = 3.08\%$$

Compounded over a number of years, the difference could become significant. While a positive growth rate is generally assumed, positive growth is not always the case. Negative growth rates have been experienced by typewriter manufacturers and most recently by old-line long-distance phone carriers. Local phone carriers may experience negative growth rates if computer and telephone traffic is switched to local cable. For the remainder of this book, when we say dividend yield, we mean the projected dividend yield.

Capital Gains Yield

Capital gains yield is the yield resulting from appreciation of the underlying security. It is independent of changes in dividends, except to the extent that increasing or decreasing dividends raises or lowers the current market value of a stock, Po. Pe1 is the estimated value of the stock price one year from the present. The capital gains yield can be computed using Eq. 8–3.

$$\text{Capital gains yield} = \frac{Pe1 - Po}{Po} \qquad \text{(Eq. 8–3)}$$

Example

Suppose we expect a stock to be worth $45 in a year, Pe1, and it is worth $40 today, Po.

$$\text{Capital gains yield} = \frac{\$45 - \$40}{\$40} = 12.5\%$$

Total Return

Total return on a stock is the return of both dividend yield and capital gains yield, as shown in Eq. 8–4.

$$\text{Total return} = \text{Dividend yield} + \text{Capital gains yield} \qquad \text{(Eq. 8–4)}$$

Combining the preceding examples,

$$\text{Total return} = 12.5\% + 3.08\% = 15.58\%$$

COMPUTING STOCK VALUE

If one were going to buy a stock and hold it forever, its value would be the present value of the future cash flows from the stock, that is, the discounted value of the dividend stream. Techniques have been developed to discount dividend cash flows under three different scenarios: zero growth, constant growth, and changing growth.

Perpetuity

A perpetuity is a security that pays a constant dividend forever, with no sale value at the end. The expected price of a perpetuity, Pe, at time zero, that is, now, is given by Eq. 8–5. We speak of the expected value of price because on any given day a security's price may be higher or lower than an estimate based on the present value of cash flows.

$$\text{Expected price of a perpetuity} = Pe0 = \frac{Do}{Kr} \quad \text{(Eq. 8–5)}$$

where Do is the dividend, and Kr is the required rate of return for a security of this risk.

Example

Top Hat Manufacturing pays a constant dividend of $1.25 per year. The required rate of return on stocks of this riskiness is 18%. What is the expected market price today?

$$Pe0 = \frac{\$1.25}{18\%} = \$6.94$$

Suppose the required rate of return, Kr, for a stock of Top Hat's riskiness were only 12%. What would you expect its price to be?

$$Pe0 = \frac{\$1.25}{12\%} = \$10.42$$

Notice that a stock's price is highly dependent on its perceived risk, independent of its dividend. We have seen that one of the factors bearing on risk is the volatility of earnings based on normal fluctuations in competition and the business cycle. However, from time to time, some companies find it necessary to restate their earnings from prior periods. Restatements usually occur because the spirit and letter of generally accepted accounting principles were not followed. Such restatements cause a dramatic, negative shift in the perception of a company's risk.

The hypothetical we have been discussing is for a *zero growth* stock. Though such stocks are theoretically possible, in the real world, one should be cautious of a "zero growth" stock. The world is very competitive, and most companies must grow or die.

Constant Growth

The earnings and dividends of most stocks are expected to grow over time. If, for example, they grew at the same rate as the gross domestic product (GDP), including inflation, one might expect them to grow at the rate of 5% to 8% per year.

Where the rate of growth of a stock is assumed to be constant, say g, the expected price of a stock may be computed using Eq. 8–6, which is also known as the Gordon model.

$$Pe0 = \frac{Do \times (1 + g)}{Kr - g} = \frac{D1}{Kr - g} \qquad \text{(Eq. 8–6)}$$

Example

Suppose Tardis Machines Corporation's last annual dividend was $2.00; its growth rate is 10% per year, and the required yield on a security of comparable riskiness is 14%. What would you expect the current price of Tardis to be?

$$Pe0 = \frac{\$2.00 \times (1 + 10\%)}{14\% - 10\%} = \frac{\$2.20}{4\%} = \$55.00$$

Note that this equation does not work, and has no meaning, if the growth rate for a company equals or exceeds the required rate of return. This is an inherent limitation in the Gordon model. By implication, if the required rate of return and the growth rate are very close, say, less than 1% different, the validity of the model's results should also be questioned because of inherent limits in the precision of growth rate and the required rate of return.

Non-constant Growth Stock

While mature companies in stable markets, with unchanging technology, may have constant growth, many new companies go through a period of rapid growth before settling down. Obviously, the expected value of a stock growing 30% forever, will be different from a stock that grows 30% per year for three years and then settles down to a comfortable 10%. So how do we compute the expected price, Pe0, for such a stock? We do it in several steps.

a. Compute the dividends for the period of the rapid growth.
b. Compute the estimated price of the stock at the end of the period of rapid growth.
c. Discount the dividends for the period of rapid growth, and the expected stock price at the end of the period

of rapid growth, back to the present using *the required rate of return.*

Example

Suppose Ion Propulsion Systems anticipates growth of 50% per year, while they ramp up for a government contract. Thereafter, they expect to grow 10% per year. Their last dividend was $0.10. The required rate of return is 15%. What is the expected price for Ion Propulsion?

a. Using the dividend growth and formula, we project dividends for three years.

$$D1 = Do \times (1 + g) = \$0.10 \times (1.50) = \$0.15$$
$$D2 = D1 \times (1 + g) = \$0.15 \times (1.50) = \$0.225$$
$$D3 = D2 \times (1 + g) = \$0.225 \times (1.5) = \$0.3375$$

b. To compute the expected price, Pe3, at the end of the period of rapid growth, we can use the Gordon model, Eq. 8–5, adjusting for the fact that we are computing the price at year 3, Pe3, using the dividend at the end of year 3, D3 in place of Do. Also note that the growth rate is now only 10%, down from 50%, but the required rate of return, Kr, remains at 15%.

$$Pe3 = \frac{D3 \times (1 + g)}{Kr - g} = \frac{D4}{Kr - g}$$

$$= \frac{\$0.3375 \times (1 + 10\%)}{15\% - 10\%} = \frac{\$0.37125}{5\%} = \$7.43$$

c. Discount, at the required rate of return, Kr, the dividend stream *and* the expected price at the end of the growth period, Pe3.

$$Peo = \frac{D1}{1 + 15\%} + \frac{D2}{(1 + 15\%)^2} + \frac{D3}{(1 + 15\%)^3} + \frac{Pe3}{(1 + 15\%)^3}$$

$$= \frac{\$0.15}{1.15} + \frac{\$0.225}{1.3225} + \frac{\$0.3375}{1.521} + \frac{\$7.43}{1.521}$$

$$= \$0.130 + \$0.170 + \$0.222 + \$4.885$$

$$= \$5.41$$

STOCK YIELD

The Gordon model is also important because it may be rewritten to compute the yield, that is, the expected rate of return, of a stock. The expected rate of return of a stock, Ke, is given by Eq. 8–7.

$$Ke = \frac{D1}{Po} + g \qquad \text{(Eq. 8–7)}$$

D1 is computed by multiplying Do $\times$ (1 + g) = D1. Examining this equation, it is clear that D1 / Po is the dividend yield, and g, the expected rate of growth (of the stock price), represents the capital gains yield. Therefore, Ke represents the total yield on the stock.

Example

Thinking Machines Corporation has been growing at the rate of 20% per year. It just declared a dividend of $0.32, and its market price is $37.50. What is the expected yield on Thinking Machines?

$$Ke = \frac{D0 \times (1 + g)}{P0} + g = \frac{\$0.32 \times (1 + 20\%)}{\$37.50} + 20\%$$

$$= \frac{\$0.384}{\$37.50} + 20\% = 1.02\% + 20\% = 21\%$$

In the preceding problem, does it matter that the company's policy is to pay a particular percent of earnings as dividends? No. The important thing is that dividend payout growth is constant. Whether corporate policy changes to reduce, increase, or maintain a constant dividend, the important thing to determine is the *next* dividend.

STOCK VALUATION BASED ON CASH FLOW

The methods discussed earlier are the classical methods of stock valuation. However, practitioners, financial analysts, investment bankers, and mergers and acquisitions specialists, tend to value assets more on the cash they can generate than the dividends they pay. One reason is that cash flow provides the power to do things: invest in new products, break into new markets, and hire the best people away from competitors. Another reason is that fewer and fewer companies, especially high-growth companies, pay dividends. Instead, they usually reinvest cash to grow their business.

Cash generated from operations, as opposed to sale of assets, is earnings before interest, taxes, depreciation, and amortization, EBITDA. Earnings before interest is used as a benchmark because interest is a function of how the enterprise is financed, not how efficiently it operates. Taxes are paid only if a company makes money, and there are so many ways to reduce a company's tax liability that comparisons of after-tax earnings might not be meaningful. Depreciation and amortization are noncash expenses and do not diminish the cash generated by the company. Therefore, they must be added back to earnings before interest and taxes, also called operating income, to get cash flow.

Cash flow in any particular year provides little insight into future prospects. To value a company properly, it is necessary to discount and sum future cash flows. Here, the modified Gordon model can be useful. Instead of dividends, think in terms of cash flow, as shown in Eq. 8–8. Let CV represent company value.

$$CV = \frac{CF \times (1 + g)}{Kr - g} \qquad \text{(Eq. 8–8)}$$

where g is growth rate, and Kr is the discount rate for a company of this risk.

Of course, to estimate the value of an individual share of stock, the company value, CV, would have to be divided by the number of shares. The stock valuation problem becomes somewhat more complex when the company has issued convertible bonds, convertible preferred, options and warrants.

Example
Kringle Corporation has EBITDA of $2 million, its growth rate is 10% per year, and the required rate of return for securities of similar risk is 17%. There are 400,000 shares outstanding. What is the value per share?

$$CV = \frac{\$2,000,000 \times (1 + 10\%)}{17\% - 10\%} = \$31,428,571$$

Since there are 400,000 shares outstanding, this value must be spread evenly across all shares to get the price per share.

$$Pe0 = \frac{\$31,428,571}{400,000} = \$78.57$$

STOCK VALUATION BASED ON EARNINGS

When analysts talk about earnings, they usually mean earnings before interest and taxes, EBIT. Companies are often valued as a multiple of earnings. The multiple varies from industry to industry and from time to time through the business cycle. Watching firm and industry valuation is important when raising capital, for example, pricing shares for an initial public offering (IPO), setting terms for convertible bonds and preferred stock, and issuing options.

Benchmarking can be used to determine the multiples for an industry at any point in time. List the major companies in a specific industry. Determine each company's value by multiplying the price per share times the shares outstanding, and dividing the result by its EBIT. The resulting multiplier can be used to value a company. Once a company's value is determined, divide it by the shares outstanding to value individual shares. Equation 8–9 provides the formula for computing an industry multiple.

$$\text{EBIT multiple} = \frac{\sum Pi \times Si}{\sum EBITi} \qquad \text{(Eq. 8–9)}$$

where Pi is the price of an individual share of benchmark stock i
             Si is the number of shares of stock i outstanding
             $EBITi$ is the EBIT for stock i

Consider the data in Figure 8–1, which analyzes industry data to find an EBIT multiplier.

Example

NewVu Company, a privately owned manufacturer of flat panel displays, is negotiating with a venture capitalist and wants to sell them enough shares to raise a certain amount of money. To do that,

FIGURE 8-1

Analysis of Earnings Multiplier for the Flat Panel Display Industry

Company	Share Price	Shares Outstanding	Market Value	EBIT	Multiplier
Trialon Industries	$23.00	4,000,000	$ 92,000,000	$ 20,000,000	4.6
Pixel Dynamics	$49.00	500,000	$ 24,500,000	$ 6,000,000	4.1
Martin Electronics	$30.00	1,200,000	$ 36,000,000	$ 9,000,000	4.0
Action Electronics	$ 5.00	1,000,000	$ 5,000,000	$ 850,000	5.9
Global Manufacturing	$30.00	12,000,000	$360,000,000	$ 95,000,000	3.8
			$517,500,000	$130,850,000	
				EBIT multiplier	4.0

they need to determine a per share value. They have an EBIT of $1.2 million and 200,000 shares authorized. Equation 8–10 can be used to compute that share price.

$$\text{Share value} = \frac{\text{EBIT} \times \text{Industry multiplier}}{\text{Shares}} \quad \text{(Eq. 8–10)}$$

Given the industry multiplier from Figure 8–1 of 4.0, they can compute share price from their other data.

$$= \frac{\$1.2 \text{ million} \times 4.10}{200,000} = \$24.00$$

When using comparative data, like the industry multiplier, there are two areas in which caution is required. The first is in defining what constitutes the industry. Standard industrial classification (SIC) codes are so broad they can be used only as a starting point; then businesses within an SIC code have to be culled by hand to identify truly comparable businesses. The other area in which caution is indicated is in purity of play. Few publicly traded companies are narrowly focused in one industry, product line, or market niche. It may be necessary so tease a business's segment information out of its financial statements before the data can be used. One alternative is to search industry and trade journals to see whether they have published multipliers or the information upon which multipliers can be based.

If a significant number of new shares is to be issued, dilution must be considered. If NewVu were issuing 100 shares, $24.00 might still be a good estimate. However, if they were issuing 100,000 new shares, company value would have to be divided by the total shares after issuance to get expected share price.

STOCK VALUATION BASED ON SALES

During the dot.com bubble, many companies were seeking investors and going public preprofit. That is, they were going public before they proved they had a profitable business model. Company value was based on a multiple of sales. The approach was to find a number of similar companies that had successfully gone public and compare the total market value of these companies to their sales. Equation 8–11 gives the formula for developing a sales multiplier.

$$\text{Sales multiplier} = \frac{\sum Pi \times Si}{\sum \text{sales } i} \qquad \text{(Eq. 8–11)}$$

where   sale i is the sales of the ith company
           Pi is the market price of the ith company
           Si is the number of shares outstanding in the ith company

Consider the example in Figure 8–2.

FIGURE 8-2

Analysis of Sales Multiplier for Internet-Based Financial Companies

Company	Share Price	Shares Outstanding	Market Value	Revenue	Multiplier
eInsurance	$12.00	10,000,000	$120,000,000	$ 75,000,000	1.6
eMortgage	$10.00	8,000,000	$ 80,000,000	$ 50,000,000	1.6
eLeasing	$23.00	4,000,000	$ 92,000,000	$ 90,000,000	1.0
eHome Equity	$19.00	2,000,000	$ 38,000,000	$ 25,000,000	1.5
eMoney4U	$ 6.00	10,000,000	$ 60,000,000	$ 60,000,000	1.0
			$390,000,000	$300,000,000	
				Sales multiplier	1.3

Equation 8–12 applies the sales multiplier to the number of shares to get an estimated share price.

$$\text{Share value} = \frac{\text{Sales} \times \text{Sales multiplier}}{\text{Shares}} \qquad \text{(Eq. 8–12)}$$

Example

eFinanceCo has sales of $4 million and 500,000 authorized shares. The sales multiplier for their industry is 1.3. What is the per share value assuming all shares are issued and outstanding?

$$\text{Share value} = \frac{\$4{,}000{,}000 \times 1.3}{500{,}000} = \$10.40 \text{ per share}$$

There are a number of cautions when using this approach. For one thing, performing an analysis of the Internet financial services industry as a whole is probably too broad to be useful. Ideally, the companies used to compute the multiplier would be as much like the company being valued as possible. Insurance companies would be compared to insurance companies, leasing companies to leasing companies, and so forth.

Another problem with this type of methodology, especially for an emerging industry, is that the market value of the benchmark companies used to determine the multiplier may fluctuate wildly. The lesson, if you are an entrepreneur trying to raise capital, is that timing is everything. If you are an investor, and don't want to invest when values are at the top of the market, look at sales multipliers over time to get a more consistent view of a company's share valuation.

The problem with pre-earnings valuation is the lingering fear that a company's financial model might not be sufficiently grounded to generate cash and profits without further infusions of capital, if it can generate earnings at all.

On the other hand, professionals often value their practices as a multiple of revenue. Among them are accountants who might, for example, value their accounting practice at three times revenue. Factors that make a sales based valuation less risky for a professional practice include the fact that such practices are often long established, and the expectation that professionals will bill two to three times their salary, which provides a way to convert revenue to an estimate of gross profit.

SUMMARY

There are several methods for estimating the fair value of a stock. The estimate of the fair value is not the same as the market value. However, the theory is that despite the random forces acting on the marketprice of a stock, price will return to the vicinity of its theoretical, estimated price. Classical stock valuation models work only for companies that pay cash dividends. However, many high-growth stocks pay no dividends.

Financial analysts, investment bankers, and others now focus more on earnings or cash flow as a basis for valuing a stock. Cash flow models discount earnings before interest taxes depreciation and amortization, EBITDA. These cash flows can be discounted using a modified Gordon model that discounts cash flows at a required rate of return.

The earnings method of valuation uses benchmarks to establish multipliers for specific industries. The EBIT multiplier is the market value of a company divided by its earnings before interest and taxes, EBIT. Industry multipliers are multiplied times a company's EBIT to get the company value, which is then divided by the number of shares to get value per share.

The cash flow and EBIT multiplier methods are very important in valuing non-public companies. Such valuations are used to negotiate terms with new investors, determine bonds convertibility features, and set offering prices when a company goes public.

Sales multipliers can also be used to value a company, but this valuation technique should be used with caution unless the company being valued is long established and the parties have reasonable expectations about the makeup of the firm's revenue and expenses. Whether using the cash flow, EBIT, or sales multiplier method, selection of appropriate companies for use in development of the multiplier is extremely important.

Cost of Capital

The cost of capital is important because it shapes financial decisions about (1) the firm's optimal capital structure, (2) which projects to invest in, and (3) whether shareholder wealth is being created or destroyed. Generally, the cost of capital is discussed in terms of the weighted average cost of capital, WACC. It includes the cost of debt, preferred stock, retained earnings, and new equity.

The weighted average cost of capital changes (usually increases) as more new capital is raised. These changes are not gradual. Rather, the WACC usually remains constant for some interval of new capital, then increases abruptly. The marginal cost of capital, MCC, is the cost of capital at each of these step increases. The optimal capital structure will be function of the requirements of those supplying capital, and the return on the firm's capital. The spread between the return on a firm's capital and the cost of capital is a measure of whether shareholder wealth is being created or destroyed.

In this chapter, we will explore the factors that influence the cost of capital, capital structure, and whether shareholder value is being created or destroyed.

COST OF DEBT CAPITAL

The real cost of debt is its after-tax cost, as given by Eq. 9–1, where Kd is the net cost of debt capital. If a company pays $10,000 in interest to get $100,000 worth of debt capital, what does it really cost the company? If the company is in the 20% tax bracket, and deducts the interest from operating income before paying taxes, it saves $2,000 because it has lowered its tax bill by $2,000 ($10,000 interest deduction × 20% tax that would have applied to that $10,000 if it had not been paid out as interest).

$$Kd = \text{Interest rate} \times (1 - \text{Tax rate}) \qquad \text{(Eq. 9–1)}$$

Example
Given the interest rate on new debt for a particular company is 13%, and the company's tax rate is 30%, what is its after-tax cost of debt?

$$Kd = 13\% \times (1 - 30\%) = 13\% \times 70\% = 9.1\%$$

COST OF PREFERRED STOCK CAPITAL

The cost of capital for preferred stock is simply the dividend divided by the par value of the stock. Preferred dividends are not tax advantaged, that is, are not tax deductible. The equation for the cost of existing preferred stock is given in Eq. 9–2.

$$Kp = \frac{Dp}{Ps} \qquad \text{(Eq. 9–2)}$$

where   Kp is the cost of the preferred stock
         Dp is the dividend on the preferred stock
         Ps is the face, or par, value of the preferred stock

Example
Consider a preferred stock with a par value of $1,000 and an annual dividend of $70.

$$Kp = \frac{\$70}{\$1,000} = 7.0\%$$

The incremental cost of capital for newly issued preferred stock must take into account the cost involved in issuing new stock. The costs of issuing new stock are called flotation costs. The cost of newly issued preferred stock capital is given by Eq. 9–3.

$$Kps = \frac{Dps}{(Ps - F)} \qquad \text{(Eq. 9–3)}$$

where Kp, Dps, and Ps have the same meanings as before, and F is flotation costs.

Example

The annual dividend on a $1,000 share of preferred stock is $70. Flotation costs are $66 per share. What is the cost of preferred stock capital?

$$Kps = \frac{\$70}{(\$1,000 - \$66)} = \frac{\$70}{\$934} = 7.5\%$$

COST OF COMMON EQUITY: RETAINED EARNINGS, STOCK AT PAR, AND ADDITIONAL PAID IN CAPITAL

Retained earnings, stock at par, and additional paid in capital are types of common equity, each with its own account on the balance sheet. The cost of these types of equity is the same, so they will be treated together.

Retained earnings represent the after-tax profit that owners have left in the business instead of paying it out as dividends. Stock at par is the product of a stock's par value times the number of shares issued. Par value for common stock is its stated or legal value. Par bears no relationship to market value. Par value for common stock is usually set very low: $1.00 or $0.01. Some stock is no par value stock. Paid in capital is the difference between the price that a company issues stock for and the par value. Taken together, we will refer to retained earnings, stock at par, and additional paid in capital as common equity. There are several ways to cost this equity, no one of which is clearly the "right way" under all circumstances.

Cost of Common Equity Based on Dividends

One method of estimating the cost of common equity is using the stock yield equation, Eq. 9–4, based on the Gordon model.

$$Ks = \frac{D1}{Po} + g = \frac{Do \times (1 + g)}{Po} + g \qquad \text{(Eq. 9–4)}$$

where   Ks is the cost of common equity
         Do and D1 are the last and next annual dividends, respectively
         Po is the current stock price
         g is the growth rate

Example

Alpha Company's last dividend was $0.90, its growth rate is 12% per year, and its current price is $31. What is its yield?

$$Ks = \frac{\$0.90 \times (1 + 12\%)}{\$31} + 12\%$$

$$= \frac{\$1.008}{\$31} + 12\% = 3.3\% + 12\% = 15.3\%$$

The theory that allows us to equate a cost of capital to stock yield is that the market ultimately determines what common equity costs. The yield is the minimum amount that the market will accept to provide capital to a company. The yield demanded by the market therefore equates to the cost a company must pay for equity. In part, the yield versus cost is a matter of perspective. Suppliers of capital demand yield; users of capital see cost.

Cost of Common Equity Based on the Capital Asset Pricing Model

The capital asset pricing model (CAPM), given in Eq. 9–5, provides another way to value common equity by comparing it to overall market performance.

$$Ks = Krf + ERP \times B = Krf + (Km - Krf) \times B \quad (Eq. 9–5)$$

where   Ks is the cost of capital
         Krf is the risk-free rate of return, usually the yield of a one-year T-bill
         ERP is the equity risk premium, which is the same as the market yield, Km, less the risk-free rate of return
         B is beta, the degree of correlation between movements in the stock market as a whole and movements in the particular stock in question

Example

The risk-free rate of return, Krf, is 5.5%; the market yield, Km, is 15%; and the beta, B, for Alpha Company is 0.9. What is the cost of common equity using CAPM for the stock in question?

$$Ks = 5.5\% + (15\% - 5.5\%) \times 0.9$$
$$= 5.5\% + 8.6 = 14.1\%$$

The CAPM model uses expectations about risk-free returns, market returns generally, and the return of a particular stock to estimate the market's expectations about the minimum yield that would be required to induce the market to provide capital to a company. Since one person's yield is another person's costs, we can use required yield as the cost of common equity.

Bond Yield Method

Bonds are constantly being evaluated by the marketplace, and many are rated by Moody's and other rating services. One way to determine the cost of equity capital is to base it on the yield of bonds sold by the company, or the yield on bonds sold by companies of similar risk. Since equity is usually riskier than investments in debt, an additional risk premium, based on judgment, is added to this bond yield to estimate the required rate of return on equity, as shown in Eq. 9–6. The judgment risk premium is usually 3% to 5%. However, this judgment can be informed by the equity risk premium, which is the difference between the return on the market as a whole and the risk-free rate of return. The required yield is used to estimate the cost of equity capital. The equation is

$$Ks = \text{Bond yield to maturity} + \text{Judgment risk premium} \quad \text{(Eq. 9–6)}$$

Note that bond yield to maturity is not the coupon rate on a bond. Rather, it is the discount rate that, when applied to all interest payments and the bond's terminal value, discounts cash inflows so that they exactly equal the bond's market price (see Chapter 6).

Example
Alpha Company's bonds yield 12%. Alpha Company is fairly typical of companies in its industry, and the judgment risk premium is set at 4%. What is its cost of common equity capital?

$$Ks = 12\% + 4\% = 16\%$$

Overall Cost of Common Equity Capital

There is nothing inherent in the methods of computing the cost of common equity that forces them to converge to a single number. Just as there are many ways to value stocks, there are many ways to estimate the cost of common equity. As a practical matter, the three methods of computing the cost of common equity capital would probably all be considered, and some central measure of tendency (such as an average) would be used as the cost of common equity capital.

Reasonableness check: Estimates of the cost of common equity should be within one or two percentage points of one another. However, if the cost using one method is far different from the others, recheck the formula, input data, and computations.

Building on the preceding examples, we can compute a reasonable estimate of cost of common equity by averaging the estimates.

Dividend yield model	15.3%
Capital asset pricing model	14.1%
Bond yield method	16.0%
	45.4%

$$\text{Method average} = \frac{45.4\%}{3} = 15.1\%$$

COST OF NEW COMMON EQUITY CAPITAL

Capital can be raised by selling new common stock, but flotation costs drive the cost of this form of equity higher than existing common equity. The reason that cost increases is that, rather than the company getting the market price, Po, the company gets only the market price less flotation costs.

Dividend Yield Method

Consider a modified version of the Gordon model to compute the cost of new equity capital, as shown in Eq. 9–7.

$$Ke = \frac{D1}{Po - F} + g = \frac{Do \times (1 + g)}{Po - F} + g \qquad \text{(Eq. 9–7)}$$

where   Ke is the yield from new equity
Do and D1 are the last and next dividends
g is the growth rate
F is flotation costs
Po is the offering price

Example

Suppose a stock has a dividend of $0.90 per share, a growth rate of 12%, a current price of $31, and flotation costs of $3 per share. What would be the cost of this capital using the dividend yield model?

$$Ke = \frac{\$.90 \times (1 + 12\%)}{\$31 - \$3} + 12\% = \frac{\$1.008}{\$28} + 12\% = 15.6\%$$

This is 0.3% higher than for existing equity (15.6% versus 15.3%), which doesn't seem like much because most of the yield is embedded in the company's growth rate. If the last dividend, Do, were $3.65 and the growth rate only 3%, the cost of existing common equity would be about the same.

$$Ke = \frac{\$3.65 \times (1 + 3\%)}{\$31} + 3\% = \frac{\$3.76}{\$31} + 3\% = 15.1\%$$

But the cost of new common equity shares would be significantly higher.

$$Ke = \frac{\$3.65 \times (1 + 3\%)}{\$31 - \$3} + 3\% = \frac{\$3.76}{\$28} + 3\% = 16.4\%$$

The point is that these equations should not be used blindly. Judgment should be used in their application, and part of applying judgment is understanding how sensitive formulas will be to the facts of a particular situation.

Capital Asset Pricing Model and Bond Yield Method for Cost of New Common Equity

Flotation costs also affect the cost of new common equity in the capital asset pricing and bond yield method. However, it affects these methods in a somewhat different way.

Most new stock is sold through underwriters who line up institutional investors and brokers to purchase large blocks of stock on the day a new issue is first offered. By lining up investors in advance, they offset what would be the natural tendency of stock prices to drop rapidly if the market were suddenly glutted by a large number of shares. They also relieve issuing companies of the burden of finding buyers. In return for this and other services, underwriters get 4% to 7% of the value of shares issued, with smaller companies paying at, or close to, the high end of the range. In addition to underwriters' fees, there are other costs associated with issuance of stock, including registration with the SEC and sometimes with states, compilation and production of the prospectus, auditing, and other fees. These additional charges can increase flotation costs another 2% to 3%.

Consider the effect of these flotation costs on the cost of capital. If $100 of retained earnings cost 14.1% under the capital asset pricing model, that is the same as saying a "theoretical buyer" of that retained earnings would expect to receive $14.10 for every $100 he or she invested. But suppose instead of the yield of $14.10 being generated on $100 of retained earnings, $14.1% had to be generated on $100 of new stock less 9% flotation costs.

$$\text{Cost of new stock equity} \atop \text{CAPM method} = Ke = \frac{\$14.10}{(\$100 - 9\% \times \$100)}$$

$$= \frac{\$14.10}{\$91.00} = 15.5\%$$

Why is the $100 value of the stock issued reduced, but the $14.10 "yield" not reduced? Investors expect the entire yield they are purchasing. They don't care that the company issuing the stock gets substantially less than the $100 they invest.

Generalizing this example, we see the cost of newly issued stock under the CAPM model and under the bond yield model is given by Eqs. 9–8 and Eq 9–9, respectively.

$$\text{Cost of new equity} \atop \text{CAPM method} = Ke = \frac{Ks \times Pn}{Pn \times (1 - F\%)} = \frac{Ks}{(1 - F\%)}$$

$$(\text{Eq. 9–8})$$

$$\text{Cost of new equity} \atop \text{bond yield method} = Ke = \frac{Ks \times Pn}{Pn \times (1 - F\%)} = \frac{Ks}{(1 - F\%)}$$

$$(\text{Eq. 9–9})$$

where Ke is the cost of newly issued stock under either the CAPM or bond yield method
Ks is the cost of existing common equity
Pn is the price of the security
$F\%$ is the flotation cost expressed as a percentage of the issue price

Example

Suppose a $31 stock were being issued; flotation costs, as a percent of stock price were 9.6%; the cost of retained earnings under the CAPM and bond yield methods were 14.1% and 16%, respectively. What would the cost of newly issued common stock be for each method?

$$\text{CAPM} \qquad Ke = \frac{14.1\%}{(1 - 9.6\%)} = 15.6\%$$

$$\text{Bond yield} \qquad Ke = \frac{16\%}{(1 - 9.6\%)} = 17.7\%$$

Overall Cost of Newly Issued Common Equity

The cost of newly issued equity can be estimated by averaging the estimates of the three methods described earlier.

Dividend yield model	15.6%
Capital asset pricing model	15.6%
Bond yield method	17.7%
	48.9%

$$\text{Method average} = \frac{48.9\%}{3} = 16.3\%$$

COST-FREE CAPITAL

Not all capital has a direct cost. When a company buys something on credit, they are borrowing money on which they don't pay interest. Accrued payroll is also a form of free capital. It is a very short-term loan by the employees to a company until the next payday. Even though these and other noninterest-bearing liabilities may be a temporary form of financing, they should be considered in computing the overall weighted cost of capital.

WEIGHTED AVERAGE COST OF CAPITAL (WACC)

Many firms try to balance capital raised from various sources, and develop a model of the optimum mix of debt, preferred equity, common equity, and other sources. But why keep a balance? For one thing, banks are reluctant to finance more than a certain percent of a company's assets. Once a firm's debt/equity ratio exceeds 4:1, the number of banks that want to lend the next dollar thins out rapidly. Another reason for maintaining a certain mix of capital sources is that bond indentures, or provisions in preferred stock agreements, might require it. Tax considerations also affect a firm's optimum capital mix, and of course, firms want to minimize their overall cost of capital.

There are two ways to use the weighted average cost of capital. The first is to evaluate a firm's historical performance. Is the firm's yield greater than its cost of capital? If not, management is slowly liquidating the firm. On the other hand, if management is generating more with its assets than the cost of capital supporting those assets, we say management is adding economic value.

The second way to use the weighted average cost of capital is to model a firm's future performance based on raising various amounts of capital from different sources. Some new capital is cost free, as when accounts payable increase. The cost of some sources of capital increases or decreases, as when dividends are increased or decreased, or when bank interest rates float up or down. The ability to model capital costs is important in making strategic plans about growth and acquisitions, as well as planning for cyclic economic downturns.

Equation 9–10 is the most general form of the weighted average cost of capital equation. Note that not every term will be used under all circumstances. If no new common or preferred stock is to be issued, the relative weight of those terms will be zero. The weight of each term is equal to how many dollars of assets it supports. On the other hand, there are many kinds of debt: term loans, line of credit, commercial paper, corporate bonds, and so forth, each of which carries its own interest rate. So while Eq. 9–10 models debt, terms will have to be introduced for each form of debt at interest. Of course, each interest term will be adjusted for tax effects.

$$
\begin{aligned}
\text{WACC} = {} & \text{Wf} \times 0\% \text{ (Cost-free capital)} && \text{(Eq. 9–10)} \\
& + \text{Wd} \times \text{Kd} \times (1 - \text{Tax Rate}) \text{ (Debt capital)} \\
& + [\text{Wp} \times \text{Kp} + \text{Wpn} \times \text{Kpn}] \text{ (Preferred capital)} \\
& + [\text{Ws} \times \text{Ks} + \text{We} \times \text{Ke}] \text{ (Common equity capital)}
\end{aligned}
$$

where   Wf is the weight or percentage of accounts payable
         and other noninterest-bearing liabilities
         Wd, Wp, Wpn, Ws, and We are the weights, or
         percentages, of debt, preferred stock, newly issued
         preferred stock, common equity, and newly issued
         common shares, respectively

Notice that the terms Wp × Kp and Wpn × Kpn are in one
set of brackets, and Ws × Ks and We × Ke are in another set of
brackets. This is done to draw attention to the fact that there may
be two different costs for preferred, depending on whether it is
pre-existing or newly issued, and there may be two different costs
for common equity, depending on whether it is pre-existing or from
newly issued stock.

Figure 9–1 provides a format for computing the actual weights
of each component of capital. The same formula can be used to develop targets for each type of capital.

Example

Micron's capital structure consists of: (1) 15% accounts payable and
other non-interest-bearing debt, (2) 45% bank debt on which they
pay 10% interest, (3) 5% preferred stock, (4) 15% retained earnings,

FIGURE 9–1

Format for Computing Relative Weight of Various Types of Capital

Capital		Weighting Percent
Liabilities		
Accounts payable	$13 M	
Accrued payroll	$ 1 M	
Noninterest-bearing debt	$14 M	Wf = $14 M/$94 M = 14.9%
Bank debt	$42 M	Wd = $42 M/$94 M = 44.7%
Total liabilities	$56 M	
Preferred stock	$ 5 M	Wp = $ 5 M/$94 M = 5.3%
Retained earnings	$14 M	Ws = $14 M/$94 M = 14.9%
Newly issued stock	$19 M	We = $19 M/$94 M = 20.2%
Total equity	$38 M	
Liabilities plus equity	$94 M	100%

and (5) 20% stock at par plus additional paid in capital. They are in the 30% tax bracket. They have outstanding preferred stock with a $75 coupon rate for every $1,000 of par value. They have estimated their cost of common equity at 14.6%. What is their present WACC?

$$\text{WAAC} = 15\% \times 0\% + 45\% \times 10\% \times (1 - 30\%)$$
$$+ 5\% \times \frac{\$75}{\$1,000} + [15\% + 20\%] \times 14.6\%$$
$$= 0\% + 45\% \times 10\% \times 70\% + 5\% \times 7.5\% + 35\% \times 14.6\%$$
$$= 0\% + 3.15\% + 0.375\% + 5.11\%$$
$$= 8.635\%$$

WHEN SHOULD NEW COMMON STOCK BE ISSUED?

Debt is relatively cheap compared to stock because it is tax advantaged, and flotation costs drive up the cost of issuing new common stock. So what would trigger the added expense of issuing new stock?

There are several reasons to issue new common stock. One reason is that unless a company maintains a satisfactory debt/equity ratio, banks and others will be reluctant to lend to a company. But there are other reasons as well. A company might want to get out from under restrictive covenants imposed on them by providers of debt, or they may simply need more working capital for expansion.

However, each of these objectives may be met in part or as a whole through retained earnings. So before deciding the amount of any new stock issue, a company would need to determine how far they could go on new retained earnings.

Example
Suppose Micron Energy has determined to keep their capital mix 40% equity and 60% debt. They have $100,000 in new retained earnings, and they want to know how much new capital they can raise with it while maintaining their target capital structure. Setting aside the issue of preferred stock for a moment, we can see that Eq. 9–11

provides a means of computing the amount of capital capacity that can be generated with retained earnings.

Capital capacity = Retained earnings/Target percent of equity%

$$= \$100,000/40\% = \$250,000 \qquad \text{(Eq. 9–11)}$$

where   Capital capacity is the total amount of capital they can raise while maintaining their capital structure
Retained earnings is new retained earnings
Target percent of equity% is the company's goal for the percent of assets financed by equity

Proof   Retained earnings = Capital capacity × 40% = $250,000 × 40% = $100,000

So what happens if the company needs more than $250,000 in new capital for the period in question? The alternatives are to change the capital model, by, for example, increasing the debt–equity ratio, which is fairly conservative in this example, or increasing the amount of common equity by issuing new stock. However, as new stock is issued to raise equity, the weighted average cost of capital goes up because it is burdened by flotation costs.

Example

Micron's board of directors wants to raise $2,000,000 of capital this year. Retained earnings are only $100,000. Interest is 12%, their tax rate is 40%, and they have decided not to issue any preferred stock. Their optimum capital structure *for new capital* is 80% debt, of which 5% will be raised by increasing accounts payable and 75% will be a bank loan, and 20% common equity. The cost of common equity (which includes retained earnings) is 14.5%, and the cost of new common stock is 16%. What will be their WACC?

To solve this problem, we must determine how much of the $2 million capital goal retained earnings will support; then, of the remainder, we must solve for how much new common equity must be issued.

a.   Compute the amount of new capital that new retained earnings will support.

New capital = Retained earnings/Target percent of equity

$$= \$100,000/20\% = \$500,000$$

b. Compute the remaining amount of capital to be raised.

$$\text{Remaining capital to be raised} = \$2,000,000 - \$500,000 = \$1,500,000$$

c. Compute the amount of new equity from common stock that must be raised.

New equity from common stock = $\$1,500,000 \times 20\% = \$300,000$

d. Compute the weight of the new retained earnings.

$Ws = \$100,000/\$2,000,000 = 5\%$

e. Compute the weight of the newly issued common stock.

$We = \$300,000/\$2,000,000 = 15\%$

Applying Eq. 9–11 to Micron's capital structure, as shown in Figure 9–2, we can see that shifting their debt/equity ratio on the margin has reduced their weighted average cost of capital.

Even with the modest changes in incremental capital, Micron's weighted average cost of capital is decreasing. Were they to make a significantly greater use of debt, which is costing them net 7%, they could probably drive their cost of capital below 8%. Balanced against that is the reality that the more debt they use, the more volatile their net income will be, the greater their risk relative to the market, and the greater their risk as perceived by bond rating services, which will increase the yield demanded by the market.

Reasonableness check: Is the weighted average cost of capital between the cost of the most expensive component and the least expensive component? If not, there is a math or formula error somewhere. Did the weighted average cost of capital go up when new equity, burdened by flotation costs was used? If not, check formulas and math.

If the cost of preferred stock capital is cheaper than the cost of new common equity capital, why not use all preferred stock to raise the target $2 million? An excellent question, the answer to which turns in part on the market demand for preferred stock. Most investors want to participate in capital gains, an opportunity not afforded to preferred shareholders unless there is a conversion option. Or, investors want an interest-bearing bond that they perceive

Micron Energy Weighted Cost of Capital Before and After Changing Capital Structure

Account	Current Balance	Weight	Cost of Capital Net	Weighted Cost of Capital	Sources of New Capital	New Capital Structure	New Weights	Cost of Capital Net	Weighted Cost of Capital
Accounts payable and non-interest-bearing liabilities	1,500,000	15.0%	0.00%	0.00%	300,000	1,800,000	15.00%	0.00%	0.00%
Bank loan liabilities	4,500,000 6,000,000	45.0%	7.00%	3.15%	1,300,000 1,600,000	5,800,000 7,600,000	48.33%	7.00%	3.38%
Retained earnings	1,500,000	15.0%	14.60%	2.19%	100,000	1,600,000	13.33%	14.60%	1.95%
Preferred stock	500,000	5.0%	7.50%	0.38%		500,000	4.17%	7.50%	0.31%
Capital stock at par	100,000	1.0%	14.60%	0.15%		100,000	0.83%	14.60%	0.12%
Additional paid in capital	1,900,000	19.0%	14.60%	2.77%		1,900,000	15.83%	14.60%	2.31%
New capital stock at par					3,000	3,000	0.03%	16.00%	0.00%
New paid in capital					297,000	297,000	2.48%	16.00%	0.40%
Equity	4,000,000				400,000	4,400,000			
Liabilities and equity	10,000,000	100.0%		8.64%	2,000,000	12,000,000	100.00%		8.47%

as safer because interest is paid before preferred dividends. In designing a capital structure, all is balance.

COST OF LEASED CAPITAL

Although few textbooks talk about it, in the real world, many corporations raise a substantial amount of their capital through financial leases. A sophisticated analyst would consider how this affects his or her weighted average cost of capital. Don't think leases are just for vehicles and equipment. In today's financial environment, whole turnkey plants can be leased. The cost of capital for leased assets should be the net cost of imputed interest, adjusting for prepayments and deposits (see Chapter 7).

Other Sources of Capital

There many sources of capital an entrepreneur can use. However, most of these can be classified and treated like debt, preferred and common equity for purposes of computing the weighted average cost of capital. An important consideration in determining the cost of all these financing devices is to include processing, application, finders, or other fees as part of the cost.

MARGINAL COST OF CAPITAL

The concept of marginal cost of capital addresses the incremental cost of new capital. The cost of capital tends to rise as more capital is demanded. Suppose, in planning for next year, a company determines they will need an additional $5,000,000 for plant and equipment, expansion into new territories, and to finance anticipated sales growth. If, for example, all incremental capital needs could be funded through increases in accounts payable, the incremental cost would be zero. However, there is a practical limit to the amount of credit that vendors will extend. The next increment of capital might be bank loans. Bank loans cost more than zero, so they are a more expensive way to finance the company. However, because of tax effects, they can be fairly economical. Again, banks will lend only so much before other, more expensive sources must be considered. Should retained earnings be kept in the company to finance growth or paid out to the shareholders as dividends?

The decision to keep some or all of the retained earnings in the company represents another increment of capital, at a higher cost than bank loans. Second mortgages might cost more than bank loans and less than retained earnings. However, sometimes banks demand a blanket lien on assets, and that will severely limit mortgages on existing real estate. Leasing represents another increment of capital. Leases are usually more expensive than bank loans. Issues of new common stock are more expensive still, and so it goes.

For example, to raise between $500,000 and $2,000,000, the cost might be 15%, whereas the cost to raise between $0 and $500,000 might be 11%, and the cost between $2,000,000 and $5,000,000 might be 18%. The marginal cost of capital (MCC) can best be visualized by graphing the cost of capital on the y axis and the amount of capital that can be raised on the x axis, as shown in Figure 9–3.

Each dollar range on the graph is the blended rate for a set of capital inputs. Each step in the graph indicates the introduction of some new funding source. For example, the first step might be the blended rate of accounts payable, which has no cost, retained earnings and the amount of the bank loan that could be obtained with the incremental retained earnings. The next increment might include funds from issuance of common stock and the bank loans that increment of capital would support. Arguably, the lowest cost-funding source will always be used first, so the graph will always rise from left to right as the amount of capital needed increases.

FIGURE 9–3

Graph of Marginal Cost of Capital

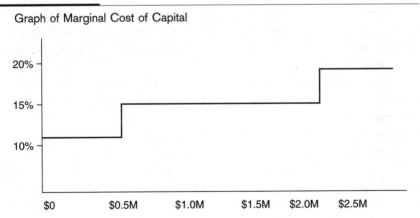

Using Marginal Cost of Capital

Obviously, the most productive projects are approved first, and they use up the lowest cost capital. At some point, the cost of new capital is going to exceed the *return on the next project* on the list. At that point, it is no longer worthwhile to raise money for the next project. The capital budget is done (see Chapter 10 for methods to compute the return on projects).

DECISION RULES FOR THE OPTIMAL CAPITAL BUDGET

The optimal capital budget is a balance between the marginal cost of capital and the return a company can get on its projects.

Most companies prepare a list of projects they want to fund and rank them by rate of return. Some call this list an investment opportunity schedule. All things being equal, an economically rational company will fund projects with the highest internal rate of return (IRR) before funding projects with lower returns.

We have seen that as a company raises more and more capital, the marginal cost of capital rises. A rational company would use the lowest cost capital first before using progressively more expensive capital.

If the amount of capital for projects were plotted on the x axis and project yield (IRR) were plotted on the y axis, we could graph both the cost of capital and the project return. Economic self-interest thus gives us two curves that will intersect when optimal capital budget is reached.

Where the marginal cost of capital exceeds the internal rate of return on a project, the company has reached its optimal capital budget. In Figure 9–4, the optimal capital budget is reached at about $330,000.

Notice that these "curves" are actually more like steps. The width of a step in the case of IRR is the amount of money it takes to fund a project. Suppose the left part of an IRR step exceeds the marginal cost of capital, and the right part of the step is less than the marginal cost of capital. In that event, the project should be rejected. If, however, the project can be segmented so that the project only proceeds to the point where it has used only low cost capital, it should be accepted.

F I G U R E   9–4

Graph of Investment Opportunities Versus Marginal Cost of Capital

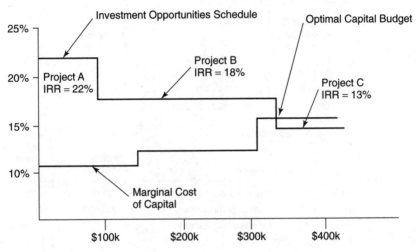

Example

Figure 9–5 provides an analysis of the marginal cost of capital and investment opportunities schedule for Merchantville Electric Motors Manufacturing. What is their optimal capital budget?

Project B, which requires $500,000 and has an internal rate of return (IRR) of 18%, would be funded with $200,000 of funds with an MCC of 11% and $300,000 of funds with an MCC of 13%.

Project C, which requires $1,000,000 and has an IRR of 17%, will *not* be funded because it would need the remaining $100,000 of 13% money, $400,000 of 15% money, and $500,000 of 18% money. A general rule is that if any part of a project requires money that is more costly than the IRR on the project, it should be rejected.

Project D, which requires $40,000 and has an IRR of 16%, will be funded with $40,000 of 13% money.

Project A, which requires $80,000 and has an IRR of 14%, will *not* be funded in its entirety because it would have used the remaining $60,000 of 13% money plus $20,000 of 15% money. Since the 15% money has a cost higher than the IRR of the project, it will not be funded. However, replacement of vans is a project that can be segmented. If each replacement van cost $20,000, the company

FIGURE 9-5

Marginal Cost of Capital and Investment Opportunities Schedule for Merchantville Electric Motors Manufacturing

Marginal Cost of Capital

Dollar Range		Percent
$0	$ 200,000	11%
$200,000	$ 600,000	13%
$600,000	$ 800,000	15%
$800,000	$2,000,000	18%

Investment Opportunities Schedule

Name	Description	Capital Required	Internal Rate of Return
A.	Purchase high-mileage vans	$ 80,000	14%
B.	Automate Micromotor assembly line	$ 500,000	18%
C.	Build Mantua Motor assembly factory	$1,000,000	17%
D.	Retrofit stamping machine	$ 40,000	16%

would replace three vans for $60,000 (3 × $20,000) using the remaining 13% money. Figure 9–6 summarizes the allocation of funds to projects.

FIGURE 9-6

Summary of Merchantville Electric Motors Manufacturing Projects to Be Funded

Project	Internal Rate of Return	Amount Funded	Source and Cost of Funds	Amount Used from Source
B Automate assembly line	18%	$500,000	11%	$200,000
			13%	$300,000
D Retrofit stamping machine	16%	$ 40,000	13%	$ 40,000
A Replace low-mileage vans	14%	$ 60,000	13%	$ 60,000
Optimal capital budget				$600,000

SUMMARY

Liabilities and equity are different kinds of capital that are used to finance a company's assets. The cost of capital can vary widely based on a company's capital structure. The cost of capital is used as a benchmark to evaluate management effectiveness. If the company's yield exceeds the cost of capital, management is adding economic value for the shareholders. If, however, the company's yield is less than the cost of capital, management is slowly liquidating the company to the detriment of shareholders.

The cost of capital for debt is the cost net of tax savings. The cost of capital for preferred shares is the dividend divided by the par value of a share. Preferred dividends are not tax deductible and are therefore not tax advantaged. Three methods of computing the cost of common equity discussed in this chapter are the stock dividend yield, the capital asset pricing model, and the bond yield model. Each has good and bad points. As a practical matter, it would be prudent to compute and consider all three before settling on an estimate of the cost of common equity capital. Common equity includes retained earnings, stock at par value, and additional paid in capital. Capital from new preferred or new common shares is more expensive than capital from existing shares because it is burdened with flotation costs. Other sources of capital that should be considered include accounts payable and other non-interest-bearing liabilities and leases. In determining the cost of leased capital, use the imputed interest rate net of any tax savings.

The marginal cost of capital (MMC) is a concept that examines the incremental cost of adding new capital sources to a mix. Arguably, the least expensive sources are used first, and more expensive sources, such as new common shares, are added last. The MCC can be graphed with the cost of capital on the y axis and additional increments of capital on the x axis. This graph can be visualized as a series of steps rising from the left to the right. The MCC is used in conjunction with a company's list of proposed projects. If projects are sorted in order of decreasing return, they can be graphed over the MCC curve. The optimal capital budget is where the two curves intersect. The reason is that the next increment of funds will cost more than the next project on the list will yield.

CHAPTER 10

Capital Budgeting

Capital budgeting is the process of evaluating projects that require a significant investment of current capital in exchange for payoffs that may not materialize for a number of years. Capital budgeting is important because commitment of resources to one project means foregoing profits from competing projects. Capital projects usually involve long-term commitment of resources, which means it is often difficult to change course in response to changing market conditions. Even if a project is canceled part way through its life, stocks, bonds, or loans used to fund the project will continue to burden the company. Betting the company on the wrong capital project(s) can be disastrous.

Companies face many difficulties when deciding on a program of capital expenditures, including (1) forecasting business conditions in the future when payoffs occur, (2) determining whether projects have a sufficient return to warrant allocation of capital, (3) accounting for project risk, and (4) translating future payoffs to current dollars.

In this chapter, we will examine five methods of evaluating and ranking capital projects, and discuss the strengths and weaknesses of each.

METHODS FOR EVALUATING CAPITAL PROJECTS

There are five basic methods for evaluating capital projects. Companies often use two or more methods to rank projects as a reasonableness check on their analysis. The methods are as follows:

1. Payback method: This involves determination of the amount of time it will take to recover an investment.
2. Discounted payback method: Cash flows are discounted, then the amount of time necessary to recover an investment in present dollars is computed.
3. Net present value (NPV): This is the present value of the cash inflows less the present value of the cash outflows (investments).
4. Internal rate of return (IRR): This is the yield on a project. It is defined as the discount rate that will make the net present value equal to zero.
5. Modified internal rate of return (MIRR): This involves finding a discount rate that will yield an NPV = 0 using the following procedure: (1) compute the future value of all cash flows to the terminal date of the project, and (2) discount the resulting amount back to the present. The MIRR is the discount rate that makes NPV = 0.

PAYBACK METHOD

If all cash inflows were the same in every period, one could simply divide cash inflows by cash outflows. However, with uneven cash flows, one must subtract inflows from outflows year by year until the final year. In the final year, divide the residue of the outflow amount by the last inflow.

Example
A project costs $100,000 in year 0, and pays back $30,000 in year 1, $50,000 in year 2, and $70,000 in year 3.

Subtracting $30,000 and $50,000 from $100,000 for years 1 and 2 leaves a residue of $20,000. The residue of the $20,000 cash outflow (investment)/$70,000 cash inflow in year 3 = 0.286. Taken together, the payback is 2 years + 0.286 year or 2.286 years. Figure 10–1 provides a format for computing payback.

$$\text{Partial year payback} = \text{Residue of initial investment}/ \quad \text{(Eq. 10–1)}$$
$$\text{Year's cash inflow}$$
$$= \$20,000/\$70,000 = 0.286 \text{ year}$$

When using the payback method, projects with the shortest payback rank ahead of projects with longer paybacks. Since payback provides information on how quickly investments are recovered, it addresses liquidity and cash flow issues, both of which are extremely important to small businesses.

While the payback method is simple and widely used, it has two major flaws: (1) it doesn't consider the time value of money, and (2) it tends to favor projects with near-term payback, compared to a project that has a greater payback over the long run.

Consider two projects, A and B. Both require an investment of $100,000. Cash inflows for project A are $50,000 for three years, at which time the project ends. Cash inflows for project B are $40,000 for eight years. The payback method will rank project A ahead of project B, even though project B will generate more cash over its lifetime.

FIGURE 10-1

Format for Computing Payback

		Remaining to Be Paid Back
Investment (cash outflow)		
Year 0	$100,000	$100,000
Payback (cash inflows)		
Year 1	$ 30,000	$ 70,000
Year 2	$ 50,000	$ 20,000
Year 3	$ 70,000	

DISCOUNTED PAYBACK METHOD

The discounted payback method is similar to the payback method except that all future cash inflows and outflows are discounted back to the present. Discounted payback is a method for determining how long it will take for the project to pay for itself in *present dollars*.

Example

A project costs $100,000 in year 0. Cash inflows are Y1 = $30,000, Y2 = $50,000, Y3 = $70,000, where year 0 is the present, and Y1, Y2, and Y3 are the inflows in one, two, and three years, respectively. Assume a discount rate of 12%. Figure 10–2 provides a format for computing discounted payback.

Projects with the shortest discounted payback ranked highest. This method has an advantage over the simple payback method because it considers the time value of money. Since it provides information on how quickly investments are recovered, it addresses liquidity and cash flow issues. However, it still suffers from one of the payback method's shortcomings. It doesn't consider the value of cash generated beyond the payback date.

Let's look at projects A and B in more detail (see Figure 10–3). Both require a $100,000 investment, and A pays $50,000 for three

F I G U R E   10–2

Format for Computing Discounted Payback

	Year 1	Year 2	Year 3
Discounting inflows	$\dfrac{\$30,000}{(1 + 12\%)}$	$\dfrac{\$50,000}{(1 + 12\%)^2}$	$\dfrac{\$70,000}{(1 + 12\%)^3}$
	$30,000/1.12	$50,000/1.254	$70,000/1.405
	$26,786	$39,872	$49,822
Outflows	$100,000		
Less DF Y1	−$26,786		
Less DF Y2	−$39,872		
Residue	$33,342		

Residue/inflow in year 3 = $33,342/$49,822 = 0.669

Payback = 2 years + 0.669 = 2.669 years

FIGURE 10-3

Analysis of the Impact of Cash Generated Beyond the Discounted
Payback Period

Present Value Factors	Project A		Project B	
	Cash Inflow	Discounted Cash Flow	Cash Inflow	Discounted Cash Flow
PV(10%, 1) = 0.9091	$50,000	$ 45,455	$40,000	$ 36,364
PV(10%, 2) = 0.8265	$50,000	$ 41,325	$40,000	$ 33,060
PV(10%, 3) = 0.7513	$50,000	$ 37,565	$40,000	$ 30,052
PV(10%, 4) = 0.6830			$40,000	$ 27,320
PV(10%, 5) = 0.6209			$40,000	$ 24,836
PV(10%, 6) = 0.5645			$40,000	$ 22,580
PV(10%, 7) = 0.5132			$40,000	$ 20,528
PV(10%, 8) = 0.4665			$40,000	$ 18,660
Present value of cash inflows		$124,345		$213,400

Investment	$100,000		$100,000	
Less				
Year 1	$ 45,455		$ 36,364	
Year 2	$ 41,325		$ 33,060	
			$ 30,052	
Residue	$ 13,220		$ 524	

Residue divided by inflow in payback year	$\dfrac{\$13,220}{\$37,565} = 0.35$	$\dfrac{\$524}{\$27,320} = 0.02$
Payback =	2.35 years	3.02 years

years, whereas B pays $40,000 for eight years. For purposes of this
example, assume a discount rate of 10%.

Project B generates far more cash over its lifetime than project A, even though project A ranks higher than project B in both
the payback and discounted payback method. Fortunately, there
is a method that considers the present value of the cash generated over the life of a project. It is the net present value method.

NET PRESENT VALUE

Net present value (NPV) is the discounted value of cash inflows less discounted cash outflows, as shown in Eq. 10–2. Net present value is designed to determine whether the project will increase or decrease shareholder wealth on a risk-adjusted basis, and by how much.

$$NPV = PV(\text{cash inflows}) - PV(\text{cash outflows}) \quad \text{(Eq. 10–2)}$$

where NPV is the net present value, and PV is the present value of the cash inflows and outflows, respectively.

When there is only one cash outflow at the beginning of a project, which is typical for many projects, PV(cash outflows) simply equals invested capital. However, where there are multiple cash outflows, each must be discounted back to the present. Two examples of projects with cash outflows at the end of their useful life are strip mines where the land must be reclaimed, and nuclear power plants that must be decommissioned.

Example

A project has cash inflows of Y1 = $30,000, Y2 = $50,000, and Y3 = $70,000. The project costs $100,000 in year 0. Assume a discount rate of 12%. This problem could be solved by using either the present value tables in Appendix C or Eq. 10–3.

$$PV(K, n) = \frac{1}{(1 + K)^n} \qquad \text{(Eq. 10–3)}$$

$$
\begin{aligned}
NPV &= \$30,000 \times PV(12\%, 1) \\
&\quad + \$50,000 \times PV(12\%, 2) \\
&\quad + \$70,000 \times PV(12\%, 3) \\
&\quad - 100,000 \\
&= \$30,000 \times 0.89286 + \$50,000 \times 0.79719 \\
&\quad + \$70,000 \times 0.71178 - \$100,000 \\
&= \$26,786 + \$39,860 + \$49,825 - \$100,000 \\
&= \$16,471
\end{aligned}
$$

As a general rule, if the net present value is greater than zero, the project is worth funding.

The advantages of this method are that (1) it is fairly straight-forward; (2) unlike the payback and discounted payback methods, it recognizes the value of cash inflows beyond the payback period; and (3) it quantifies the risk-adjusted increase in shareholder wealth from the project.

The disadvantage is that it is difficult to compare NPV to any benchmark. For example, suppose project A has an NPV of $10,000 and project B has an NPV of $25,000. Which is the better project? On the face of it, project B would seem better. However, suppose project A required an investment of only $100,000, whereas project B required an investment of $10 million. To make a sensible analysis of the two projects, one would have to consider alternative uses of the incremental $9.9 million required for project B. If alternative uses provide an NPV greater than the incremental $15,000, project B would have to be rejected in favor of Project A and the other alternative projects.

INTERNAL RATE OF RETURN (IRR)

Internal rate of return (IRR) is the discount rate at which a project will have a net present value of zero. Internal rate of return is another name for the yield on funds invested in a project.

How does one compute IRR? Thinking about the problem for a moment, it is a lot like a bond yield problem. This class of problems is generally too complex to use tables. Some texts suggest that this class of problem is impossible without a financial calculator or computer, and leave people to trial and error. But we know we can do better. How? Consider how Eq. 10–2 can be rewritten to yield the equation for the internal rate of return, Eq 10–4.

$$NPV = PV(\text{cash inflows}) - PV(\text{cash outflows})$$

We know that NPV = 0, so the equation becomes

$$0 = PV \text{ cash inflows} - PV \text{ cash outflows} \quad \text{(Eq. 10–4)}$$

In *most* cases, there is one cash outflow at project inception. So we can further rewrite the equation as

$$\text{Cash outflow} = PV(\text{cash inflows}) \quad \text{(Eq. 10–5)}$$

We could substitute a range of test IRR values into the present value function for cash inflows and generate a series of numbers, some higher than the cash outflow (the investment) and some lower. If we plotted the generated numbers on the y axis, and the corresponding test IRRs on the x axis, we could graph a curve. If we found, on the y axis, the actual cash outflow, and drew a horizontal line across to where it intersected the curve, we could read down to the x axis to find the correct IRR. But that is still not as efficient as we want it to be. So consider this computational alternative.

a. Select a test IRR and compute a test present value of a cash inflow.

b. From our bond problems, we know that if the test cash inflow is less than the cash outflow (investment), our IRR is too high. The discount rate, our IRR, is "sanding down" cash inflows too fast. If the test cash inflow is higher than the cash outflow, IRR is too low.

c. Select another IRR using informed judgment, based on the first test computation.

d. Interpolate using the two data points thus created to estimate the actual IRR.

Example
Consider a project with cash inflows of Y1 = $30,000, Y2 = $50,000, and Y3 = $70,000. The project costs $100,000 in year 0. Having just computed the NPV for this problem, we know that 12% is an insufficient discount rate to achieve an NPV of zero. Ideally, a test discounted cash inflows would bracket the initial investment of $100,000. Assume an IRR1 of 18% and compute a value test1.

test1 = $30,000 × PV(18%, 1) + $50,000 × PV(18%, 2)
        + $70,000 × PV(18%, 3)
      = $30,000 × 0.84746 + $50,000 × 0.71818 + $70,000 × 0.60863
      = $25,423.80 + $35,909.00 + $42,604.10
      = $103,936.90

We see that IRR1 was insufficient to discount cash inflows down to the amount of the cash outflows (investment), so we need to select a higher value for IRR2. If, on the other hand, IRR1 had discounted the cash inflows to a value less than cash outflows, IRR1 was too high, and we would have to select an IRR2 that is lower. For this problem, however, we need a higher IRR2. Selecting 24% and applying it to the facts of the case, we can compute a test2.

$$\text{test2} = \$30,000 \times \text{PV}(24\%, 1) + \$50,000 \times \text{PV}(24\%, 2)$$
$$+ \$70,000 \times \text{PV}(24\%, 3)$$
$$= \$30,000 \times 0.80645 + \$50,000 \times 0.65036$$
$$+ \$70,000 \times 0.52449$$
$$= \$24,193.50 + \$32,518 + \$36,714.30$$
$$= \$93,425.80$$

This is less than the investment (cash outflow) of $100,000. Since test1 and test2 bracket the cash outflow, we can conclude we have bracketed the "actual" IRR. However, suppose IRR2 yielded a test2 that was still greater than the investment. In that case, we would know that we had to select a higher discount rate, perhaps 30% or more until test1 and test2 bracket the investment.

Adapting the interpolation formula we used in Chapter 5, we get equation Eq. 10–6.

$$\frac{\text{test 2} - \text{test 1}}{\text{IRR2} - \text{IRR1}} = \frac{\text{Cash outflow} - \text{test1}}{\text{IRR} - \text{IRR1}} \quad \text{(Eq. 10–6)}$$

$$\frac{\$93,425.80 - \$103,936.90}{24\% - 18\%} = \frac{\$100,000 - \$103,936.90}{\text{IRR} - 18\%}$$

$$\frac{-\$10,511.10}{6\%} = \frac{-\$3,936.90}{\text{IRR} - 18\%}$$

Multiplying both sides by -1 and cross-multiplying by (IRR $-$ 18%) and 6%, respectively gives

$$(\text{IRR} - 18\%) \times \$10,511.10 = \$3,936.90 \times 6\%$$

Dividing both sides by $10,511.10 gives

$$\text{IRR} - 18\% = (\$3,936.90 / \$10,511.10) \times 6\%$$
$$\text{IRR} = 0.37455 \times 6\% + 18\%$$
$$= 2.247\% + 18\% = 20.247\%$$

Proof We can prove that 20.247% is a good estimate of the internal rate of return for this project by plugging it back into the

NPV equation. If the NPV is zero, we know our IRR is correct because, by definition, IRR is the discount rate that makes NPV equal
to zero.

Since there are no tables for 20.247%, it would be impossible
to perform this proof without the present value formula we discussed in Chapter 5, which is given in Eq. 10–6.

$$PV(K, n) = \frac{1}{(1 + K)^n} = 1/(1 + K)^n$$

Proof

$$
\begin{aligned}
NPV &= \$30,000/(1 + 20.247\%) \\
&+ \$50,000/(1 + 20.247\%)^2 \\
&+ \$70,000/(1 + 20.247)^3 \\
&- \$100,000 \\
&= \$30,000/(1.20247) \\
&+ \$50,000/(1.20247)^2 \\
&+ \$70,000/(1.20247)^3 \\
&- \$100,000 \\
&= \$30,000/1.20247 \\
&+ \$50,000/1.44593 \\
&+ \$70,000/1.73869 \\
&- \$100,000 \\
&= \$24,948.65 + \$34,579.82 + \$40,260.20 - \$100,000
\end{aligned}
$$

$$\text{Difference} = \$99,788.67 - \$100,000 = -\$211.33$$

The variance in the solution is about 0.2% ($-\$211.33/\$100.000$).
Precision in computing the internal rate of return can be improved
further, if necessary, by (1) using the present value formula to compute test1 and test2, and increase the number of decimal points in
the computation beyond that in the tables; (2) selecting IRR1 and
IRR2 closer to the "actual" value of the internal rate of return, which
we have estimated fairly closely already. Recall that interpolation
is based on a calculus trick that says if points on a curve are fairly
close, the slopes of the lines between them are almost exactly equal.
By selecting IRR1 and IRR2 closer to the "actual" IRR, precision can
be improved.

Internal rate of return calculations can be modeled on a spreadsheet, as can the analysis of variance to determine whether the selected IRR1 and IRR2 were close enough to the actual IRR to converge to an answer with the requisite amount of precision.

Projects with the highest internal rate of return rank higher than projects with a lower IRR. Projects with an IRR greater than the cost of capital should be considered for funding. Those with an IRR equal to or less than the cost of capital should not be considered.

The advantage of internal rate of return is that it is directly comparable to competing uses of funds. IRR can be compared to the yield of stocks and bonds, and to the yield of other projects. It can also be used to determine the optimal capital budget by ranking projects in terms of their IRR and comparing them to the marginal cost of capital. IRR can also provide an idea of the "cushion" in a project. If, for example, a project has an IRR of 15% and the cost of capital is 12%, the cushion is 3%.

The disadvantage of IRR is that it is complex. Another problem is that it doesn't always produce a unique solution. When there are multiple cash outflows, for example, in the case of strip mines needing land restoration or nuclear power plants needing decommissioning, there are multiple IRRs that can drive NPV to zero. A technique called modified internal rate of return overcomes this difficulty.

MODIFIED INTERNAL RATE OF RETURN (MIRR)

Under certain circumstances, when there is more than one cash outflow (investment), IRR can give multiple solutions. It is beyond the scope of this book to describe the underlying mathematics other than to say that when factoring a polynomial, sometimes more than one value is a solution.

So what is modified internal rate of return? Like NPV and IRR, MIRR analyzes a capital budgeting problem as a series of cash inflows and outflows over time. NPV is used to determine whether discounted cash inflows exceed discounted cash outflows. IRR is used to find the discount rate that will make the present value of cash outflows equal the present value of cash outflows. Sound familiar so far?

Modified internal rate of return looks to the end of a project first. The future value of all the cash flows, *except the initial investment*, is computed to get a so-called terminal value of the investment. This terminal value is then discounted back to the present. MIRR is the discount rate that, when applied to all cash flows except the initial investment, makes the net present value zero. Clear? Right now you are probably wondering if these people are insane.

But since a large number of business and financial managers use MIRR, we must master it.

Example
A project has cash inflows of Y1 = $30,000, Y2 = $50,000, and Y3 = $70,000. The project costs $100,000 in year 0. Selecting a test MIRR1 of 20%, we can apply the algorithm for finding the "actual" MIRR.

  a. What is the terminal date of the project? Three years.

  b. Assume an MIRR1 of 20%. What is the *future value* of all cash inflows and outflows at project completion in year 3 (not including the initial investment)?

Year 1	Year 2	Year 3
$30,000 × FVIF(20%, 2)	+ $50,000 × FVIF(20%, 1)	+ $70,000 = Terminal value
$30,000 × 1.44	+ $50,000 × 1.2	+ $70,000 = Terminal value
$43,200	+ $60,000	+ $70,000 = $173,200

  c. Discount the terminal value to the present.

test1 = $173,200 × PV(20%, 3) = $173,200 × 0.5787 = $100,230.84

This amount is higher than the original investment of $100,000, which implies the discount rate is not "wearing down" the cash flow enough. The implication is to try a discount rate that is higher. Let MIRR2 = 24%, and compute another test value.

  a. What is the terminal date of the project? Three years.

  b. Assume an MIRR2 = 24%. What is the terminal value of the project?

Year 1	Year 2	Year 3
$30,000 × FV(24%, 2)	+ $50,000 × FV(24%, 1)	+ $70,000 = Terminal value
$30,000 × 1.5376	+ $50,000 × 1.24	+ $70,000 = Terminal value
$46,128	+ $62,000	+ $70,000 = $178,128

c. Discount the terminal value to the present value.

test2 = \$178,128 × PV(24%, 3) = \$178,128 × 0.52449 = \$93,426.35

Since test1 and test2 bracket the initial investment of \$100,000, we can infer MIRR1 and MIRR2 bracket the "actual" MIRR. We now have enough information to use the interpolation formula, Eq. 10–7, which is a modified version of the IRR interpolation formula.

$$\frac{\text{test2} - \text{test1}}{\text{MIRR2} - \text{MIRR1}} = \frac{\text{Cash outflow} - \text{test1}}{\text{MIRR} - \text{MIRR1}} \quad \text{(Eq. 10–7)}$$

$$\frac{\$93,426.35 - \$100,230.84}{24\% - 20\%} = \frac{\$100,000 - \$100,230.84}{\text{MIRR} - 20\%}$$

$$\frac{-\$6,804.49}{4\%} = \frac{-\$230.84}{\text{MIRR} - 20\%}$$

Multiplying both sides by −1, then multiplying both sides by (MIRR − 20%) first, then by 4% gives

$$(\text{MIRR} - 20\%) \times \$6,804.49 = \$230.84 \times 4\%$$
$$\text{MIRR} - 20\% = (\$230.84/\$6,804.49) \times 4\%$$
$$\text{MIRR} = 0.136\% + 20\% = 20.136\%$$

Projects with the highest MIRR rank higher than projects with lower MIRR. Projects with an MIRR greater than the cost of capital can be profitably funded. Those with an MIRR equal to or less than the cost of capital should not be funded.

One advantage of MIRR is that it is directly comparable to the yield on other investments. MIRR can be used in place of IRR to find the optimal capital budget. The highest ranking projects should be funded first, using the capital with the lowest marginal cost of capital (MCC). When MCC equals or exceeds MIRR, the optimal capital budget has been reached. MIRR also provides some indication of the amount of "cushion" in a project. For example, if the cost of capital is 12%, and the IRR on a project is 15%, there is a 3% "cushion" in the project. The major drawback to MIRR is that it is somewhat complex.

Comments on Interpolation Methodology

How can essentially the same interpolation equation solve bond yield, yield to call, IRR and MIRR problems? Is it a trick? Yes, a calculus trick. It is a trick that works on a large variety of problems. Recall that a function is just a machine that creates outputs from inputs. Theoretically, we could generate thousands of inputs, feed them into the function, and create thousands of outputs. Inputs and outputs can be graphed. The intersection of some known quantity, the market value of a bond or the amount of an initial investment, will correspond to a point on the graph above the "actual" value we are trying to determine. But rather than generating thousands of test inputs, we use our best judgment to select a few test inputs, maybe as few as two. The calculus trick is to say that the slope of the line between our two test inputs and outputs is almost equal to the slope of the line between the point defined by one test input and its output on the one hand, and the point described between a known value, for example, the market value of a bond or the amount of an investment, and the input we are trying to determine.

Our interpolation trick can be used for almost any function with the following conditions: the function is continuous, and the selected test inputs are fairly close to the actual input we are trying to determine. The solution found from interpolation can be "proved" by using it as an input to the function and determining whether the output is equal or close to the known value. The quality of the solution can be determined by subtracting the output of the proof from the known value and dividing the difference by the known value. If the resulting variance is unacceptably large, use the solution of the interpolation as a test input and repeat the algorithm.

COMPARISON OF CAPITAL BUDGETING METHODS

Figure 10–4 provides a summary of the advantages and disadvantages of various capital budgeting methods. Most companies use several methods to assure project ranking is appropriate under a variety of circumstances.

SUMMARY

There are five basic methods of evaluating capital projects. Payback and discounted payback focus on how soon a company can

FIGURE 10-4

Comparison of Capital Budgeting Decision Methods

Technique	Advantages	Disadvantages	Decision Rule
Payback	Simple	Does not consider the time value of money or payback in out years	Select shortest payback period
Discounted payback	Fairly simple	Does not consider big payback in out years	Select shortest payback period
NPV	Not too complex Quantifies wealth creation	NPV is not directly comparable to alternative investments. Does not consider size of investment	Reject NPV < 0 Generally select greatest NPV
IRR and MIRR	Can compare directly to other investments and marginal cost of capital	Complex and bizarrely complex	Select highest IRR or MIRR

recoup invested capital. Discounted payback is superior to payback because it considers the time value of money.

Net present value (NPV) compares the present value of cash inflows to cash outflows (investments). If NPV is positive, the project will increase shareholder wealth. If it is zero or negative, it will not increase shareholder wealth and should be rejected.

Internal rate of return (IRR) and modified internal rate of return (MIRR) are used to find the discount rate that will make a project's NPV equal zero. This discount rate is also the yield on a project and can be directly compared to the cost of capital and alternative investments. MIRR is superior to IRR because it provides a unique solution for projects that have multiple cash outflows. On the other hand, it is conceptually more complex.

Interpolation can be used to estimate IRR and MIRR to any degree of precision desired. The degree of precision in an estimate can be determined by using the estimate of IRR or MIRR in the NPV equation to determine whether the result is zero. If it isn't, the variance, or relative degree of error, can be measured by dividing the computed NPV by the investment. If the variance is too large, other test IRRs and MIRRs can be used to compute new, more precise estimates of IRR and MIRR, respectively.

CHAPTER 11

Cash Flow Estimation for Capital Budgeting

Fancy formulas for ranking capital projects have little meaning unless the cash flow data going into them are correct. In this chapter, we shall explore principles for project cash flow estimation. These principles are also broadly applicable to operating cash budgets. Cash budgets different from typical operating budgets that focus on profit and loss.

CAPITAL BUDGETING GROUND RULES

Capital budgeting decisions are based on *cash flows*, not accounting income. This overriding principle informs decision making throughout the process of developing a cash flow model. The other overriding principle is to understand that, like finance, capital budgeting is about shaping the future. It is a forward-looking process, and little weight is given to anything that happened prior to the date budgeting decisions are being made. These principles give rise to a number of rules about cash flow estimation.

1. Incremental cash flows: Only incremental cash flows are relevant. Cash that will flow into or out of the company whether or not the project is undertaken is irrelevant.
2. Sunk costs: Expenditures made prior to the capital budgeting decision, also called sunk costs, are never

included in the decision-making process or in the estimation of cash flows.

Sunk costs are the result of past actions and cannot be changed. However, sunk costs may reduce future costs. For example, if a project can be built on a foundation that already exists, it will indirectly affect the capital budgeting decision by lowering future costs.

3. Opportunity costs: Opportunity costs should be charged against the project. For example, if a truck already owned by the company could be either sold for $20,000 or used in a capital project, the market value of the truck should be charged to the project.

4. Shipping and installation: Shipping and installation costs should be included in capital budgeting costs.

5. Cash net of tax: Cash flows should be considered net of tax. For example, if $50,000 per year of operating profit is expected, and the company is in the 30% bracket, the relevant cash flow from the operating profit is $35,000 ($50,000 less $15,000 of taxes).

6. Changes in depreciation: When an undepreciated asset is being replaced by another asset, the difference in depreciation should be considered, as well as the tax effects on this change in depreciation.

For example, suppose an old machine had an annual depreciation of $10,000, and a new machine has an annual depreciation of $25,000. Depreciation will not be allowed on the old machine once it is replaced. So the incremental depreciation (which becomes part of the incremental cash flow) is the relevant amount. The incremental depreciation is $15,000 ($25,000 new machine less $10,000 old machine). Changes in depreciation have tax consequences. If a company in the 30% bracket increases its depreciation by $15,000, that will reduce its taxes by $4,500 ($15,000 × 30% tax rate).

7. Working capital: Most projects require changes in working capital. If a new manufacturing plant is being brought online, arguably that will increase sales, which will require more accounts receivable and inventory. Some of that will be financed through increased

accounts payable and payroll accruals. So the *net change in working capital* is the relevant cash flow item to budget.

When the project winds down, accounts receivable will be collected, and inventory sold and not replaced. The net working capital should be recovered. Recovery of this working capital is also relevant for a capital budget.

8. Salvage: If plant or equipment purchased for the capital project can be sold at the end of the project, the salvage value of that plant and equipment should be counted as a cash inflow. Gain or loss on sale of salvage has tax consequences that must be netted against proceeds. Selling costs should also be considered in net cash flows as, for example, when real estate is sold through a broker.

9. Net cash flows: In some years, there will be cash outflows for plant, equipment, upgrades, restoration of land, and so forth at the same time that there are cash inflows from operations, salvage, or recovery of working capital. Cash inflows and cash outflows for any given year should be netted to a single number for the year.

10. Impact on other projects: Another factor to consider is whether sales from this new project are going to cannibalize existing sales or, on the other hand, enhance existing sales. It may be difficult to quantify the incremental cash flow impact on other projects, but such a potential impact should always be on a checklist of cash flow estimation issues. If it is determined that the proposed project will affect cash flow in other projects, the net affect of that cash flow should be recognized.

CAPITAL BUDGETING FORMAT

Virtually every capital project has three phases.

1. Investment: Investment outlays are expenditures needed to get the project up and running. This includes plant and equipment, as well as increases in net working capital for accounts receivable, inventory, and training payroll.

2. Operating cash flows: Operating cash flows are cash flows over the life of the project.

3. Terminal cash flows: Terminal cash flows include the salvage value of plant and equipment at the end of a project, as well as recovery of working capital.

Example

Parker Packaging estimates it can double sales if it purchases and installs a new box-making machine. The cost of the machine is $200,000, shipping and installation costs are $40,000. Accounts

---

FIGURE 11-1

Parker Packaging Cash Flow Estimates for New Box-Making Machine

Investment Outflows

1. Machine purchase and installation ($200,000 + $40,000)	$240,000
2. Increase in working capital ($200,000 − $100,000)	$100,000
Total initial investment	$340,000

Operating Cash Flows

1. Operating profits	$ 70,000
2. Depreciation ($240,000/6)	$ 40,000
Total operating cash flows	$110,000

Terminal Cash Flows

1. Salvage value of machine	$ 20,000
2. Recovery of working capital	$100,000
Total terminal cash flows	$120,000

Relevant cash flows are

Year 0	Outflow	$340,000
Year 1	Inflow	$110,000
Year 2	Inflow	$110,000
Year 3	Inflow	$110,000
Year 4	Inflow	$110,000
Year 5	Inflow	$110,000
Year 6	Inflow	$230,000

receivable and inventory combined will double from $100,000 to $200,000 as the result of increased sales. The machine has a life expectancy of six years and a salvage value of $20,000. After-tax profits attributable to the machine will be $70,000 per year. Year 6 inflows are the result of operating cash inflows of $110,000 plus the terminal cash flow of $120,000, for a total of $230,000. Figure 11–1 is an analysis of the relevant cash flows over the life of the project.

REPLACEMENT EQUIPMENT

Capital budgeting for replacement plant, property, and equipment is generally the same as for a new project. However, you must remember to take into account changes in net depreciation.

INFLATION AND PRICE PRESSURE

Inflation can affect the dollar value of revenue and cost projections in capital budgeting cash flow. Depreciation is usually not affected by inflation, but operating costs, especially wages and fringe benefits, almost always rise. On the other hand, revenue does not always rise. As products mature from novelties to commodities, there is an inevitable price squeeze. Not so very long ago, a personal computer cost half as much as a Ford Mustang, and a long distance call was $1.00 per minute. The affect of product maturity on costs and prices should be factored into cash flow estimates.

SPREADSHEET MODELING

To facilitate estimation of cash flow under a variety of circumstances, companies often develop a spreadsheet that explicitly recognizes revenue, cost of goods sold, overhead, and depreciation. As assumptions change throughout the capital budgeting process, annual cash flow estimates can be quickly updated. In addition, use of a spreadsheet template facilitates cash flow estimation for numerous projects. Figure 11–2 is a detailed analysis of cash flow estimation for Molecular Engineering's new plant. The following example is general enough to be adapted for most capital projects.

FIGURE 11-2

Detailed Analysis of Cash Flows for Molecular Switch Plant

MOLECULAR ENGINEERING CORPORATION
Cash Flows—Molecular Switch Plant

	Year 0	Year 1	Year 2	Year 3	Year 4
Investment outlays					
1. Building and land	2,000,000				
2. Equipment	3,000,000				
3. Increase in net working capital	400,000				
Total net investment	5,400,000				
Operating cash flows					
1. Switch revenues		4,000,000	5,000,000	6,000,000	6,000,000
2. Cost of goods sold 50% of sales		2,000,000	2,500,000	3,000,000	3,000,000
3. Selling costs 7.5% of sales		300,000	375,000	450,000	450,000
4. Fixed costs		800,000	800,000	800,000	800,000
5. Depreciation building		40,000	40,000	40,000	40,000
6. Depreciation equipment		750,000	750,000	750,000	750,000
7. Pretax operating income		110,000	535,000	960,000	960,000
8. Taxes @ 30%		33,000	160,500	288,000	288,000
9. After-tax income		77,000	374,500	672,000	672,000
10. Add back depreciation		790,000	790,000	790,000	790,000
11. Operating cash flows		867,000	1,164,500	1,462,000	1,462,000
Terminal year cash flows					
1. Salvage value of plant and equipment					1,900,000
2. Less book value of plant and equipment					1,840,000
3. Gain or loss on salvage					60,000
4. Taxes on gain or loss @ 30%					−18,000
5. Plus cash from salvage value sale					1,900,000
6. Salvage cash net of tax					1,882,000
7. Return of net working capital					400,000
8. Net terminal cash flows					2,282,000
	Outflow	Inflow	Inflow	Inflow	Inflow
Relevant cash flows	5,400,000	867,000	1,164,500	1,462,000	3,744,000

Example

Molecular Engineering Corporation is considering a fabrication plant for molecule-sized computer switches. Buildings and land will cost $2,000,000, and equipment will cost $3,000,000. The net increase in working capital needed to support the switch plant is about $400,000. These are the initial cash outflows.

Revenue from plant operations will increase over its four-year life as productivity increases. Revenue is estimated at $4,000,000 the first year, $5,000,000 the second year, and $6,000,000 the last two years. The cost of goods sold is 50% of revenue, and selling costs are about 7.5% of revenue. Fixed costs are $800,000 per year. Building and equipment depreciation are $40,000 and $750,000 per year, respectively. The tax rate is 30%. Operating cash flows net were based on this information.

At the end of the project, Molecular plans to liquidate its investment. They think they can sell the plant and equipment for $1,900,000, at which time it will have a book value of $1,840,000. Since they will have a gain on the sale of the property, a taxable event, they have to deduct taxes on the gain when computing the net cash inflow. They will also be able to recover about $400,000 of net working capital. Terminal cash flows will be based on the foregoing information. Figure 11–2 is a format that can be used to combine all the information on the proposed plant into one spreadsheet.

SUMMARY

Sound capital budgeting decisions depend as much on an estimation of a project's cash flow as they do on the method of ranking capital projects. Only the incremental cash used or generated by a project from the point in time the decision is being made is relevant. Sunk costs should never be considered. Cash flows are net of tax, which means that the tax effects of changes in depreciation and the gain or loss on salvage impact cash generated or used. The investment in working capital at the beginning of a project must be considered, as well as recovery of working capital when the project winds down. Other elements of cash flow that must be considered are installation and shipping costs; opportunity costs, that is, the fair market value of resources used in the project; and the impact of a particular project on the cash flow of other projects.

Almost every project has three phases: (1) investment outlays, (2) operating cash flows, and (3) terminal year cash flows. The net cash flow in any given year is the relevant cash flow for use in the capital budgeting process.

Product Costing

Product costing is important for a number of reasons. Unless product costs are under control, gross margins will be inadequate, which means not enough gross profit will be generated to cover overhead, financing costs, and profit.

Product cost is important in setting price and in finding competitive advantage. Product cost is especially important in mature or commodity products in which companies compete on price. Product cost is an important factor in estimating cash flow for capital budgeting and financing purposes. Product cost is also important in planning production volumes and performing break-even analysis. And it is important in make-versus-buy and outsourcing analysis.

In this chapter, we will discuss the two major approaches to product costing. Full absorption cost is used for cost of goods sold, and inventory valuation. The other approach used in managerial accounting focuses on incremental costs and is designed to analyze the economic impact.

COST VERSUS EXPENSE

A cost is a sacrifice of resources. Suppose an unused mailroom department truck is commandeered by the manufacturing department to haul raw materials for one of its capital projects. If the fair market value of that truck were $5,000, the sacrifice of that resource to production would be considered a cost.

An *expense* is an accounting concept that tries to match revenues with the costs that generated them.

Example

Survivalist Homes, Inc. purchases 200 tons of steel at $600 per ton to build homes. They use 100 tons this year to build and sell four homes. What is their cost for steel? What is the expense for steel?

The cost is $120,000 (200 tons of steel × $600 per ton). However, their steel expense is only $60,000 (100 tons of steel used × $600 per ton). The remaining 100 tons of steel is an asset called inventory.

FINANCIAL ACCOUNTING VERSUS MANAGERIAL ACCOUNTING

Financial accounting and managerial accounting are two different disciplines with different objectives. Although some concepts overlap, what is important are the differences. Financial accounting is about making a fair and accurate representation of what happened in the past. With the caveat that the past is not always a prologue, it does provide substantial clues to business performance.

Managerial accounting is primarily concerned with helping management make the best possible decisions about the future allocation of resources. It is informed by historical, financial reporting data, but is not constrained by it. If historical direct labor costs have been $20 per hour, and management knows its union negotiated a $2 per hour raise, it would be folly to base future plans on the historical information versus what is known about future pay rates.

Full Absorption Costing

The full absorption costing method is used to cost products for purposes of inventory valuation and cost of goods sold. The reason it is called full absorption costing is that it fully absorbs (or accounts for) all manufacturing overhead, whether fixed or variable. Equation 12–1 is used to compute full absorption cost.

Full absorption cost = Direct labor   (Eq. 12–1)
+ Direct material
+ Variable factory overhead
+ Fixed factory overhead

Variable Costing

Variable costing addresses only the incremental or marginal cost of the next unit of production. Variable costing is used in break-even analysis and sometimes in capital budgeting cash flow estimation where manufacturing overhead is a sunk cost. Variable costing is also used in economics to determine the maximum number of units that should be produced. When incremental cost exceeds incremental revenue, no more of a good should be produced. Variable costing is used in managerial accounting. Equation 12–2 gives the components of variable cost.

Variable cost = Direct labor   (Eq. 12–2)
+ Direct material
+ Variable factory overhead
+ Variable sales cost
+ Variable administrative overhead

Example

Lomax Corporation produces leather briefcases. Direct labor is $3.00 per briefcase, direct materials are $4.00, variable manufacturing overhead is $1.00. Fixed manufacturing overhead is $25,200 per year. Lomax expects to produce 8,400 briefcases per year, giving a fixed manufacturing overhead allocation of $3.00 per briefcase. Marty Ong, the company's only salesperson, gets $2.00 for every briefcase he sells. Figure 12–1 is an analysis of full absorption costing versus variable costing.

We stipulated that Lomax expects to make 8,400 briefcases per year. Without an estimated production volume, fixed manufacturing overhead cannot be calculated because there is no basis for allocating factory overhead to units of production. Suppose production volume were estimated at only 3,600 briefcases. Fixed factory overhead would rise to $7 per briefcase ($25,200/3,600), bringing

Analysis of Full Absorption Costing Versus Variable Costing

TWO VIEWS OF PRODUCT COSTING

Cost Component	Full Absorption Cost Financial Reporting	Variable Cost Managerial Accounting
Direct labor	$ 3.00	$ 3.00
Direct materials	$ 4.00	$ 4.00
Variable manufacturing overhead	$ 1.00	$ 1.00
Fixed manufacturing overhead ($25,200/8,400 units)	$ 3.00	
Variable administrative cost (sales commission $2)		$ 2.00
Financial reporting cost (inventory and COGS)	$11.00	
Variable cost		$10.00

the full absorption cost of one briefcase to $15 ($3 + $4 + $1 + $7). Since production can vary from month to month, fixed manufacturing costs are usually allocated over a year's worth of production.

Recall that for many companies, cost of goods sold can be calculated using Eq. 12–3.

Cost of goods sold = Beginning inventory   (Eq. 12–3)
          + Purchases − Ending inventory

Since we know that full absorption cost as defined in Eq. 12–1 is used to compute the value of inventory as well as the cost of goods sold, we can use it to expand Eq. 12–3 into Eq. 12–4.

Cost of goods sold = Beginning inventory   (Eq. 12–4)
          + Purchases [direct labor
          + direct material
          + variable factory overhead
          + fixed factory overhead]
          − Ending inventory

Example

Lomax's beginning inventory was 200 briefcases at a (full absorption) cost of $11 each. It is estimated the factory will make 8,400 briefcases during the year, and annual, fixed factory overhead is $25,200. About $25,200 of raw materials, $33,600 of direct labor, and $8,400 of factory supplies were purchased. Ending inventory was 300 briefcases. What is the full absorption cost if exactly 8,400 briefcases were manufactured?

Full absorption cost = $3 direct materials ($25,200/8,400)
            + $4 direct labor ($33,600/8,400)
                + $1 variable manufacturing overhead
                ($8,400/8,400)
                + $3 fixed factory overhead
                ($25,200/8,400)
        = $11

There was no unabsorbed factory overhead in this example based on the estimated number of units, 8,400, and a fixed manufacturing cost burden of $3 per briefcase. Therefore, there is no unallocated overhead to book.

What was the cost of goods sold?

Cost of goods sold = $2,200 beginning inventory (200 × $11)
            + $92,400 purchases [$25,200 raw materials
            + $33,600 direct labor
                + $8,400 variable manufacturing
                + $25,200 of *allocated* fixed
                    manufacturing overhead]
                − $3,300 ending inventory
                (300 briefcases × $11)
        = $2,200 + $92,400 − $3,300 = $91,300

UNALLOCATED MANUFACTURING OVERHEAD

Over the course of a year, plans, sales, and production are likely to change. What if production overshoots, or undershoots, estimates? If production undershoots targets, that means that services, in the form of manufacturing overhead provided to the factory floor, are not being fully utilized. Underutilization is considered wastage, and rather than charging those unallocated costs to the product, or to the cost of goods sold, unallocated costs should be reclassified into an overhead account like expense for unallocated manufacturing overhead.

If production overshoots goals, then factory overhead should be allocated first to items remaining in inventory at year-end, then to the cost of goods sold. More than 100% of factory overhead cannot be allocated.

Example

Suppose Lomax purchased a year's worth of raw materials, but only ran the plant nine months per year because of slow sales. Arguably, rather than making 8,400 briefcases per year, they would make only 6,300 (9 months/12 months per year × 8,400).

As we have seen, the full absorption cost at 8,400 briefcases per year is $11 per briefcase. The full absorption cost does not change. But what happens to the unused direct materials and the unallocated fixed manufacturing overhead?

If $25,200 of raw material is purchased (enough for 8,400 briefcases) and only $18,900 is used to actually make briefcases (6,300 × $3), then the balance, $6,300 ($25,200 − $18,900) becomes raw materials inventory. Since it is inventory, the unused material represents an asset, not an expense. However, the same cannot be said for fixed manufacturing overhead.

Of the total fixed manufacturing overhead of $25,200, only $18,900 (6,300 brief cases × [$25,200/8,400]) was applied to products. This leaves unallocated fixed manufacturing overhead of $6,300, which should be written off to expense for unallocated fixed manufacturing overhead. Why not just allocate it to briefcases? There are two reasons: (1) the amount of manufacturing overhead supplied, but not used, is waste, and applying waste to a product cost inappropriately inflates the value of inventory, and (2) waste should be brought to the attention of management by segregating it into a separate account.

What is the impact of unallocated factory overhead on the cost of goods sold? Nothing. It is still $11 per briefcase, as we can see from the following example that assumes all finished goods are sold.

Cost of goods sold = $2,200 beginning inventory (200 units × $11)
                  + $25,200 purchases ($25,200 raw material)
                  + $25,200 direct labor (9 months/
                    12 months × $33,600)
                  + $6,300 variable manufacturing
                    overhead,
                  + $18,900 allocated factory overhead
                    ($25,200 × 6,300 units/
                    8,400 units planned)
                  − $6,300 ending inventory
                    (raw material)
                = $2,200 + 75,600 − $6,300 = $71,500

In the prior example, the cost of goods sold was $91,300 for 8,300 brief cases, or $11 each. In this example, because of the factory shut down, only 6,300 briefcases were made. The cost of goods sold is $71,500, and the cost per briefcase is still $11 each ($71,500/[200 briefcases in beginning inventory and 6,300 briefcases manufactured]).

Exceeding Production Targets

Suppose Lomax exceeds production goals by 600 briefcases on the year making a total of 9,000 without increasing its plant capacity or fixed manufacturing overhead. What is the full absorption cost of its briefcases?

Full absorption cost = $3 direct materials
                     + $4 direct labor
                     + $1 variable manufacturing overhead
                     + $3 fixed manufacturing overhead
                       ($25,200/8,400 intended
                       production run)
                   = $11

The full absorption cost remains the same, but all fixed manufacturing overhead will be fully absorbed by the first 8,400 production units. That means 600 units have no fixed manufacturing overhead. So, arguably, we have 8,400 units at $11 each, and 600 units at $8 each. But which are which? Are the low-cost units always produced at year-end?

To get a sensible answer, recall that full absorption costing is used to value inventory and measure the cost of goods sold for financial reporting and tax purposes. The consistency that full absorption costing provides under a number of circumstances helps assure the outside readers of financial reports that statements will be comparable from company to company and period to period. Thus it contributes toward meeting the goals of generally accepted accounting principles.

Some accountants may disagree, but a good argument can be made for the proposition that any units remaining in inventory at year-end are the $11 units. This avoids understating inventory. The effect of manufacturing 600 units at $8 is to lower the cost of goods sold. Analytically, then, how is this efficiency in the manufacturing process translated into a reduced cost of goods sold? Consider the following example:

Cost of goods sold = $2,200 beginning inventory (200 × $11)
+ $97,200 purchases [$27,000 (9,000 units × $3) direct materials
+ $36,000 (9,000 units × $4) direct labor
+ $9,000 (9,000 units × $1) variable manufacturing
+ $25,200 of *allocated* fixed manufacturing overhead]
− $3,300 ending inventory (300 briefcases × $11)
= $2,200 + $97,200 − $3,300 = $96,100

Under the conditions in this hypothetical, the average cost of goods sold declined to $10.80 per unit ($96,100 cost of goods sold/8,900 units sold) from $11.00.

The number of unsold units was computed using Eq. 12–4, a modified version of the equation used to compute cost of goods sold.

Number sold = Number in beginning inventory
+ Number of units produced
− Number in ending inventory
= 200 + 9,000 − 300 = 8,900

EXPENSES VERSUS INVENTORY

Notice that something extraordinary is going on here. We usually think of payroll, rent, depreciation, lubricants, and raw materials as expenses. However, GAAP accounting allows a magic transformation of expenses into a store of value called inventory. Suppose $10,000 of cash is spent on the payroll, something we usually think of as an expense. If $5,000 of that is direct manufacturing labor, then that labor can be reclassified, and becomes part of a product's cost. If the product is not sold, the value of that labor becomes inventory. So even though we have paid $5,000 in payroll, it remains a company asset. Likewise, cash paid for raw materials becomes raw material inventory, and then is transformed via the manufacturing process into finished goods inventory. When inventory is sold, the costs that went into the inventory are recognized as a cost of goods sold expense.

FULL ABSORPTION COST OF PURCHASED MERCHANDISE

What is the full absorption cost of merchandise purchased for resale? The cost of purchased merchandise includes its purchase price, plus shipping in, import taxes, and costs for finishing, repackaging, or labeling and stocking. Equation 12–5 shows the most common elements of full absorption cost for purchased merchandise, but any other costs necessary to make goods "ready for sale" should also be included.

Full absorption cost = Purchase price (Eq. 12–5)
+ Shipping in
+ Import taxes
+ Costs for assembly or finishing
+ Repackaging costs
+ Labeling costs
+ Stocking costs

Example
Berlin Mart is going to sell teak bookcases made in Chile. The bookcases cost $60 each. Import duties are $6, and inward shipping costs

are $12 each. The bookcases come broken down on pallets. Berlin Mart assembles the bookcases prior to sale. Labor for assembly is $10 per bookcase. There is no manufacturing overhead. What is the "full absorption cost" of these bookcases?

Full absorption cost = $60 merchandise cost
+ $6 import duties
+ $12 inward shipping cost
+ $10 preparation cost

What does "full absorption cost" mean when there is no manufacturing overhead to absorb? Return to the purpose of full absorption cost. It is the cost used for valuing inventory and measuring the cost of goods sold. In many companies, items manufactured for sale sit side by side with items purchased for resale. Full absorption costing allows comparable treatment of both types of items.

MAKE OR BUY DECISIONS

Good product costing is critical to informed make or buy decisions. Many businesses elect to purchase goods for resale rather than manufacturing them themselves. The correct comparison is between the full absorption cost of manufacturing goods in house versus the full absorption cost of purchased goods. Buy decisions that look correct on the surface can be costly if purchased goods must be extensively "prepared" for sale. Such preparation is simply the vendor's way of shifting the burden back to the buyer.

The question often arises whether variable costs are the correct basis of comparison because fixed manufacturing costs will be fixed even if manufacture of goods is outsourced. The answer is that fixed manufacturing costs are fixed only over the short term. In the long term, fixed costs can be reduced or eliminated.

Another approach companies are using to reduce cost is to purchase subassemblies that have internal components preassembled and tested. An example would be if an auto manufacturer purchased an engine with all its wiring, antipollution controls, and fuel assemblies, and all they had to do was bolt the engine to a chassis. Whether to make the engine from parts or purchase a preassembled engine turns on the full absorption cost of each alternative.

Real-world costs that are often buried in direct labor, direct material, variable factory overhead, and fixed factory overhead are the costs of errors, rework, and inferior quality materials. Whether making or buying products, these costs must be explicitly recognized and accounted for.

MANAGERIAL ACCOUNTING

Managerial accounting is just a fancy name for cost accounting. The objective of managerial accounting it to provide management with information they can use to make better decisions.

Contrast this with generally accepted accounting principles (GAAP), which is a set of financial reporting rules designed to inform bankers, regulators, investors, and other external, interested parties about the performance of a company. GAAP exists to make financial reports comparable from company to company, and from period to period for the same company. Because comparability is one of the primary reasons for GAAP accounting, its rules must cover a broad range of circumstances. Full absorption costing uses GAAP rules to value inventory and the cost of goods sold (COGS).

Managerial accounting is much more flexible. Though there are some rules, these rules are tailored to help managers make decisions.

Another major difference is that financial reporting is concerned with what happened in the past. Managerial accounting is concerned with the future. The past may inform managerial accounting, but it need not control it. For example, if labor cost per unit of production has been $100, and management knows a new union contract is going to increase labor cost by 4%, they would use $104 as the labor cost in data analysis.

Full absorption costing includes direct labor, direct material, variable factory overhead, and fixed factory overhead. It does not include administrative costs such as accounting, marketing, executive, or payroll services.

Managerial accounting, on the other hand, is concerned with all the incremental costs of producing an incremental unit whether or not those costs spring from the factory floor. Incremental is just another way of saying variable cost per unit. Variable costs include direct material, direct labor, and variable manufacturing overhead, the same as in full absorption costing. However, variable costs *exclude* fixed manufacturing overhead, which is charged to the company whether or not one more unit is produced. Managerial accounting may also take into account variable administrative costs associated with producing one more unit, whereas financial accounting would not.

Economists tell us that as long as marginal revenue exceeds marginal cost, the next unit of production should be built. Marginal revenue is unit price, but what is marginal cost? Marginal cost is also another way of saying variable cost per unit.

Consider the following hypothetical. It is Christmas Eve, and your salesperson Marty Ong hands you an order for 50 briefcases at $10.75 each. Do you accept the order? Look again at the Lomax data in Figure 12–1.

The relevant question is whether incremental revenue exceeds incremental cost. We know incremental revenue is $10.75. Your accountant might tell you not to accept the order because you are selling below your full absorption cost of $11.00. But suppose you have already fully absorbed your manufacturing overhead? Your cost of goods sold on this order is only going to be $8 anyway ($3 direct labor + $4 direct materials + $1 variable manufacturing overhead).

Even if you have not full absorbed your overhead, the appropriate incremental cost is *not* the full absorption cost. It is the variable cost. Here the variable cost is $10 ($3 direct labor + $4 direct materials + $1 variable manufacturing overhead + $2 variable administrative cost, that is, sales commission). Since the incremental (variable) revenue $10.75 exceeds the incremental (variable) cost, the order should be accepted from a purely economic point of view.

The impact from an accounting point of view is that these briefcases are sold at a loss of $0.25 each. What about the marketing perspective? From Marty's point of view, he wants to make the sale and get the commission, but Marty's view is not the company's view. The company must ask questions like am I setting price expectations too low for this customer? Will they want a $10.75 deal on all future sales? In this example, the accounting loss is easy to rectify by asking Marty whether he is willing to accept a $1.75 commission on the deal. If he is, the transaction is a wash from an accounting point of view, and the sale makes a contribution toward overhead.

Over the long run, accepting a price below the full absorption cost can be ruinous. On the other hand, fixed manufacturing costs are fixed only in the short run. If the only way to sell goods is below full absorption cost, that is a strong signal that a company's cost structure is too high.

GROSS PROFIT VERSUS CONTRIBUTION

Gross profit and contribution are designed to answer different questions. Gross profit deals with the question of financial statement profitability. It is how much revenue is left over after the cost of goods are subtracted. Gross profit is given by Eq. 12–6.

$$\text{Gross profit} = \text{Revenue} - \text{Cost of goods sold} \quad \text{(Eq. 12–6)}$$

This equation can be rewritten to find the gross profit on each unit sold by substituting price for revenue and unit full absorption cost per unit for cost of goods sold, as shown in Eq. 12–7.

$$\text{Gross profit per unit} = \text{Price} - \text{Full absorption cost per unit}$$
$$\text{(Eq. 12–7)}$$

Contribution deals with how much each additional unit contributes toward covering fixed costs and profits after variable costs are covered. Equation 12–8 gives the formula for contribution.

$$\text{Contribution} = \text{Price} - \text{Variable costs} \quad \text{(Eq. 12–8)}$$

Contribution margin is the percent of each dollar of sales that contributes to covering fixed costs and goes toward profits after variable costs are covered. The equation for contribution margin is given by Eq. 12–9.

$$\text{Contribution margin} = \text{Contribution}/\text{Price} \quad \text{(Eq. 12–9)}$$

Both gross margin and contribution margin are useful concepts, but they are useful only in answering the right questions.

FIGURE 12-2

Analysis of Lomax's Gross Margin and Contribution Margin

Full Absorption Cost		Managerial Accounting	
Price	$20	Price	$20
Full absorption cost	$11	Variable cost	$10
Gross profit	$ 9	Contribution	$10

Gross margin = $9/$20 = 45%
Contribution margin = $10/$20 = 50%

Example

Lomax sells briefcases for $20 each. Its full absorption cost is $11 per unit. Its variable cost is $10 per unit. What is the gross profit on a per unit basis? What is the contribution margin on a per unit basis? Figure 12–2 is an analysis of Lomax's gross margin versus contribution margin.

Effect of Overproducing on Gross Profit, Contribution Margin, and Cost of Goods Sold

In computing the gross profit on a per unit basis, fixed manufacturing overhead is applied based on expected production levels. The effects of lower (or higher) cost beginning inventory, and the effects of producing more than anticipated, thus "running out of" fixed manufacturing overhead, are automatically adjusted for in the cost of goods sold.

Gross profit on a per unit basis considers only price less the full absorption cost. However, the average cost of goods sold may be more or less than the gross profit on a per unit basis because beginning inventory may have a cost that is higher or lower than the current full absorption cost.

Contribution margin, on the other hand, is unaffected by the cost of beginning inventory, or by underproducing (and underapplying fixed manufacturing overhead) or overproducing (running out of fixed manufacturing overhead). Contribution margin is concerned only with incremental revenue and expenditures.

SUMMARY

Product costing is important for computing cost of goods sold and valuing inventory. It also informs pricing decisions and provides a starting point for analyzing the efficiency of the production process. Costs are not the same as expenses. A cost is a sacrifice of resources, whereas an expense is an accounting concept designed to help match revenue with the costs that generated that revenue.

Financial reporting in conformance with generally accepted accounting principles is based on historical performance and is designed to make financial statements comparable from company to company and year to year.

Managerial accounting is a different discipline with different rules. The objective of managerial accounting is to help management make decisions about current and future transactions. It is not bound by historical information although it may be informed by it. Managerial accounting is concerned with issues like the incremental (variable) cost of a product. This information is useful in many applications such as break-even analysis, opportunistic pricing, and economic analysis of production levels.

Full absorption cost for a manufacturing operation includes direct labor, direct material, variable factory overhead, and fixed factory overhead. Full absorption cost for a business that purchases goods for resale includes the purchase price, transportation in, import duties, and any other costs necessary to make goods ready for sale.

Full absorption cost has no meaning without production targets to allocate fixed manufacturing overhead to units of production. Underproduction results in unallocated overhead that is booked as a manufacturing overhead expense rather than being charged to the cost of inventory. Overproduction lowers the cost of goods sold.

Variable cost includes direct labor, direct material, variable factory overhead, variable selling expense such as commissions, and variable overhead such as shipping costs.

Gross margin is a percentage computed by dividing gross profit (revenue less cost of goods sold) by revenue. Gross margin can be computed on a per unit basis using price for revenue and full absorption cost for cost of goods sold.

Contribution margin is a percentage computed by dividing contribution (price less variable costs) by price. Contribution margin represents the percentage of each dollar of revenue that contributes to covering fixed costs and profits.

Since financial reporting and managerial accounting have different objectives, it is necessary to understand when to apply financial reporting principles and when to apply managerial accounting principles. Different tools are necessary for different tasks.

CHAPTER 13

Break-Even Analysis and Modeling

Business models are an important planning tool because (1) they help focus the attention of management on key profit drivers, (2) they can help identify obstacles and thereby help refine strategies, (3) they facilitate testing alternative strategies before resources are committed, and (4) they can be used to test the reasonableness of goals. Break-even analysis is a powerful tool for business modeling. It embraces information on price, cost, operating expenses, and profit goals in a way that helps management think through strategy and related operating plans.

In this chapter, we will start with a simple break-even analysis, and step by step, push the boundaries of this technique to show how it can be used to model a wide variety of circumstances.

BREAK-EVEN ANALYSIS

Break-even analysis is concerned with the amount of activity, sales volume, or number of units of production it takes to make a zero profit. Zero profit is not the ultimate goal. However, it provides a starting point for building a robust set of models.

Equation 13–1 parallels a profit and loss statement with revenue less different classes of costs to get profit.

$$\text{Revenue} - \text{Variable costs} - \text{Fixed costs} = \text{Profit} \quad \text{(Eq. 13–1)}$$

We can rewrite equation Eq. 13–1 as Eq. 13–2, which expresses revenue and some expenses in terms of unit revenue and unit costs. This equation can be further transformed into an equation for break-even analysis. We can obtain revenue by multiplying price (P) times number of units sold, and we can obtain variable costs by multiplying variable cost per unit (VC) times number of units.

$$\text{Price} \times \text{Units} - \text{VC} \times \text{Units} - \text{Fixed costs} = \text{Profits} \quad \text{(Eq. 13–2)}$$

Factoring units out of revenue and variable cost and re-grouping terms yields Eq. 13–3. Price less variable costs in the first term of the equation is the contribution margin discussed in Chapter 12.

$$(P - VC) \times \text{Units} - \text{Fixed costs} = \text{Profits} \quad \text{(Eq. 13–3)}$$

Since, by definition, profits equals zero when the break-even number of units is made and sold, we can rewrite Eq. 13–3 to get Eq. 13–4, the equation for break-even.

$$(P - VC) \times \text{Units} = \text{Fixed costs} \quad \text{(Eq. 13–4)}$$

Consider this simple example. Loren plans to rent a cart in a mall for $800 per month to sell home-baked cookies. Her cookies sell for $5.00 per pound. Her ingredients, packaging, and labeling cost her $2.00 per pound. How many pounds of cookies will she have to sell per month just to break even? Stated another way, how many pounds of cookies will she have to sell before she begins to make a profit? Plugging Loren's data into Eq. 13–3 and setting profits equal to zero, we get the following:

$$\$5/\text{lb} \times \text{pounds} - \$2/\text{lb} \times \text{pounds} - \$800 = 0 \text{ (break-even profit)}$$
$$(\$5/\text{lb} - \$2/\text{lb}) \times \text{pounds} = \$800$$
$$\text{pounds} = \frac{\$800}{(\$5/\text{lb} - \$2/\text{lb})}$$
$$= \$800/\$3/\text{lb} = 267 \text{ lb}$$

What are the implications of this computation for the small, or even large, business owner? For one, this gives Loren a good estimate of the amount of product she must sell at a minimum. Suppose she decides she wants to keep her cart open only during peak hours: 11:00 a.m. to 2:00 p.m. weekdays, and 11:00 a.m. to 7:00 p.m.

Saturday and Sunday. This is about 31 hours per week. Assuming four weeks per month, she will be open 124 hours per month, and must sell about 2.2 pounds of cookies per hour (267 lb/124 hours per month). That may not be an unreasonable goal.

Suppose, on the other hand, Loren plans to pay herself some minimal rate per hour. Can break-even analysis be used to compute sales volume under those circumstances? Of course, but with some minor modifications. Assume she wants to be paid $10 per hour for the time she is at her cart. Then her "fixed costs" will increase by $1,240 (124 hours per month × $10 per hour). Recomputing the break-even point using Eq. 13–2 we get:

$5/lb × pounds − $2/lb × pounds
$$− (\$800 + \$1,240) = 0$$
$$(\$5 − \$2) × pounds = \$2,040$$
$$\$2,040/\$3 = 680 \text{ lb of cookies}$$
$$\text{per month}$$

Thinking about the economic model of her "company," she now has to sell about 5.5 pounds of cookies per hour to break even (680 lb/124 hours per month).

While thinking about how she is going to bake 680 pounds of cookies per month, she realizes she has not allocated value to the time she spends baking. She estimates she can bake about 20 pounds per hour with her home oven. This implies she will have to spend 34 hours per month baking (680 lb/20 lb per hour). At $10 per hour, she will have to add $340 into her cost model, but where?

Since baking is directly proportional to sales, she decides it is a variable cost. She therefore assigns an additional $0.50 per pound (labor rate $10 per hour/20 lb per hour) to her variable costs. Again using Eq. 13–2, the break-even model then becomes

$5/lb × pounds − $2.50/lb × pounds
$$− (\$800 + \$1,240) = 0$$
$$(\$5 − \$2.50) × pounds = \$2,040$$
$$\$2,040/\$2.50 = 816 \text{ pounds of cookies}$$

Loren must now ask herself a number of questions based on this break-even analysis. Will she be able to sell 6.6 pounds of cookies per hour (816 lb/124 hours per month) on a consistent basis?

Does she want to work an estimated 158 hours per month? This is virtually a full-time job. Was her objective just to work part time? Or was it to build a business? Is there any upside potential on this business? That is, if she is working 158 hours per month, will she be able to grow her income beyond $10 per hour? These are all questions that entrepreneurs have to ask themselves.

As with any good entrepreneur, Loren wants to work *on* her business not *in* her business. She contracts with Ralph, a home-maker who will bake and package cookies to her specifications for $2.25 per pound. Selling from her cart at the mall requires mini-mal skills, only someone to reliably and honestly make change. She hires someone to manage the cart for her at $8 per hour, including employer payroll taxes. How does this change Loren's break-even model? By substituting the labor of a specialist (the homemaker baker) for her own labor, she increases productivity, which reduces her variable costs. By substituting less skilled labor for her semi-skilled labor on the cart, she reduces "store" overhead. These changes will reduce her break-even point as follows:

$$(\$5/lb - \$2.25/lb) \times \text{pounds} - (\$800 + \$8/hr$$
$$\times\ 124\ \text{hours}) = 0$$
$$\$2.75 \times \text{pounds} - \$1{,}792 = 0$$
$$\text{pounds} = \frac{\$1{,}792}{\$2.75} = 652\ \text{pounds}$$

In deciding whether her business is feasible, Loren must as-sess how likely it is to sell 652 pounds of cookies (more than a quar-ter of a ton) each month. Loren sees that she has to average only 5.3 pounds of cookies per hour (652 lb/124 hours per month) and decides her goal is still reasonable.

MODELING PROFIT

Break-even analysis can be used to model profit by thinking of the target profit as another fixed cost to be covered by the contribu-tion margin from sales. Modifying Eq. 13–4 to include profits we get Eq. 13–5.

$$(P - VC) \times \text{Units} = \text{Fixed costs} + \text{Profits} \quad \text{(Eq. 13–5)}$$

Example

As an entrepreneur, Loren doesn't just want to break even. She wants to make $1,000 per month profit. Given P is $5, VC is $2.25, FC is $800 for the cart and $992 for a sales clerk, she writes her new "break-even" formula as follows:

$$(\$5.00 - \$2.25) \times \text{pounds} = (\$800 + \$992) + \$1,000$$
$$\$2.75 \times \text{pounds} = \$2,792$$
$$\text{pounds} = 1,015$$

As an entrepreneur, Loren is now in a better situation to assess her business. Is it practical to sell half a ton of cookies each month? If it is not feasible to sell 1,015 pounds of cookies per month or 8.2 pounds per hour, what are her strategic options?

She could extend hours, but then she would have to compare marginal revenue to marginal cost. If marginal revenue were greater than marginal cost, extended "store" hours would be useful from an economic point of view. Marginal revenue is $5 per pound × the number of pounds of cookies sold at "off peak" hours. Marginal cost is the variable cost of the product sold plus additional sales staff overhead of $8 per hour.

She could test the market to see whether she could raise the price of her cookies. But since higher prices tend to reduce sales volume, she would have to determine the net effect of such actions. (These issues are discussed in more detail in Chapter 16.) She could also look for a homemaker who will bake cookies for less than the $2.25 per pound that Ralph charges. On the other hand, she might consider outsourcing her cookies to a bakery.

The break-even analysis principles applied to Loren's cookies can be generalized to almost all service and manufacturing businesses. The importance of these models is to help management think through the effects of each of their decisions on pricing, variable costs, overhead, and profit targets.

Unfortunately, many businesspeople think profit is something left over after the bills are paid. Buy low, sell high, and pray for profits. That kind of thinking cedes far too much control to customers, suppliers, employees, and random chance. Reasonable profit targets should be set based on the goals of the company, industry performance, and other strategic factors. Once profit targets are set, break-even analysis and other planning techniques like pricing theory should be considered to see how goals can be reached or, on the other hand, to prove goals are unrealistic under the circumstances. Either way, the decision on how to proceed should be one made by management after deliberate consideration and analysis, and not left to chance.

SALES VOLUME BREAK-EVEN

For many businesses, number of units has no meaning when planning and budgeting. Examples include grocery stores, department stores, law firms, and manufacturers who make a wide variety of products or a variety of sizes of one product. For these businesses, a break-even analysis based on sales dollars is more meaningful.

An equation that facilitates break-even analysis based on sales volume can be derived from Eq. 13–1 by making several modifications. First, we leave revenue in dollars and don't try to break it down into the price for individual products. Second, let operating expenses, also called overhead, substitute for fixed costs. Finally, we use cost of goods sold as a surrogate for variable costs.

As we saw, the difference between cost of goods sold and variable costs is that cost of goods sold is burdened by fixed manufacturing overhead, and variable costs are not, whereas variable costs are burdened by things like variable selling and administrative costs, and cost of goods sold is not. On the other hand, we know that fixed manufacturing costs are fixed only over the short run. Over the long run, all costs are variable. Using cost of goods sold as an estimator of variable costs has proven useful for this class of problem. It helps management address many of the same issues that were addressed by Loren as she thought through her business model.

Sales and revenue are the same thing in this type of analysis. The only difference is that revenue is a GAAP term that has a technical meaning that is most relevant to the issue of when revenue is recognized. Rewriting Eq. 13–1 using sales in place of revenue, cost of goods sold (COGS) in place of variable costs, and overhead in place of fixed costs, we get Eq. 13–6.

$$\text{Sales} - \text{COGS} - \text{Overhead} = \text{Profits} \qquad \text{(Eq. 13–6)}$$

We know that sales less COGS is gross profit. Gross margin is gross profit divided by sales. We can also write COGS as sales less gross margin times sales, as shown in Eq. 13–7.

$$COGS = Sales - Sales \times Gross\ margin \qquad (Eq.\ 13–7)$$

Why do we want to do that? The reason is that the fewer the variables we can express a relationship in, the easier it is to solve a problem. Factoring sales out of the equation, we get Eq. 13–8.

$$COGS = Sales \times (1 - Gross\ margin) \qquad (Eq.\ 13–8)$$

Substituting Eq. 13–8 into Eq. 13–6, we get Eq. 13–9.

$$Sales - Sales \times (1 - Gross\ margin) - Overhead = Profits$$
$$(Eq.\ 13–9)$$

Example

Executive Furniture, founded in 1950, makes a variety of furniture from end tables to highboys, ranging in price from $200 to $2,000 wholesale. They have had only one manufacturing plant located in Asheville, North Carolina. They are considering building a new manufacturing facility in Salem County, New Jersey, to be closer to the Boston–Washington population corridor. The gross margin on sales is 30%. Overhead, including debt service, will be $7 million. What sales volume will provide break-even?

$$Sales - Sales \times (1 - 30\%) - \$7\ million = 0$$
$$Sales - 0.7 \times Sales - \$7\ million = 0$$
$$Sales \times 0.3 = \$7\ million$$
$$Sales = \$7\ million/0.3 = \$23.33\ million$$

Suppose the ROA (return on assets) threshold set by the board of directors requires that the plant's operating profit be $3 million per year. Using break-even analysis, can we estimate the needed sales volume? Of course. The minimum profit demanded by the board can be considered, in a sense, a "fixed cost," another element of the overhead on the project as shown in Eq. 13–10.

$$Sales - COGS - Overhead - Profits = 0 \qquad (Eq.\ 13–10)$$

$$Sales - Sales \times (1 - 30\%) - \$7\ million - \$3\ million = 0$$

$$\text{Sales} - 0.7 \text{ Sales} - \$7 \text{ million} - \$3 \text{ million} = 0$$
$$\text{Sales} \times 0.3 = \$10 \text{ million}$$
$$\text{Sales} = \$10 \text{ million}/0.3 = \$33.33 \text{ million}$$

RELEVANT RANGE

Break-even analysis works only within some relevant range. The relevant range is often dictated by current production capacity. When production capacity needs to be increased, the break-even point changes because fixed costs change. When planning and forecasting, a company may have several alternative growth paths, each with its own break-even point. As we have seen in the foregoing examples, Loren set her goals and then manipulated the variables in the break-even equation to meet them. Large companies should do the same.

REALITY TESTING

One of the most important things an entrepreneur or company can do with break-even analysis is reality testing. If a goal is not in the "reality space" of a company, no matter how much management demands, goal will not be achieved and the exercise may be a waste of time, effort, company moral, and resources. Sometimes, limits are physical. Suppose Loren had an expense structure, and articulated profit goals that required her to sell ten tons of cookies per month to break even at one cart. The physical limits of the cart just wouldn't stand up to that much wear even if she could get the necessary sales. Other limits might include the number of hours per week Loren could work, the number of potential customers visiting the mall, and so forth.

If goals can't be reached after reasonable limits are reached in a business model, it is often necessary to step back and adjust other parameters such as price, cost, the number of hours the "store" is open, and so forth. If goals still can't be met after all reasonable adjustments have been made, then the goals themselves must be questioned. If, for example, Loren needed to make $25,000 per month before it was feasible for her to give up her job as an orthopedic surgeon, and break-even analysis determined that goal couldn't be reached, then perhaps the enterprise isn't for her. This same type of analysis applies to a company trying to decide whether to introduce a new product, open a new plant, or go into another line of business.

BREAK-EVEN AND RISK

We have seen how break-even analysis can be used to model sales, costs, and profit. But suppose there is some degree of uncertainty in the sales forecast. Can we use break-even analysis to account for that risk?

In the real world, there is always some level of risk of unforeseen costs, lost customers, and failure to meet sales projections. Boards of major corporations, as well as entrepreneurs (and their bankers), want to know what steps are being taken to hedge against that risk.

As target profits can be added to fixed costs to model break-even, a risk factor can be added to fixed costs to find a target profit *plus some margin for uncertainty*. Equation 13–11 gives the formula for managing risk.

$$\text{Revenue} - \text{Variable cost} - \text{Fixed costs} \quad \text{(Eq. 13–11)}$$
$$- \text{Target profits} - \text{Uncertainty} = 0$$

How do we quantify uncertainty? One way, of course, is simply to use management judgment to pick an amount. For example, management may say they want a 10% hedge against uncertainty. In that case, uncertainty is just target profits times management's hedge percent. A more quantitative approach might be to compute the standard deviation of profits, described in detail in previous chapters, and apply that to target profits.

Example

Grippen Foods has one product, a home-style soup sold in jars. Their wholesale price is $1.00, variable costs are $0.75, fixed costs for the soup plant are $300,000, target profits are $1,000,000, and one standard deviation on profits has been calculated at $150,000. The Grippen board wants to know what the target sales should be so they can be 95% confident of making at least $1,000,000 profit.

As we saw in Chapter 4, absent other information, we can assume most data are normally distributed. Normal distribution can

FIGURE   13-1

Analysis of Grippen Profit Targets to Be 95% Confident of Making at Least $1 Million of Profit

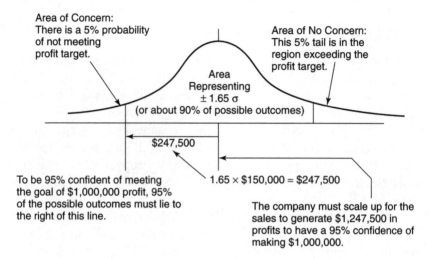

be assumed only when there are a large number of data points in play. In this case, Grippen based its analysis on the soup consumption of the average consumer. Since there are a very large number of people in this class, it would be safe to assume a normal distribution. The probability of any particular even occurring from the set of all possible outcomes can be represented by an area under a normal distribution curve as shown in Figure 13–1.

To be 95% confident of making at least $1 million in profits, Grippen must draft a plan that would cause 95% of probable profit outcomes to be to the right of (greater than) the $1 million mark. Stated differently, they need to set a sales goal high enough so that when variability of their data is taken into account, there is still a 95% probability of meeting their profit goal. Given a standard deviation of $150,000, 95% of the area under normal distribution probability curve will lie to the right of $1 million if the target is $1,000,000 + 1.65 standard deviations.

$$\text{Target profit} = \$1,000,000 + 1.65 \times \text{Standard deviation}$$
$$= \$1,000,000 + 1.65 \times \$150,000$$
$$= \$1,247,500$$

Using $1,247,500 as the new profit target gives

$$\$1.00 \times \text{Units} - \$0.75 \times \text{Units} - \$300,000$$
$$- \$1,247,500 = 0$$
$$\text{Units} \times (\$1.00 - \$0.75) = \$300,000 + \$1,247,500$$
$$\text{Units} \times \$0.25 = \$1,547,500$$
$$\text{Units} = \$1,547,500/\$0.25 = 6,190,000 \text{ jars of soup}$$

How would a business use such information? For one thing, they might ask whether their current plant capacity can produce the needed number of units. They might ask whether marketing can sell that number of units, whether they need to hire more salespeople, open new territories, and have enough trucks to deliver the product. In addition, they might ask whether they have enough working capital to fund that level of production.

Suppose they cannot produce 6.2 million units at their current plant and are reluctant to expand? They could try to re-engineer the product to lower unit variable costs, increase price if the market will bear it, reduce fixed costs, or accept a lower confidence level. Break-even analysis can therefore be a very useful tool in strategic planning.

Suppose they lower unit costs to $0.74, and increase price to $1.09 while maintaining a $300,000 fixed cost and a $1,000,000 profit target, and lower the acceptable confidence level to 90%. How does that change break-even?

Unless other information is given, we can assume the sales distribution has two equal tails. The 10% of the area in the left tail represents an unacceptable profit level. The rightmost tail, which also represents 10% of the probability space, is acceptable. We need to find a standard deviation that represents the central 80% of the probability distribution. From the tables in Chapter 4, we know that plus or minus 1.28 standard deviations represents that amount of area. So we need to set our profit target at $1,000,000 + 1.28 standard deviations.

$$\text{New profit target} = \$1,000,000 + 1.28 \times \text{Standard deviations}$$
$$= \$1,000,000 + 1.28 \times \$150,000$$
$$= \$1,192,000$$

Given the new profit target, the break-even equation becomes

$1.09 × Units − $0.74 × Units − $300,000

$$- \$1{,}192{,}000 = 0$$
$$\text{Units} \times (\$1.09 - \$.74) = \$1{,}492{,}000$$
$$\$1{,}492{,}000 / \$0.35 = 4{,}262{,}857 \text{ units}$$

SUMMARY

Business models can help management test and refine plans prior to implementation. They can identify obstacles and test alternative strategies. Break-even analysis is one type of model that, with suitable modifications, can be applied to a large variety of problems.

Break-even analysis can be used to model the effects of changes in variable costs or the cost of goods sold and changes in fixed costs or overhead. It can also be used to model profit goals.

Break-even analysis works only over a relevant range. If required sales or unit volume exceeds plant capacity, more plant will have to be added changing fixed costs and or overhead. Fixed costs are fixed only over the short term. Over the long term, all costs are variable. If the model provides unsatisfactory results, that may be a signal that the company's cost structure should be changed.

One of the most important uses of break-even analysis is reality testing. If model solutions require plant and equipment, capital investments, or a number of customers that are unrealistic, something needs to be changed before a sensible plan can be developed.

Break-even analysis can also be combined with other business tools to build more sophisticated models. Principles of pricing theory and changes in price and sales volume can be input to break-even models. Statistical analysis can also be used in some situations to measure the confidence with which goals can be achieved. The flexibility of break-even analyses makes it a very powerful modeling tool that can be used in a large variety of circumstances.

CHAPTER 14

Working Capital and Cash Budgeting

To a business, cash isn't everything, but it rates right up there with oxygen. Cash fuels business, and without cash, or cash equivalents, everything stops. One of the most important things a controller or chief financial officer can do for a company is to make sure there is enough cash to keep the business going.

In this chapter, we will discuss working capital and cash budgeting under a variety of circumstances: start-up; ongoing operations; and opening a facility. We will also discuss a line of credit as a cash management tool; and how accounts receivable, inventory, and accounts payable can be both sources and uses of cash.

WORKING CAPITAL

Working capital, sometimes called net working capital, is defined as current assets less current liabilities. Current assets are assets that can be converted to cash fairly quickly, that is, assets expected to be converted to cash within a year. Current liabilities are liabilities that are due within a year.

Bankers and investment analysts frequently look at net working capital to determine whether a company has the capacity to pay its bills as they become due. The current ratio (current assets/current liabilities) and the quick ratio ([current assets − inventory]/current liabilities) are two related measures of whether a company has the capacity to pay its bills.

The problems with these ratios are they are based on data at a point in time, and they assume a fairly static level of business operations. Controllers and chief financial officers must be able to project future cash demand and match that demand to collections and other sources of cash.

CASH BUDGETING

For a service industry, payroll is usually the largest component of cost. Employees expect paychecks within a few days of the end of a pay period. Clients pay much later. Consider a temporary staffing service that pays employees weekly and bills weekly. The cash for payroll and employment taxes is paid out immediately. However, most clients pay in 30 days (even if terms are due on invoicing).

So at a minimum, there must be enough cash to cover the payroll since receipts from collections are probably a month in the future. But is it just one payroll that must be covered? No. Under the best circumstances (that is, customers actually pay in 30 days), the temporary staffing service will have to cover four, perhaps five, payrolls before invoices from the first week's work are collected. Cash required is therefore equal to weekly payroll times the number of payrolls until the first collection. Stated as an equation this is

$$\text{Cash required} = \text{Payroll} \times \frac{\text{Average collection time}}{\text{Days per payroll}} \qquad \text{(Eq. 14-1)}$$

For example, suppose weekly payroll is $1,000 and average time to collect is 30 days. Then, on average, we will have to fund about 4.3 payrolls, assuming weekly pay days, before collection (30 days average collection time/7 days per payroll). Since the average payroll is $1,000, we will need cash of about $4,300 ($1,000 × 4.3). If we wanted to be conservative, we might round 4.3 up to 5 payrolls, bringing the cash needed to $5,000 ($1,000 × 5).

We have seen a measure of the time between billing and collections before. Remember days sales outstanding (DSO)? DSO is 365 days per year/accounts receivable turnover. In a large corporation, where the behavior (or misbehavior) of any one customer cannot significantly change collection patterns, DSO can be substituted for average collection days.

Example

Sally plans to start Sally's Temps by providing 200 hours of secretarial time at $12 per hour. She pays her workers $9 per hour, including taxes. She pays and bills weekly. Average collection time is 35 days. How much cash is required for Sally to get started?

Cash required = (200 hours × $9/hr)

$\quad\quad\quad\quad\quad\quad$ × 35 days average collection/7 days per pay

$\quad\quad$ = $9,000

Another way to think about the cash required is to break it down into two parts: the average payroll per day (payroll/days per pay) and the number of days that must be funded before collection.

After Sally gets paid $2,400 for her first 200 hours of service (200 hours × $12/hr), she will arguably have enough cash to fund subsequent payrolls because each future payroll will only cost $1,800 (200 hours × $9/hr), leaving a positive cash flow of $300 per week. But suppose Sally gets another client who wants 200 hours per week of service? What will her cash demand be then? The same type of analysis will apply. The incremental cash required will equal the average daily cash outflows (that is, for payroll) times the number of days until collection. Growth, whether from startup or an ongoing business, will consume additional cash that must be provided from somewhere.

For the moment, let us set aside the $300 cash flow per week generated by operations. At 12% interest, not unusual for a small business, it would take about $800 per month, or about $200 per week, to pay back the initial $9,000 investment in a year, leaving very little for nonpayroll operational expenses. (See Chapter 5 for details on loan computations.) We see from Sally's Temps that cash management can be troublesome when sales grow.

Relatively few businesses can change sales volume simply by adding more labor. Most require other inputs. For example, a telemarketing company requires both labor hours and telephone time. If a telemarketer is on the phone 40 minutes per hour, and it costs $0.08 per minute for phone time, phone charges are $3.20 per hour. If labor costs, including taxes are $13.30 per hour, and volume increases by 100 telemarketing hours per week, costs increase by

$1,650 [($13.30 + $3.20) × 100 hours]. But does cash outflow increase by $1,650 per week? Probably not. While wages must be paid within a week of the end of the payroll period, phone bills are usually paid in 30 days. Required cash can then be broken into two components, as shown in Eq. 14–2 and Eq. 14–3, respectively.

Required cash payroll = Daily payroll × Collection period

(Eq. 14–2)

Required cash phone = Daily phone   (Eq. 14–3)
                  × (Collection period − Payment period)

To this point, we have assumed that payroll payment and billing occur on the same day. However, nonpayroll expenses usually become accounts payable. Therefore, the company has to finance only the number of days between the payment date and collection (collection period − payment period), as shown in Eq. 14–3.

Given payroll is weekly, the clients are invoiced weekly, the average client collection period is 65 days, the phone company invoices 10 days after the end of the period, and gives 30 days for payment, how much cash is required to fund the 100-hour per week increase in telemarketing?

Required cash payroll
      = ($13.30/hr × 100 hr/wk/7days) × 65days = $12,350
Required cash phone = ($3.20/hr × 100 hr/wk/7 days)
                  × (65 days − 40 days) = $1,143
                                        _____
Total cash to fund expansion $13,493

Suppose the telemarketing company could reduce collection time to 58 days, and increase its terms with the telephone company to 60 days. What would its incremental cash requirement be?

Required cash payroll = ($13.30/hr × 100 hr/wk/7 days)
                  × 58 days = $11,020

Since the cash related to the phone utilization will be collected before the bill is due, no incremental cash will be required to fund the increase in phone usage, and cash required to fund payroll would be reduced because the collection period has been shortened. The difference in cash needed to fund growth drops by $2,473

($13,493 − $11,020). Since telemarketing companies grow by thousands or even tens of thousands of hours per month, the savings in the capital needed for growth is significant. For example, the cash needed to fund a new contract for 10,000 hours per month under the old facts would be $1,349,300, whereas only $1,102,000 is needed under the new facts, a savings of almost a quarter of a million dollars.

OPENING A NEW FACILITY

Cash demand tends to spike when a new facility is opened. The reasons for this are (1) facilities must be purchased or rented some time prior to their productive use so they can be properly outfitted; (2) if a facility is rented, a deposit and month's rent in advance are usually required; (3) equipment must be purchased and installed; (4) engineers or architects may have to be retained to lay out the facility; (5) payment for services or lease payments on equipment usually start before a facility starts generating revenue; (6) staff must be hired and trained; (7) inventory must be purchased; (8) the new facility might not reach 100% productivity immediately; (9) if the new facility is a retail establishment, advertising expenditures will have to be made to let the public know where it is located; and (10) even after production begins, credit sales delay receipt of cash.

Cash Flow Break-Even

Cash flow break-even is the point in a project, an investment, or a company at which it consistently generates enough cash to pay its bills and meet debt service. It is the point at which it produces positive cash flow on a consistent basis. Cash flow break-even is important for two reasons. First, it marks the beginning of the period in which it is self-sustaining. This is an important milestone for banks and investors. Second, it provides a terminal point for a project's detailed startup cash budget. Unless a company knows when a new facility is going to be self-sustaining, that is, generate at least as much cash as it draws, there is no way to tell how much startup capital is necessary. The net of all the cash outflows is the amount that must be secured prior to starting the project.

When we say cash must be secured, we mean we must have identified sources of cash and have in hand firm commitments for cash as needed. In opening a facility, that may mean having cash reserves; bank financing in place; or a strategic investor ready, willing, and able to provide the requisite cash.

Detailed Cash Budget

Before a project is undertaken, a detailed estimate of all the cash inflows and outflows from inception to cash flow break-even should be constructed. Unfortunately, no simple equation can accurately forecast when cash flow break-even will occur. The best method is to schedule cash outflows and inflows, preferably using spreadsheet software, on a week-by-week basis, until cash flow break-even is achieved.

Example

J. Leaderman, a catalog company, decides to open a number of retail outlets. The plan for a typical store follows. Store rent is $10,000 per month, the deposit is $20,000, the lease begins two months prior to opening so the facility can be refurbished. Refurbishing is completed two weeks before the opening and costs $60,000, half payable before the work is done, and half on completion. A staff of 12 is hired 2 weeks prior to opening at an average wage, including payroll taxes, of $11 per hour; each person works 35 hours per week. Payroll is paid weekly. Inventory is delivered to the store 2 weeks prior to opening and costs $120,000 wholesale; terms are 30 days. Advertising for six weeks is purchased and paid for in advance for $50,000. Projected sales are $10,000, $20,000, and $30,000 for the first three weeks and $40,000 per week thereafter. Credit card sales will be 80% of the total, and the credit card company pays on an average of 42 days. Gross margin is 30%. What is the cash required to open this store and operate it until *cash flow break-even*?

Modeling even this simple case, we find that through the first nine weeks of store operations, it has used about $318,000 more cash than it generated. Only after 10 weeks of operations, and 18 weeks after the initial investment was made, does it reach cash break-even. A pro forma cash flow budget for the new J. Leaderman store is shown in Figure 14–1.

FIGURE 14-1

J. Leaderman New Facility Cash Budget

Week	Activity	Memo Amount	Cash Outflow	Cash Inflow	Net Cash/Wk
1	Sign lease pay deposit and one month rent		30,000		
2	Begin refurbishing		30,000		
4	Pay rent		10,000		
5	Complete refurbishing		30,000		
6	Staff hired				
	Inventory arrives				
7	Payroll $11/hr × 35 hr × 12 people		4,620		
	Advertising preopening to wk 4		50,000		
8	Payroll $11/hr × 35 hr × 12 people		4,620		
	Pay rent		10,000		
			169,240		−169,240
9	Week 1 sales $10,000 about 20% cash	10,000		2,000	
	Payroll $11/hr × 35 hr × 12 people		4,620		
	Misc. operating expense, electricity, etc.		1,000		
			5,620	2,000	−3,620
10	Opening + week 2 sales $20,000 about 20% cash	20,000		4,000	
	Payroll $11/hr × 35 hr × 12 people		4,620		
	Order new inventory 70% × prior wk sales	7,000			
	Misc. operating expense, electricity, etc.		1,000		
			5,620	4,000	−1,620
11	Opening + week 3 sales $30,000 about 20% cash	30,000		6,000	
	Payroll $11/hr × 35 hr × 12 people		4,620		
	Order new inventory 70% × prior wk sales	14,000			
	Pay for initial shipment of inventory		120,000		
	Misc. operating expense, electricity, etc.		1,000		
			125,620	6,000	−119,620
12	Opening + week 4 sales $40,000 about 20% cash	40,000		8,000	
	Payroll $11/hr × 35 hr × 12 people		4,620		
	Order new inventory 70% × prior wk sales	21,000			
	Misc. operating expense, electricity, etc.		1,000		
			5,620	8,000	2,380
13	Opening + week 5 sales $40,000 about 20% cash	40,000		8,000	
	Payroll $11/hr × 35 hr × 12 people		4,620		
	Order new inventory 70% × prior wk sales	28,000			
	Pay for first inventory reorder		7,000		
	Pay rent		10,000		
	Misc. operating expense, electricity, etc.		1,000		
			22,620	8,000	−14,620

FIGURE 14-1

J. Leaderman New Facility Cash Budget (*Continued*)

Week	Activity	Memo Amount	Cash Outflow	Cash Inflow	Net Cash/Wk
14	Opening + week 6 sales about 20% cash	40,000		8,000	
	Collect first week's credit card sales			8,000	
	Payroll $11/hr × 35 hr × 12 people		4,620		
	Order new inventory 70% of prior wk sales	28,000			
	Pay for second inventory reorder		14,000		
	Misc. operating expense, electricity, etc.		1,000		
			19,620	16,000	−3,620
15	Opening + week 7 sales about 20% cash	40,000		8,000	
	Collect second week's credit card sales			16,000	
	Payroll $11/hr × 35 hr × 12 people		4,620		
	Order new inventory 70% of prior wk sales	28,000			
	Pay for third inventory reorder		21,000		
	Misc. operating expense, electricity, etc.		1,000		
			26,620	24,000	−2,620
16	Opening + week 8 sales about 20% cash	40,000		8,000	
	Collect third week's credit sales			24,000	
	Payroll $11/hr × 35 hr × 12 people		4,620		
	Order new inventory 70% of prior wk sales	28,000			
	Pay for fourth inventory reorder		28,000		
	Misc. operating expense, electricity, etc.		1,000		
			33,620	32,000	−1,620
17	Opening + week 9 sales about 20% cash	40,000		8,000	
	Collect fourth week's credit card sales			24,000	
	Payroll $11/hr × 35 hr × 12 people		4,650		
	Order new inventory 70% of prior wk sales	28,000			
	Pay for fifth inventory reorder		28,000		
	Pay rent		10,000		
	Misc. operating expense, electricity, etc.		1,000		
			43,650	40,000	−3,650
18	Opening + week 10 sales about 20% cash	40,000		8,000	
	Collect fifth weeks' credit card sales			32,000	
	Payroll $11/hr × 35 hr × 12 people		4,650		
	Order new inventory 70% of prior wk sales	28,000			
	Pay for sixth inventory reorder		28,000		
	Misc. operating expense, electricity, etc.		1,000		
			33,650	40,000	6,350
					−311,500

Turning from cash flow to profit, for a moment, let us consider the profitability of the store, shown in Figure 14–2, which is the Leaderman store pro forma, *once it is in full operation*. On an annualized basis, Leaderman expects about $175,000 profit on sales of $2,000,000 per year, or about 8.75% before taxes and interest. This would generally be regarded as an excellent profit for a retailer.

The concern of this chapter, however, is to inform Leaderman, in a realistic way, how much capital is needed before these profits can be realized. If Leaderman runs out of resources before achieving cash flow break-even, Leaderman will have to forego projected profits and probably take a loss on the investment to that point.

We can also contrast the cash flow budgeting Leaderman needs to do with capital budgeting. If Leaderman *only* considered the net cash flows over the course of the year, as it would when preparing a capital budget, it might never realize the extent of the cash drain in the first five months of operation. Suppose J. Leaderman decided to open five or ten stores at a time. They could be hit with unexpected negative cash flows of $1.5 million to $3.0 million, respectively, in the early months.

Although businesses must grow or die, periods of rapid expansion are usually periods of extreme risk. Part of the risk involves failure to properly forecast revenue and expenses. However, much of the risk comes from failure to adequately plan for and manage cash demand.

FIGURE 14–2

J. Leaderman Store Pro Forma

Sales:	$40,000/wk	
Cost of goods sold @ 70%	$28,000/wk	
Gross profit		$12,000/wk
Less		
Labor (12 people × $11/hr × 35 hr/wk)	$ 4,620/wk	
Rent ($10,000/month/4 wk/mo)	$ 2,500/wk	
Misc. expenses, electricity, etc.	$ 1,000/wk	
Depreciation on leasehold improvements	$ 385/wk	
		$ 8,505/wk
Profit before interest and taxes		$ 3,495/wk

Contingencies

As we have seen in several other contexts, plans never unfold perfectly. Operating costs could be underestimated, there could be delays in obtaining building permits and construction, or revenue projections could be overoptimistic. Even if a new facility replicates a proven format, the unexpected could occur. Consequently, all cash budgets should have a contingency built in. The amount and nature of the contingency will depend on the nature of operations or projects being planned. For example, a 30-day delay in opening a retail store is not unheard of. A contingency line item in the budget might anticipate this by budgeting for an additional month of rent, staff salary, and miscellaneous operating expenses.

LINE OF CREDIT

A line of credit is a bank facility that allows a company to borrow money as needed for payroll, accounts payable, or other purposes. It is only meant as temporary financing. As a general rule, a company draws down on its line of credit (that is, they borrow money from the bank through this facility) and pay it back when they can. There is no fixed payment schedule. However, interest must be kept current (that is, paid monthly).

A line of credit does, however, come with a number of conditions. For example, a bank may require a monthly report of aged accounts payable, aged accounts receivable, and net tangible assets. Often a bank will compute a company's borrowing capacity by first multiplying net tangible assets (cash, accounts receivable, inventory, plant and other assets, but not patents and other intellectual property, goodwill, amounts due from officers, or accounts receivable over 90 days) less non-bank liabilities, by some percentage, usually 70% or 80%. This gives the company's credit capacity. Next, a bank subtracts all outstanding bank loans, and line of credit balances from capacity. If the result of this computation is negative, the company must immediately pay down their line of credit until total outstanding loans are less than or equal to the company's credit capacity.

Example
Mid Pennsauken Bank has extended Guido's Printed Circuits a $100,000 line of credit. Every month they must compute their

tangible net assets and borrowing capacity. What would be Guido's capacity if it has $1,000 cash, $200,000 of accounts receivable, $70,000 of which are over 90 days old, $30,000 of inventory, and an asset called due from officer of $10,000. Guido has no plant or equipment since it rents everything. It's only non-bank liability is $50,000 of accounts payable. Mid Pennsauken Bank defines borrowing capacity as 70% of net tangible assets, excluding officers loans and accounts receivable over 90 days old. Guido's borrowing capacity is analyzed in Figure 14–3.

Every bank has a slightly different form and format for computing tangible net assets and borrowing capacity. They use different percentages, and some exclude accounts receivable over 60 days. In addition, a given bank may change its tangible net assets and borrowing capacity formulation over time. The best approach when considering a bank is to ask what their specific terms are for computing these items. If you are in an industry that pays on average 60 days after invoicing, you can't afford to use a bank that excludes accounts receivable over 60 days old.

Banks usually require a line of credit to be "cleaned up" once per year. By this, banks mean that they want the line of credit paid down to zero. Many banks require it to be zero for at least a month. They do this for two reasons. First, banks are always looking for escape hatches, ways to get out of loans if a company's performance deteriorates. The period when the line of credit is paid down to zero is an opportune time to shed a client. Second, banks are constantly testing companies. The requirement that the line of credit be paid off for at least a month is a test to see whether a company

FIGURE 14-3

Analysis of Guido's Borrowing Capacity

Cash:		$ 1,000
Accounts receivable	$200,000	
Less accounts over 90 days	−$ 70,000	
		$130,000
Inventory		$ 30,000
Tangible assets		$161,000
Less accounts payable		$ 50,000
Net tangible assets		$111,000
		× 70%
Borrowing capacity		$ 77,700

has sufficient cash from operations to keep going or whether they are juggling money from account to account on an indefinite basis. In other words, does the company need the line of credit to meet temporary cash needs, or does the company rely on the line as permanent financing?

SEASONAL CASH DEMAND

Sales volume varies seasonally for many businesses. Examples include the toy business, which peaks before Christmas, and the lawn care business, which peaks in the summer. Since there is often a lag between the time work is done and the time when a business is paid, seasonal sales create a spike in cash demand. (If expenditures and receipts were perfectly synchronized, cash management would be trivial.)

Few truly seasonal businesses have enough cash to see them through from a period of high production costs to the period when cash is collected. A line of credit is ideally suited to fund this kind of periodic cash demand. Figure 14–4 is the cash demand for a seasonal business plotted over a year.

When negotiating with a bank for a line of credit, it is vitally important that a company have a realistic forecast of their annual cash demand. Banks are reluctant to extend additional credit to companies that have run out of cash midway through the year because of bad planning.

Therefore, a forecast of cash demand is an essential element of both an annual plan and any bank negotiation. The amount of the line of credit should be the difference between the maximum cash demand and the minimum cash demand, plus some contingency. Banks get nervous when a company borrows their entire line of credit. So in the best-case scenario, having some amount of unused line helps maintain bank confidence, and in a worse-case scenario, provides a cushion against adverse events.

On the other hand, a line of credit should be no more than can be repaid over the course of the year. If, as in Figure 14–4, cash demand never fully reverses because the business is growing year to year, that growth should be funded through term loans, which have extended payment terms.

F I G U R E   14–4

Cash Demand for a Seasonal Business Plotted over a Year

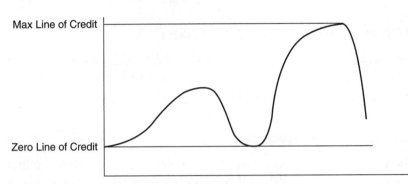

Example

Klag Sports Equipment expects to open two stores this year. They have budgeted $40,000 per month for 12 months to get these stores up and running. July and August are peak sales months, and because a large volume of purchases are made by credit card, collections for summer sales will not be completed until the beginning of October. To prepare for summer sales, Klag plans to purchase $250,000 more than its usual monthly amount of raw materials in April, and run its factory overtime from April through June at an additional cost of $400,000.

How much of this cash budget should be financed with permanent financing, that is, through a bank term loan, or equity if it is available, and how much should be financed with a line of credit?

Opening new stores is a long-term investment in the company. Arguably, it could take a year or more for start-up cash to be recouped. Therefore, the $480,000 invested in new stores (12 months × $40,000 per month) should be financed on a permanent basis. This assumes that some contingency has been built into the startup budget.

On the other hand, cash expenditures for $250,000 of raw materials and $400,000 of factory overtime should probably be financed with a line of credit since cash collections will be complete in a few months. That makes the minimum line of credit request $650,000. If they want a 10% contingency in their line, they should request at least $715,000. If they round up to the next $50,000, a fairly common occurrence for loans under $1 million, they would request $750,000 for a line of credit.

MANAGING WORKING CAPITAL

Net working capital is defined as the difference between current assets and current liabilities. Current accounts can be a source of cash for expansion if carefully managed.

Accounts Receivable

When a company sells on credit, it is lending money to its customers, a use of cash. When it collects accounts receivable, it is generating cash. Accounts receivable turnover, Eq. 14–4, expresses the relationship between credit sales and accounts receivable.

$$\text{Accounts receivable turnover} = \frac{\text{Credit sales}}{\text{Average accounts receivable}}$$

(Eq. 14–4)

Sales to other businesses are usually credit sales. Sales to consumers are usually a mix of cash and credit sales, with most credit sales being on credit cards.

Example

Smith Brothers has sales of $6 million, of which $5 million are credit sales. Their average accounts receivable is $1 million. Given this information, we can compute their accounts receivable turnover.

$$\text{Accounts receivable turnover} = \frac{\$5,000,000}{\$1,000,000} = 5.0$$

Ratios, in a vacuum, are not very informative. Two things can be done to make sense of an accounts receivable turnover ratio. One is to compare it to ratios of other companies in the industry to see how the company ranks. Higher turnover ratios are better. The other, more intuitive, way to use this information is to convert it to days sales outstanding (DSO) using the formula in Eq. 14–5.

$$\text{DSO} = \frac{365}{\text{Accounts receivable turnover}}$$

(Eq. 14–5)

What is the Smith Brothers DSO?

$$DSO = \frac{365}{5.0} = 73 \text{ days}$$

DSO represents the average number of days a company is lending money to its customers, and as such, is a much more intuitive measure of credit and collections performance. It is one thing to tell your collections staff their accounts receivable turnover is 5.0 and they better improve. Unless you carefully explain the ratio in comparison to other companies' turnover ratios, your instructions might elicit only blank stares. On the other hand, if you tell your collections staff that customers are paying their bills an average of 73 days after shipment, that has impact. It is something they can understand.

Accounts Receivable as a Use of Cash

As a business grows, its credit sales grow, which means in effect, that it is lending more money to its customers. Increases in accounts receivable must be funded, and that drives cash demand. Suppose Smith Brothers planned a marketing campaign that they believed would increase their sales by 20%. How much additional cash would they need to fund those increased sales? If only cash sales increased, the answer would be zero. However, if credit sales increase 20%, then accounts receivable will increase, generating new cash demand. We can modify Eq. 14–4 to recognize the effect of sales growth, giving us Eq. 14–5, which shows how that growth affects accounts receivable.

$$\frac{\text{Accounts receivable}}{\text{turnover}} = \frac{\text{Prior credit sales} \times (1 + \text{Sales growth})}{\text{New average accounts receivable}}$$

Applying the Smith Brothers data, we find the following:

$$5.0 \text{ turns} = \frac{\$5,000,000 \times (1 + 20\%)}{\text{New average accounts receivable}}$$

$$\text{New average accounts receivable} = \frac{\$6,000,000}{5.0 \text{ turns}} = \$1,200,000$$

From this, we can compute the incremental cash needed to fund the increase in accounts receivable, as shown in Eq. 14–6.

Cash needed = New average accounts receivable   (Eq. 14–6)
                    − Old accounts receivable

The cash demand created by sales growth can be forecast through use of the accounts turnover ratio. Why not estimate the increases as a percentage of sales growth? In the real world, we may want to improve collections (which will increase the turnover ratio) as we are growing sales. The formula above allows us to model both effects at the same time.

Accounts Receivable as a Source of Cash

Accounts receivable can be a source of cash as well as a use of cash. An accounts receivable turnover ratio is not necessarily immutable. Improving credit and collection practices, screening customers for their ability and willingness to pay, tightening payment terms, and more diligent collection efforts, can increase the turnover ratio.

Suppose Smith Brothers wanted to raise $100,000 from their $1,200,000 accounts receivable and still support $6,000,000 of credit sales. What would they have to do in terms of improving their accounts receivable turnover ratio? We can address such questions by adapting Eq. 14–4 to the issue of raising cash and recasting it as Eq. 14–7.

$$
\begin{aligned}
\text{New accounts receivable turnover} &= \frac{\text{Credit sales}}{\text{Accounts receivable} - \text{Amount to be raised}} \\[2mm]
&= \frac{\$6,000,000}{\$1,200,000 - \$100,000} \\[2mm]
&= \frac{\$6,000,000}{\$1,100,000} = 5.45 \text{ turns} \qquad \text{(Eq. 14–7)}
\end{aligned}
$$

Translating that into DSO to make the requirement easier for the collections staff to understand, we see

$$
\text{DSO} = \frac{365}{5.45} = 67 \text{ days}
$$

So, in the Smith Brothers example, the staff would be challenged to reduce average collections from 73 days to 67 days.

Changing the question slightly, suppose after some research, management found that average collections for the industry were 40 days, and they challenged the collections staff to reduce DSO from the current 73 days to 50 days. How much cash could be raised?

To answer this question, we start with the DSO goal and compute the required accounts receivable turns using Eq. 14–5. Applying it to the facts of the Smith case, we find

$$50 \text{ days} = \frac{365}{\text{New accounts receivable turns}}$$

$$\frac{\text{New accounts}}{\text{receivable turns}} = \frac{365}{50} = 7.3 \text{ turns}$$

Feeding the new turns back into the accounts receivable turnover ratio, Eq. 14–4, we find

$$7.3 \text{ turns} = \frac{\$6,000,000 \text{ credit sales}}{\text{New average accounts receivable}}$$

$$\frac{\text{New average}}{\text{accounts receivable}} = \frac{\$6,000,000}{7.3} = \$821,918$$

When we compare this to our prior accounts receivable of $1,200,000, we find we can squeeze $378,082 ($1,200,00 − $821,918) of cash out of accounts receivable by improving collections.

Notice how we began the analysis. We didn't just throw a bunch of numbers into an equation and turn the crank. We started with goals, goals for raising an amount of cash, or goals for staff performance, and then, and only then, did we use the equations to model either what we needed to do to reach a goal or the beneficial effects of reaching some goal.

Finance is about shaping the future, and a company can't shape its future without information that can be clearly communicated to those who must implement management's decisions. So one aspect of financial analysis and decision making is to make goals understandable.

Accounts Receivable and Collection Agencies

If a company hasn't had success collecting one or more of its accounts, it should consider turning them over to a collection agency. Collection agents are tough people in a tough business. However, experience shows them to be reliable allies. The two benefits of using a collection agency are that they can be extremely effective in converting overdue accounts to cash, and they relieve a company's staff from wasting time on difficult accounts.

However, there are drawbacks to using a collection agency. One is that their fee is usually 25% to 35% of what they collect, and they might not collect a customer's entire balance. The reason is they usually ask for the right to compromise a bill in exchange for prompt payment. The other drawback is that sending an account to a collection agent impairs customer relations. To a businessperson, this latter argument is weak. The objective of business isn't to make a sale; it is to get paid. Clients who can't or won't pay their bills should be struck off salespersons' customer lists anyway.

Contracts with collection agencies usually give them the power to compromise and settle claims. That means whatever amount they get is all that a customer will ever have to pay on the invoices in question. Collection agencies remit net; that is, they take their fee from the amount collected and pay the company that hired them the balance. Since this is by definition less than the client's accounts receivable balance, the difference between the amount remitted and the book balance will have to be written off.

Example

Emerson Powell owes CPL Antiques $10,000. CPL refers the matter to the Bonebreak Collection Agency. Bonebreak finds Powell and negotiates an $8,000 settlement of the claim if Powell pays in 48 hours. Powell pays Bonebreak $8,000. Bonebreak takes a 30% fee, as per the contract they signed with CPL, and remits $5,600 to CPL Antiques. CPL Antiques makes the following journal entry to close out the Powell affair.

	Debit	Credit
Cash	$5,600	
Bad debt expense	$4,400	
Accounts receivable		$10,000
(Powell account)		

The Powell account is reduced to zero, as it must be; otherwise, there would be an uncollectible balance in the accounts receivable ledger forever. Zeroing out Powell's account may strike some as unfairly generous to Mr. Powell, but it is not. To CPL Antiques the writeoff is only business. But like most companies, CPL will probably put Powell on a list of people that they will not extend credit to in the future.

One problem with collections, whether a company is collecting themselves or turning collections over to an agency, is that what isn't documented can't be collected. Companies need to keep meticulous records of goods sold: make, model, serial number, color, size, weight, date of shipment, and so forth. For services rendered, a company should keep copies of deliverables, if any, hours applied, names of those providing service, and the dates and hours of service rendered.

A final word on collection agencies: fees are negotiable. The larger and more recent accounts receivable are, the lower the fees. The smaller and older the accounts receivable, the higher the fees. The implication is turn over accounts sooner rather than later.

Strategic Analysis: Raising Cash from Accounts Receivable
Though accounts can and should be analyzed one at a time, businesspeople need to think strategically about raising cash. That means looking at the overall financial landscape and making the hard decisions that are necessary to push the company to the next level.

Example
Suppose Jake's Plumbing decided to open a "branch office" in the next valley by buying and outfitting a two-ton truck as a rolling shop/hardware store/warehouse. Jake needs $75,000 to buy and outfit his branch office. His line of credit and bank loans are fully extended. What does he do? Consider the following financial information on Jake's, as shown in Figure 14–5.

Analyzing accounts receivable, we see two problems. The first problem is that $90,000 is over 90 days old. Allowing accounts receivable to age out to 90 days reduces borrowing capacity. In addition, "old" accounts receivable "lock up" assets. If Jake has tried to collect these accounts without success, he should turn them over to a collection agency immediately.

FIGURE 14-5

Jake's Plumbing Financials

Assets			Liabilities	
Cash	$ 5,000		Accrued payroll	$ 30,000
Receivables 0 to 90 days	$ 500,000		Accounts payable	$ 155,000
Receivables 91 to 365 days	$ 90,000		Line of credit	$ 160,000
Inventory	$ 260,000		Current portions of loans	$ 155,000
Total current assets	$ 855,000		Total current liabilities	$ 500,000
Equipment:	$ 50,000		Bank loans	$ 160,000
Plant:	$ 95,000		Equity	$ 340,000
Total assets	$1,000,000		Total liabilities and equity	$1,000,000

Income Statement

Revenue:	$4,000,000	*operating expenses include
Cost of goods sold	$3,000,000	depreciation of $20,000
Gross profit	$1,000,000	
Operating expenses*	$ 950,000	
Profit before interest and tax	$ 50,000	

If he uses a collection agency, and they collect all $90,000 outstanding, not usually the case, he will net $63,000 ($90,000 turned over to collections less a 30% fee of $27,000). In that case, he will have to write off the $27,000 as a bad debt expense. But by taking this one action, Jake has found a way to fund substantially all the investment in his rolling branch office. But what else can he do?

Examining his accounts receivable turnover ratio, we see it is 6.8:1 [$4,000,000 credit sales/$590,000 average accounts receivable]. Jake's DSO is about 53.7 days [365 days/6.8]. If invoices are due on presentment, or even due in 30 days, an average collection time of 53.7 days is pretty bad. Even if Jake sells his accounts receivable over 90 days old, and computes the turnover on the remaining accounts, his ratio will still be 8:1 [$4,000,000 credit sales/$500,000], and his DSO will be 45.6 days.

Suppose Jake got his accounts receivable turnover ratio up to 12:1. That would mean DSO would drop to 30.4 days [DSO = 365/ accounts receivable turnover ratio]. At a ratio of 12:1, and a DSO of 30.4 days, Jake needs only $333,333 to finance this present sales volume [$4,000,000/12].

What happens to the difference between the $500,000 in accounts receivable and the $333,333? It is converted to $166,667 of cash. So by taking action on overdue accounts and instituting better credit and collection efforts, Jake can raise $229,667.

What has Jake done? The issue at the beginning of the problem was how to raise $75,000 at a point where the bank wouldn't lend him any more money. By thinking strategically and taking appropriate actions, Jake can have his new rolling branch office, and pay off a substantial portion of his bank debt.

Inventory

Inventory can be either a source or a use of cash. Purchasing inventory uses cash; selling inventory generates cash. The performance of inventory can be measured through inventory turnover, as seen in Eq. 14–8.

$$\text{Inventory turns} = \frac{\text{Cost of goods sold}}{\text{Average inventory}} \quad \text{(Eq. 14–8)}$$

Example

Smith Brothers has an average inventory of $800,000 on cost of goods sold of $2,400,000. What is their inventory turns?

$$\text{Inventory turns} = \frac{\$2,400,000}{\$800,00} = 3.0$$

As with an accounts receivable turnover ratio, an inventory turnover ratio by itself has little meaning. Comparison to the industry average is one way to give it meaning. Higher turnover ratios are better than low turnovers. Another way to give it meaning is to convert it to days in inventory (DII). This is a measure of how long inventory—raw material, work in progress, and finished goods—is owned by the company. It starts when the company receives raw material, usually at their shipping dock, and ends when the goods are shipped. The formula for days in inventory is given by Eq. 14–9.

$$\text{DII} = \frac{365}{\text{Inventory turns}} \quad \text{(Eq. 14–9)}$$

In the case of Smith Brothers, we find their DII is

$$DII = \frac{365}{3.0} = 121.7 \text{ days}$$

Inventory and Cash Demand

What are the implications for the investment in inventory if a company improves their sales? More sales mean a greater cost of goods sold, which will mean greater activity in the plant and more raw material, work in process, and finished inventory. Increases in inventory, whether manufactured or purchased, mean more cash will be required. How can this cash demand be estimated?

If we posit that Smith's cost of goods sold was $2,400,000 on $5,000,000 of sales, we know their gross margin was 52% (sales of $5,000,000 − COGS of $2,400,000 = gross profit of $2,600,000; gross profit of $2,600,000/sales of $5,000,000 = gross margin of 52%), then we can translate sales into COGS without having to know purchases.

We can adapt Eq. 14–8 by using sales × (1 − gross margin) instead of COGS, to get Eq. 14–10.

$$\text{Inventory turnover} = \frac{\text{Sales} \times (1 - \text{Gross margin})}{\text{Average inventory}} \quad \text{(Eq. 14–10)}$$

Equation 14–10 can further be rewritten to adjust for growth in sales to get Eq. 14–11.

Inventory turnover

$$= \frac{\text{Sales} \times (1 + \text{Growth}) \times (1 - \text{Gross margin})}{\text{New average inventory}} \quad \text{(Eq. 14–11)}$$

Applying this to forecast 20% growth in Smith Brothers sales, we find

$$3.0 = \frac{\$5,000,000 \times (1 + 20\%) \times (1 - 52\%)}{\text{New average inventory}}$$

$$\text{New average inventory} = \frac{\$6,000,000 \times 48\%}{3.0} = \frac{\$2,880,000}{3.0}$$

$$= \$960,000$$

Cash demand for new inventory is given by Eq. 14–12.

Cash needed = New average inventory − Old average inventory

(Eq. 14–12)

Applying this to the facts of Smith Brothers, we find

Cash needed = $960,000 − $800,000 = $160,000

To support increased sales, Smith will have to increase inventory by $160,000, which creates a cash demand of $160,000. Although $160,000 might not seem like much, consider what will happen in a few years if Smith continues to grow at 20% per year. In a few years, they will need to raise half a million per year in addition to all the money they would have raised and invested in inventory up to that point. But is there a better way?

Inventory as a Source of Cash

Just as purchasing inventory is a use of cash, shedding inventory can be a source of cash. In raising cash from inventory, we want to have goals to work toward; otherwise, it will be impossible to measure progress and hold people accountable. Equation 14–8 can be modified to give Eq. 14–13, which indicates what it takes to raise a certain amount of cash from inventory.

$$\text{Inventory turns} = \frac{\text{Cost of goods sold}}{\text{Average inventory} - \text{Amount to be raised}}$$

(Eq. 14–13)

Suppose Smith Brothers wanted to raise $200,000 from their current inventory of $800,000, while supporting $2,400,000 in cost of goods sold. What would their inventory turns have to be?

$$\text{Inventory turns} = \frac{\$2,400,000}{\$800,000 - \$200,000} = \frac{\$2,400,000}{\$600,000} = 4.0$$

Translating inventory turns into the more intuitive days in inventory (DII), we find

$$\text{DII} = \frac{365}{4.0} = 91.25 \text{ days}$$

This means that if Smith can find a way to get inventory into and out of their plant in an average of 91.25 days instead of the current 121.7 days, they can raise $200,000 in cash from inventory.

It is one thing to crunch numbers in a model, but how, on a practical level, does a company increase inventory turns? There are several ways. First, adjust inventory levels to more appropriately support sales. Second, purchase raw materials only as needed, rather than stockpiling them. Third, manufacture goods only as needed. Fourth, redesign the manufacturing process so that material passes through the plant in a minimum amount of time. Redesign of the manufacturing process is the province of production management, and a good production management text will provide guidance in that area.

Defining Appropriate Levels of Inventory

Many managers talk about the big picture and being big-picture managers. Unfortunately, much of what is needed to improve company performance is in the details. Setting appropriate inventory levels is one example of the need to analyze things at a detailed level.

In almost every company, materials are purchased, inventoried, and sold via a stockkeeping unit, or SKU (pronounced "skew"), part number, or some other alphanumeric tag. We will call all these SKUs in the following discussion. If inventory and sales are tracked by SKU, it should be possible to compute inventory turnover at the SKU level. Adapting Eq. 14–8 to the level of SKUs gives Eq. 14–14.

$$\text{SKU turnover} = \frac{\text{Number of parts sold} \times \text{Unit cost}}{\text{Average number in inventory} \times \text{Unit cost}}$$

$$(\text{Eq. } 14\text{--}14)$$

Suppose SKU number 1234 cost $30.00, 4,000 of these parts were sold last year, and the average inventory of SKU number 1234 was 2,900. What is the turnover for SKU 1234?

$$\text{SKU 1234 turnover} = \frac{4,000 \times \$30.00}{2,900 \times \$30.00} = \frac{\$120,000}{\$87,000} = 1.38 \text{ turns}$$

Translating SKU turns into days in inventory by adapting Eq. 14–9 to the SKU level, we get Eq. 14–15.

$$\text{SKU DII} = \frac{365}{\text{SKU turns}} \qquad \text{(Eq. 14–15)}$$

For the Smith Brothers, SKU 1234, DII is

$$\text{SKU 1234 DII} = \frac{365}{1.38} = 264.5 \text{ days}$$

This means that SKU 1234 is in inventory for an average of 264.5 days. Stating this another way, there is a 264.5-day supply of this part. Is such a supply really necessary? Suppose it was determined that a 30-days supply were needed. We could use that to back into SKU turns and from there SKU inventory levels.

$$\text{SKU 1234} = 30 \text{ days} = \frac{365}{\text{SKU 1234 turns}}$$

$$\text{SKU 1234 turns} = \frac{365}{30} = 12.1$$

Since the cost cancels out in the numerator and denominator of Eq. 14–4, we can rewrite the inventory turnover equation as Eq. 14–16.

$$\text{SKU turns} = \frac{\text{Units sold}}{\text{Average units in inventory}} \qquad \text{(Eq. 14–16)}$$

$$\text{SKU 1234 turns} = 12.1 = \frac{4,000}{\text{New target inventory level}}$$

$$\text{Target inventory level} = \frac{4,000}{12.1} = 331$$

We are now in a position to compute the excess inventory using Eq. 14–17 and quantify the cash raised if we could sell excess inventory at cost.

$$\frac{\text{Excess}}{\text{inventory}} = \text{Current average inventory} - \text{Target inventory level}$$
$$\text{(Eq. 14–17)}$$

For SKU 1234,

$$\text{Excess inventory} = 2,900 - 331 = 2,569$$

At a unit cost of $30 each, Smith has the potential of raising $77,070 (2,569 units at $30 each) by better managing this one part alone.

Since SKU data is computerized in most companies, it would be relatively easy to compute DII for all parts. In most companies two trends will emerge. First, some SKUs are probably moving through inventory fairly quickly, whereas some inventory is moving at a glacial pace, if at all. Second, there is probably excess inventory across most SKUs.

Suppose, after analysis, the company determines the supply it needs of each part. The excess inventory can be sold down, or sold off, to raise cash. The potential from this type of analysis is significant and can often dramatically reduce inventory. Figure 14–6 is what a SKU level inventory analysis might look like.

Once a SKU level analysis is performed, clear goals can be set for purchasing, manufacturing management, and whoever is responsible for selling excess inventory. Remember, financial analysis and decisions are pointless if they don't result in plans that are specific and measurable enough to be executed.

Accounts Payable as a Source of Cash

All liabilities are a source of financing whether accrued payroll or bank loans. For most companies, vendor financing, in the form of accounts payable, is a major source of capital. As bills are paid down, cash is used. When purchases are made on credit, accounts payable becomes a substitute for cash. Proper management of accounts payable is therefore very important in maximizing the cash a company has to invest in new, profit-making projects, or in the alternative, to avoid the cost of bank debt.

Example
Marty's Software receives cash as it collects accounts receivable and uses cash to pay its bills. It pays its bills in an average of 28 days. How much cash could it raise if it extended the average payment to 32 days? To determine that, we first have to find his accounts payable turnover, then the number of days it takes him to pay his

FIGURE 14-6

SKU Level Inventory Analysis

SKU	Average Units of Inventory	Annual Sales/Use in Units	Cost per Unit	SKU Turnover	Actual SKU DII	Target SKU DII	Target SKU Turns	Target Units of Inventory	Excess Units	Excess Inventory Value
1234	2,900	4,000	$ 30.00	1.38	265	30	12.17	329	2,571	$ 77,136.99
1345	300	1,500	$ 9.00	5.00	73	30	12.17	123	177	$ 1,590.41
1456	890	2,000	$ 15.00	2.25	162	15	24.33	82	808	$ 12,117.12
1478	3,000	15,000	$ 8.00	5.00	73	30	12.17	1,233	1,767	$ 14,136.99
1490	500	4,000	$125.00	8.00	46	45	8.11	493	7	$ 856.16
1510	1,000	4,000	$ 25.00	4.00	91	45	8.11	493	507	$ 12,671.23
1520	850	8,000	$900.00	9.41	39	30	12.17	658	192	$173,219.18
1650	900	5,000	$ 50.00	5.56	66	60	6.08	822	78	$ 3,904.11
										$295,632.19

bills on average, which we shall call days to pay, or DTP. Accounts payable turnover can be computed using Eq. 14–18.

$$\text{Accounts payable turnover} = \frac{\text{Purchases}}{\text{Average accounts payable}}$$

(Eq. 14–18)

However, to use this equation, we must find purchases, an amount not typically provided on financial statements. To find out what purchases were over the course of a year, we start with an intuitive, fairly easy idea. Think about everything we had in our possession some time during the year. If we sold it, we call it cost of goods sold, and if it was left over at the end of the year, it would be ending inventory. We must have purchased everything we had during the course of the year, except for the beginning inventory.

Expressing this as a formula gives us Eq. 14–19.

Purchases = Cost of goods sold + Ending inventory   (Eq. 14–19)
          − Beginning inventory

Suppose Marty's beginning and ending inventory were $150,000 and $155,000, respectively, and cost of goods sold was $2,000,000. Then using Eq. 14–19, purchases would be

Purchases = $2,000,000 + $155,000 − $150,000
          = $2,005,000

Using Eq. 14–18, we find accounts payable turnover is

$$\text{Accounts payable turnover} = \frac{\$2,005,000}{(\$150,000 + \$155,000)/2}$$

= 13.1 accounts payable turns

We can use accounts payable turnover in Eq. 14–20 to find the number of days it takes on average for Marty's Software to pay its bills.

Days to pay (DTP) = 365/Accounts payable turns   (Eq. 14–20)
                  = 365/13.1 = 28 days

Suppose Marty's is thinking about increasing its average days to pay to 32. How much will that increase his accounts payable?

Remember increasing accounts payable is like increasing an interest-free line of credit.

$$\text{Target days to pay} = 32 \text{ days} = \frac{365}{\text{New accounts payable turns}}$$

$$\frac{\text{New accounts}}{\text{payable turns}} = 365/32 \text{ days} = 11.4$$

$$= 11.4 = \frac{\$2,002,000}{\text{New average accounts payable}}$$

$$\frac{\text{New average}}{\text{accounts payable}} = \frac{\$2,002,000}{11.4} = \$175,614$$

$$\frac{\text{Cash generated by}}{\text{extending payments}} = \text{New average accounts payable}$$
$$- \text{ Old average accounts payable}$$
$$= \$175,614 - \$152,500$$
$$= \$23,114$$

By extending payments, Marty's Software has generated another $23,114 to use in the business. But if the average number of days to pay exceeds vendor expectations, they may decide not to extend the company credit at all. As with all business matters, there must be a balance between the interests of the company and the interests of those who supply goods, services, and labor to the company.

Accounts Payable as a Measure of Customer Creditworthiness

Some companies take any customer that comes through the door. That isn't always the wisest strategy. Remember the objective isn't to close the sale, it's to get paid. Therefore, customers that want to make a significant purchase on credit should be screened for creditworthiness. One fairly simple method of screening is to compute the customer's days to pay.

Example
Pundit Manufacturing wants to purchase $500,000 of programming time from Marty's software over the course of a year. Pundit's beginning and ending accounts payable were $3.3 million and

$3.5 million, respectively. Its cost of goods sold was $9.8 million. Its beginning and ending inventory was $2.4 million and $2.6 million, respectively. How long does it take to pay its accounts on average?

We can find purchases using Eq. 14–19.

Purchases = $9.8 M cost of goods sold + $2.6 M ending inventory

− $2.4M beginning inventory

= $10 M

We can use this in Eq. 14–18 to find the accounts payable turnover.

$$\text{Accounts payable turnover} = \frac{\$10 \text{ M}}{(\$3.5 \text{ M} + \$3.3 \text{ M})/2}$$

$$= 2.94$$

From this, we can use Eq. 14–20 to compute Pundit Manufacturing's days to pay.

$$\text{Days to pay} = \frac{365}{2.94} = 124.1$$

If Marty's goal is to collect in 20 or 30 days, Pundit's average payment is so far out of the profile that they should be rejected as a client. Even if Pundit promised to pay Marty's Software in 30 days, it would be unrealistic to think they could sustain a 30-day payment period in the face of demands from their other vendors. Besides, any company that doesn't pay bills for four months is a credit risk per se. The only alternatives Marty's Software has are to demand cash or demand a letter of credit from a bank guaranteeing payment.

When should this type of credit analysis be performed? The question turns in part on a company's risk tolerance. Is the company willing to risk 10% of their monthly profits on a new client? If so, then a credit analysis should be made of customers wanting credit at that level.

For example, if Marty's Software generates profits of $50,000 per month, and their risk tolerance is 10% of profits, then they are willing to risk a $5,000 sale without checking the buyer's credit. If a customer wants to buy $5,100 of programming services on credit, then the company should be asked to complete a credit application since they exceed Marty's credit risk threshold. If a company wants a Unix systems programmer to speak to their staff for a day, and the charge is $1,000, that contract would be under Marty's risk threshold, and a credit application probably wouldn't be required.

There is no theoretically correct risk threshold. Some companies may be willing to risk only 5% of monthly profits; others might be willing to risk 20% of monthly profits. However, it is incorrect, both theoretically and practically, not to set credit thresholds and get credit applications for those exceeding the threshold.

Where do we get the data to make these computations? If a company is publicly held, financial information is available on the Securities and Exchange Commission website, specifically in the Edgar database. The website address is www.sec.gov. If a company is not publicly traded, they should have to complete a credit application. Privately held companies are often reluctant to provide financial statements. One approach is to ask only for the data needed to compute their average days to pay. That includes beginning and ending inventory, beginning and ending accounts payable, and cost of goods sold.

Other questions that are useful on a credit application are:

1. Are you profitable?
2. Are you in violation of any bank covenants?
3. Do you plan to file for bankruptcy?
4. Is there anything that you know of that might increase the risk of bankruptcy?

Getting a good customer credit application has implications for bankruptcy. If, for example, a company provides false information to a vendor to get credit, and files bankruptcy within three months of providing that false information, the company extending the credit might have a right to reclaim goods out of bankruptcy or the claim might be nondischargable in bankruptcy. This is especially important for big-ticket, easily identifiable items.

If, however, the company says either (1) they are too new to have financial statements, or (2) they don't want to provide even this minimal data, you can assume they are not a good credit risk.

SUMMARY

Cash is like oxygen. Take it away, and a company dies. Cash budgets are different from accounting budgets. A company can have an accounting profit and be loosing cash.

Working capital is one, broad measure of a company's cash position. It is defined as current assets less current liabilities. Current assets include cash and assets expected to be converted to cash within a year. Current liabilities are liabilities that come due within a year. A company with zero or negative working capital is in trouble and may not have enough cash to pay its bills as they become due.

Cash budgeting is important because cash outflows from business operations usually precede cash inflows. Whereas revenue and the cost of goods sold may be recognized at the same time, the cash needed to manufacture or purchase goods for sale usually precedes cash collections.

In a steady-state, no-growth situation, cash inflows can be expected to meet or exceed cash outflows. However, in a startup or growth situation, cash demand can exceed inflows. For simple businesses, the excess cash demand can be estimated using a variety of formulas. However, for a more complex operation, the only way to comprehensively estimate cash is by constructing a detailed, week-by-week cash flow budget. Cash flow break-even is the point at which a project or facility consistently generates more cash than it uses. Detailed cash flow budgets should be prepared from project inception through cash flow break-even.

A bank line of credit is one way to manage temporary cash shortfalls. A line of credit is best used for a seasonal business or a business trying to finance a specific, short-term project. Banks usually require a line of credit to be "cleaned up," that is, paid down to zero for about a month each year. Therefore, a line of credit is not a good vehicle for permanently financing growth. Term loans are better.

In addition to increased cash demand for operating expenses during a period of growth, increases in accounts receivable and inventory also use cash. Credit sales are like lending customers money, and increased credit sales increase the demand for cash. Increased sales will also require increased inventory to support those sales. Formulas based on turnover ratios help estimate cash demand for these working capital accounts.

The accounts receivable turnover ratio can be translated to days sales outstanding (DSO), which is the average number of days it takes to collect on a sale. The inventory turnover ratio can be translated into days in inventory (DII), which is a measure of how long a company holds inventory on average. Both DSO and DII are more intuitive measures of performance and easier to explain to the staff than turnover ratios.

Accounts receivable and inventory can be sources of cash as well as uses of cash. Increasing accounts receivable or inventory turnover reduces the average balance in these accounts, freeing up cash for other uses. One technique for identifying excess inventory is to compute turnover ratio by part or stockkeeping number (SKU). That can be used to compute days in inventory by SKU, which can be compared to the target inventory levels by SKU. Excess inventory can be sold to raise cash.

Accounts payable can also be a source of cash. However, caution should be exercised because any company that consistently pays bills later than suppliers expect may find they are no longer welcome as customers. Accounts payable analysis can also be used to determine how long it takes a customer to pay their bills. Screening customers for their ability and willingness to pay is an important component of accounts receivable management.

CHAPTER 15

Master Budgets and Variance Analysis

An annual or operating budget is just another paperwork exercise if management loses sight of the reasons for budgeting. Budgets are a planning device in that they provide fairly detailed goals for sales, production, and other activities. Budgets help assess the feasibility of company goals. It is one thing to say the objective is to double sales; it is another to systematically think about the resources it will take to double sales and double output. Budgets also provide a way to identify variances from goals. Finally, budgets are one way to measure management performance.

In the broadest possible terms, an operating budget is a way of quantifying a company's business plan. It captures key elements of operation such as sales, product price, variable production and administrative costs, fixed costs, and forecast profits.

If a company compiles a budget, and finds profits are unsatisfactory, it is far easier to adjust budgets and the plans that underlie them, than to make adjustments once resources have been committed and operations are underway. Of course, budgets must have some basis in reality. If management just keeps throwing numbers into a spreadsheet until a profit appears without coordinating budgets with operational plans, the budget collapses into just so much paperwork.

In this chapter, we will explore several types of budgets from simple to complex and show how they can be used as tools to manage the company's operations on an ongoing basis.

BASIC BUDGETS

Even the most basic budget has certain features. These include various categories of fixed and variable costs, forecast number of units sold, unit price, and budget versus actual. These data should be familiar from break-even analysis. With the estimated number of units, we can compute revenue and variable costs. Of course, the fixed costs remain unchanged with (moderate) changes in sales volume. We can therefore compute a budget and estimate operating profits. Figure 15–1 is an analysis of cost and production plans for Pitcarn Pumps.

What is the probability that actual sales are going to equal forecast sales? In the real world, practically zero. Sales will either be higher or lower. So in comparing the forecast budget to the actual budget, the first type of variance to be teased out should be based on changes in sales volume.

For example, suppose direct materials are budgeted at $3,200,000, but purchasing spends $3,300,000. Is that good or bad? We can answer that question only by knowing how many units were produced. If direct material for 80,000 units was budgeted ($3,200,000 = $40 × 80,000), but 88,000 units were produced, then

FIGURE 15-1

Analysis of Cost and Production Plans for Pitcarn Pumps

Pitcarn Pumps plans to make and sell 80,000 units			
Revenue (price × units)		$150 × $80,000	$12,000,000
Variable manufacturing costs/unit			
Direct materials	$40		
Direct labor	$25		
Variable manufacturing overhead	$15		
		$80 × 80,000	$ 6,400,000
Variable administrative costs/unit		$20 × 80,000	$ 1,600,000
Commissions		5% × $150 × 80,000	$ 600,000
Contribution margin			$ 3,400,000
Fixed manufacturing overhead			$ 1,500,000
Fixed marketing costs			$ 120,000
Fixed administrative costs			$ 800,000
Operating profit			$ 980,000

the actual direct material cost per unit was only $37.50 ($3,300,000/88,000). So even though manufacturing costs in total dollars went up, the cost per unit went down, which is good.

On the other hand, if fixed manufacturing overhead is budgeted at $800,000 and it went up to $810,000, there is a $10,000 unfavorable variance because, by definition, fixed costs should not vary with sales volume. So variances break out into two major classes. (1) variances due to differences in operating volume, and (2) variances due to differences in price or costs.

Differences (variances) are not, per se, good or bad. But if they have a significant impact on profits, such variances should be analyzed to determine (1) where the responsibility, if any, lies, and (2) whether such variances, if unfavorable, can be minimized, or if favorable, maximized.

MASTER BUDGETS

Master budgets, also called flexible budgets, are operating budgets used to monitor and control companywide operations. These budgets have three major columns, and the differences between these columns are the variances to be analyzed. Figure 15–2 is the general format for master budgets and variances.

What do we mean by standard prices and costs? Standard prices and costs are the prices and costs used in the initial budget. Arguably, prices are set by the marketing department's consideration of competing products, price elasticity, and other factors. Standard costs, sometimes called engineered costs, are the projected costs for raw materials, direct labor, variable manufacturing overhead, fixed manufacturing overhead, and fixed and variable administrative costs.

FIGURE   15–2

General Format for Master Budgets and Variances

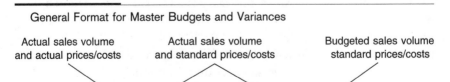

Actual sales volume and actual prices/costs		Actual sales volume and standard prices/costs		Budgeted sales volume standard prices/costs
	Price/cost variances		Sales volume variances	

Though historical or accounting data might inform standard costs, they should not control it. Standard costs are the costs management *believes* will be incurred in the future. For example, if direct labor has been $19.00 per hour, and management knows that workers will receive a 4% raise, they should include that 4% increase in the manufacturing labor budget.

Why compute two sets of variances? Think about the logic of the budget. If the original budget calls for manufacture of 80,000 units, and the marketing department sells 10% more than planned, are we going to criticize manufacturing for using 10% more materials or labor? Of course not. So this two-step process separates the effect of sales volume variances from the effects of variances due to inefficient manufacturing and purchasing.

Example

Pitcarn Pumps expects to sell 80,000 pumps at $150 each. Engineering and cost studies indicate that variable manufacturing costs should be about $80 per pump. Variable administrative costs should be about $20 per pump, and the primary variable marketing cost is a 5% sales commission, which at a price of $150 should be about $7.50 per pump. Fixed manufacturing, marketing, and administrative costs are estimated at $1,500,000, $120,000, and $600,000, respectively. Based on this information, Pitcarn constructed the planned budget, which is the far right-hand column (column 7) of the master budget shown in Figure 15–3.

The far left-hand column of Figure 15–3 (column 1) reflects actual sales and costs. The flexible budget (column 5) shows what sales and costs *should have been* using the original engineered cost estimates *adjusted for the actual sales volume*. The columns between these three columns analyze sources of the variances.

Looking at the flexible budget (column 5), we see the actual sales volume of 100,000 pumps, at the planned price of $150 per pump, should have yielded sales of $15,000,000. The variance (difference) between the planned revenue of $12,000,000 (column 7) and flexible budget sales of $15,000,000 (column 5, which assumes the standard price,) was $3,000,000. Notice the F next to the $3,000,000 variance under sales volume variance (column 6)? We usually designate all variances as either favorable, F, or unfavorable, U.

FIGURE 15-3

Pitcarn Pumps Master Budget

PITCARN PUMPS Plan vs. actual	Commission	Actual 5%	Price Var. Mfg. Var. Admin.	140.00 80.50 25.00	Budget	Price Var. Mfg. Var. Admin.	150.00 80.00 27.00
	(1)	(2)	(3)	(4)	(5)	(6)	(7)
	Actual Based on Sales Volume of 100,000	Purchasing and Production Variances	Marketing and Admin. Variances	Sales Price Variance	Flexible Budget Actual Sales Volume 100,000	Sales Volume Variance	Plan Budget Based on Units of 80,000
Sales (revenue):	14,000,000			−1,000,000 U	15,000,000	3,000,000 F	12,000,000
Less variable							
Manufacturing costs	8,050,000	−50,000 U			8,000,000	−1,600,000 U	6,400,000
Marketing and admin.	2,500,000		150,000	50,000 F	2,700,000	−540,000 U	2,160,000
Contribution margin	3,450,000	−50,000	150,000	−950,000	4,300,000	860,000	3,440,000
Less fixed							
Manufacturing costs	1,490,000	10,000 F			1,500,000		1,500,000
Marketing costs	118,000		2,000 F		120,000		120,000
Admin. costs	590,000		10,000 F		600,000		600,000
Operating profits	1,252,000	−40,000	162,000	−950,000	2,080,000	860,000	1,220,000

Favorable variances are not necessarily good, and unfavorable variances are not necessarily bad. If the marketing department has a $120,000 advertising budget, but does not advertise, they will have a favorable variance, though the consequences could be lowered sales, which is bad. The designations *favorable* and *unfavorable* simply mean a variance tends to increase, or decrease, operating profits.

Comparing the flexible budget (column 5) variable manufacturing and variable marketing and administrative costs to the planned costs, the flexible budget costs are greater than planned costs, but this is what we would expect since the company produced and sold 100,000 pumps instead of 80,000 pumps. Nevertheless, since these variances tend to decrease profits, they are classified as unfavorable.

Notice that there are *no* variances between the planned (column 7) and flexible (column 5) budget *fixed costs*. And why should there be? Fixed costs, by definition, are independent of sales volume.

Returning to sales for a moment, we see actual sales (column 1) were $14,000,000, whereas planned sales (column 7) were only $12,000,000. How do we account for this difference? At the planned price of $150 per pump, and 100,000 pumps, we should have had $15,000,000 in sales per the flexible budget (column 5), yet actual sales (column 1) were only $14,000,000. The difference between actual and flexible sales is accounted for by the unfavorable sales price variance (column 4) of $1,000,000. Given this sales price variance, management should investigate why unit prices were cut.

Did market competition force prices down? If so, in the next budget cycle, the company should work to lower pump manufacturing costs so that profit margins can be maintained. On the other hand, sales staff may be inappropriately discounting the merchandise, which caused the price variance. Only a management inquiry will be able to tell for certain.

Looking at variable manufacturing costs, we see actual costs (column 1) of $8,050,000 exceeded planned costs (column 7) of $6,400,000 by $1,650,000! However, before firing the plant manager, consider the source of the unfavorable variance. Of the total variance, $1,600,000 was caused by increased production volume (column 6), and only $50,000 was caused by a combination of purchasing and production inefficiencies (column 2).

Consider variable marketing and administrative costs. Based on the flexible budget (column 5), we would expect them to be $2,700,000, whereas they were only $2,500,000 (column 1), giving a favorable variance of $200,000. Where did this favorable variance come from? And why analyze favorable variances? They are analyzed (1) to find out whether there is a mistake in the budget analysis, and (2) to determine whether there is an opportunity to further increase the favorable price or cost trend.

So before we give the marketing or administrative manager a bonus for the $200,000 favorable variance, notice that $50,000 (column 4) was lost commissions due to the lower unit prices. On balance, most companies would rather have sold their pumps for $150 (as compared to $140), gotten the extra $1,000,000 in revenue, and *paid* another $50,000 in commissions! The favorable commission variance (commission savings) can be obtained by multiplying the commission rate, 5%, times the unfavorable sales price variance, $1,000,000 (column 4). The remaining $150,000 favorable variance (column 3) was due to reduced spending.

Variances in fixed costs, in this example all favorable, are just the differences between the flexible budget fixed costs and the actual fixed costs.

In practice, things like variable manufacturing costs would be broken down into direct labor, direct materials, and variable manufacturing overhead. Direct labor might be further analyzed into components representing straight time versus overtime, and manufacturing time versus down time. Labor might also be broken down by department or process. Direct materials may be analyzed into inefficiencies in using material, for example, the amount of scrap or the number of pumps that had to be diverted to the rework department, compared to variances resulting from changes in materials prices.

Each line of the budget would be broken into enough detail so that responsibility for variances could be assigned to specific departments or individuals with the objective of prompting corrective action. Of course, as with anything, there must be a balance. If budgets are too detailed, the detail will obscure the overall picture. Excess detail is also costly to accumulate and analyze. So judgment is required in preparation and management of any budget.

Most businesses have monthly, and some weekly, budgets. The principles of budget analysis are the same. Planned sales and costs are compared to flexible sales and costs. Flexible sales and costs are simply a restatement of the planned budget using *actual sales volumes*. Once variances due to changes in volume are analyzed, changes due to other factors can be more readily identified by comparing actual sales and costs to flexible sales and costs.

Return to the general format for master budgets and variance analysis. We have been analyzing the flexible and planned budgets and the results of sales volume variances. Figure 15–4 summarizes the format for analyzing actual, planned, and flexible variances.

Example

Suppose for GenX ComX, the planned, or engineered, price was $2.40 per comic; variable manufacturing costs were $1.50; commissions at 10% were $0.24; and fixed manufacturing, marketing, and administrative costs were $750, $200, and $300, respectively. Suppose 2,100 copies were actually sold. Assume the actual (wholesale) price was only $2.35; variable costs per copy were $1.48; and actual fixed manufacturing, marketing, and administrative costs were $790, $150, and $310. Figure 15–5 provides a flexible budget analysis for GenX ComX.

In analyzing sales variances, we see that actual sales of $4,935 were less than the $5,040 expected for 2,100 copies ($2.40 × 2,100). This creates an unfavorable sales price variance of $105.

The reduced selling price means commissions at 10% are also reduced by about $11 (10% × $105 rounded), giving rise to a favorable marketing cost variance.

F I G U R E   15–4

Format for Analyzing Actual to Flexible Budget Variances

Actual Budget	**Flexible Budget**	**Planned Budget**
Actual sales volume and actual prices/costs	Actual sales volume and standard prices/cost	Budgeted sales volume standard prices/costs

Price/cost variances   Sales volume variances

FIGURE 15-5

Flexible Budget for GenX ComX

	Actual* Budget	Manufacturing Variance	Marketing and Admin. Variance	Price Variance	Flexible† Budget
Sales	$4,935			−$105 U	$5,040
Less variable costs					
Manufacturing	$3,108	$42 F			$3,150
Administrative and marketing	$ 494	____	____	$11 F	$ 504
Contribution margin	$1,333			$94 U	$1,386
Less fixed costs					
Manufacturing	$ 790	−$40 U			$ 750
Marketing	$ 150		$50 F		$ 200
Administrative	$ 310	____	−$10 U	____	$ 300
Operating profit	$ 83	$2 F	$40 F	$94 U	$ 136

*Actual budget is the actual number of units sold, actual prices, and actual costs.
†Flexible budget is the actual number of units sold and budgeted prices and costs.

Looking at fixed marketing and administrative costs, we see that there is a $50 favorable marketing variance, partly offset by a $10 unfavorable administrative variance.

Variable manufacturing costs had a favorable variance of $42 because the unit cost of production dropped from $1.50 to $1.48 (2,100 units × [$1.50 − $1.48]). However, fixed manufacturing cost had an unfavorable variance because manufacturing overspent its budget by $40.

Don't despair at the low profits comic book fans and entrepreneurs. If GenX ComX can hold its actual cost structure and raise sales to 10,000 copies per issue, operating profits jump to $5,090 per issue.

MASTER BUDGETS VERSUS FINANCIAL STATEMENTS

Master budgets are extremely useful management tools, but they are not financial statements; they are a managerial accounting device. This is frequently a source of management frustration because they may be tracking to budget, but still show poor performance on financial statements.

Recall that managerial accounting and generally accepted accounting principles (GAAP) have different objectives. Managerial accounting is focused on improving management's internal, decision-making process. Master budgets build on managerial accounting principles. Financial reporting, on the other hand, is used to make statements comparable from company to company and year to year. Financial reporting follows GAAP rules. Since the objectives of these systems are different, we shouldn't expect them to yield the same results. Nevertheless, it is useful to discuss some of the ways they differ.

Master budgets assume products are made and sold in the same period. If more is made than is sold, the costs associated with unsold units must be taken out of the master budget and booked as inventory. This should be no problem for variable manufacturing costs: direct labor, direct materials, and variable factory overhead. However fixed manufacturing overhead becomes problematic. The fixed manufacturing overhead associated with unsold units is recorded as part of inventory. So comparing budgeted fixed manufacturing overhead with actual fixed manufacturing overhead, without making an adjustment for unsold units will create nonexistent variances.

Likewise, if units are sold from inventory, sales might be properly stated, but the amount of variable manufacturing costs for the period might look low, thus creating favorable variances that do not exist.

Unless workers are paid daily, there is likely to be accrued payroll at the end of any budget period. Accruals, of necessity, are estimates, and estimates often have a distorting effect. Further, at the beginning of each new period, the prior period's payroll accrual must be reversed, and this reversal may create differences between the operating profit on the master budget and the operating profit on a financial statement.

Purchasing and accounts payable are other sources of discrepancies. For example, actual amounts in master budgets are frequently based on invoices. If invoices are not timely received and processed, master budget costs may be understated. Accountants adjust for delayed invoicing in financial statements by accruing for anticipated expenses.

If preparation of master budget and variance reports is delayed too long by waiting for invoices, they lose effectiveness as a tool. If accruals are made for purchased materials, those accruals can have their own pernicious effects.

In a sophisticated manufacturing environment, some of these problems can be overcome by linking the master budget to the purchasing and receiving system. This will tell the master budget what material has been ordered, its price, and whether it was received. So, the effect of delays in receiving and processing invoices can be minimized.

Bill of materials programs can tell what material was transferred from inventory to the factory floor, and perpetual inventory systems can provide the unit cost of materials actually used. A bill of materials (BOM) system contains a detailed parts list for every product a company makes. If, for example, a company wants to make a batch of lawnmowers, the BOM system tells material men how many engines to pull, how many mower blades, how many nuts, how many bolts, how many feet of wire, and so on. A good BOM system will tell a company ahead of time whether it has all the parts in stock to build all the mowers on the production plan before they start so that no labor time will be wasted.

So while it is possible to synchronize master budgets and financial statements, it is no trivial matter. Nevertheless, master budgets have proved to be extremely useful tools in managing a company.

SUPPLEMENTAL BUDGETS

Most companies have supplemental, departmental-level, budgets that roll up into a master budget. Such supplemental budgets help each department better manage its own operation. Supplemental budgets have formats similar to master budgets. However, their goal might not be to maximize operating profits because few departments have sales. Their goals may be to minimize unfavorable variances given any particular sales volume.

SUMMARY

Operating budgets are designed to guide a company's operations for a period of time, usually a year. A budget is a quantification of a company's plan. It has a shorter time horizon than a capital budget and usually isn't concerned with the acquisition of long-term assets and their payback.

Conventional operating budgets forecast sales and production levels in advance for a year and then measure variances against these targets. Master, also called flexible, budgets are designed to isolate two types of variances: those due to sales volume changes and those due to operational inefficiencies. Unless sales volume variances are isolated from other variances, it will be difficult or impossible to know who is responsible for unexpected results.

Master budgets and financial reports are difficult to reconcile because each has different goals and is based on a different set of principles. Master budgets are designed to help management make better decisions about internal operations. They are based on managerial accounting principles. Financial reporting is based on generally accepted accounting principles that are designed to make financial statements comparable from company to company and year to year.

Companies often have supplemental operating budgets that break down costs and responsibilities to departments and lower levels. These operating budgets are designed to track variances and affix responsibility at the lowest possible level in the organization. These budgets roll up to line items in master budgets.

CHAPTER 16

Pricing Theory

Proper pricing is as important to a company's fortune as having a good cost structure, investing in the right capital projects, and having budget controls in place to assure management's plan is being properly executed.

Pricing affects gross margins, and gross margins affect a company's profitability. Pricing affects the amount of cash a company can generate from operations. Pricing also affects competitiveness. If a company prices its products too high, it may price itself out of the market. If it prices too low, it may be giving away profits it could have had.

In this chapter, we will discuss a number of approaches to pricing. None of them is right in every situation. We will discuss the pros and cons of each in enough detail so that informed judgments can be made about pricing strategy. We will also discuss the competitive forces acting on a company to drive price. In the final analysis, however, several approaches may be needed to identify and validate the optimum product price.

COST-CENTERED PRICING

Many companies base prices on their costs. This has a certain logic since any company that prices their products below cost will soon be out of business. By cost, we mean full absorption cost.

Cost-based pricing is easy to use, and it is easy to build in either a target gross profit or a target gross margin.

Example

Gentlemen's Clothing Emporium finds that good-quality men's suits can be purchased wholesale for $100 each. Gentlemen's wants a gross profit of $75 per suit. Therefore, they price their suits at $175 retail. If the wholesale price of men's suits rises to $115, Gentlemen's will raise their prices to $190 ($115 cost + $75 target gross profit).

Another, and more common, cost-centered pricing approach is to use a target profit margin. If, for example, Gentlemen's wants to make 40% gross margin on a suit that costs $100. They could use Eq. 16–1 to determine the price of the suit.

$$\text{Price} = \text{Cost} + \text{Gross margin} \times \text{Price} \qquad \text{(Eq. 16–1)}$$

This can be rewritten as Eq. 16–2.

$$\text{Price} - \text{Price} \times \text{Gross margin} = \text{Cost} \qquad \text{(Eq. 16–2)}$$

Factoring out price, we get Eq. 16–3.

$$\text{Price} \times (1 - \text{Gross margin}) = \text{Cost} \qquad \text{(Eq. 16–3)}$$

Dividing both sides by $(1 - \text{gross margin})$, we get Eq. 16–4, which can be directly used to compute a price given a cost and target gross margin.

$$\text{Price} = \frac{\text{Cost}}{(1 - \text{Gross margin})} \qquad \text{(Eq. 16–4)}$$

Applying the facts of Gentlemen's Clothing Emporium to Eq. 16–4, we can solve for price.

$$\text{Price} = \frac{\$100}{(1 - 40\%)}$$

$$= \frac{\$100}{60\%} = \$166.67$$

To simplify the application of prices to hundreds or thousands of products, Eq. 16–4 can be modified further. Rather than using dollar cost in the numerator, suppose they use percent of cost (cost %) as shown in Eq. 16–5. In that circumstance, the answer provided by the equation won't be a dollar price applicable to just one garment; it will be price in terms of a percent of the cost of the item.

$$\text{Price} = \frac{\text{cost }\%}{(1 - \text{Gross margin})} \qquad \text{(Eq. 16–5)}$$

Applying the facts of Gentlemen's Clothing Emporium to Eq. 16–5, the only variable we put into the equation is the target gross margin. The output or answer we get from the equation is price stated as a percentage of cost. Here cost is 100% of cost.

$$\begin{aligned} \text{Price} &= \frac{100\% \text{ of cost}}{(1 - 40\%)} \\ &= \frac{100\% \text{ of cost}}{60\%} \\ &= 166.67\% \text{ of cost} \end{aligned}$$

What happens if we use this approach to price the $100 suit?

$$\begin{aligned} \text{Price} &= 166.67\% \times \$100 \\ &= \$166.67 \end{aligned}$$

Can we apply this in the case of a suit that costs $115? Yes, very simply.

$$\begin{aligned} \text{Price} &= 166.67\% \times \$115 \\ &= \$191.67 \end{aligned}$$

Once management decides the gross margin they need, they can translate that into a percentage of cost that is easily applied by staff, and more easily applied by computer. Obviously, if the target margin is 40%, a store might want to round up or down a little on individual products.

This strategy has the benefit of simplicity, but it also has its drawbacks. Changes in pricing tend to be driven by changes in cost, and target gross margin to the exclusion of market forces.

MARKET-CENTERED PRICING

Market-centered pricing holds that internal costs are largely irrelevant to price setting, assuming, of course, that there is *some* profit in a product. The weakness in cost-centered pricing is that it doesn't adjust to market forces, temporary competition, shifts in perception, and so forth. In other words, cost-centered pricing is somewhat arbitrary. Market-centered pricing attempts to overcome these problems.

Market Pricing and Changes in Cost

Suppose, for example, Raj Patel has a 20% gross margin target for his gasoline station, and he can buy gasoline at $0.84 per gallon. If all competing gas stations purchase gas at the same price and have the same gross margin target, the price of gasoline will be $1.05 everywhere. However, suppose Patel finds a source of gasoline that is $0.75 per gallon when his competitors are paying $0.84 per gallon. Should he reduce his gas price from $1.05 per gallon to $0.94 per gallon? He would under cost-centered pricing.

One argument is that by following a cost-based strategy, he is maintaining his gross margin at 20%, and by lowering his prices, he can win customers from competing gas stations. However, there are two counterarguments to this.

The first is that Patel was making $0.21 per gallon under the old cost pricing structure ($1.05 − $0.84), and by maintaining margins in a lowered price structure, he is reducing his gross profit per gallon to $0.19 ($0.94 − $0.75).

The second counterargument is that he should let the marketplace set the price. If competing gas stations continue to charge $1.05, then Mr. Patel could charge about $1.05 and keep the increased margin. In effect, by letting the marketplace set the price, he is maximizing his available gross profit, getting $0.30 per gallon ($1.05 − $0.75).

On the other hand, if Patel's price rises to $0.90 per gallon, and competing gas stations maintain their price at $1.05, market-based pricing suggests he should leave his price at $1.05. The logic is that if he tries to maintain a 20% gross margin and raises his price to $1.13, he will lose sales to competitors.

Market Pricing and Defining the Relevant Market

Market pricing is more difficult than cost-based pricing because the market price must be determined. The market price is a function of the relevant marketplace, that is, the marketplace in which a company's customers are likely to shop. Although almost anything can be purchased over the Internet, the vast majority of purchases are still made in brick-and-mortar stores, in part because people want to touch, feel, and try merchandise, and in part because people want to receive goods instantly. So for a conventional retailer, the primary relevant market is other conventional retailers, and for an Internet company, the relevant market is other Internet companies, recognizing there is some degree of crossover between the Internet market and the conventional market.

Take the example of Wilson Computer Center, which is trying to set a retail price on the latest IBM personal computer. Figure 16–1 is an analysis of the prices charged by the five stores within 10 miles that sell the same computer. Wilson's strategy is not to be the low-cost retailer, but to be about average. Given his competitors' prices, what should Wilson charge?

Where there are a lot of sellers in the relevant market, and one of them prices a product significantly higher than other sellers, an argument can be made to eliminate the highest price as being either out of touch with the market or as having some special feature not obvious from competitive research. Eliminating the price outlier, Wilson would set his price at about $1,550 [($1,400 + $1,500 + $1,600 + $1,700)/4].

An important concept to remember is that market prices are like shifting sand. It is inevitable they will move. If market-centered pricing is going to drive your decisions, then you must have a constant stream of intelligence about competitors prices. This doesn't mean tracking the price of thousands of items in dozens of stores. It does mean that certain bellwether products sold by competitors

FIGURE 16–1

Analysis of Price Charged by Competitors

Competitor	Price
Mad Max Computer Stuff	$1,400
Center City Computer	$2,100
Moe Larry Curly's Nyuck Nyuck Stores	$1,500
Berlin Mart	$1,600
Federal National Computer	$1,700

should be tracked. Bellwether items are items that attract customers to a store, catalog, or company, and that are directly comparable.

Market Pricing and Value Pricing

Another aspect of market pricing is value pricing. Value pricing holds that for most products there are one or more ways to compute a price performance, or price–value ratio. For example, suppose one store sells Cherrios for $3.50 per box, and another store sells Cherrios for $5.00 per box. Does the low-price store always prevail? Not necessarily. If the $3.50 box contains 15 ounces and the $5.00 box contains 45 ounces, the higher priced Cheerios win because of the superior price performance, $0.11 per ounce ($5.00/ 45 ounces) versus $0.23 per once ($3.50/15 ounces). Many products have price–performance characteristics that can make a higher priced good a better value good.

Consider Jersey Farm Machinery, which has designed a light-duty tractor for municipal, park, estate, and light construction work. It is larger than most lawn tractors, yet smaller than most commercial tractors. Research indicates that purchasers of both farm and construction equipment tend to view horsepower as a relevant measure of performance. The light-duty tractor has 80 horsepower. The Jersey research department has compiled the information in Figure 16–2 to perform a value analysis for competing tractors.

Using horsepower as an indicator of perceived value, and including all four competitors, what should the price be on Jersey's

FIGURE 16–2

Value Analysis for Competing Tractors

Product	Horsepower	Price	Cost per Horsepower
Red Devil Garden Tractor	40	$ 4,600	$115
John Deere Model A Tractor	150	$18,750	$125
Powatan Industrial Tractor	120	$15,600	$130
Kubota Light Tractor	140	$16,800	$120

light-duty tractor? Based on horsepower value, the price per horse-power should be about $122.50 [($115 + $125 + $130 + 120)/4]. If Jersey is pricing an 80-horsepower tractor, its price should be about $9,800.

Many products are priced to reflect this sort of value. Airplanes' performance is measured by cost per seat mile, computers are measured by processor speed, disk drives are measured by storage capacity, and so forth.

ENGINEERED COST

Engineered cost is a strategy in which a product's probable, or target market price, is established *prior to its design*. Given the target price, product features, and forecast sales volume, the engineering team attempts to design a product and related production methods that will deliver the product at a cost that maintains the company's target profit margin.

Example

Z Engineering makes small flat panel displays. They want to make large screen, television flat panel displays. Market research indicates they can sell 500,000 such displays if they can get the wholesale price down to $600 each. The company has a target gross margin of 40% on all new products. That means that engineering must design, and manufacturing must be able to build, screens that cost no more than $360 ($600 × 60%). Remember the cost of goods sold plus the gross margin of 40% must equal 100%; therefore, the cost of goods sold must be 60%.

Engineered cost is an important strategic concept. As products mature, and competitors enter the marketplace, competition will inevitably drive prices down. If a company is sophisticated enough, it will ask what its product's price will be in six months, a year, two years, and take appropriate measures to maintain target gross margins. One way to do that is to give the product engineering and manufacturing departments goals well in advance so that they can refine products and operations to keep costs tracking down with product price.

PRICE ELASTICITY

Price elasticity is a concept that deals with the combined effects of demand and prices on total revenue. Ordinarily, if a company cuts prices, they will sell more units, and if they raise prices, they will sell fewer units. The question is if prices are lowered or raised, what will happen to total revenue? That question gives rise to the concepts of elastic and inelastic demand.

Elastic Demand

Elastic demand is defined as a situation in which cutting prices *increases* total revenue. Even though the revenue generated by each unit is less than before, enough additional units will be sold to earn back that lost revenue and generate more. To say a product's demand is elastic is to say it is very sensitive to price.

Inelastic Demand

Inelastic demand is defined as a situation in which cutting prices *decreases* total revenue. Even though the number of units sold increases, it doesn't increase enough to offset the effects of the lower price received from each unit sold. To say a product's price is inelastic is to say it is not sensitive to price.

Example 1

Phil's Hardware in Dry Hole, Texas, is the only store within 40 miles that sells plumbing supplies. In the average year, Phil sells 24 sinks at $80 each. Phil decides to cut his prices to $75, and the next year he sells 25 sinks. Is Phil's market for sinks elastic or inelastic?

Under the old pricing structure, sinks generated $1,920 in revenue ($80 × 24), and under his new price structure, Phil's revenue is $1,875 ($75 × 25). So even though unit sales went up, total revenue decreased. Therefore, we conclude the sink demand in Dry Hole, Texas, is inelastic.

The concepts of elasticity and inelasticity also apply to price increases. Sometimes raising prices reduces sales volume so much that total revenue decreases. We say this demand is elastic, meaning sales volume is very sensitive to price changes. On the other hand, if raising prices increases total revenue, we say that demand is inelastic.

Example 2

Phil, of Phil's Hardware in Dry Hole, Texas, knows he has little competition in the sink trade. Therefore, instead of cutting prices, he raises them from $80 per sink to $99. As a result of his price increase, Phil's unit sales drop from 24 sinks to 22. Phil's revenue under the old price structure was $1,920 ($80 × 24), and revenue under his new price structure is $2,178 ($99 × 22), an increase of $258. Since revenue increased even though prices increased, we conclude the market for sinks in Dry Hole is inelastic.

Price Elasticity and Gross Profits

Changes in total revenue don't tell the whole story. A second-level analysis of price elasticity considers the effect of volume changes on gross profit. If prices are reduced in a highly elastic market, total revenue increases, but as the number of units sold goes up, the cost of goods sold goes up. Each unit sold has a lower gross margin. Taken to the extremes, this can seriously impact gross profit.

Consider the case of MegaMart, Inc. Last year they sold 500 pairs of Lee Jeans at $33 per pair. Research indicated that the price of jeans was elastic, so they cut price to $29 and sold 700 pairs. Revenue from Lee Jeans increased to $20,300 ($29 × 700) from $16,500 ($33 × 500). The change in total revenue confirmed that the price of jeans was elastic. But what happens if we consider the effect of this price change on gross profit? The effects are analyzed in Figure 16–3.

FIGURE 16–3

Analysis of Price Elasticity and Gross Profit

	Unit Cost Is $28		Unit Cost Is $15	
Price	$33	$29	$33	$29
Units	500	700	500	700
Total revenue	$16,500	$20,300	$16,500	$20,300
COGS	$14,000	$19,600	$ 7,500	$10,500
Gross profit	$ 2,500	$ 700	$ 9,000	$ 9,800

We see from Figure 16–3 that if Lee Jeans cost MegaMart $28 per pair, then even though revenue increases from $16,500 to $20,300, gross profit decreases from $2,500 ($16,500 − 500 × $28) to $700 ($20,300 − 700 × $28); not a good thing. On the other hand, if the cost of Lee Jeans were $15, gross profit would grow from $9,000 ($16,500 − 500 × $15) to $9,800 ($20,300 − 700 × $15). So though the concept of price elasticity is a very powerful tool for strategic analysis, it cannot be used without considering its effects on gross profits.

PRODUCT LIFE CYCLE

Most products have a life cycle that affects pricing decisions. Sometimes the life of a product is long, for example, televisions, sheet rock, and Barbie dolls; sometimes the product life is short, for example, certain toys and fashions. As a product progresses through its life, its characteristics in the market change. These changes help inform pricing decisions. Generally, there are four phases to a product's life cycle: introduction, growth, maturity, and decline.

Phase	Description and Market Characteristics
Introduction	The product is new, price is usually high, and there is a scarcity of suppliers. Not all uses for the product have been identified and worked out. At this stage, it is purchased by early adopters, people who try new products and services just for the sake of trying them. During this period, price is relatively inelastic because of lack of competition and the indifference of early adopters to price within a broad range.
Growth	Customers become broadly aware of the product or service and its features. There is a general acceptance of the product category. There is often a fight to determine who will set industry standards. During this period, demand may exceed production capacity. The product can command a premium price.
Maturity	Many companies bring production capacity online. Products become standardized. Consumers are sufficiently knowledgeable to identify key value features. Competitive pricing begins in earnest. Pricing flexibility is limited.
Decline	The product has become standardized; the industry consolidates and is dominated by a relatively few large companies. High quality and many features are demanded. Low-price producers fight for market share. Non-low-cost producers are driven from the market. Customers become very price sensitive. The price becomes elastic.

Different products have different life cycles. Personal computers have gone from the hobby–experimentalist phase in the 1970s when computers were often sold as electronic kits to a commodity appliance. Some toys and novelties are introduced, grow, mature, and decline in 18 months.

Each phase of a product's life cycle gives rise to a different pricing strategy. First, recognize when prices are inelastic and maximize gross margin during those times by keeping price relatively high. Second, understand that eventually price competition is going to squeeze prices and profit margins, so plan to engineer costs down as the product matures. Third, the life cycle can be manipulated to a certain extent if the product is "reinvented," that is, if the product or its features are changed enough for the market to perceive it as "new" and reward that newness with premium prices.

TRANSFER PRICING

Large companies often have divisions that buy and sell from one another. The question is what should Division A of a company charge Division B for their products? Should they sell at cost? If so, what do we mean by cost? Full absorption cost or just variable cost?

Suppose Division A can sell a product in the marketplace for $40 per ton, but it only costs them $20 per ton to make. If Division A sells in the marketplace, its gross profit is increased by $20 maximizing its profitability. If Division B can't buy from Division A, it might have to go to the market to purchase its resources, increasing its cost and consequently reducing its profits.

It should be obvious that there is some degree of built-in rivalry between divisions, for maximizing the profit of one reduces the profit of the other.

A better question to ask is what maximizes the profits of the *whole company*? There is a rule of thumb that can be verified experimentally. The rule depends on whether the selling division is operating at full capacity or not. Note that this rule assumes the selling division has the option to, and capability of, selling its products in the marketplace.

Part I: If the selling division, Division A, is not operating at capacity, it should sell to Division B at variable cost. *Reasoning:* If

Division A is not operating at capacity, it should be indifferent to making one more unit for Division B provided that Division B reimburses it for its variable costs because there is *no lost opportunity* to sell that incremental unit at the market price.

Part II: If the selling division, Division A, is operating at capacity, it should sell to Division B at the market price. *Reasoning:* If Division A sells at cost to Division B, *it forgoes the opportunity* for a sale at market price.

Why is correct transfer pricing important? It is important so that each division will make economically rational decisions. In the absence of this kind of economic rule, divisions could be subsidizing one another, masking true costs and leading management to make incorrect decisions about product or division profitability.

Example 1

Paveco operates both a gravel pit and a road construction company, each of which is organized as a division of Paveco. The gravel pit has a capacity of one million tons per month, and can sell gravel for $20 per ton. Variable costs are $4 per ton. The gravel pit is operating at 400,000 tons per month when the construction company orders 500,000 tons of gravel. Since the gravel pit is operating at less than capacity, it can fulfill the construction division's order without loosing any outside sales. The gravel division sells to the construction company for $4 per ton.

Example 2

It is spring, and there is a building boom. The gravel division is operating at capacity when the construction division orders 500,000 tons of gravel. The gravel division offers to sell at $20 per ton. After some complaining, the purchasing manager for the construction company phones around to see if anybody can beat the gravel division's price. If he finds a company that will sell him gravel at $18 per ton, then the gravel division has maximized their (and the company's) profits, and the construction division has minimized their costs (and maximized the company's profits).

Example 3

Suppose the next best gravel price the construction company can find is $21 per ton? In that case, the construction company can buy from their sister division at the full price of $20, and still be ahead.

There is a dark side to transfer pricing. It is easy to see how costs, and therefore profits, can be shifted from division to division if transfer prices are set by company mandate rather than through economic optimization. The reason that many companies want to transfer profits from one division to another is that some divisions are in low-tax jurisdictions, and some are in high-tax jurisdictions.

Under some circumstances, the tax saving in successfully implementing such a strategy can be enormous, far greater than the informational value in making economically rational purchasing decisions. Of course, taxing authorities understand the potential for manipulation and carefully monitor transfer pricing.

OPPORTUNISTIC PRICING

There are often occasions when marketing wants to sell products for less than target prices to generate sales and cash flow, or to acquire market share. Manufacturing sometimes suggests accepting product orders below target prices to increase plant utilization. The question is whether, and when, such sales should be accepted.

Analytically, one should never sell for less than variable costs because each such sale would cost the company money. Variable costs include direct labor, direct materials, and variable factory overhead. Variable costs also include variable administrative expenses, if any, and sales commissions.

If a company sells for less than full absorption costs (which does not include commissions and variable administrative costs, but does include an allocation of fixed factory overhead), the company is at risk of being charged with predatory pricing. In addition, if it sells for less than full absorption cost, the difference would be booked at a loss.

So there are two ways of computing the minimum price a company should charge, variable costs and full absorption costs, and the higher of the two should set the minimum.

What about selling products or services below target profit margins? A great deal of experience has shown that if sales are made to regular customers below target prices, and therefore below target profit margins, it is very difficult to convince the customer to pay an increased price later. In effect, discounting creates new customer price expectations and may lower the psychological price point at which the customer is willing to buy.

So should target profit margins always be maintained? Not necessarily. There are three instances when opportunistic pricing, that is, pricing below normal targets, can be highly productive.

1. Different product: When the product offered is sufficiently different from the normal products offered to a customer that it won't change price expectations for regular products.
2. Market domination: When there is a drive for the dominant market share, and dominance brings with it some competitive advantage, for example, the ability to set standards and leverage that into future price increases.
3. Irregular customer: When the sale is made to someone who is not a regular customer and is not in the company's target market.

Example
Sprite Machinery makes small backhoes for light-duty work, like trenching fiber optic cables, landscaping, and for working in cramped quarters. Their variable costs are $10,800, their full absorption cost is $10,200, and their target profit margin is 40%, which means Sprite backhoes are priced at $17,000. They sell their backhoes from Maryland south to Florida, and west to the Mississippi. They have no interest in expanding nationwide. They planned to make 200 units this year, which would fully absorb their factory overhead of $500,000. However, demand is down, and the plant has scheduled the manufacture of only 180 units. A Canadian cable company offers to purchase 15 backhoes at $12,000 each. Should Sprite sell at that price?

If they sell for less than their variable costs of $10,800, they will be selling at an actual loss. If they sell for less than their full absorption cost of $10,200, they will be taking a loss on paper, and they risk charges of predatory pricing. So taking these two rules together, the minimum should be $10,800.

The next question is whether such a sale would lower the price point expectations of their regular customers. Since the Canadian cable company is well outside their usual target market, *and* the cable company is not likely to resell backhoes to Sprite's regular customers, this particular sale should not affect customer pricing expectations.

The economic analysis indicates that this offer should be accepted because it contributes $1,200 per unit to fixed costs ($12,000 − variable costs of $10,800); contributes $1,800 per unit to gross profits ($12,000 − full absorption cost of $10,200); and absorbs $37,500 of factory overhead, which would not otherwise be absorbed (15 units × $500,000 fixed manufacturing overhead/200 planned units).

MICROECONOMICS PRICING

Another way to understand pricing is through the lens of microeconomics. Classical theory says price is set by supply and demand, but what does that mean? And how does it inform pricing strategy?

Demand

Demand is the amount of a product customers are willing to buy at any given price. As a general rule, the higher the price, the less people demand. Conversely, the lower the price, the more people demand. The principal reason is the *substitution effect*. As price rises, people find more economical substitutes for the good being offered. As price drops, people substitute the good in question for other goods. Demand can be graphed as shown in Figure 16–4.

FIGURE 16–4

Demand Curve

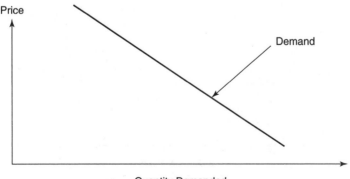

Supply

Supply is the amount producers are willing to supply at any given price. As a general rule, the higher the price, the more suppliers are willing to produce. The lower the price, the less suppliers are willing to produce. Supply can be plotted as shown in Figure 16–5.

Price Equilibrium

Price equilibrium occurs at the point at which the demand curve intersects the supply curve. At that price point, the quantity people are willing to supply exactly matches the amount people are willing to buy. This is sometimes called the market-clearing price because there are no unsold goods and no unmet demand. Figure 16–6 plots the supply and demand curves, and shows the equilibrium quantity is Q0 and the equilibrium price is P0.

What happens if a price is set too high? If price is too high, say, P1, people will purchase only Q1 units because, by definition, the demand curve is the quantity people will buy at any given price. Of course, at price P1, a company will want to produce Q2, giving rise to a surplus (inventory overstock) equal to Q2 − Q1. Figure 16–7 is an analysis of supply and demand if price is set above the equilibrium point.

FIGURE 16-5

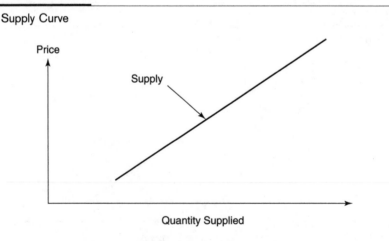

Supply Curve

FIGURE 16-6

Supply and Demand Curves with Equilibrium Price and Quantity

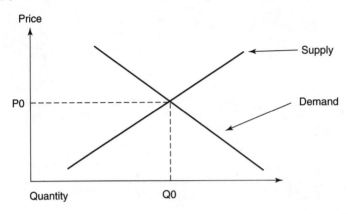

The flip side of surpluses is shortages. We can see the effect of setting price too low in Figure 16–8. If price is set below equilibrium, say, P2, then buyers will demand Q2 units, whereas suppliers will want to produce only Q1 units. This will create a shortage of Q2 − Q1. This is why price controls create shortages.

FIGURE 16-7

Analysis of Supply and Demand with Price Set Above the Equilibrium Point

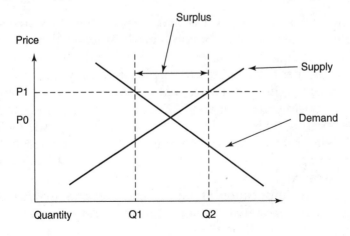

FIGURE 16-8

Analysis of Supply and Demand with Price Set Below the Equilibrium Point

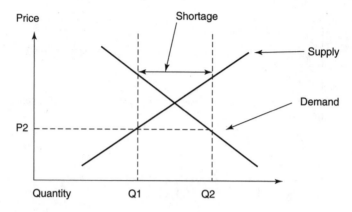

Strategic Implications of Supply and Demand

What are the strategic implications of this supply and demand analysis? First, the profitability of certain products, product lines, and even companies often depends on their reaching a certain sales volume. One way to reach those volume targets is to adjust price, sliding down the demand curve. However, few if any companies can reduce price indefinitely. So supply and demand analysis can be used to test the reasonableness of assumptions regarding unit sales volume.

The second implication is that chronic inventory overstocks are a signal that price may be too high. It is always less expensive to reduce production volumes and sell all goods than to keep production volumes high and retain surplus inventory for a prolonged period of time. The reasons are that (1) inventory ties up working capital, reducing the company's financial flexibility; (2) carrying charges such as warehousing, insurance, interest, and inventory taxes erode profit margins; (3) goods in storage frequently deteriorate from age, accident, or inadvertence; and (4) there is the risk of obsolescence.

The third implication of supply and demand analysis is that chronic shortages signal an opportunity to raise price. As price rises, fewer units will be demanded. However, the price of each unit sold will increase without adding to cost. Gross margins will therefore be greater.

Are companies the hapless victims of market forces? Are they leaves blowing in the wind? Not at all. Among the factors that shape demand curves are individual preferences or, stated differently, perceptions of value, and the availability of substitutes.

Shifting the Demand Curve

It is generally believed that individual perceptions of value can be manipulated through customer service, warranties, word of mouth, channels of distribution, and of course, advertising. Manipulation of perceptions can shift the demand curve to the right. Rightward movement of the demand curve means that more will be demanded at any given price. This causes the equilibrium price to increase.

Perceptions can also be negative. Consider what happened to the demand for Firestone Tires when it was alleged they were responsible for vehicle rollovers (a charge that Firestone denies). Nevertheless, the perception of that brand was negatively affected. The demand curve shifted left, that is to say, people are willing to buy less at any given price. The supply and demand curves for Firestone tires would then intersect at a lower combination of price and quantity.

Figure 16–9 is a graphic representation of the effect on equilibrium price of shifting the demand curve.

At price P0, Q0 units are demanded. However, if through advertising, or some other mechanism, perceptions are manipulated so that demand shifts to D1, the equilibrium price will shift from P0 to P1, while the quantity demanded will increase from Q0 to Q1. Likewise, if perceptions are negative, the demand curve will shift left causing price and quantity to drop to P2, Q2.

Product Differentiation

Supply and demand analysis assumes there are close substitutes for the goods a company produces. Fords and Mercurys are close substitutes. Fords, Mercurys, Chryslers, and Buicks might also be close substitutes. A Ford is a less perfect substitute for a Porsche. Intel and AMD microprocessors might be close substitutes, but IBM's OS2 was not a good substitute for Windows XP.

FIGURE   16-9

Effect on Equilibrium Price of Shifting the Demand Curve

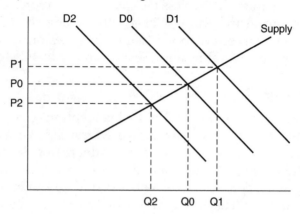

Where there are no close substitutes for a product, a firm is said to have *market power*, that is, they can control price and the quantity they want to produce over some range. Market power is usually used to keep price as high on the demand curve as possible. Firms with market power usually enjoy higher than average profits.

The pricing implication is that firms should make their products look and feel "unique." That is, they should have a combination of characteristics for which there are no close substitutes. This is why marketers are always trying to differentiate their products from others.

Consumer Surplus

An interesting feature of supply and demand is the unity of price. For most products, a market-clearing price is set where supply equals demand, but look at the graph closely. Consider the demand curve in Figure 16–10. There are some people on the curve who are willing to pay more than the market-clearing price, just as there are some people who would only buy below the market-clearing price.

Customer C1 is willing to pay price P1. The difference between the market-clearing price P and P1 represents "excess value"

FIGURE 16–10

Analysis of Prices Individual Customers Will Pay Compared to the
Market-Clearing Price

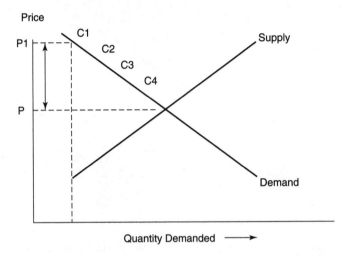

for customer C1. Economists call this "consumer surplus." Likewise, customers C2, C3, and C4 are all willing to pay more than the equilibrium price. In a perfect (seller's) world, a firm would be able to charge every customer exactly what the value of a good is to that customer. C4 would pay more than price P, C3 would pay more than C4, and so forth, maximizing revenue. There is a way to approximate this through market segmentation.

Market Segmentation

If a company can segregate its customers into groups with different demand curves, each of those groups will have a different price–quantity equilibrium point. The more demand curves a seller can isolate, the closer they can approximate the situation wherein they can charge each customer exactly what he or she is willing to pay. This is illustrated in Figure 16–11, which analyzes demand curves for different market segments, labeled MS1 for market segment number one, MS2 for market segment number two, and so forth.

FIGURE 16-11

Analysis of Price Points by Market Segment

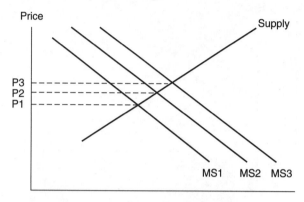

Quantity Demanded

Segmenting customers into different demand curves representing different market segments, MS1, MS2, MS3, yields different equilibrium prices, P1, P2, P3.

One can think of this as the market for premium, standard,
and economy products. Many strategies are used to segment customers, including the following:

1. Customer self-image: Customers that perceive themselves
   to be "upscale" might prefer channels of distribution that
   they consider more exclusive. These include department
   stores versus mass merchandisers.

2. Brand awareness: Heavy advertising causes people to
   perceive products as different when the differences may
   be skin deep.

3. Packaging: Packaging might convey the feeling that
   products are different, when they may be fundamentally
   the same.

4. Physical location: Goods sold in New York, London, or
   Paris might be perceived to be different from goods sold
   in Kansas City.

5. Features: Sometimes features that are minimal in cost and
   function can be used to differentiate products.

Many other factors can be used to segregate customers into market segments and therefore onto different demand curves. However, such segmentation will work only if some mechanism can be devised to prevent customers on the MS3 demand curve from purchasing at the prices available to those on the MS1 demand curve. Often those barriers are only psychological.

Pharmaceutical companies sell the same medicine for premium prices in the United States, for lower prices in Canada, and sometimes for very low prices in Africa and South America. They have lobbied for, and have obtained, laws that make it illegal to purchase their drugs in a lower priced country and then "reimport" them into the United States. For them, market segmentation is based on statute.

Most companies don't resort to legal action to support market segmentation. They segment through manipulation of perceptions and addition of features that only minimally affect cost, but have a major effect on the perceived value of the product. For example, Ford and Mercury share most of the same parts, but Mercurys generally command a higher price.

Brands and Imperfect Information

The supply and demand analyses we have examined so far assume customers have prefect information about the goods and services in the marketplace. But information is expensive, both in terms of the dollar cost of information and the time it takes to acquire information. As a result, few buyers have perfect information. They make a rational decision to accept a certain level of ignorance about goods in the marketplace. Rational ignorance balances the cost of incremental information against its value in terms of better purchasing decisions.

One way for purchasers to reduce the amount of information they need is to purchase goods with a reputation for quality and value. The symbol of that quality–value combination is embodied in a brand name. Campbell Soup, IBM, Toyota, McDonald's are all brand names with which purchasers associate a tremendous amount of information. For example, from the late 1960s to the early 1980s, the IBM brand name allowed it to price its computers 10% to 20% higher than those of competitors and still increase sales.

Many marketing studies indicate that purchasers want a sense of safety more than anything. Brands provide that sense of safety. In so doing, they increase perceptions of product value, and therefore shift the demand curve to the right. That gives rise to higher equilibrium prices for branded goods, assuming the brand has a favorable image.

SUMMARY

There are a variety of ways to set price. No one method is right under all circumstances. Cost-based pricing starts with the product's cost and a target gross margin and solves for the price. The problem with this approach is that it ignores market information about what people are willing and able to pay. As a result, prices might be set uncompetitively high with the risk of significantly reduced sales, or they may be set below market rates, forgoing available gross profit. The benefits of cost-centered pricing are that it's simple to use and easy to price with a target gross margin in mind.

Market-centered pricing holds that costs are irrelevant, provided that there is some gross profit. Identification of the correct prices for comparison is the key to using market-centered pricing. Competitors should be in the relevant geographic market and the same channel of distribution. Competitive prices change continuously, so it is important to have some mechanism to routinely collect pricing data. Value pricing is a form of market-centered pricing that compares price–performance ratios as opposed to comparing prices directly. The key to value pricing is determining the features that are the basis for determining price versus performance or price versus value.

Engineered cost starts with a forecast of what a product's price is going to be at some point in the future and subtracts the target gross profit to determine the maximum unit cost. Engineering and production refine design and manufacturing parameters until a product meets stated cost objectives. Engineered cost is useful in strategic analysis because it focuses on the needs of the market in the future.

Price elasticity is a concept that deals with the change in total revenue as a result of raising or lowing prices. If the price of an item is cut and the quantity demanded goes up so much that total revenue increases, the price is elastic. If the price of an item is cut and total revenue declines, the price is inelastic. Price elasticity is a measure of sensitivity to price. Where markets are inelastic, that is, not sensitive to price, price increases can generate more revenue on sales of fewer units. Caution is indicated when cutting prices in elastic markets. Though total revenue rises, so do the number of units sold and the cost of goods sold. From the perspective of the business, the real question should be does gross profit rise or fall. This can be determined only by modeling gross profit.

All products have a four-phase life cycle: introduction, growth, maturity, and decline. During introduction and growth, prices are usually inelastic, and premium prices should be sought. However, in maturity and decline, prices become elastic as customers become sensitive to price. The life cycle can be reset back toward the growth phase by "reinventing" the product so that it is perceived as new in the marketplace.

Transfer pricing deals with the issue of what one division of a company should charge another division for their product. Generally, where the selling division is working at less than capacity, it should sell to other divisions at variable cost because it is no burden to do so. On the other hand, if the selling division is working at capacity, the buying division should purchase at market rates so that the seller will not have to forgo available profits. Transfer pricing rules are designed to maximize overall company profit without having one division subsidize another and thereby mask the economic value of each.

Opportunistic pricing deals with circumstances in which sales should be made at less than the target price. Sales should never be made lower than variable costs because that would cause an economic loss on every unit. Sales should not be made at less than the cost of goods sold because that would result in a loss on the income statement. Selling below target prices is risky because it lowers customer price expectations. Selling below target prices can be useful when (1) the product is different from normal products; (2) there is a drive for market dominance, and dominance brings with it some competitive advantage, for example, the ability to set standards and leverage future price increases; or (3) the sale is made to someone who will never be a regular customer.

Microeconomics holds that the optimum price is the one at

which the supply and demand curves intersect. The demand curve is a graph of the quantity customers are willing to buy at any given price. It slopes down and to the right. The supply curve is the quantity that suppliers are willing to supply at any given price. It slopes up and to the right. At some price, the quantity of units demanded by customers exactly equals the quantity supplied by suppliers. This is the equilibrium, or market-clearing price. If prices are set higher than the equilibrium price, suppliers will produce more of a good than customers are willing to buy. This will result in overstocks. Excess inventory is therefore a signal that price is too high. If price is set below the equilibrium price, customers will demand more than suppliers are willing to supply, and there will be shortages. This is why price controls fail.

Shifting the demand curve to the right can increase both the equilibrium price and the quantity demanded. Demand is based on perceptions. Perceptions can be manipulated by customer service, warranties, word of mouth, channels of distribution, and advertising.

Some customers on the demand curve are willing to pay more than the market-clearing price. In a perfect sellers world, a company would be able to charge every customer the maximum he or she were willing to pay. This effect can be simulated if customers can be segmented into different markets with different demand curves. Those willing to pay more will be on a demand curve that intersects the supply curve at a higher price. However, one of the requirements for this segmentation to work is a mechanism to prevent customers from jumping to the lowest price demand curve. These mechanisms can be regulatory, geographic, or psychological.

Brands are an important factor in setting price. Traditional supply and demand relies on perfect information in the marketplace. However, perfect information is costly in terms of time and money. People are willing to accept less than perfect information if they can feel "safe" about a purchase, that is, if they can rely on the seller to do what is promised. Brands are a mechanism for carrying a tremendous amount of information about a product. Customers are usually willing to pay a premium for this information and the implied safety it carries. However, brands can have negative connotations as well. Therefore, protecting the brand and the premium it can command are very important.

Advanced Cost Concepts and Allocation of Resources

Business is complex, and management is always probing for ways to get new insights into company operations. This chapter discusses a variety of approaches to analyzing cost, performance, and allocation of resources that don't fit neatly within other chapters.

COST DRIVERS

The term *cost driver* is used in two different senses in accounting and financial literature. In activity-based costing, a cost driver is a means of allocating costs to products based on units of service. In a strategic planning context, a cost driver is a cost that dominates all other costs. Let us consider a cost driver in the strategic sense first.

Optimizing the operation of a production line, a factory, or a business depends on identifying those variables, functions, or materials that *dominate* a product's cost. Once primary cost drivers are identified, managerial and engineering effort can be focused on minimizing those costs and increasing efficiency. In the event that cost drivers cannot be controlled, for example, oil to an oil refinery, clear identification of cost drivers can help management more accurately predict how changes in the cost of resources are going

FIGURE 17-1

Analysis of Oil Refinery Cost Components

Cost Component	Amount	Percentage
Crude oil	$11,000,000	58%
Union labor	$ 3,000,000	16%
Interest	$ 2,500,000	13%
Catalysts	$ 1,000,000	5%
Fixed overhead	$ 1,000,000	5%
Other supplies	$ 500,000	3%
	$19,000,000	100%

to change product costs. Consider Figure 17–1, an analysis of the cost structure for an oil refinery.

In this example, the price of crude oil is the dominant cost driver, followed by union labor and interest. For management to optimize their refinery's economic performance, they should focus most heavily on controlling crude oil costs.

If oil prices rise 10% to $12,100,000, total production costs will rise to $20,100,000, or about 5.8%. However, if union labor rises 10% to $3,300,000, total production costs rise only 1.6%. This is not to say minimizing crude oil prices is important and minimizing labor costs isn't. Rather, this type of analysis helps management focus on the costs with the largest potential savings. For example, a 2% improvement in the yield from crude oil, $220,000 (2% × 11,000,000), is the same as making a 22% reduction in catalysts or fixed overhead.

Some of these cost drivers are variable costs, for example, crude oil, labor, and catalysts, and some are fixed or semivariable, for example, fixed overhead and interest. Some of these costs are part of the cost of goods sold, and some of these costs are not, specifically, interest. Nevertheless, the top three items represent 87% of costs. They are therefore the principal cost drivers for this refinery.

The advantages of using a cost driver analysis are that it is easy to use and it is easy to explain to the management responsible for these costs on a day-to-day basis. The disadvantage to this type of analysis is that it doesn't provide direct guidance for action.

ACTIVITY-BASED COSTING

Activity-based costing is built on the premise that specific activities, or functions, are necessary to transform raw materials into finished goods. Rather than just applying direct labor and indirect labor in bulk to a product to find its cost, activity-based costing uses *transforming* activities to allocate costs to various products or departments.

Example

Pitcarn Corporation makes pump housings of various sizes. The activities necessary to make a pump housing are casting, grinding, painting, inspecting, and testing. The casting department costs $120,000 per year for direct labor, the working supervisor, employee taxes, sand for molds, and fuel for the furnace. With this $120,000 per year, they can cast 36,000 pounds of pump housings, not including the price of the metal. If all pumps were of the same size and weight, the number of castings might be a good cost driver. Last year, the department cast 12,000 pump housings, which implies each pump should be charged $10 for casting department work ($120,000/12,000 pumps).

Suppose pump housings vary widely in weight, that is, by a factor of 2 or more. In that case, pounds per castings might be a better cost driver. A pump housing weighing 2 pounds would be charged $6.67 (2 pounds × $120,000/36,000 pounds of castings). On the other hand, a 20-pound pump housing would be charged $66.67 (20 pounds × $120,000/36,000 pounds of castings).

Another possible cost driver is the number of hours it takes to cast a particular size pump. Last year, the casting department applied 6,000 labor hours to making castings. A pump housing that takes 15 minutes of casting labor would be charged $5 of casting department costs (1/4 hour × $120,000/6,000 labor hours), whereas a pump housing that takes 2 hours to cast would be charged $40 (2 hours × $120,000/6,000 hours).

Again ask, why are we doing this? What difference could it make? The reasons a company needs to understand their cost structure *in depth* include the following:

1. Identification of expensive operations so they can be re-engineered
2. To better understand the profitability of a particular product mix
3. For pricing decisions
4. To better understand what it takes to become a low-cost producer

Pitcarn Corporation's management may want to employ activity-based costing to measure productivity, determine the optimum product mix, or determine whether costs could be reduced if processes were re-engineered or automation introduced. They might even be trying to decide whether they should subcontract out certain functions. To do that, they need to follow a number of rules so that their analyses provide consistent results. Two of these include

1. Cost of labor should include employer taxes, and ideally workers' compensation costs (since it is illegal not to pay these costs) and fringe benefits, if any.
2. When departmental costs are being considered, the cost of working supervisors should be considered *with their related employer taxes, workers' compensation, and fringe benefits.*

Example
Pitcarn Corporation's casting department has the following costs:

6,000 hours direct labor	$10/hr
Department supervisor salary	$30,560
2,000 gallons of fuel oil	$0.90/gallon
Sand, tools, and misc. supplies	$5,000
Sales commission	$20/pump
Employer taxes	15%
Workers' comp.	6%
Fringe benefits	4%

What is the allocable cost of the casting department?

Labor = (6,000 hr × $10/hr + $30,560)
        × (1 + [15% employer tax + 6% workers' comp.
        + 4% fringe])
      = $90,560 × (1 + 25%) = $113,200

Other costs = 2,000 gallons of fuel oil × $0.90 + $5,000 sand, etc.
            = $6,800

Total cost to allocate: $113,200 + $6,800 = $120,000

Sales commission, though a variable cost associated with each pump, is not included as a cost for activity-based costing purposes.

In trying to decide whether something should be included with a department's cost for purposes of activity-based costing, ask whether the cost is necessary for the department to do its job. If we were considering the casting department, we would not include costs for accounting, payroll, or human resources *for activity-based costing*. Why? We might allocate accounting, payroll, or HR for some cost purposes, but activity-based costing relates more *directly to producing the product*.

Should we include facility costs? This is somewhat problematic. If the casting department is in a large building with the company's other activities, we might not allocate it, focusing more narrowly on the incremental costs of running the department. However, if the casting department overflowed into a building that the company had to rent, that incremental cost would probably be considered part of the cost of the casting department. Ask the question, if this activity were subcontracted out, would the cost be eliminated? This is an extremely important issue in corporate restructuring because outsourcing has proved to be a good way to optimize production costs.

JOB COSTING

The cost concepts we have discussed so far are primarily used in process costing. Process costing is appropriate where there are a large number of homogeneous items, that is, items with the same characteristics. As items become more expensive, they are often customized. As a result, the cost of two items produced by the same company may be radically different. The classic example is a builder who builds a four-bedroom, three-bathroom house for one client, and a three-bedroom, two-bathroom house for another.

Concepts used to account for customization are also used to account for things like professional services. In such cases, accounts are set up for each customer (frequently called work in process, or WIP, accounts) and costs are allocated to accounts as services are rendered. Examples include attorney time (for a law firm), medical costs (for a hospital), or architect's time (for a construction project).

The process begins by creating a journal entry that is posted to a T-account (one side of which is customer WIP). These T-accounts are eventually relieved, and customer WIP is transferred to cost of goods sold.

There are two important rules for journal entries and T-accounts. First, each journal entry must balance, that is, the debits (left side) must equal the credits (right side).

Second, the sum of all the debits, in all a company's T-accounts, must equal the sum of all of their credits. This second rule is embodied in the equation

$$\text{Assets} = \text{Liabilities} + \text{Owner's equity} + \text{Revenue} - \text{Expenses}$$
$$(\text{Eq. 17--1})$$

This equation also provides an important clue to whether something is a debit or a credit. Notice assets are on the left (or debit) side of the equal sign. When assets increase (as we hope they will), the entry is a debit. When assets decrease (as they sometimes must—after all what is the point of having cash if you can't spend it), the entry is a credit.

Example
Murray, an architect, has an associate and a secretary. He pays the associate $30 per hour and the secretary $15 per hour. They work 40 hours, making their salaries $1,200 ($30 × 40) and $600 ($15 × 40), respectively, for a total of $1,800 per week. What is the journal entry to record their wages?

	Debit	Credit
Payroll expense	$1,800	
Cash		$1,800

Note that the journal entry balances, and the total of Murray's debits balance total credits.

Of the 40 hours the associate worked, 20 hours are billable to Sam's Bar & Grill, and 10 hours are billable to Mrs. Jones. Since Murray expects projects for these clients to continue for some time, he sets up work in process (WIP) accounts to capture project costs.

As a result, Murray *reclassifies* $600 (20 hours × $30 per hour) of his payroll expense to Sam's WIP account, and $300 ($30 × 10) to Mrs. Jones's WIP account.

	Debit	Credit
Sam's WIP	$600	
Mrs. Jones's WIP	$300	
Payroll expense		$900

Why bother? For one thing, the WIP account data will be used to compute cost of goods sold; for another, WIP account data will be used as the basis of client billing. Billing the client is the second most important thing a company does. The most important, of course, is to get paid.

Reallocating payroll expense to clients is also important to identify and track unbilled time. Notice in the example that the associate was paid for 40 hours, but only had 30 billable hours! This unbilled, or unbillable, time is somewhat like unallocated factory overhead in that it represents waste. (In the real world, an architect's associate, lawyer, accountant, or consulting engineer is expected to bill 50 hours for every forty they are paid!)

Two additional journal entries are usually made to close out a project. First, *bill the client*. Suppose Murray marks up costs by 150% for billing purposes, then the work for Sam would be billed at $1,500 ($600 + 150% × $600), and the work for Mrs. Jones would be billed at $750 ($300 + 150% × $300).

	Debit	Credit
Accounts receivable—Sam's	$1,500	
Accounts receivable—Mrs. Jones	$ 750	
Revenue		$2,250

Second, relieve (that is, zero out) the WIP accounts.

	Debit	Credit
Cost of goods (services) sold	$900	
WIP—Sam's		$600
WIP—Mrs. Jones's		$300

Why is it important for management to know this kind of detail? First, management must have some common vocabulary they can use to discuss issues with the accounting department. If you, management, are talking in Pascals, and they are talking in Newtons per meter squared, or you are talking in degrees Kelvin when they are talking in degrees Centigrade, the results could be nasty. Second, accurate job costing can influence calculations of gross profit (and bonuses) and can influence future pricing and follow-on sales.

Consider an example using union labor. Suppose Burlington Bridge Constructors has two projects going on simultaneously. One at Pequad Creek, and one at Hope Creek. The United Iron Workers Union has contracted 10 men, 40 hours per week for 2 weeks (800 total labor hours) at $25 per hour. Payroll is therefore $20,000, and the journal entry is

	Debit	Credit
Payroll	$20,000	
Cash		$20,000

One issue to consider when contracting for a block of time, whether from a union, consulting company, or temp company, is that productive utilization of that time is the responsibility of you the purchaser. The WIP journal entries, assuming 400 hours of union labor were allocated to Hope Creek, and 350 hours were allocated to Pequad, follow:

	Debit	Credit
Hope Creek WIP ($25 × 400)	$10,000	
Pequad Creek WIP ($25 × 350)	$ 8,750	
Overhead unallocated labor ($25 × 50)	$ 1,250	
Payroll		$20,000

Construction companies, especially those that broker union labor on cost plus fixed fee contracts, can only bill labor allocated to a project. Since 50 of the 800 labor hours are not allocated, they are unbillable under a cost plus contract. This unbillable time is usually closed out to an overhead expense account. This form of overhead is important to track because it represents a form of waste that is a measure of project management efficiency. After this entry, all labor hours are totally accounted for, and the payroll expense account is relieved (returned to zero).

COST DRIVERS AS A METHOD FOR OVERHEAD ALLOCATION

Overhead is often allocated to production departments for budgeting purposes. Suppose departments A and B are payroll and data processing, respectively. They might allocate their costs to production departments C and D based on the cost drivers of number of employees and number of computer hours, respectively. For example,

> Payroll department costs are $6,000 per month. Data processing costs are $20,000.
>
> Department C has 25 employees and uses 50 hours of computer time a month.
>
> Department D has 75 employees and uses 450 hours of computer time a month.

Total C + D employees = 100. Department C has 25% (25 employees/100 total in the production departments); 75% (75 employees/100 total employees in the production departments) are in department D.

> Department C payroll overhead costs: 25% × $6,000 = $1,500
>
> Department D payroll overhead costs: 75% × $6,000 = $4,500

Total C + D computer hours = 500. Department C uses 10% (50 hours/500 hours); 90% (450 hours/50 hours) are used by department D.

> Department C computer costs: 10% × $20,000 = $2,000
>
> Department D computer costs: 90% × $20,000 = $18,000

What about allocating payroll and computer costs to overhead departments A and B? Under many schemes, overhead is allocated only to production departments on the theory that if production increases or decreases, allocable overhead will likewise increase or decrease. If a production department is eliminated altogether, for example, if a department's work is outsourced, the related overhead will be eliminated as well. Other arguments for allocating overhead to production departments are (1) production will be incentivised to use as little of the overhead resource as possible if they know they are being charged for usage, and (2) production departments will put pressure on overhead departments to minimize costs since ultimately those costs are borne by production.

TRADITIONAL OVERHEAD ALLOCATION

A more traditional method of allocating costs, especially nonproduction or overhead costs, is to allocate costs in layers. Three common layers for cost allocation are production departments, overhead departments, and overhead costs (not directly created by a department).

For example, if rent is $20,000 per month for an office of 20,000 square feet, rent may be allocated to departments (both overhead and production) based on the number of square feet they use. The cost of the building's alarm system might be allocated on square feet, or it might be so minimal it is aggregated with other miscellaneous facility costs before allocation.

Example
Rent is $20,000 per month, alarm systems $200 per month, guards $5,000 per month, and utilities $2,000 per month. Total facility cost would then be $20,000 + $200 + $5,000 + $2,000 = $27,200 per month. If the facility were 20,000 square feet, the cost per month per square foot would be $1.36/square foot/month.

If overhead departments A and B used 1,000 and 4,000 square feet, respectively, their facility charge would be $1,360 (1,000 × $1.36) and $5,440 (4,000 × $1.36), respectively. If production departments C and D used 5,000 and 10,000 square feet, their charges would be $6,800 (5,000 × $1.36) and $13,600 (10,000 × $2.36), respectively.

Another common method to allocate overhead costs is based on a percentage of direct costs. For example, departments A, B, C, and D might have direct costs of $50,000, $150,000, $300,000, and

$500,000, making total direct costs $1,000,000. Direct costs usually include salaries, materials, and any other cash expenditures made on behalf of the department. If overhead, that is, the president's salary, the secretary's salary, and the cost of a leased Porsche for the president totaled $200,000 per year, it would be allocated to the departments as follows: department A, $10,000 ($200,000 × [$50,000/$1,000,000]); department B, $30,000 ($200,000 × [$150,000/ $1,000,000]); department C, $60,000; and department D, $100,000. You can see that in every case the overhead allocation is the same percent of direct costs. Therefore, overhead is often referred to as the "percent of overhead burden." There are an endless variety of methods for allocation overhead. The balance to be achieved is between cost and the benefit the information will provide. The important thing is to have a rational and consistent basis for the allocation.

Caution: Sometimes overelaborate overhead or cost allocation schemes lead to the wrong economic outcome. For example, one corporation located in eastern Pennsylvania had 17 divisions, and corporate overhead was allocated to each. Each operation was profitable on its own, but when corporate overhead was allocated, the smallest division showed a loss. The company sold that division, and a year later, after allocating corporate overhead to the remaining 16 divisions, it again found that divisions were profitable on their own, but one division was unprofitable after corporate overhead was allocated. They then sold the "unprofitable" division. On reallocating overhead to the remaining fifteen divisions, they found they still had one "unprofitable" division.

Each time they sold a division, the remaining divisions were burdened with a greater share of the corporation's overhead, which never decreased and always grew. The problem was not in the profitability of the divisions but that the corporation's overhead was excessive.

JOINT PRODUCTS:
TWO PRODUCT PROBLEM

Companies must often decide whether to sell raw material, perform some processing on the material, or process material into finished goods. This decision, sometimes called the two product problem, is informed by the contribution margin at each stage of production. If further processing decreases the contribution margin, then further processing should be avoided and the goods sold as is. If the contribution margin is the same whether the goods are partly or completely processed, the goods should be sold earlier in the process rather than later because additional processing ties up working capital. In this decision model, it is assumed the equipment to process goods to completion is available.

Example

Alpha Computer makes power supplies that have a variable cost of $18 and sell for $30. Alpha also has the ability to assemble computers by adding purchased components to their power supplies. Variable costs for the finished computers are $250, and they can sell them for $300. Should Alpha sell power supplies, or add other components and sell finished computers?

The contribution margin on power supplies is 40% ([$30 − $18]/ $30), whereas the contribution margin on computers is only 16.7% ([$300 − $250]/$300). Therefore, the company should prefer the sale of power supplies.

THEORY OF CONSTRAINTS

In most systems, operations, factories, there is one variable, one thing that limits the production of the enterprise. For example, airports often find their passenger capacity is limited by the number of airline docking gates. Fewer gates mean fewer planes can land and take off, thereby limiting passengers.

The purposes of the theory of constraints are to (1) help management identify the critical, or limiting, resource so that attention can be focused narrowly on acquiring more of that resource, (2) avoid acquiring resources that cannot be used because of constraints elsewhere in the system, and (3) quantify the marginal revenue to be gained through a marginal increase in the constraining resource.

A branch of operations research called linear programming has developed to analyze resource allocation. Linear programming is both sophisticated and complex. It is also beyond the scope of this book. However, the concept of constraints is not.

Example

August is running a bakery, selling bread for $1.50 per loaf. She has a hundred pounds of flour, fifty pounds of yeast, and a dozen eggs. What's the problem? Not enough eggs. Assume for purposes of this illustration that the recipe for bread is 1 pound flour, 2 cups of water, 3 eggs, and an ounce of yeast (don't try to bake bread from these ingredients). How do we analytically determine where the constraint is? One way is to list all the raw materials, then divide each material by the amount of that material in a unit of production, to determine how many units that resource can support. The material that provides the least units is the constraint. Figure 17–2 is an analysis of bakery resources.

In this example, the constraint is on the number of eggs. So the answer is to buy more eggs. Not more flour, not more yeast. So this analysis has met the first and second objectives of the theory of constraints, that is, to identify the constraining resource and avoid acquiring nonconstraining resources. That raises the question, how many eggs can we buy before we encounter the next constraint?

Examining Figure 17–2, we find that the next lowest number of loaves, 100, is for flour. We already have enough eggs to bake 4 loaves of bread, but we need enough eggs to bake an additional 96 loaves (100 − 4). Since it takes 3 eggs to bake a loaf, we need 288 eggs (3 × 96), or 24 dozen (288/12 eggs/dozen). The analysis can continue to find out how much flour and eggs are needed to consume all the yeast.

The incremental cost of eggs is $21.60 ($0.90/dozen × 24 dozen). However, the incremental revenue from this investment is

FIGURE 17-2

Analysis of Bakery Resources

Ingredient	Cost Unit	Amount in Inventory	Units per Loaf	Max No. of Loaves
Flour	$0.20/pound	100 pounds	1 pound	100
Yeast	$8/pound	50 pounds	1 ounce	800*
Water	$0.001/gallon	Unlimited	2 cups	Unlimited
Eggs	$0.90/dozen	12	3	4

*One ounce to the loaf of bread, 16 ounces per pound × 50 pounds = 800 ounces = 800 loaves.

CHAPTER 17

$144 (96 loaves × $1.50). Clearly, it is advantageous to buy more eggs and expand production. This satisfies the third objective of constraint theory, which is to determine the marginal revenue and cost of acquiring more of the constraining resource.

The theory of constraints can also be applied to factory equipment, component parts, trucks, people, and so forth.

Consider the example of Pitcarn Pumps, which has three pump product lines: (1) agricultural, which sells pumps for irrigation; (2) municipal, which sells pumps for sewage lines; and (3) commercial, which sells pumps for HVAC equipment. Within Pitcarn's plant, there are four operations: foundry, to make pump housings; machining, to grind and fabricate parts; assembly; and testing. Each of these four operations has a maximum capacity of 600 hours per week. Data on manufacturing costs and capacity are given in Figure 17–3.

Another foundry will cost $500,000 but will double foundry capacity. Milling machines can be added to the factory floor for $40,000, and each milling machine will increase capacity by 120 hours per week. Another assembly line can be constructed for $200,000, but it will double capacity. Another testing facility can be added for $30,000, which will increase test capacity by 120 hours per week.

In its current configuration, what variable (operation) provides the constraint on plant capacity? Note that the gross margin for agricultural pumps is 33% ($300/$900); for municipal pumps

FIGURE 17–3

Analysis of Pitcarn Pumps Manufacturing Operations

	Agricultural Pumps		Municipal Pumps		Commercial Pumps	
Price	$900		$4,000		$600	
Variable costs	$600		$2,000		$400	
Contribution margin	$300	Plant Capacity	$2,000	Plant Capacity	$200	Plant Capacity
Foundry hours per unit	1.5	400 pumps	10.0	60 pumps	1.0	600 pumps
Machining hours	2.0	300 pumps	20.0	30 pumps	1.5	400 pumps
Assembly hours	1.0	600 pumps	3.0	200 pumps	0.5	1,200 pumps
Testing hours	0.5	1,200 pumps	2.0	300 pumps	0.5	1,200 pumps

it is 50% ($2,000/$4,000); and for commercial pumps it is 33% ($200/$600). Since municipal pumps provide the greatest contribution margin, we should begin the analysis there. We see the limiting constraint is machining hours, which limits production to 30 pumps per week. By adding enough capacity to machine another 30 pumps per week, we reach the next level constraint, which is on foundry capacity. Since each municipal pump requires 20 machining hours, the total number of machining hours necessary is 600 hours (20 hours × 30 pumps). If each milling machine can provide 120 hours, the number of machines needed is 5 (600/120).

The incremental annualized revenue is $6,240,000 ($4,000 per pump × 30 pumps × 52 weeks) compared to an incremental annualized cost of $3,720,000 (variable costs of $2,000 × 30 units/week × 52 weeks plus $600,000 for 5 milling machines costing $120,000 each; assume milling machines have a one year life for this example). Where the incremental revenue exceeds the incremental cost for resources, resources should be acquired to eliminate the constraint.

As long as Pitcarn can sell all the municipal pumps they can make, they should continue to add capacity in this high margin product line, provided incremental revenue exceeds incremental cost. However, if market demand shifts to other product lines, the constraint analysis will have to be performed anew.

Note: In this problem, we are concerned with purchase of capital equipment, not expendable resources. So although comparing incremental cost to incremental revenue is useful for a cash flow analysis, this approach should not be used to forecast sales and profits.

PROFIT LADDER

A profit ladder is a way of analyzing profitability by applying the least costly resources to the highest priced products first, then applying higher cost resources to lower priced products. The objective is to find out whether high gross margin products are covering losses on low or negative margin products. This is often a problem when production is being outsourced on a product-by-product basis without considering the firm's production cost structure as a whole.

Consider the example of a company that provided service on an hourly basis. The services produced by this company's subcontractors were identical to company-produced services and to each other so that units were interchangeable from a customer perspective.

This particular company prided themselves on making a profit on every contract. On analyzing their business, it was found that they had a contract billable at $31/hr that they subcontracted out for $23 per hour; a contract billable at $25/hr that they subcontracted out for $19 per hour; a contract billable at $21/hr that they subcontracted out for $16 per hour; and a contract billable at $19/hr that they subcontracted out for $15 per hour. For simplicity sake, assume each contract was for 10,000 hours of work per month. They summarized their contracts in Figure 17–4.

The company was very pleased with themselves until an outside consultant suggested they rearrange their contracts and subcontractors into a profit ladder, that is paring the highest revenue contract with the least costly resources. When they did, as shown in Figure 17–5, they found things were different from what they expected.

Notice that (1) by rearranging the allocation of subcontractors to contracts, neither total revenue, total expenses, nor total gross profit changed; and (2) the $19/hr contract was a loser. The recommendation was obvious; terminate the $19 per hour contract, and discontinue use of the $23 per hour subcontractor. Implementing those recommendations increased gross margin by $40,000 per month.

FIGURE 17–4

Current Analysis of Subcontractor Gross Profits

Contracts	I	II	III	IV	Total
Billable rate per hour	$31	$25	$21	$19	
Subcontract rate per hour	$23	$19	$16	$15	
Gross profit per hour	$ 8	$ 6	$ 5	$ 4	
Gross profit per contract	$80,000	$60,000	$50,000	$40,000	$230,000

FIGURE 17-5

Profit Ladder Analysis of Subcontractor Gross Profits

	I	II	III	IV	Total
Billable rate per hour	$31	$25	$21	$19	
Subcontract rate per hour	$15	$16	$19	$23	
Gross profit per hour	$16	$ 9	$ 2	−$ 4	
Gross profit per contract	$160,000	$90,000	$20,000	−$40,000	$230,000

A profit ladder analysis of Ashville Airlines is more complex because all resources are not exactly alike. Ashville Airlines covers five daily routes. They have a flat rate structure of $80 per person per trip. An analysis of operating costs and route revenue follows. All five routes are fewer than 400 miles, and any plane can fly to any city on their route. Ashville is a startup airline and cannot afford to fund losing routes. Figure 17–6 is an analysis of current air operations.

Suppose we perform a profit ladder analysis, matching the lowest cost resources with the highest revenue sources. Can gross profits be increased? This is not a "pure" profit ladder analysis because plane capacity limits the extent to which resources can be reallocated to revenue sources. Figure 17–7 is a profit ladder analysis of air operations.

FIGURE 17-6

Analysis of Current Air Operations

Route	Plane	Plane Capacity	Daily Operating Costs	Average Passengers per Trip	Trips per Day	Revenue	Daily Gross Profit
Route I	A	100	$11,000	60	4	$19,200	$ 8,200
Route II	B	75	$ 9,000	40	4	$12,800	$ 3,800
Route III	C	60	$ 8,000	35	4	$11,200	$ 3,200
Route IV	D	60	$ 7,000	30	4	$ 9,600	$ 2,600
Route V	E	40	$ 6,000	25	4	$ 8,000	$ 2,000
			$41,000			$60,800	$19,800

FIGURE 17-7

Profit Ladder Analysis of Air Operations

Route	Plane	Average Passengers per Trip	Average Revenue 4 Trips × $80	Cost per Plane	Gross Profit
I	B	60	19,200	9,000	10,200
II	D	40	12,800	7,000	5,800
III	E	35	11,200	6,000	5,200
IV	C	30	9,600	8,000	1,600
V	A	25	8,000	11,000	−3,000
			60,800	41,000	19,800

The lowest cost resource, plane E, doesn't have the capacity to handle the traffic for the high revenue route, I, so it is eliminated. Planes C and D, the next lowest cost resources, have the capacity only to service the average number of passengers. Since, statistically, the average is near the middle of the number expected, they only minimally satisfy the capacity criteria. Let plane B serve route I.

The lowest cost, unallocated resource, plane E, just barely meets the average demand for route II. Assign plane D, the next lowest cost resource, to route II.

The lowest cost, unallocated resource, plane E, covers more than the average number of passengers on route III and is assigned.

The next lowest cost, unallocated resource, plane C, is more than capable of covering route IV and is assigned there. The remaining plane, A, is assigned to the remaining route, V.

The total revenue of $60,800 remains unchanged by this analysis, as does the total cost of $41,000. However, if we look at the allocation of resources from the profit ladder point of view, we see that we are "loosing" $3,000 per day on route V, using plane A. Stated another way, gross profit would increase from $19,800 to $22,800 per day if route V were eliminated and planes were reallocated using a profit ladder approach. Annualizing this, we can increase gross profit $1,095,000 per year.

The increase is achieved by not incurring plane A's operating cost. Nowhere in this analysis have we discussed whether a resource like plane A should have been acquired. We are analyzing only incremental revenue and operating costs. Over the long haul, if passenger patterns hold, plane A should be sold to purchase a less expensive plane, like E, that can profitably service route V.

NEW PRODUCT SELECTION

Companies make decisions to add or drop products all the time. Such decisions turn on both sales volume and profitability. As products become less profitable, a natural consequence of product maturity (see "Product Life Cycle" in Chapter 16), companies assess four methods of improving product performance.

1. Cut costs through product redesign, simplification, and improvements in the production process.
2. Subcontract out all production, shifting company operations to sales, distribution, and service.
3. Increase the investment in advertising, sales, and marketing to take market share from competitors.
4. Reinvent the product by adding enough new features so that the market will perceive it as new and reward that newness with increased pricing tolerance.

If these four approaches cannot restore a product to profitability, it may be terminated. The question then becomes, what will take the place of the retired product? A related issue unfolds if a successful company decides to expand. What new products should be added to the product line?

A threshold question is whether the company is going to remain in their current industry, however broadly that is defined. Assume for a moment they are going to stay in their own industry; that then provokes a series of other questions.

1. How is the industry defined? If they make frozen green beans, is frozen corn in the industry? How about frozen chicken patties? Frozen dinners? Ice cream? The common links are grocery stores as the channel of distribution; and these are all food products that must be manufactured, stored, transported, and retailed with refrigeration in mind.

If they make frozen green beans, are canned beans in their industry? How about dried beans? Fresh beans? The common links are grocery store distribution and beans as a product.

2. What is the gross margin on candidate products? What is the gross margin on other products in their industry? Is the gross margin on beans, corn, chicken patties or dinners more or less? A manufacturer might be surprised at the candor and openness of their clients in terms of providing information on competitors.

3. Is there enough sales volume to justify product development and manufacture? If a company has to choose between a $10 product with a 50% gross margin and estimated sales volume of 100,000 units, and a $10 product with a 25% sales margin with an estimated sales volume of 1,000,000 units, which should they choose? The first product, even though it has twice the margin, will yield only a gross profit of $500,000 ($10 × 50% × 100,000), whereas the second product will yield a gross profit of $2.5 million ($10 × 25% × 1,000,000).

4. What is the required investment in product development, plant, property, equipment, and marketing? This is a capital budgeting question. Cost outlays and projected cash inflows can be estimated and discounted to provide the net present value and internal rate of return on a new product. This assessment becomes relatively more important when (1) the product is very different from existing products, (2) large investments in plant and equipment are required, (3) heavy marketing and advertising expenditures are anticipated to introduce the product, or (4) it is expected to take a long time to recover the initial investment.

Consider Chemco, a company that make insecticides and sells them through neighborhood garden centers. Though once profitable, margins on these products are being squeezed by increased government regulations and competitor's pricing. Regional sales managers have surveyed the garden centers in their areas for both the products they carry and the gross margin on those products.

They estimate they could capture 10% of the sales volume in any product category in Figure 17–8 within a year.

Pheromone-based bee traps have the highest gross margin at 55%, whereas vegetable fertilizer is likely to provide the highest gross profit. Although gross margin and the gross profit do not always point to the same product, they can provide powerful tools to inform the decision-making process. A capital budgeting analysis might provide a clear winner among the possible choices because a capital budgeting analysis will consider (1) development costs—a cash outflow; (2) initial marketing, advertising, and introduction costs—a cash outflow; and (3) costs for new plant, equipment, and working capital—another cash outflow versus the cash inflows over the life of the product. A good capital budgeting analysis will also consider the growth or decline of sales over the life of the product.

5. Another consideration when evaluating a new product is how the company's existing brand image works for or against that product. A new Steinway organ might achieve instant acceptance. On the other hand, a Steinway television might meet with resistance since the new product is inconsistent with the existing brand image.

FIGURE 17–8

Chemco New Product Research

Analysis of Garden Center Products	Wholesale Price	Gross Margin	Est. Sales Volume	Gross Sales	Gross Profit
A. Ant spray	$2.00	30%	100,000	200,000	60,000
B. Ant traps—chemical	$0.90	32%	60,000	54,000	17,280
C. Ant traps—pheromone based	$3.00	52%	8,000	24,000	12,480
D. Bee traps—pheromone based	$6.00	55%	5,000	30,000	16,500
E. Dandelion killer	$2.10	25%	200,000	420,000	105,000
F. Fertilizer—flowering plants	$1.25	22%	220,000	275,000	60,500
G. Fertilizer—lawn	$2.00	20%	500,000	1,000,000	200,000
H. Fertilizer—lawn, organic	$4.00	35%	120,000	480,000	168,000
I. Fertilizer—vegetable	$2.75	30%	250,000	687,500	206,250
J. Fertilizer—vegetable, organic	$3.50	40%	15,000	52,500	21,000
K. Weed killer—chemical	$2.00	33%	60,000	120,000	39,600
L. Weed killer—natural ingredients	$3.00	40%	20,000	60,000	24,000

SUMMARY

Cost analysis and resource allocation go hand in hand because they are designed to provide management with new, decision-making, insight. The term *cost drivers* is used in both a strategic and cost accounting sense. In a strategic sense, it means the key variables that dominate cost. Changing these key variables by a few percent often has greater impact than eliminating whole other cost categories.

Activity-based costing springs from the premise that products are the result of certain transforming processes, and these processes should be the basis of cost allocation. Here the term *cost driver* means the units of the transforming process. For example, machining department costs should be allocated to products based on how much machining is required by each product.

Job costing is an approach that aggregates costs for each product or service in a work in process (WIP) account that is transformed into cost of goods (or services) sold at period end. Job costing is most likely to be used for expensive, customized products such as some houses, hospital care, or legal services.

Cost drivers can be used to allocate overhead as well as direct costs. The cost driver for payroll department expenses might be the number of employees in production departments; the cost driver for computer department expenses might be the amount of computer time used. More traditional ways of allocating overhead are by the number of square feet a production department uses for facility costs or total direct labor for corporate overhead. The important thing in deciding on a cost allocation system is to balance complexity and cost against the incremental value of information to management.

Companies must often decide whether to sell raw material, perform some processing on the material, or process material into finished goods. This is called the two product problem. The decision rule is to maximize the contribution margin. If the contribution is highest in raw form, sell raw material.

In most production facilities, there is some constraint, or some resource, that limits total production. Operations research has developed a sophisticated method of resource allocation called linear programming to address this class of problem. However, there is no need to resort to linear programming for most problems. Usually constraints can be identified along with necessary corrective action by creating a table that lists functional plant capacity for several areas, the amount of resources a product needs, and the volume of products each function can create. The same type of analysis can be used for component parts or ingredients. The resource with the lowest unit capacity, or the resource that can produce the fewest products, is the constraint. The decision whether to add resources until another variable constrains the system is based on whether incremental revenue is greater than incremental cost.

Decisions on pricing and profitability are often made one product at a time or one contract at a time. A profit ladder is a way of analyzing profitability by applying the least costly resources to the highest priced products first, then applying higher cost resources to lower priced products. The objective is to find out whether high gross margin products are covering losses on low or negative margin products. Its benefit springs from the systemic nature of the analysis in which incremental revenue and expenses are paired.

Companies constantly evaluate products and product mix. The analysis of new product introduction is the same as the evaluation of replacement products for those that have been dropped. If a product is underperforming, four things can be done to resuscitate it: (1) cut manufacturing costs, (2) outsource production and concentrate on sales and service, (3) increase the investment in sales and advertising, and (4) reinvent the product so that it is perceived as new. If none of that works, the product is often dropped. That raises the question of evaluating new products to take its place. Five issues must be evaluated when considering a new or replacement product: (1) should the company stay in the same industry or try a new one; (2) what is the gross margin of potential products; (3) what is the gross profit of potential new products; (4) if research, development, plant retooling, and product introduction were compared to cash inflows from the product using capital budgeting models, how would it fair; and (5) is the new product consistent enough with the company's brand image to be credible in the market? Financial analysis can go a long way in addressing these issues, but in the end, management must apply its judgment to the facts of each particular situation.

CHAPTER 18

Labor Costs

Labor is one of the most significant costs of any company. Even in a tight labor market, this cost is highly controllable. In this chapter, we will analyze a number of ways to manage labor costs.

OVERTIME

Overtime must be paid to nonexempt workers who work over 40 hours per week. Exempt workers are managers and professionals who have decision-making responsibility that can affect a company's direction. Everyone else is non-exempt. Overtime is paid at one and a half times regular pay rates. Some union contracts require workers to be paid double time for holiday work. The premium paid for overtime can radically alter a company's cost structure.

Example
Push Marketing Inc. employs telemarketers to prospect for individuals who are ready to purchase new luxury cars. Leads are fed back to salespeople who take cars to clients' homes for test drives. Auto dealers pay Push $21 per telemarketing hour. Push can subcontract out its work at $16 per hour, or it can use its own employees. If it uses its own employees, its variable costs are telephone line charges $3 per hour, and labor $10 per hour. It is less expensive to use its own employees at $13 per hour ($10 wages + $3 phone charges) than the subcontractor's at $16 per hour.

Suppose, however, there is more demand for telemarketing hours than current staff can accommodate in a 40-hour workweek. Figure 18–1 is an analysis of the contribution margin using overtime, no overtime, and outsourcing.

We see that contribution margin dropped from 38% to 14% because overtime was used. Outsourcing to a subcontractor, though expensive, would only have reduced contribution margin to 24%. If Push Marketing were using 1,000 hours of overtime per month, the difference in the annualized contribution is significant: $36,000 (1,000 hr/month × 12 months × $3) contribution from overtime versus $60,000 (1,000 hr/month × 12 months × $5) contribution from outsourcing.

Most companies consider the premium part of overtime, that is, the differential over and above straight time as waste. More sophisticated companies analyze this waste out of labor costs and book it as a separate overhead entry so that it does not become part of the cost of inventory or the cost of goods sold. Overtime premium pay is therefore treated like any other form of scrap.

Example

Betty's Furniture manufactured 400 bookcases in August. Each bookcase took 10 hours of direct labor. Of the 4,000 labor hours used to make the bookcases, 3,200 hours were straight time, and 800 hours were overtime. Betty pays her craftspeople $16 per hour,

FIGURE 18–1

Analysis of the Contribution Margin Using Overtime, No Overtime, and Outsourcing

	Straight Time In-House Production	Time-and-a-Half In-House Production	Subcontractor Production
Revenue per hour	$21	$21	$21
Costs per hour			
Subcontractor			$16
Labor	$10	$15	
Phone	$ 3	$ 3	
	$13	$18	$16
Contribution per hour	$ 8	$ 3	$ 5
Contribution margin	38%	14%	24%

straight time. Betty's labor costs for August were $70,400. How much of this was overtime premium?

If all 4,000 labor hours were paid at straight time, her labor cost would be $64,000 (4,000 × $16). The overtime premium pay is then the difference of $6,400 ($70,400 − $64,000).

Another way to compute the amount of premium pay is to multiply the amount of the premium, $8 per hour (half of straight pay), times the number of overtime hours, 800, to get the premium pay of $6,400 ($8 × 600).

In this example, Betty's Furniture would charge only $64,000 to inventory, and would expense the $6,400 premium pay by charging it to an overhead account.

The accounting entries would be

	Debit	Credit
A. Payroll expense	$70,400	
Cash		$70,400
To record cash disbursed for payroll		
B. Inventory (bookcases)	$64,000	
Overhead overtime premium pay	$ 6,400	
Payroll expense		$70,400
To allocate labor costs to inventory and to overtime premiums		

TURNOVER COSTS

Turnover is a hidden cost of labor. Few employees are 100% productive from the day they are hired. This is especially true in knowledge-based businesses. For employees to be fully effective, they must know how their department works, and how their output affects departments down stream from them, as well as how to get what they need from other departments. Customer knowledge and maintenance of customer relations also takes time to develop. Well-developed employee–customer relations can assure the follow-on sale. Lack of employee–customer relations can result in the permanent loss of a customer.

Example
Jones Telemarketing knows from sales statistics that new employees are only about 25% effective their first month on the job, 50%

effective their second month on the job, and 75% effective their third month on the job. Thereafter, most employees improve their performance very slowly over time. Jones gives each employee two days training before they are put on the phone. Telemarketing wages, including employer taxes and workers' compensation, are $10 per hour. Jones's turnover is 200% per year, which means that, on average, an employee works for them for only four months. Jones has 100 telemarketing workstations that it uses 40 hours per week. What does turnover cost Jones per year (not counting the cost to recruit replacement workers)?

The first step in this type of analysis is to estimate the cost of bringing an employee to full productivity. In the case of Jones, the cost includes $160 for two training days ($10/hr × 8 hr/day × 2 days); plus the loss in productivity for the first month, $1,200 ($10/hr × 40 hr/wk × 4 wk/month × [1 − 25%]); plus lost productivity for the second month, $800 ($10/hr × 40 hr/wk × 4 wk/month × [1 − 50%]); plus lost productivity for the third month, $400 ($10/hr × 40 hr/wk × 4 wk/month × [1 − 75%]). That brings the total cost for a new employee to $2,560 ($160 training, plus loss of productivity for the first three months: $1,200 + $800 + $400).

The next step is to estimate, based on turnover, the number of people Jones will lose over the course of a year. Assuming everyone works 40 hours per week, with 100 workstations, and a turnover of 200%, Jones will lose 200 people over the course of a year (100 employees × 200%). Total turnover costs (not counting the cost to recruit replacements) are $512,000 ($2,560 × 200).

In knowledge-based businesses, or businesses that are heavily craft oriented, or businesses that pay substantially more than $10 per hour, turnover cost can be dramatically higher.

WORKERS' COMPENSATION

Workers' compensation is a component of labor cost. It provides coverage for the medical expenses and wages of workers injured on the job. Workers need not show their employer was at fault in order to gain coverage under a workers' compensation policy. However, in exchange for employers giving up the right to deny liability, statute generally limits the benefits workers can receive. Workers' compensation disputes, if any, usually bypass the regular court system for special Workers' Compensation Courts. Does this mean that workers' compensation costs are uncontrollable? No. There are several things a business can do to minimize workers' compensation costs.

First, a company can make sure policies are properly rated. Rates are usually quoted per hundred dollars of salary. These rates vary by job function. For example, the rate for an office worker might be $0.28 per hundred dollars of salary, whereas the rate for a machinist might be $3.47 per hundred. Therefore, the first line of defense in controlling workers' compensation costs is to make sure that people and their salaries are properly classified.

Overtime can artificially boost pay because of the overtime premium. Arguably, since the risk to an insurance company is the same no matter whether a person is on straight time or overtime, only the straight time portion of overtime should go into the calculation for policy-rating purposes.

Finally, a company can implement an aggressive loss prevention campaign. Loss control helps reduce premiums because most workers' compensation policies are experience rated. Experience-rated policies are policies in which a significant portion of the premium is related to a company's prior claims experience. Schemes for computing experience modifications vary from state to state, depending on their workers' compensation laws.

New Jersey, for example, uses several factors to determine a company's experience modification factor. Generally, a company that has a hundred $1,000 losses is charged more than a company with a single $100,000 loss. The rationale is that a single serious accident may be unavoidable, whereas a pattern of accidents indicates that management is not creating a safe workplace.

They also look at the size of a company. The loss experience of a company with a thousand employees is usually more predictive of future losses than the loss experience of a company with just a handful of employees. In effect, they are trying to determine whether loss experience is statistically significant. In New Jersey, this is called a credibility factor and becomes part of the experience modification factor.

Finally, the experience modification factor is based on a company's paid claims experience compared to other companies in the same industry. If a company's claims are greater than expected, the experience modification factor increases rates over standard rates. If a company's claims are less than expected, the experience modification factor reduces rates.

In New Jersey, the state's Compensation Rating and Inspection Bureau computes a company's experience modification factor each year using three years of claims history. Most states have bureaus or agencies that set or regulate rates.

Example

Suppose a company has a $5 million payroll. Their workers' compensation premium would be computed, as shown in Figure 18–2. Salary is analyzed by job classification to get the number of $100 units for each job classification. These units are multiplied by the appropriate rate for the job classification to get a standard premium. The total of standard premiums are multiplied by the company's experience modification factor to get the actual premium charged.

This company has had more losses than average for its industry and has an experience modification factor of 1.05, which means it will pay 105% of the standard premium of $163,930. In other words, their unfavorable loss experience cost them an additional $8,197. Experience modification factors can be less than 1.0 as well. If, for example, the company had an experience modification factor of 0.91, their premium would have been $149,176 ($163,930 × 0.91), or a savings of $14,754. In this example, by changing their claims experience from slightly worse than average to slightly better, they have saved almost half a percent of their labor cost.

Every state has its own rules for experience rating policies.

FIGURE 18–2

Workers' Compensation Premium Computation

Job Classification	Salary Dollars	Units Salary/$100	Standard Rate	Standard Premium
Office worker	$ 300,000	3,000	$0.28	$ 840
Machinist	$4,700,000	47,000	$3.47	$163,090
				$163,930
		Company experience modification factor		× 1.05
		Total premium		**$172,127**

Your state's rules can usually be obtained by calling the bureau of workers' compensation.

UNEMPLOYMENT COMPENSATION TAXES

Unemployment compensation taxes are also experience rated. Unemployment is a fund that pays individuals, usually for 26 weeks, if they become unemployed through no fault of their own. Schemes for taxing employers to provide unemployment compensation vary from stated to state. In New Jersey, for example, the rates charged are based both on an individual employer's claims experience and on the state's overall claims experience.

Every year, the state computes an unemployment trust fund reserve ratio, which is the balance in the fund after all unemployment taxes have been collected and claims paid, *divided by* total wages taxable for unemployment compensation purposes. In New Jersey, unemployment taxes are paid on the first $20,200 of an employee's wages.

Based on the state's overall unemployment trust fund reserve ratio, one of six rate tables are used. If the reserve ratio is greater than 4.5%, the table with the lowest rates is used. If the reserve ratio is less than 1%, the table with the highest rates is used. So in some sense, an employer's rates are affected by the state's economy overall.

Each year, the state also computes an employer reserve ratio. This ratio is the sum of all the unemployment taxes an employer pays, minus the sum of all claims against the employer for the year, *divided by* the employer's average wages for the last three years. The employer reserve ratio is used to find an employer's tax rate in the table the state is using for any particular year.

Assume for a moment, the state is using its lowest rate table. If an employer's reserve ratio is 17% and over, the tax rate will be just 0.3%! If, on the other hand, the employer's reserve ratio is negative (that is, claims exceeded taxes paid), an employer's tax rate can go as high as 5.4%.

Now let us assume the worst-case scenario and the state's worst (highest tax) table is being used. A company with a 17% employer reserve ratio would pay employer taxes of 1.3%, whereas an employer with a negative reserve ratio might pay as much as 7.7%.

In one state, individuals who make as little as $8,700 in wages from a company can claim up to $10,580 in unemployment benefits. So in a sense, terminating an employee is like writing a check for $10,580 because all payments from an employer's account are recovered through future taxes.

Nevertheless, unemployment taxes are manageable costs. Strategies include terminating new hires sooner rather than later if it is obvious they will not work out. If an employee earns less than a threshold amount, their total benefit (claim) will be severely limited. Keep detailed records of attendance and employee discipline. Individuals terminated for selected causes are not eligible for unemployment in most states. These causes include absenteeism, excessive tardiness, fighting, theft, and insubordination. Further, employees who simply quit are almost never eligible for unemployment compensation. States notify companies when former employees make a claim for unemployment compensation. It is up to each company to scrutinize these claims and deny those that have no merit. States administratively review reasons for denial and any documentation supporting the denial. If the state finds the denial has merit, the company's experience will not be charged for the former employee.

Each state has a bureau of employment security or some other agency that sets, tracks, and manages rates. Consult the bureaus in the states where your company has facilities, and they will provide you with detailed rating information.

Example

Mandy Industries has an annual unemployment taxable payroll of $6 million. About a year ago, the new controller noticed that a significant number of new hires were just walking off the job and filing for unemployment. She began keeping detailed records, and as a result, unemployment claims were denied for a substantial number of individuals. Since claims were down, the state reduced Mandy's unemployment tax rate from 5.8% to 4.1%. Mandy wanted to know how much the controller saved the company.

Old unemployment tax	5.8% × $6,000,000 = $348,000
New unemployment tax	4.1% × $6,000,000 = $246,000
Savings	$102,000

SUMMARY

There are a number of ways to control labor costs other than through layoffs and cutting wage rates. Overtime, that is, time and a half paid to nonexempt employees who work more than 40 hours per week, can significantly alter a company's economic model. The premium over and above regular wage rates is often segregated from cost of goods sold and inventory valuation, and is debited to a special overhead account.

Turnover is a significant, and often unrecognized, controllable labor cost. The components of turnover cost include new employee training and orientation and reduced productivity while an employee learns his or her specific job, company, and customers.

Workers' compensation assists employees injured on the job. Employers pay for workers compensation through experience-rated policies. Three ways to control these costs are (1) make sure salary is allocated to the proper rate class; (2) segregate overtime premium pay so that insurance is not charged on this premium pay; and (3) reduce claims through workplace safety measures, which in turn, will reduce claims experience.

Unemployment taxes are charged on a percentage of payroll based on a company's claims experience in terminating employees. Employees terminated for absenteeism, theft, fighting, insubordination, and other specified reasons are not eligible for unemployment. It is up to the employer to deny such claims, and those claims that are successfully denied reduce a company's claim's experience, which in turn, reduces unemployment taxes.

Taken together, improved management of overtime, turnover, workers' compensation, and unemployment taxes can reduce labor costs significantly.

APPENDIXES

Appendix A: Future Value Interest Factor: FVIF(i, n)

Appendix B: Future Value Interest Factor for an Annuity: FVIFA(i, n)

Appendix C: Present Value Interest Factor: PVIF(i, n)

Appendix D: Present Value Interest Factor for an Annuity: PVIFA(i, n)

Appendix E: Chapter Exercises

Appendix F: Exercise Answers

Future Value Interest Factor: FVIF(i, n)

Period Interest Rates

n	0.50%	0.75%	1.00%	1.25%	1.50%	2.00%	3.00%	4.00%	5.00%	6.00%	7.00%
1	1.005	1.0075	1.01	1.0125	1.015	1.02	1.03	1.04	1.05	1.06	1.07
2	1.01003	1.01506	1.0201	1.02516	1.03023	1.0404	1.0609	1.0816	1.1025	1.1236	1.1449
3	1.01508	1.02267	1.0303	1.03797	1.04568	1.06121	1.09273	1.12486	1.15763	1.19102	1.22504
4	1.02015	1.03034	1.0406	1.05095	1.06136	1.08243	1.12551	1.16986	1.21551	1.26248	1.3108
5	1.02525	1.03807	1.05101	1.06408	1.07728	1.10408	1.15927	1.21665	1.27628	1.33823	1.40255
6	1.03038	1.04585	1.06152	1.07738	1.09344	1.12616	1.19405	1.26532	1.3401	1.41852	1.50073
7	1.03553	1.0537	1.07214	1.09085	1.10984	1.14869	1.22987	1.31593	1.4071	1.50363	1.60578
8	1.04071	1.0616	1.08286	1.10449	1.12649	1.17166	1.26677	1.36857	1.47746	1.59385	1.71819
9	1.04591	1.06956	1.09369	1.11829	1.14339	1.19509	1.30477	1.42331	1.55133	1.68948	1.83846
10	1.05114	1.07758	1.10462	1.13227	1.16054	1.21899	1.34392	1.48024	1.62889	1.79085	1.96715
11	1.0564	1.08566	1.11567	1.14642	1.17795	1.24337	1.38423	1.53945	1.71034	1.8983	2.10485
12	1.06168	1.09381	1.12683	1.16075	1.19562	1.26824	1.42576	1.60103	1.79586	2.0122	2.25219
13	1.06699	1.10201	1.13809	1.17526	1.21355	1.29361	1.46853	1.66507	1.88565	2.13293	2.40985
14	1.07232	1.11028	1.14947	1.18995	1.23176	1.31948	1.51259	1.73168	1.97993	2.2609	2.57853
15	1.07768	1.1186	1.16097	1.20438	1.25023	1.34587	1.55797	1.80094	2.07893	2.39656	2.75903
16	1.08307	1.12699	1.17258	1.21989	1.26899	1.37279	1.60471	1.87298	2.18287	2.54035	2.95216
18	1.09393	1.14396	1.19615	1.25058	1.30734	1.42825	1.70243	2.02582	2.40662	2.85434	3.37993
20	1.1049	1.16118	1.22019	1.28204	1.34686	1.48595	1.80611	2.19112	2.6533	3.20714	3.86968
24	1.12716	1.19641	1.26973	1.34735	1.4295	1.60844	2.03279	2.5633	3.2251	4.04893	5.07237
28	1.14987	1.23271	1.32129	1.41599	1.51722	1.74102	2.28793	2.9987	3.92013	5.11169	6.64884
30	1.1614	1.25127	1.34785	1.45161	1.56308	1.81136	2.42726	3.2434	4.32194	5.74349	7.61226
32	1.17304	1.27011	1.37494	1.48813	1.61032	1.88454	2.57508	3.50806	4.76494	6.45339	8.71527
36	1.19668	1.30865	1.43077	1.56394	1.70914	2.03989	2.89828	4.10393	5.79182	8.14725	11.4239
40	1.22079	1.34835	1.48886	1.64362	1.81402	2.20804	3.26204	4.80102	7.03999	10.2857	14.9745
48	1.27049	1.43141	1.61223	1.81535	2.04348	2.58707	4.13225	6.57053	10.4013	16.3939	25.7289
50	1.28323	1.45296	1.64463	1.86102	2.10524	2.69159	4.38391	7.10668	11.4674	18.4202	29.457
60	1.34885	1.56568	1.8167	2.10718	2.44322	3.28103	5.8916	10.5196	18.6792	32.9877	57.9464
72	1.43204	1.71255	2.0471	2.44592	2.92116	4.16114	8.40002	16.8423	33.5451	66.3777	130.506
84	1.52037	1.8732	2.30672	2.83911	3.49259	5.27733	11.9764	26.965	60.2422	133.565	293.926
96	1.61414	2.04892	2.59927	3.29551	4.1758	6.69293	17.0755	43.1718	108.186	268.759	661.977
108	1.7137	2.24112	2.92893	3.82528	4.99267	8.48826	24.3456	69.1195	194.287	540.796	1490.9
120	1.8194	2.45136	3.30039	4.44021	5.96932	10.7652	34.711	110.663	348.912	1088.19	3357.79
240	3.3102	6.00915	10.8926	19.7155	35.6328	115.889	1204.85	12246.2	121740	1184153	
360	6.02258	14.7306	35.9496	87.541	212.704	1247.56	41821.6	1355196			

Period Interest Rates

n	8.0%	9.00%	10.00%	12.00%	15.00%	18.00%	20.00%	24.00%	30.00%	36.00%
1	1.08	1.09	1.1	1.12	1.15	1.18	1.2	1.24	1.3	1.36
2	1.664	1.1881	1.21	1.2544	1.3225	1.3924	1.44	1.5376	1.69	1.8496
3	1.25971	1.29503	1.331	1.40493	1.52088	1.64303	1.728	1.90662	2.197	2.51546
4	1.36049	1.41158	1.4641	1.57352	1.74901	1.93878	2.0736	2.36421	2.8561	3.42102
5	1.46933	1.53862	1.61051	1.76234	2.01136	2.28776	2.48832	2.93163	3.71293	4.65259
6	1.58687	1.6771	1.77156	1.97382	2.31306	2.69955	2.98598	3.63522	4.82681	6.32752
7	1.71382	1.82804	1.94872	2.21068	2.66002	3.18547	3.58318	4.50767	6.27485	8.60543
8	1.85093	1.99256	2.14359	2.47596	3.05902	3.75886	4.29982	5.58951	8.15731	11.7034
9	1.999	2.17189	2.35795	2.77308	3.51788	4.43545	5.15978	6.93099	10.6045	15.9166
10	2.15892	2.36736	2.59374	3.10585	4.04556	5.23384	6.19174	8.59443	13.7858	21.6466
11	2.33164	2.58043	2.85312	3.47855	4.65239	6.17593	7.43008	10.6571	17.9216	29.4393
12	2.51817	2.81266	3.13843	3.89598	5.35025	7.28759	8.9161	13.2148	23.2981	40.0375
13	2.71962	3.0658	3.45227	4.36349	6.15279	8.59936	10.6993	16.3863	30.2875	54.451
14	2.93719	3.34173	3.7975	4.88711	7.07571	10.1427	12.8392	20.3191	39.3738	74.0534
15	3.17217	3.64248	4.17725	5.47357	8.13706	11.9737	15.407	25.1956	51.1859	100.713
16	3.42594	3.97031	4.59497	6.13039	9.35762	14.129	18.4884	31.2426	66.5417	136.969
18	3.99602	4.71712	5.55992	7.68997	12.3755	19.6733	26.6233	48.0386	112.455	253.338
20	4.66096	5.60441	6.7275	9.64629	16.3665	27.393	38.3376	73.8641	190.05	468.574
24	6.34118	7.91108	9.84973	15.1786	28.6252	53.109	79.4968	174.631	542.801	1603
28	8.62711	11.1671	14.421	23.8839	50.0656	102.967	164.845	412.864	1550.29	5483.9
30	10.0627	13.2677	17.4494	29.9599	66.2118	143.371	237.376	634.82	2620	10143
32	11.7371	15.7633	21.1138	37.5817	87.5651	199.629	341.822	976.099	4427.79	18760.5
36	15.9682	22.2512	30.9127	59.1356	153.152	387.037	708.802	2307.71	12646.2	64180.1
40	21.7245	31.4094	45.2593	93.051	267.864	750.378	1469.77	5455.91	36118.9	219562
48	40.2106	62.5852	97.0172	230.391	819.401	2820.57	6319.75	30495.9	294633	2569612
50	46.9016	74.3575	117.391	289.002	1083.66	3927.36	9100.44	46890.4	497929	4752755
60	101.257	176.031	304.482	897.597	4384	20555.1	56347.5	402996	6864377	
72	254.983	495.117	955.594	3497.02	23455.5	149797	502400	5325512		
84	642.089	1392.6	2999.06	13624.3	125493	1091663	4479450			
96	1616.89	3916.91	9412.34	53079.9	671418	7955596				
108	4071.6	11017	29540	206798	3592252					
120	10253	30987	92709.1	805680						
240										
360										

Future Value Interest Factor for an Annuity: FVIFA(*i, n*)

Period Interest Rates

n	0.50%	0.75%	1.00%	1.25%	1.50%	2.00%	3.00%	4.00%	5.00%	6.00%	7.00%
1	1	1	1	1	1	1	1	1	1	1	1
2	2.005	2.0075	2.01	2.0125	2.015	2.02	2.03	2.04	2.05	2.06	2.07
3	3.01502	3.02256	3.0301	3.03766	3.04522	3.0604	3.0909	3.1216	3.1525	3.1836	3.2149
4	4.0301	4.04523	4.0604	4.07563	4.0909	4.12161	4.18363	4.24646	4.31013	4.37462	4.43994
5	5.05025	5.07556	5.10101	5.12657	5.15227	5.20404	5.30914	5.41632	5.52563	5.63709	5.75074
6	6.0755	6.11363	6.15202	6.19065	6.22955	6.30812	6.46841	6.63298	6.80191	6.97532	7.15329
7	7.10588	7.15948	7.21354	7.26804	7.32299	7.43428	7.66246	7.89829	8.14201	8.39384	8.65402
8	8.14141	8.21318	8.28567	8.35889	8.43284	8.58297	8.89234	9.21423	9.54911	9.89747	10.2598
9	9.18212	9.27478	9.36853	9.46337	9.55933	9.75463	10.1591	10.5828	11.0266	11.4913	11.978
10	10.228	10.3443	10.4622	10.5817	10.7027	10.9497	11.4639	12.0061	12.5779	13.1808	13.8164
11	11.2792	11.4219	11.5668	11.7139	11.8633	12.1687	12.8078	13.4864	14.2068	14.9716	15.7836
12	12.3356	12.5076	12.6825	12.8604	13.0412	13.4121	14.192	15.0258	15.9171	16.8699	17.8885
13	13.3972	13.6014	13.8093	14.0211	14.2368	14.6803	15.6178	16.6268	17.713	18.8821	20.1406
14	14.4642	14.7034	14.9474	15.1964	15.4504	15.9739	17.0863	18.2919	19.5986	21.0151	22.5505
15	15.5365	15.8137	16.0969	16.3863	16.6821	17.2934	18.5989	20.0236	21.5786	23.276	25.129
16	16.6142	16.9323	17.2579	17.5912	17.9324	18.6393	20.1569	21.8245	23.6575	25.6725	27.8881
18	18.7858	19.1947	19.6147	20.0462	20.4894	21.4123	23.4144	25.6454	28.1324	30.9057	33.999
20	20.9791	21.4912	22.019	22.563	23.1237	24.2974	26.8704	29.7781	33.066	36.7856	40.9955
24	25.432	26.1885	26.9735	27.7881	28.6335	30.4219	34.4265	39.0826	44.502	50.8156	58.1767
28	29.9745	31.0282	32.1291	33.2794	34.4815	37.0512	42.9309	49.9676	58.4026	68.5281	80.6977
30	32.28	33.5029	34.7849	36.1291	37.5387	40.5681	47.5754	56.0849	66.4388	79.0582	94.4608
32	34.6086	36.0148	37.4941	39.0504	40.6883	44.227	52.5028	62.7015	75.2988	90.8898	110.218
36	39.3361	41.1527	43.0769	45.1155	47.276	51.9944	63.2759	77.5983	95.8363	119.121	148.913
40	44.1588	46.4465	48.8864	51.4896	54.2679	60.402	75.4013	95.0255	120.8	154.762	199.635
48	54.0978	57.5207	61.2226	65.2284	69.5652	79.3535	104.408	139.263	188.025	256.565	353.27
50	56.6452	60.3943	64.4632	68.8818	73.6828	84.5794	112.797	152.667	209.348	290.336	406.529
60	69.77	75.4241	81.6697	88.5745	96.2147	114.052	163.053	237.991	353.584	533.128	813.52
72	86.4089	95.007	104.71	115.674	128.077	158.057	246.667	396.057	650.903	1089.63	1850.09
84	104.074	116.427	130.672	147.129	166.173	213.867	365.881	649.125	1184.84	2209.42	4184.65
96	122.829	139.856	159.927	183.641	211.72	284.647	535.85	1054.3	2143.73	4462.65	9442.52
108	142.74	165.483	192.893	226.023	266.178	374.413	778.186	1702.99	3865.74	8996.6	21284.3
120	163.879	193.514	230.039	275.217	331.288	488.258	1123.7	2741.56	6958.24	18119.8	47954.1
240	462.041	667.887	989.255	1497.24	2308.85	5744.44	40128.4	306130	2434771		
360	1004.52	1830.74	3494.96	6923.28	14113.6	62328.1	1394021				

Period Interest Rates

n	8.00%	9.00%	10.00%	12.00%	15.00%	18.00%	20.00%	24.00%	30.00%	36.00%
1	1	1	1	1	1	1	1	1	1	1
2	2.08	2.09	2.1	2.12	2.15	2.18	2.2	2.24	2.3	2.36
3	3.2464	3.2781	3.31	3.3744	3.4725	3.5724	3.64	3.7776	3.99	4.2096
4	4.50611	4.57313	4.641	4.77933	4.99338	5.21543	5.368	5.68422	6.187	6.72506
5	5.8666	5.98471	6.1051	6.35285	6.74238	7.15421	7.4416	8.04844	9.0431	10.1461
6	7.33593	7.52333	7.71561	8.11519	8.75374	9.44197	9.92992	10.9801	12.756	14.7987
7	8.9228	9.20043	9.48717	10.089	11.0668	12.1415	12.9159	14.6153	17.5828	21.1262
8	10.6366	11.0285	11.4359	12.2997	13.7268	15.327	16.4991	19.1229	23.8577	29.7316
9	12.4876	13.021	13.5795	14.7757	16.7858	19.0859	20.7989	24.7125	32.015	41.435
10	14.4866	15.1929	15.9374	17.5487	20.3037	23.5213	25.9587	31.6434	42.6195	57.3516
11	16.6455	17.5603	18.5312	20.6546	24.3493	28.7551	32.1504	40.2379	56.4053	78.9982
12	18.9771	20.1407	21.3843	24.1331	29.0017	34.9311	39.5805	50.895	74.327	108.437
13	21.4953	22.9534	24.5227	28.0291	34.3519	42.2187	48.4966	64.1097	97.625	148.475
14	24.2149	26.0192	27.975	32.3926	40.5047	50.818	59.1959	80.4961	127.913	202.926
15	27.1521	29.3609	31.7725	37.2797	47.5804	60.9653	72.0351	100.815	167.286	276.979
16	30.3243	33.0034	35.9497	42.7533	55.7175	72.939	87.4421	126.011	218.472	377.692
18	37.4502	41.3013	45.5992	55.7497	75.8364	103.74	128.117	195.994	371.518	700.939
20	45.762	51.1601	57.275	72.0524	102.444	146.628	186.688	303.601	630.165	1298.82
24	66.7648	76.7898	88.4973	118.155	184.168	289.494	392.484	723.461	1806	4450
28	95.3388	112.968	134.21	190.699	327.104	566.481	819.223	1716.1	5164.31	15230.3
30	113.283	136.308	164.494	241.333	434.745	790.948	1181.88	2640.92	8729.99	28172.3
32	134.214	164.037	201.138	304.848	577.1	1103.5	1704.11	4062.91	14756	52109.8
36	187.102	236.125	299.127	484.463	1014.35	2144.65	3539.01	9611.28	42150.7	178275
40	259.057	337.882	442.593	767.091	1779.09	4163.21	7343.86	22728.8	120393	609890
48	490.132	684.28	960.172	1911.59	5456	15664.3	31593.7	127062	982106	7137809
50	573.77	815.084	1163.91	2400.02	7217.72	21813.1	45497.2	195373	1659761	
60	1253.21	1944.79	3034.82	7471.64	29220	114190	281733	1679147		
72	3174.78	5490.19	9545.94	29133.5	156363	832203	2511995			
84	8013.62	1546.22	29980.6	113527	836612	6064789				
96	20198.6	43510.1	94113.4	442324	4476110					
108	50882.6	122400	295390	1723309						
120	128150	344289	927081	6713994						
240										
360										

APPENDIX C

Present Value Interest Factor: PVIF(*i, n*)

Period Interest Rates

n	0.50%	0.75%	1.00%	1.25%	1.50%	2.00%	3.00%	4.00%	5.00%	6.00%	7.00%
1	0.99502	0.99256	0.9901	0.98765	0.98522	0.98039	0.97087	0.96154	0.95238	0.9434	0.93458
2	0.99007	0.98517	0.9803	0.97546	0.97066	0.96117	0.9426	0.92456	0.90703	0.89	0.87344
3	0.98515	0.97783	0.97059	0.96342	0.95632	0.94232	0.91514	0.889	0.86384	0.83962	0.8163
4	0.98025	0.97055	0.96098	0.95152	0.94218	0.92385	0.88849	0.8548	0.8227	0.79209	0.7629
5	0.97537	0.96333	0.95147	0.93978	0.92826	0.90573	0.86261	0.82193	0.78353	0.74726	0.71299
6	0.97052	0.95616	0.94205	0.92817	0.91454	0.88797	0.83748	0.79031	0.74622	0.70496	0.66634
7	0.96569	0.94904	0.93272	0.91672	0.90103	0.87056	0.81309	0.75992	0.71068	0.66506	0.62275
8	0.96089	0.94198	0.92348	0.9054	0.88771	0.85349	0.78941	0.73069	0.67684	0.62741	0.58201
9	0.9561	0.93496	0.91434	0.89422	0.87459	0.83676	0.76642	0.70259	0.64461	0.5919	0.54393
10	0.95135	0.928	0.90529	0.88318	0.86167	0.82035	0.74409	0.67556	0.61391	0.55839	0.50835
11	0.94661	0.92109	0.89632	0.87228	0.84893	0.80426	0.72242	0.64958	0.58468	0.52679	0.47509
12	0.94191	0.91424	0.88745	0.86151	0.83639	0.78849	0.70138	0.6246	0.55684	0.49697	0.44401
13	0.93722	0.90743	0.87866	0.85087	0.82403	0.77303	0.68095	0.60057	0.53032	0.46884	0.41496
14	0.93256	0.90068	0.86996	0.84037	0.81185	0.75788	0.66112	0.57748	0.50507	0.4423	0.38782
15	0.92792	0.89397	0.86135	0.82999	0.79985	0.74301	0.64186	0.55526	0.48102	0.41727	0.36245
16	0.9233	0.88732	0.85282	0.81975	0.78803	0.72845	0.62317	0.53391	0.45811	0.39365	0.33873
18	0.91414	0.87416	0.83602	0.79963	0.76491	0.70016	0.58739	0.49363	0.41552	0.35034	0.29586
20	0.90506	0.86119	0.81954	0.78001	0.74247	0.67297	0.55368	0.45639	0.37689	0.3118	0.25842
24	0.88719	0.83583	0.78757	0.7422	0.69954	0.62172	0.49193	0.39012	0.31007	0.24698	0.19715
28	0.86966	0.81122	0.75684	0.70622	0.6591	0.57437	0.43708	0.33348	0.25509	0.19563	0.1504
30	0.86103	0.79919	0.74192	0.68889	0.63976	0.55207	0.41199	0.30832	0.23138	0.17411	0.13137
32	0.85248	0.78733	0.7273	0.67198	0.62099	0.53063	0.38834	0.28506	0.20987	0.15496	0.11474
36	0.83564	0.76415	0.69892	0.63941	0.58509	0.49022	0.34503	0.24367	0.17266	0.12274	0.08754
40	0.81914	0.74165	0.67165	0.60841	0.55126	0.45289	0.30656	0.20829	0.14205	0.09722	0.06678
48	0.7871	0.69861	0.62026	0.55086	0.48936	0.38654	0.242	0.15219	0.09614	0.061	0.03887
50	0.77929	0.68825	0.60804	0.53734	0.475	0.37153	0.22811	0.14071	0.0872	0.05429	0.03395
60	0.74137	0.6387	0.55045	0.47457	0.4093	0.30478	0.16973	0.09506	0.05354	0.03031	0.01726
72	0.6983	0.58392	0.4885	0.40844	0.34233	0.24032	0.11905	0.05937	0.02981	0.01507	0.00766
84	0.65773	0.53385	0.43352	0.35222	0.28632	0.18949	0.0835	0.03709	0.0166	0.00749	0.0034
96	0.61952	0.48806	0.38472	0.30344	0.23947	0.14941	0.05856	0.02316	0.00924	0.00372	0.00151
108	0.58353	0.4462	0.34142	0.26142	0.20029	0.11781	0.04108	0.01447	0.00515	0.00185	0.00067
120	0.54963	0.40794	0.30299	0.22521	0.16752	0.09289	0.02881	0.00904	0.00287	0.00092	0.0003
240	0.3021	0.16641	0.09181	0.05072	0.02806	0.00863	0.00083				
360	0.16604	0.06789	0.02782	0.01142	0.0047	0.0008					

Period Interest Rates

n	8.00%	9.00%	10.00%	12.00%	15.00%	18.00%	20.00%	24.00%	30.00%	36.00%
1	0.92593	0.91743	0.90909	0.89286	0.86957	0.84746	0.83333	0.80645	0.76923	0.73529
2	0.85734	0.84168	0.82645	0.79719	0.75614	0.71818	0.69444	0.65036	0.59172	0.54066
3	0.79383	0.77218	0.75131	0.71178	0.65752	0.60863	0.5787	0.52449	0.45517	0.39754
4	0.73503	0.70843	0.68301	0.63552	0.57175	0.51579	0.48225	0.42297	0.35013	0.29231
5	0.68058	0.64993	0.62092	0.56743	0.49718	0.43711	0.40188	0.34111	0.26933	0.21493
6	0.63017	0.59627	0.56447	0.50663	0.43233	0.37043	0.3349	0.27509	0.20718	0.15804
7	0.58349	0.54703	0.51316	0.45235	0.37594	0.31393	0.27908	0.22184	0.15937	0.11621
8	0.54027	0.50187	0.46651	0.40388	0.3269	0.26604	0.23257	0.17891	0.12259	0.08545
9	0.50025	0.46043	0.4241	0.36061	0.28426	0.22546	0.19381	0.14428	0.0943	0.06283
10	0.46319	0.42241	0.38554	0.32197	0.24718	0.19106	0.16151	0.11635	0.07254	0.0462
11	0.42888	0.38753	0.35049	0.28748	0.21494	0.16192	0.13459	0.09383	0.0558	0.03397
12	0.39711	0.35553	0.31863	0.25668	0.18691	0.13722	0.11216	0.07567	0.04292	0.02498
13	0.3677	0.32618	0.28966	0.22917	0.16253	0.11629	0.09346	0.06103	0.03302	0.01837
14	0.34046	0.29925	0.26333	0.20462	0.14133	0.09855	0.07789	0.04921	0.0254	0.0135
15	0.31524	0.27454	0.23939	0.1827	0.12289	0.08352	0.06491	0.03969	0.01954	0.00993
16	0.29189	0.25187	0.21763	0.16312	0.10686	0.07078	0.05409	0.03201	0.01503	0.0073
18	0.25025	0.21199	0.17986	0.13004	0.08081	0.05083	0.03756	0.02082	0.00889	0.00395
20	0.21455	0.17843	0.14864	0.10367	0.0611	0.03651	0.02608	0.01354	0.00526	0.00213
24	0.1577	0.1264	0.10153	0.06588	0.03493	0.01883	0.01258	0.00573	0.00184	0.00062
28	0.11591	0.08955	0.06934	0.04187	0.01997	0.00971	0.00607	0.00242	0.00065	0.00018
30	0.09938	0.07537	0.05731	0.03338	0.0151	0.00697	0.00421	0.00158	0.00038	
32	0.0852	0.06344	0.04736	0.02661	0.01142	0.00501	0.00293	0.00102	0.00023	
36	0.06262	0.04494	0.03235	0.01691	0.00653	0.00258	0.00141	0.00043		
40	0.04603	0.03184	0.02209	0.01075	0.00373	0.00133	0.00068	0.00018		
48	0.02487	0.01598	0.01031	0.00434	0.00122	0.00035	0.00016			
50	0.02132	0.01345	0.00852	0.00346	0.00092	0.00025	0.00011			
60	0.00988	0.00568	0.00328	0.00111	0.00023					
72	0.00392	0.00202	0.00105	0.00029						
84	0.00156	0.00072	0.00033							
96	0.00062	0.00026	0.00011							
108	0.00025									
120										
240										
360										

329

Present Value Interest Factor for an Annuity: PVIFA(*i, n*)

Period Interest Rates

n	0.50%	0.75%	1.00%	1.25%	1.50%	2.00%	3.00%	4.00%	5.00%	6.00%	7.00%
1	0.99502	0.99256	0.9901	0.98765	0.98522	0.98039	0.97087	0.96154	0.95238	0.9434	0.93458
2	1.9851	1.97772	1.9704	1.96312	1.95588	1.94156	1.91347	1.88609	1.85941	1.83339	1.80802
3	2.97025	2.95556	2.94099	2.92653	2.9122	2.88388	2.82861	2.77509	2.72325	2.67301	2.62432
4	3.9505	3.92611	3.90197	3.87806	3.85438	3.80773	3.7171	3.6299	3.54595	3.46511	3.38721
5	4.92587	4.88944	4.85343	4.81784	4.78264	4.71346	4.57971	4.45182	4.32948	4.21236	4.1002
6	5.89638	5.8456	5.79548	5.74601	5.69719	5.60143	5.41719	5.24214	5.07569	4.91732	4.76654
7	6.86207	6.79464	6.72819	6.66273	6.59821	6.47199	6.23028	6.00205	5.78637	5.58238	5.38929
8	7.82296	7.73661	7.65168	7.56812	7.48593	7.32548	7.01969	6.73274	6.46321	6.20979	5.9713
9	8.77906	8.67158	8.56602	8.46234	8.36052	8.16224	7.78611	7.43533	7.10782	6.80169	6.51523
10	9.73041	9.59958	9.4713	9.34553	9.22218	8.98259	8.5302	8.1109	7.72173	7.36009	7.02358
11	10.677	10.5207	10.3676	10.2178	10.0711	9.78685	9.25262	8.76048	8.30641	7.88687	7.49867
12	11.6189	11.4349	11.2551	11.0793	10.9075	10.5753	9.954	9.38507	8.86325	8.38384	7.94269
13	12.5562	12.3423	12.1337	11.9302	11.7315	11.3484	10.635	9.98565	9.39357	8.85268	8.35765
14	13.4887	13.243	13.0037	12.7706	12.5434	12.1062	11.2961	10.5631	9.89864	9.29498	8.74547
15	14.4166	14.137	13.8651	13.6005	13.3432	12.8493	11.9379	11.1184	10.3797	9.71225	9.10791
16	15.3399	15.0243	14.7179	14.4203	14.1313	13.5777	12.5611	11.6523	10.8378	10.1059	9.44665
18	17.1728	16.7792	16.3983	16.0295	15.6726	14.992	13.7535	12.6593	11.6896	10.8276	10.0591
20	18.9874	18.508	18.0456	17.5993	17.1686	16.3514	14.8775	13.5903	12.4622	11.4699	10.594
24	22.5629	21.8891	21.2434	20.6242	20.0304	18.9139	16.9355	15.247	13.7986	12.5504	11.4693
28	26.0677	25.1707	24.3164	23.5025	22.7267	21.2813	18.7641	16.6631	14.8981	13.4062	12.1371
30	27.7941	26.7751	25.8077	24.8889	24.0158	22.3965	19.6004	17.292	15.3725	13.7648	12.409
32	29.5033	28.3557	27.2696	26.2413	25.2671	23.4683	20.3888	17.8736	15.8027	14.084	12.6466
36	32.871	31.4468	30.1075	28.8473	27.6607	25.4888	21.8323	18.9083	16.5469	14.621	13.0352
40	36.1722	34.4469	32.8347	31.3269	29.9158	27.3555	23.1148	19.7928	17.1591	15.0463	13.3317
48	42.5803	40.1848	37.974	35.9315	34.0426	30.6731	25.2667	21.1951	18.0772	15.65	13.7305
50	44.1428	41.5664	39.1961	37.0129	34.9997	31.4236	25.7298	21.4822	18.2559	15.7619	13.8007
60	51.7256	48.1734	44.955	42.0346	39.3803	34.7609	27.6756	22.6235	18.9293	16.1614	14.0392
72	60.3395	55.4768	51.1504	47.2925	43.8447	37.9841	29.3651	23.5156	19.4038	16.4156	14.1763
84	68.453	62.154	56.6485	51.8222	47.5786	40.5255	30.5501	24.0729	19.668	16.5419	14.2371
96	76.0952	68.2584	61.5277	55.7246	50.7017	42.5294	31.3812	24.4209	19.8151	16.6047	14.2641
108	83.2934	73.8394	65.8578	59.0865	53.3137	44.1095	31.9642	24.6383	19.8971	16.6358	14.2761
120	90.0735	78.9417	69.7005	61.9828	55.4985	45.3554	32.373	24.7741	19.9427	16.6514	14.2815
240	139.581	111.145	90.8194	75.9423	64.7957	49.5686	33.3057	24.998	19.9998	16.6667	14.2857
360	166.792	124.282	97.2183	79.0861	66.3532	49.9599	33.3325	25	20	16.6667	14.2857

Period Interest Rates

n	8.00%	9.00%	10.00%	12.00%	15.00%	18.00%	20.00%	24.00%	30.00%	36.00%
1	0.92593	0.91743	0.90909	0.89286	0.86957	0.84746	0.83333	0.80645	0.76923	0.73529
2	1.78326	1.75911	1.73554	1.69005	1.62571	1.56564	1.52778	1.45682	1.36095	1.27595
3	2.5771	2.53129	2.48685	2.40183	2.28323	2.17427	2.10648	1.9813	1.81611	1.67349
4	3.31213	3.23972	3.16987	3.03735	2.85498	2.69006	2.58873	2.40428	2.16624	1.9658
5	3.99271	3.88965	3.79079	3.60478	3.35216	3.12717	2.99061	2.74538	2.43557	2.18074
6	4.62288	4.48592	4.35526	4.11141	3.78448	3.4976	3.32551	3.02047	2.64275	2.33878
7	5.20637	5.03295	4.86842	4.56376	4.16042	3.81153	3.60459	3.24232	2.80211	2.45498
8	5.74664	5.53482	5.33493	4.96764	4.48732	4.07757	3.83716	3.42122	2.9247	2.54043
9	6.24689	5.99525	5.75902	5.32825	4.77158	4.30302	4.03097	3.5655	3.019	2.60326
10	6.71008	6.41766	6.14457	5.65022	5.01877	4.49409	4.19247	3.68186	3.09154	2.64945
11	7.13896	6.80519	6.49506	5.9377	5.23371	4.65601	4.32706	3.77569	3.14734	2.68342
12	7.53608	7.16073	6.81369	6.19437	5.42062	4.79322	4.43922	3.85136	3.19026	2.7084
13	7.90378	7.4869	7.10336	6.42355	5.58315	4.90951	4.53268	3.91239	3.22328	2.72676
14	8.24424	7.78615	7.36669	6.62817	5.72448	5.00806	4.61057	3.9616	3.24867	2.74027
15	8.55948	8.06069	7.60608	6.81086	5.84737	5.09158	4.67547	4.00129	3.26821	2.7502
16	8.85137	8.31256	7.82371	6.97399	5.95423	5.16235	4.72956	4.0333	3.28324	2.7575
18	9.37189	8.75563	8.20141	7.24967	6.12797	5.27316	4.81219	4.07993	3.30369	2.76681
20	9.81815	9.12855	8.51356	7.46944	6.25933	5.35275	4.86958	4.11026	3.31579	2.77185
24	10.5288	9.70661	8.98474	7.78432	6.43377	5.45095	4.9371	4.14281	3.32719	2.77604
28	11.0511	10.1161	9.30657	7.98442	6.53351	5.5016	4.96967	4.15657	3.33118	2.77727
30	11.2578	10.2737	9.42691	8.05518	6.56598	5.51681	4.97894	4.1601	3.33206	2.7775
32	11.435	10.4062	9.52638	8.11159	6.59053	5.52773	4.98537	4.1624	3.33258	2.77763
36	11.7172	10.6118	9.67651	8.19241	6.62314	5.5412	4.99295	4.16486	3.33307	2.77773
40	11.9246	10.7574	9.77905	8.24378	6.64178	5.54815	4.9966	4.1659	3.33324	2.77777
48	12.1891	10.9336	9.89693	8.29716	6.65853	5.55359	4.99921	4.16653	3.33332	2.77778
50	12.2335	10.9617	9.91481	8.3045	6.66051	5.55414	4.99945	4.16658	3.33333	2.77778
60	12.3766	11.048	9.96716	8.32405	6.66515	5.55529	4.99991	4.16666	3.33333	2.77778
72	12.451	11.0887	9.98954	8.33095	6.66638	5.55552	4.99999	4.16667	3.33333	2.77778
84	12.4805	11.1031	9.99667	8.33272	6.66661	5.55555	5	4.16667	3.33333	2.77778
96	12.4923	11.1083	9.99894	8.33318	6.66666	5.55555	5	4.16667	3.33333	2.77778
108	12.4969	11.1101	9.99966	8.33329	6.66666	5.55556	5	4.16667	3.33333	2.77778
120	12.4988	11.1108	9.99989	8.33332	6.66667	5.55556	5	4.16667	3.33333	2.77778
240	12.5	11.1111	10	8.33333	6.66667	5.55556	5	4.16667	3.33333	2.77778
360	12.5	11.1111	10	8.33333	6.66667	5.55556	5	4.16667	3.33333	2.77778

Chapter Exercises

We don't expect basketball players to become proficient by simply showing them a picture of a basketball. We expect them to practice. How can we expect businesspeople to become proficient at financial analysis unless they are given an opportunity to practice? The exercises provided in this book give professionals the practice they need to gain proficiency and confidence at solving problems.

CHAPTER 1 EXERCISES

1. Modern Medical has revenue of $2,000,000, the cost of doctors, nurses, and medical supplies is $1,500,000. Office rent, administrative staff, utilities, and so on are $450,000. The income tax rate is 30%.
   a. What is their cost of goods sold?
   b. What is their gross profit in dollars?
   c. What is their gross margin in percent?
   d. What is their earnings before taxes?
   e. What is their net income?
   f. What is their profit margin in percent?

2. Modern Medical can increase revenue by $300,000 if it adds another doctor to its staff. The doctor will cost $275,000 per year, including employer taxes, fringe, and medical malpractice insurance. For purposes of this exercise, consider medical malpractice insurance part of the cost of goods sold. Given the information from this

and the preceding problem, complete the following
summarized P&L statement for Modern Medical.

	Dollars	Percent
a. Revenue		
b. Cost of goods sold		
c. Gross profit		
d. Overhead:		
e. Earnings before taxes		
f. Taxes		
g. Net income		

3. Sybase had operating profit of $200,000. Depreciation on
   office equipment was $6,000, on computers was $11,000,
   and on their building was $25,000. How much cash did
   Sybase generate from operations?

4. Wilson Corporation had operating profit of $78,000,
   depreciation on plant property and equipment was
   $18,000, and amortization of leasehold improvements
   (not a cash expense) was $14,000. How much cash did
   Wilson generate from operations?

5. Given the balances in Wilson's working capital accounts,
   classify each as a source or use of cash, and quantify them.

	1998	1999	Source of Cash Amount	Use of Cash Amount
a. Accounts receivable	$230,000	$410,000		
b. Accounts payable	$450,000	$425,000		
c. Accrued payroll	$ 78,000	$102,000		

6. Given the summary financial statements for Murray's
   Boutique, construct a statement of cash flows.

MURRAY'S BOUTIQUE: BALANCE SHEET

	2002	2001	Change
Cash	105,000	60,000	
Accounts receivable	100,000	80,000	
Inventory	75,000	80,000	
Plant and equip.	40,000	40,000	
Total assets	**320,000**	**260,000**	

MURRAY'S BOUTIQUE: BALANCE SHEET (*Continued*)

	2002	2001	Change
Accounts payable	200,000	150,000	
Accrued payroll	20,000	10,000	
Bank loan	40,000	40,000	
Liabilities	260,000	200,000	
Equity	60,000	60,000	
Liabilities and **equity**	320,000	260,000	

MURRAY'S BOUTIQUE: INCOME STATEMENT

Revenue	850,000
COGS	650,000
Gross profit	200,000
Operating expenses	50,000
Depreciation	30,000
EBIT	120,000
Interest	10,000
EBT	110,000
Taxes	20,000
Net income	90,000

MURRAY'S BOUTIQUE: STATEMENT OF CASH FLOWS

Cash from operations	_____
	_____
Total from operations	
Changes in working capital	_____
	_____
	_____
Total from working capital	
Acquisitions and divestitures	_____
Financing activities	_____
Change in cash position	_____

CHAPTER 2 EXERCISES

1. Gray Wire & Cable has net income of $3.1 million; interest expense is $1.5 million; it is in the 40% tax bracket; at the end of year 2, its assets were $44 million, and at the end of year 1, its assets were $36 million. What is its ROA?

2. Wire Connector Co. has net income of $110,000; interest expense of $40,000; and they are in the 25% tax bracket. Assets at the end of year 1 were $1,250,000, and at the end of year 2, $1,750,000. What is their ROA?

3. Gray Wire & Cable has net income of $3.1 million on revenue of $24 million; interest expense is $1.5 million; it is in the 40% tax bracket. What is its profit margin?

4. Wire Connector Co. has net income of $110,000 on sales of $1,500,000. Interest was $40,000; and they are in the 25% tax bracket. What is their profit margin?

5. Gray Wire & Cable has revenue of $24 million. Assets at the end of year 1 were $36 million, and at the end of year 2 were $44 million. What is its asset turnover?

6. Wire Connector Co. had sales of $1,500,000. Assets at the end of year 1 were $1,250,000, and at the end of year 2 $1,750,000. What is its asset turnover ratio?

7. Gray Wire & Cable has revenue of $24 million. Accounts receivable at the end of year 1 was $2.3 million, and at the end of year 2 was $2.5 million. What is its accounts receivable turnover? What is its days sales outstanding?

8. Wire Connector Co. had sales of $1,500,000. Assets at the end of year 1 were $250,000, and at the end of year 2 were $300,000.
   a. What is its accounts receivable turnover?
   b. What is its days sales outstanding?

9. Gray Wire & Cable has beginning inventory of $400,000, purchases of $6,000,000, and ending inventory of $500,000.
   a. What is its inventory turnover ratio?
   b. On average, how many days does its stock stay in inventory?

10. Wire Connector Co. had revenue of $1,500,000 and cost of goods sold of $1,200,000. Their beginning inventory was $130,000, and their ending inventory was $140,000.
   a. What is their inventory turnover?
   b. What is their average days in inventory?

11. Gray Wire & Cable has sales of $24 million. Plant assets at the end of year 2 were $23 million; at the end of year 1, $19 million. What is its plant asset turnover?

12. Wire Connector Co. has sales of $1,500,000. Plant assets at the end of year 1 were $550,000, and at the end of year 2 $750,000. What is their plant asset turnover?

13. Gray Wire & Cable has net income of $3.1 million, preferred dividends of $250,000, total equity at the end of year 2 of $12.5 million and at the end of year 1, $12.0 million. What is its ROE?

14. Wire Connector Company has net income of $110,000 and preferred dividends of $10,000. Equity at the end of year 1 was $600,000, and equity at the end of year 2 was $670,000. What is its ROE?

15. Gray Wire & Cable has assets averaging $40 million and an ROA of 10%.
   a. What is the income generated by its assets?
   b. What would be its ROE if assets were entirely financed by common equity?
   c. What would be its ROE if assets were 70% financed by 9% debt at a 40% tax rate?

16. Wire Connector Company's ROA is 7.3% on average assets of $1,500,000.
   a. How much income before interest and taxes do their assets generate?
   b. What would their ROE be if they were financed entirely by shareholder equity?
   c. What would their ROE be if they financed 60% of their assets with 10% debt at a 25% tax rate?

17. Gray Wire & Cable has net income of $3.1 million and preferred dividends of $250,000. On January 1, it has common share outstanding of 800,000 shares. On July 1,

they issued an additional 200,000 shares. What is its earnings per share?

18. Wire Connector Company had net income of $110,000 and preferred dividends of $10,000. On January 1, the company had 200,000 shares outstanding. On December 2 (30 days from the end of the year), the company issued another 50,000 shares. What are their earnings per share?

19. If Gray Wire & Cable had an EPS of $3.17, and a market price of $40 and $55 on September 1 and December 1, respectively, what would have been their price/earnings (P/E) ratios on those days?

20. If Wire Connector had an EPS of $0.53 and a market price of $9.00 on April 15, and a market price of $13.25 on October 31, what would have been its P/E ratios on those days?

21. Gray Wire & Cable historically has a P/E of 16. Over the last year, its P/E ratio has fluctuated widely. Given P/E data for several dates, determine whether the stock was probably overvalued, undervalued, or properly valued compared to historical norms on each of the following dates: (a) 1/1 P/E: 17.4, (b) 4/15 P/E: 14.5, (c) 8/20 P/E: 11, (d) 12/14 P/E: 23.

22. Wire Connector historically has a P/E of 18. Given Wire's P/E ratio for various dates, determine whether Wire was probably undervalued, overvalued, or properly valued based on the following dates: (a) 1/1 P/E: 13, (b) 3/31 P/E: 17, (c) 6/30 P/E: 20, (d) 11/30 P/E: 26.

The following balance sheets will be used for Exercises 23 through 26.

Assets	Gray Wire & Cable	Wire Connector
Cash and securities	$12,000,000	$ 300,000
Accounts receivable	$ 500,000	$ 300,000
Inventory	$ 500,000	$ 400,000
Plant property and equip.	$23,000,000	$ 750,000
Other long-term assets	$ 8,000,000	
Total assets	$44,000,000	$1,750,000

Liabilities	Gray Wire & Cable	Wire Connector
Accounts payable	$ 1,800,000	$ 310,000
Accrued payroll	$ 120,000	$ 110,000
Line of credit	0	$ 100,000
Term loan current	$ 300,000	$ 30,000
Leases current	$ 600,000	$ 60,000
Current liabilities	$ 2,820,000	$ 610,000
Loan long term	$15,000,000	$ 400,000
Leases long term	$ 2,400,000	$ 300,000
Total liabilities	$20,220,000	$1,310,000
Equity	$23,780,000	$ 440,000
Total liability and equity	$44,000,000	$1,750,000

23. Compute the current ratio for Gray Wire & Cable.

24. Compute the current ratio for Wire Connector Co.

25. Compute the quick ratio for Gray Wire & Cable.

26. Compute the quick ratio for Wire Connector Company.

27. Gray Wire & Cable has net income of $3.1 million of which $0.2 million is due to sale of an office building. They also made $0.3 million investing in corporate bonds. Average current liabilities are $2.82 million. Depreciation is $2.3 million. What is the ratio of cash flow to average current liabilities?

28. Wire Connector Company has net income of $110,000, of which $10,000 was interest earned on T-notes. Average current liabilities are $610,000. Depreciation was $75,000. What is the ratio of cash flows from operations to average current liabilities?

29. Gray Wire & Cable has total liabilities of $20,220,000 and equity of $23,780,000. What is their debt equity ratio?

30. Wire Connector Company has total liabilities of $1,310,000 and equity of $440,000. (a) What is their debt equity ratio? (b) If they use $200,000 of cash to pay off $100,000 of accounts payable and the $100,000 line of credit, what will be their debt equity ratio?

31. Gray Wire & Cable has net income of $3.1 million, interest of $1.0 million, and taxes of $400,000. What is their interest coverage ratio?

32. Wire Connector Company has net income of $110,000, interest of $90,000, and taxes of $30,000. What is their interest coverage ratio?

CHAPTER 3 EXERCISES

1. Assume that Krf, the rate paid on a 1-year T-bill is 4%, estimate the required rate on a 90-day T-bill.

2. What is the required rate of return, K, for a 10-year, Minsk Brick Works bond given the following: Krf = 4%; default risk premium = 8%; liquidity premium = 3%; and maturity risk premium = 2%.

3. You are analyzing a five-year Allegheny Hospital bond with a quoted rate of 13%. You know that 1-year T-bills yield 4.5%; the maturity risk premium on five-year T-notes is 0.5%; and the liquidity premium for the Allegheny bond is 1%. How much of the Allegheny bond's quoted rate is due to default risk?

4. Given the maturity risk premium on a 20-year G.E. corporate bond is 2.1%, what would you expect the maturity risk premium on a 20-year T-note to be?

5. Assume Prudy's Bond Service has made the following assessment of premiums for various bond ratings:

Rating	Default Risk Premium	Liquidity Premium for This Quality
AAA	0.5%	0.5%
AA	0.8%	0.5%
A	1.0%	0.5%
BBB	1.2%	0.5%
C	2.5%	1.0%

One of their studies indicates that the maturity risk premium on a ten-year bond is 2%. One-year T-bills are yielding 4.3%. If your company wants to float a $1,000,000 ten-year bond, and their rating is AAA, what would you expect the quoted rate to be?

6. One of your cargo planes crashes due to poor maintenance, and Prudy's downgrades your company's bond rating to C. If your company wants to float a

$1,000,000 ten-year bond, what would the quoted rate of interest have to be, based on the preceding table?

7. Given the rate on a one-year T-bill is 4.5% and the rate on a two-year T-note is 4%, what rate is expected on a one-year T-bill purchase one year from now?

8. Given the rate on a one-year Commerce Bank CD is 5%, and the rate on a two-year Commerce Bank CD is 4.8%. What rate is expected on a one-year Commerce Bank CD if purchased one year from now?

9. Three companies want to sell bonds for capital projects. They hired a bond underwriting company to determine how to price their bonds to raise various amounts of capital. The companies have bonds ratings of AAA, BBB, and CCC, respectively. They surveyed 30 professional money managers and found the following information. Plot the money supply curve for each of the companies.

Interest Rate	Cumulative Number of Money Managers Who Would Purchase Million-Dollar Bonds at Given Credit Ratings		
	AAA Rated	BBB Rated	CCC Rated
5%	1	0	0
6%	2	0	0
7%	5	1	0
8%	9	3	1
9%	12	6	3
10%	16	9	7
11%	21	12	8
12%	30	18	13

10. Industrial Development Bonds are being sold by the governments listed. Merrill Walstreep & Company plans to purchase these bonds in the issuing countries' currency, and repackage them as $1 million U.S. debt units. While Merrill is going to charge a brokerage fee for repackaging these debt instruments, they assume no risk, and do not guarantee return of principal and interest to investors. Merrill surveys the top 30 insurance companies and the top 20 money center

banks, and finds the information shown in the table. Plot the capital supply curves for the first $50 million for each country.

| Interest Rate | Cumulative Number of Money Managers Who Would Buy a Million-Dollar Industrial Development Bond from These Countries | | | |
	Russia	Canada	England	Brazil
6%	0	0	1	0
8%	0	2	10	0
10%	0	10	20	1
12%	2	20	30	3
14%	5	30	50	7
16%	8	40	100	10
18%	10	80	200	20
20%	13	100	400	30

CHAPTER 4 EXERCISES

Computation of yield and risk is best performed by learning the tabular computation format in Figure 5–1. The following exercises are designed to familiarize you with the format by presenting partially completed problems and allowing you to finish them.

1. AT&T accounts for 50% of the revenue of Ajax Telemarketing Company. A half a dozen smaller clients account for the other 50% of their work. They have been trying to win Sears as a client for the last year, and there is a 10% probability they will get the Sears account. The marketing department thinks there is a 20% chance of bringing in four small clients, which will also increase revenue. However, there is a 20% chance they will lose AT&T. Compute the expected yield, standard deviation, and coefficient of variation. Note that this problem is set up a little differently in that the probability and rate of return columns are reversed. Data are sometimes presented in this format. However, it has no effect on the outcome of the computation. Other variables and columns, however, should not be switched.

(1)	(2)	(3)	(4)	(5)	(6)	(2) × (6)
	Prob-	**Rate of**				
Scenario	**ability**	**Return**	**(2) × (3)**	**Ki − Ke**	**(Ki − Ke)²**	**(Ki − Ke)² × Pi**
Win Sears	0.1	50%	5%	50% − 10% = 40%	1600	160
Win four small clients	0.2	20%	4%	20% − 10% = 10%		
No change	0.5	10%	5%			
Lose AT&T	0.2	−20%	−4%			

Expected return = Ke = 10%

$$\sigma = \sqrt{\quad}$$

Coefficient of variation =

2. The marketing department of Xenon Corporation has predicted a range of revenues, and assigned a probability of reaching each revenue target. The accounting department has used that information to model ROE for each level of revenue. Compute the expected ROE, the standard deviation, and the coefficient of variation.

(1)	(2)	(3)	(4)	(5)	(6)	(7)
		Expected				
Revenue	**Probability**	**ROE**	**Value**	**Ki − K**	**(Ki − K)²**	**(Ki − K)² × Pi**
$20 M	0.1	25%				
$18 M	0.2	20%				
$16 M	0.3	15%				
$14 M	0.2	10%				
$12 M	0.1	5%				
$10 M	0.1	0%				

3. Compute expected yield, standard deviation, and coefficient of variation given the following historical data:

Year	Yield	Ki − Ke	(Ki − Ke)²
1995	15%		
1996	−5%		
1997	20%		
1998	18%		

$$\Sigma \, (Ki − K)^2 = \quad$$

Ke =

$$\sigma = \sqrt{\quad}$$

Coefficient of variation =

4. Wild West Wranglers is a company out of Pecos, Texas, that buys, restructures, and sells companies in bankruptcy or about to go into bankruptcy. The yield on their stock follows. Compute their expected yield K, standard deviation, and coefficient of variation.

Year	Yield	Ki – Ke	(Ki – Ke)^2
1996	100%		
1997	–40%		
1998	100%		
1999	–10%		
		Σ (Ki – K)^2 =	_____

$K = \quad /4 =$

$$\sigma = \sqrt{\underline{}}$$

Coefficient of variation =

5. Lolly Bank and Trust has the following ROE history. What is their expected yield, standard deviation, and coefficient of variation?

Year	ROE	Ki – Ke	(Ki – Ke)^2
1999	18%		
1998	14%		
1997	13%		
1996	15%		
1995	9%		_____

$$\sigma = \sqrt{\underline{}}$$

Coefficient of variation =

6. Suppose market research indicates that men and women are equally likely to purchase a sports car. Then the company would have to compute the average height and standard deviation for all people. Since a more diverse group is being analyzed, we would expect the standard deviation to be larger. Suppose research found the

expected height (He) of the men and women together was 67 inches, and its standard deviation was 5 inches. If the company wanted to design so that 95% of its target market was comfortable, what height range should it design for?

7. The manufacturing department of the company wants a 95% level confidence (probability) that model cars will completely sell out. Based on an expected sales of 100,000 units and a standard deviation of 6,000 units, how many should the company make?

8. Autoworld Imports is ordering Porsches for their year-end clearance. Carrying costs for Porsches are very high, so they want to be 90% confident of selling whatever they order. The sales manager estimates that she can sell 37 Porsches this year. The general manager calculates that the standard deviation is 3.5 Porsches. How many should the general manager order to be 90% confident of selling out by year-end?

9. Steel Specialty Corporation's stock rises 25% when the market rises 5%, and the stock drops 25% when the market drops 5%. What is the stock's beta?

10. Stock in Marla's Auto Centers usually rises about 10% when the market rises 20%, and drops 10% when the market drops 20%. What is the beta for Marla's Auto Centers?

11. What is the beta of the following portfolio?

Stock	Amount Invested	Beta	Weight
Microsoft	$ 50,000	1.2	
Xcellent Energy	$ 20,000	0.5	
Wild West Wranglers	$ 30,000	3.0	
	$100,000		100.0%

12. Camden Capital Investments has invested in the following. What is the beta of their portfolio?

Stock	Amount Invested	Beta	Weight
Microsoft	$ 500,000	1.2	
Wyeth Labs	$1,000,000	0.9	
Cold Fusion Associates	$ 500,000	4.0	
Internet.com	$1,000,000	4.0	
Super Food Stores	$ 500,000	0.6	
Voorhees Water Company	$1,500,000	0.5	
			100.0%

13. What is the expected yield of the following portfolio?

Stock	Amount Invested	Ke	Weight
Microsoft	$ 50,000	20%	
Xcellent Energy	$ 20,000	10%	
Wild West Wranglers	$ 30,000	40%	
	$100,000		100.0%

14. Compute the required yield of Wild West Wranglers given an equity risk premium of 8%, a Wild West beta of 3.0, and a Krf of 4.5%.

15. Compute the required yield of Microsoft given an equity risk premium of 7%, a Microsoft beta of 1.2, and a Krf of 4.2%.

16. Compute the required yield on Steel Recyclers, Inc. given it has a beta of 1.5, market yield is 12%, and the risk-free rate of return is 4.8%.

CHAPTER 5 EXERCISES

1. What is the future value of a $1,000 investment in a five-year CD with an APR of 5%?

2. Your company has just bought a two-year Wild West Wrangler bond with an APR of 12% compounded monthly. The face amount of the bond is $100,000. The bond interest is accumulated and paid at maturity. At the end of two years, the face amount of the bond and

accumulated interest will be paid to your company. How much will they receive?

3. You purchased a $20,000, five-year Commerce CD, with an APR of 6%, compounded semiannually. How many dollars will you get in five years?

4. K-9 Security Systems has current revenue of $600,000 per year. Five years ago, they had revenue of only $149,000. What is their compound annual sales growth rate?

5. Master Corporation has an EPS of $1.30 per share. Ten years ago, their EPS was only $0.55 per year. What is the compound annual growth rate of their EPS?

6. Assume $5,000 is invested for two years in a 4% CD, interest compounded quarterly. What is the CD payoff at maturity?

7. What is the present value of a $100,000 note with a discount rate of 6%, payable in 50 years?

8. What is the present value of a five-year, $1,000,000 note with a discount rate of 8%, discounted quarterly?

9. Using the present value formula, rather than the tables, compute the present value of a $10,000, two-year, 8% note, discounted semiannually?

10. What is the present value of $2,000 deposited into a 5% IRA every year for 15 years?

11. Your employer agrees to deposit $1,000 per year into a fund for each of the next five years if you continue working for her. The fund yields 8%. What is the present value of those contributions?

12. What are the payments on a $18,000, 30-month, truck loan at 12%?

13. You are thinking about buying a $135,000 house at the shore. The owner is willing to finance the purchase at 8%, with payments due quarterly (not monthly). However, the owner wants to finance the house for only 10 years. What are the quarterly payments?

14. Compute the present value of $2,000 deposited into a 5% IRA every year for 15 years using the present value of an annuity formula.

15. Compute the present value of a deposit of $1,000 per year into a fund yielding 8% for each of the next five years using the present value of an annuity formula.

16. You plan to be the first person in your class to retire and take it easy. You believe you can save $15,000 per year for the next eight years, making a single payment per year to your investment portfolio. Your broker says you can reliably earn 15% per year every year in the stock market. How much will you have to retire on in eight years?

17. After thinking things over, you decide you can save only $1,000 per quarter, and you decide to invest in a fund that has a blend of stocks and risk-free securities. This fund has a yield of only 8%. How much will you have after ten years?

18. Recompute how much you will have to retire on using the future value of an annuity formula, not the tables. The facts are you can save $1,000 per quarter, and you decide to invest in a fund that has a yield of only 8%. How much will you have to retire on after ten years?

CHAPTER 6 EXERCISES

1. Compute the value of a Minsk Brick Works bond with a par value of $500,000 that makes an annual interest payment of $60,000. The bond matures in two years. Bonds of similar "quality" yield 20%.

2. Compute the value of a G.E. corporate bond with a par value of $1,000,000, a five-year maturity, interest paid semiannually, and a coupon rate of 7%. Bonds of similar quality yield 6%. Hint: Compute the value of a semiannual interest payment first, then compute the Kd and n needed for your present bond valuation equation.

3. Suppose your broker has a 30-year, $100,000, Santa Fe Railroad bond with a coupon rate of 2.75%, interest payable semiannually. Bonds of similar quality yield 8%. The bonds will mature in 3 years. What is the value of such a bond? Remember to adjust Kd, the

discount, or yield rate, and *n*, the number of periods for compounding before actually computing the bond value.

4. Wild West Wranglers is offering a $100,000, ten-year bond, with a 10% APR, interest payable quarterly. The bond is callable after three years with a call premium of 7.5%. Bonds of similar quality yield 16%. What should you offer for the bond? Before you answer this question, first compute (a) the period interest rate that will be used to compute each interest payment, (b) the amount of each interest payment, (c) the period discount rate used in the bond valuation equations, (d) the number of periods used to compute the value to maturity, (e) the bond value assuming it is held to maturity, (f) how many periods would be used to value the bond to call, assuming the bond will be called in three years, and (g) the value to call.

5. Microsoft has a ten-year bond, with a face value of $10,000, and a coupon rate of 8.5%, interest payable annually. It was issued two years ago, and matures in eight years. It is callable *five years from date of issue* with a call premium of 5%. Bonds of a similar quality yield 6%. Since interest rates are dropping, it is certain Microsoft will call the bond. What is the bond value assuming it will be called?

6. What is the yield on a $10,000 Bruno Credit Corporation bond, with an APR of 10%, interest payable annually, which has four years to maturity? The price of the bond is $9,200. Hint: To solve this problem, values test1 and test2 will have to be computed using informed judgment to select k1 and k2. Use k1, k2, test1, test2, and the market value of the bond to solve for the yield, *K*, using the following interpolation formula.

$$\frac{test2 - test1}{k2 - k1} = \frac{Vm - test1}{K - k1}$$

7. What is the yield on a Wild West Wrangler bond with a face value of $250,000, a coupon rate of 10%, interest

paid semiannually, and that matures in six years? The bond is currently selling for $210,000.

8. Uganda National Railway bonds, $100,000 denomination, are priced at 62% of face value. They mature in six years, have a coupon rate of 6%, and pay interest annually. What is their yield?

9. The Minsk Brick Works has issued a ten-year, $1,000,000 bond with a coupon rate of 15%, interest payable annually. The bond has a call provision that allows Minsk to call the bond two years after issue at a premium of 10%. The International Monetary Fund is putting together a debt relief program that will allow former Soviet Block debtors to refinance at 2%, so it is certain the bonds will be called in two years. The bond is selling for $980,000. What is its yield to call? Hint: The rate at which Minsk can refinance is irrelevant, so ignore it. The interpolation formula used to solve this problem is as follows:

$$\frac{\text{test2} - \text{test1}}{\text{k2} - \text{k1}} = \frac{\text{Vm} - \text{test1}}{\text{K} - \text{k1}}$$

10. Campbell's Soup issued a $100,000, 20-year bond, with a 9% coupon, interest payable annually, seven years ago. They have the right to call the bond ten years after issue for a call premium of 6%. Because interest rates have dropped so dramatically, it is certain they will call the bonds in three years. The bond is currently selling for $103,500. What is its yield to call?

11. Microsoft issued a $500,000 bond that will be called in four years. The coupon rate on the bond is 8%. Interest is paid *semiannually*. The call premium is 7.5%. The bond is selling for $520,000. What is its yield to call?

CHAPTER 7 EXERCISES

1. Murry, of Murry's Cheesesteak fame, is going to finance a new, stainless-steel kitchen by leasing it from Sharkleaseco. The kitchen appliances and equipment he

picked out sell for $18,000. The equipment lease will be four years. Monthly payments will be $500.94. Given only this information, what is the imputed interest rate on Murray's leased equipment?

2. Murry hires a Rutger's finance student as a part-time bookkeeper. The student looks over the fine print in Murray's lease with Sharkleaseco and discovers that Murray had to make the first and last three payments at the lease signing.

   a. How much is Murray actually financing?

   b. How many more monthly payments must he make?

   c. What is the effective interest rate on the lease?

   d. Given that "excess interest," defined as the difference in rates between what Murray thought he was paying, from Exercise 1, and what he is actually paying from 2 (c), times the amount that is actually being financed from 2 (a), and his gross margin on every cheesesteak is $0.50, how many cheesesteaks will he have to sell to cover the "excess interest"?

3. Replicant Technologies has just gotten a contract from Genetics, Inc. to grow genetically engineered bacteria that produce proteins used in various medical applications. The five-year contract is contingent on Replicant building a plant to Genetics's specifications. The plant will cost $2 million. Replicant's bank has had the loan application for a month without committing, saying they need more information and a blanket lien on the personal assets of all Replicant officers and directors. Replicant asks the 1950 Leasing Company to submit a bid. 1950 will provide a 60-month lease for the plant at $46,020 per month. There is no fine print. What is the imputed interest rate?

4. Replicant's outside directors ask New Age Leasing for a bid, and New Age agrees to a 60-month lease at $44,000 per month, with $130,000 deposit, and the first and last month's lease payments in advance. What is the imputed interest rate on the New Age lease?

5. a. Prepare an amortization table for the first three monthly payments for Murray's Cheesesteaks,

assuming the amount actually financed is $15,996.30, the imputed rate is 18.2%, and there are 44 payments remaining.

b. Prepare the journal entry to record the acquisition of assets subject to his lease.

c. Prepare the journal entries for the first month's *actual* payment.

d. Assuming the lease agreement were signed just before the fiscal year-end, *estimate* the current portion of leases payable based on the first three months of the amortization table.

CHAPTER 8 EXERCISES

1. Tux Manufacturing has paid a constant dividend of $0.85 per year since 1965. Analysts expect Tux to pay this dividend forever. Stocks of similar riskiness yield 11%. What is the expected price for Tux Manufacturing?

2. Doctor Explorations has a dividend of $1.35 per share, and is growing at the rate of 15%. The required rate of return on a company of comparable riskiness, Kr, is 18%. What would you expect the price of Doctor Explorations to be?

3. The EPS (earnings per share) of Strategic Consulting, Inc. has been growing at the rate of 15% per year. Dividend policy is to pay out 80% of earnings as dividends to stockholders. This means that dividends grow at the same rate as earnings. The last dividend was $1.60 per share. The stock is currently selling for $22.50 per share. What is the expected rate of return on Strategic?

4. DNA Systems just got their antibaldness drug approved by the FDA. They expect 100% growth for the next three years as they ramp up for production. Thereafter, they expect 12% growth rate for the foreseeable future. Their last dividend was $0.50. The required rate of return, Kr, is 15%.

a. Compute the expected dividends for the next three years using the formula: Dt + 1 = Dt × (1 + *g*), to get D1, D2, and D3.

   b. Compute the expected price at the end of the period of high growth using the formula

$$\text{Pet} = \frac{\text{Dt} \times (1 + g)}{\text{Kr} - g} = \frac{\text{Dt} + 1}{\text{Kr} - g}$$

   c. Discount the dividends, D1, D2, and D3, and the expected value of the stock, Pe3, back to the present value using the required rate of return Kr = 15% to get the expected price Pe0.

5. Jack's Telemarketing expects to grow 50%, per year for four years. Thereafter, it is expected to grow 15% per year. Jack's last dividend was $0.80. The required rate of return is 18%.

   a. Compute the expected dividends for the next four years: D1, D2, D3, and D4.

   b. Compute the expected price at the end of the period of high growth using the formula

$$\text{Pe4} = \frac{\text{D4} \times (1 + g)}{\text{Kr} - g} = \frac{\text{D5}}{\text{Kr} - g}$$

   c. Discount the dividends, D1, D2, D3, and D4, and the expected value of the stock, Pe4, back to the present value using the required rate of return Kr = 18%. What is its expected price, Pe0?

CHAPTER 9 EXERCISES

1. What is the incremental cost of debt capital for a company where the interest rate for new bonds is 15%, and the company's marginal tax rate is 25%?

2. What is the incremental cost of debt capital for a company that has an available line of credit at the prime rate plus 1%, where the prime rate is 8.5%? Assume the company's marginal tax rate is 40%.

3. Kravitz International wants to sell $10,000 preferred stock with an annual dividend of $750. Flotation costs are $900 per share. What is the cost of capital for this new preferred stock issue?

4. Composite Materials, Inc. wants to raise $10,000,000 through issue of 10,000 shares of preferred stock at par. Each share of stock will throw off an annual dividend of $85. Their flotation costs are 6%. What is the cost of capital for this preferred stock?

5. Consider the following information: last dividend = $1.00, growth rate = 4%, current price = $10. The risk-free rate is 4.2%, the market risk premium is 8%, and the stock's beta is 1.1. Long-term bond yield is 9.5%, and the judgment risk premium for equity is 4%. What is the cost of new retained earnings using (a) the stock yield method, (b) the CAPM method, and (c) the bond yield plus judgment premium method?

6. Your boss at Morgan Standish asked you to compute the cost of capital for retained earnings of Pinelands Publishing. From your *Value Line* research and other Morgan Standish files, you have discovered the following: Pineland's last dividend was $0.40 per share. Their cash flow for the last five years has been growing at a steady 11% per year. Their current stock price is $22. Their long-term bonds have a yield to maturity of 8.5%. Pinelands has a beta of 0.85. Right now the equity risk premium is 6%, and the risk-free rate of return is 4.9%. Morgan Standish's policy is to use a 5% judgment risk premium on any company that, like Pinelands, has under $100 million in revenue. Compute the cost of new retained earnings capital using (a) the stock yield method, (b) the CAPM method, and (c) the bond yield and judgment risk premium method.

7. Fractal Systems wants to issue new stock. Their underwriter finds they have been growing at 7.5% per year, and the best price for a technology stock is $20. Furthermore, the new underwriter insists their next dividend, D1, be $1.00 per share. The underwriters have agreed to do the flotation for 9.5% of share price. What is their cost of new equity capital?

8. K-9 Security has the following capital structure: 80% debt, with an *after tax* rate of 6.5%; 1% preferred stock, which

costs *net of flotation* 8%; and 19% equity, which costs 15%. What is the weighted average cost of capital, WACC?

9. Given the following information about Dunn Labs, what will be their WACC? Debt = 50%, preferred = 20%, and common equity = 30%. Price, $43; dividend, $3.00; growth rate, −2%; annual preferred stock dividend, $82 per $1,000 share with flotation costs of 7.5% per share; and interest, 11%. Though sales have risen slightly year to year, they lost money for the last two years, so their tax rate is zero.

10. Brooklyn Refinancing Corporation wants to raise $20,000,000 to expand its portfolio of second mortgages and substandard auto loans. Bank financing agreements limit Brooklyn to 75% debt. They can borrow money at 13%, and they are in the 40% tax bracket. New retained earnings are $200,000. Brooklyn can privately place $1,000,000 of preferred stock at 12%, and preferred floatation costs are 7.5%. Their current stock price is $15; dividends are $0.75, and have been growing at 20% per year; and flotation costs are $3 per share. Compute the weighted average cost of capital considering the following strategy.

   a. What is the weighted average cost of new capital using only new retained earnings (25%) and debt (75%)?

   b. What is the weighted average cost of new capital from the preferred stock offering with a blend of 25% preferred and 75% debt?

   c. What is the weighted average cost of new capital maintaining a mix of 25% newly issued common stock and 75% debt?

   Hint: The first task in solving this problem is to define the intervals for the weighting. It has already been demonstrated that the amount that can be financed through new retained earnings is as follows:

   $$\frac{\text{New capital from}}{\text{retained earnings}} = \text{Retained earnings/Equity\%}$$

   $$\frac{\text{New capital from}}{\text{preferred stock}} = \text{Preferred/Preferred\%}$$

The balance of the $20,000,000 to be raised will come from newly issued common equity 25% and 75% debt.

11. Cinnaminson Soups wants to expand. Their bank will lend them $300,000 at 12% interest on the condition they will not enter any capital leases. In the alternative, the bank will provide a $50,000 line of credit and allow them to lease whatever equipment they want. Charleasco is willing to finance, via lease, a new $500,000 plant at an imputed interest rate of 20%. Cinnaminson is in the 30% tax bracket; assume imputed interest is tax deductible. The only way Cinnaminson can raise more than $600,000 is to issue new common stock. Since they have two mutually exclusive ways of raising capital, depending on whether they borrow $300,000 from the bank or only $50,000 and use lease financing, they have two different marginal cost of capital curves. What should they do? What is their optimal capital budget?

Marginal Cost of Capital (thousands of dollars)

With Maximum Bank Financing		Cost	With Minimal Bank Financing		Cost
Bank financing	$0 to $300	8.4%	Bank financing	$0 to $50	8.4%
New retained earnings	$300 to $350	10.5%	New retained earnings	$50 to $100	10.5%
New common stock	$350 to $600	18.0%	Charleasco	$100 to $600	14.0%

Capital Projects for Expansion (cost in thousands of dollars)

A. Purchase adjoining property and 4 to 50 gallon kettles	$ 65	15%
B. Build new, automated plant	$500	17%
C. Purchase automated jar filler machine	$ 30	23%
D. Lease and refurbish unused soup plant	$300	13%
E. Invest in marketing and advertising campaign	$ 9	25%
F. Purchase and refurbish unused Campbell Soup plant	$900	17%

CHAPTER 10 EXERCISES

1. Glass Co. wants to invest $200,000 in a furnace. Cash inflows from the project will be $50,000, $100,000, and $100,000 in years 1, 2, and 3. What is the payback period?

2. Powdered Metals Corp. wants to invest $500,000 in a
   metal press. Cash inflows from this project will be Y1 =
   $250,000, Y2 = $300,000, Y3 = $350,000, Y4 = $400,000.
   What is the payback period?

3. Packett Machine Tools wants to buy a numerically
   control milling machine that costs $2,000,000. The cash
   inflows from this milling machine, net of all operating
   costs, are Y1 = $500,000, Y2 = $1,000,000, Y3 =
   $1,000,000, Y4 = 1,000,000. The discount rate is 15%.
   What is the discounted payback period?

4. Mega Corporation wants to buy Mini Corporation. It is
   an all-cash purchase. The price is $600,000. The discount
   rate on this investment is 20%. The projections are that
   Mini Corporation will throw off the following cash
   during the next five years. What is the discounted
   payback period?

Y1	$100,000
Y2	$150,000
Y3	$225,000
Y4	$350,000
Y5	$500,000

5. Packett Machine Tools wants to buy a numerically
   control milling machine that costs $2,000,000. The cash
   inflows from this milling machine, net of all operating
   costs, are Y1 = $500,000, Y2 = $1,000,000, Y3 = $1,000,000,
   Y4 = $1,000,000. The discount rate is 15%. What is
   the NPV?

6. Mega Corporation wants to buy Mini Corporation for
   cash. The price is $600,000. The discount rate on this
   investment is 20%. The projections are that Mini
   Corporation will throw off the following cash during
   the next five years. What is the net present value of the
   acquisition?

Y1	$100,000
Y2	$150,000
Y3	$225,000
Y4	$350,000
Y5	$500,000

7. Powdered Metals Corp. wants to invest $500,000 in a metal press. Cash inflows from this project will be Y1 = $250,000, Y2 = $300,000, Y3 = $350,000, Y4 = $400,000. The discount rate is 18%. What is the NPV of this project?

8. Powdered Metals Corp. wants to invest $500,000 in a metal press. Cash inflows from this project will be Y1 = $250,000, Y2 = $300,000, Y3 = $350,000, Y4 = $400,000, Y5 = $400,000. What is the internal rate of return (IRR) of this project? Hint: Let IRR1 = 24%. *To facilitate practice calculations, only use whole dollars.*

9. Packett Machine Tools wants to buy a numerical control milling machine that costs $2,000,000. The cash inflows from this milling machine, net of all operating costs, are Y1 = $500,000, Y2 = $1,000,000, Y3 = $1,000,000, Y4 = 1,000,000. What is the IRR?

10. Powdered Metals Corp. has re-evaluated their metal press project and has decided that materials technology is moving so fast that the project must be self-liquidating in four years to be worthwhile. Recalculate IRR using the following information. Invest $500,000 in a metal press. Cash inflows from this project will be Y1 = $250,000, Y2 = $300,000, Y3 = $350,000, Y4 = $400,000. What is the IRR of this project?

11. Calculate the modified internal rate of return (MIRR) for Powdered Metals Corp.'s metal press project. The investment is $500,000. Cash inflows from this project will be Y1 = $250,000, Y2 = $300,000, Y3 = $350,000, Y4 = $400,000.

12. Galaxy Paint Corporation wants to build a temporary plant in Gibbsboro to make paint for a large housing complex being built in the area. The temporary plant will cost $120,000. Demand for the paint will evaporate when the housing complex is complete in three years. Cash inflows are Y1 = $40,000, Y2 = $60,000, and Y3 = $40,000. What is the MIRR of the temporary plant?

CHAPTER 11 EXERCISES

1. Bernard Broadcasting is considering replacing its 250,000-watt television transmitter with a 2,000,000-watt transmitter. The upgrade will allow it to reach another 300,000 households and increase advertising revenue by $3 million per year. As a result, they expect accounts receivable to increase by $270,000. The transmitter will cost $800,000, and installation costs will be $150,000. Net profit after tax will increase by $400,000 per year. The transmitter will be obsolete in ten years, at which time, it can be sold for $20,000. Compute relevant cash flows over the life of the project.

2. Johnson Telemarketing wants to open a 200-workstation telemarketing center in Glassboro. Because of changes in the industry and technology, the life of the project is expected to be four years. The building will cost $800,000, and for tax purposes will be depreciated over 40 years. Two years ago, Johnson paid $50,000 for an option to purchase the land that will cost an additional $100,000 if the project is approved. Computer and telephone equipment will cost $400,000 and will be depreciated for tax purposes over four years, straight line. Net working capital to fund accounts receivable will be about $500,000. Revenue will be $35,000 per workstation. Cost of sales (cost of services sold) is about 75%. Sales and marketing costs are 5%. Fixed costs are $150,000 per year. The company's tax rate is 40%. After four years, the computer and phone equipment will have a salvage value of $10,000. The building and land will have a salvage value of $740,000. Compute the relevant cash flows. Use the following format to compute the relevant cash flows.

Johnson Telemarketing: Cash Flow Estimation for Glassboro Facility

	Year 0	Year 1	Year 2	Year 3	Year 4
Investment Outlays					
1. Building and land					
2. Equipment					
3. Increase in NWC					
Total net investment					

Operating Cash Flows

1. Revenue
2. Cost of goods sold 75% of sales
3. Selling costs 5% of sales
4. Fixed costs
5. Depreciation building
6. Depreciation equipment
7. Pretax operating income
8. Taxes @ 40%
9. After-tax income
10. Add back depreciation
11. Operating cash flows

Terminal Year Cash Flows

1. Salvage value of plant and equipment
2. Less book value of plant and equip.
3. Gain or loss on salvage
4. Taxes on gain or loss @ 40%
5. Plus cash from salvage value sale
6. Salvage cash net of tax
7. Return of networking capital
8. Net terminal cash flows

	Outflow	Inflow	Inflow	Inflow	Inflow

Relevant Cash Flows

CHAPTER 12 EXERCISES

1. Bilo Builders has 6,000 cinder blocks left over from construction of the city hall. Bilo is planning to build a retail complex that will use 4,000 cinder blocks. New cinder blocks can be purchased for $1.50 each. Bilo's leftover cinder blocks, because they have to be cleaned up, have a fair market value (FMV) of $1.00 each. Bilo decides to use its leftover cinder blocks in the retail complex. What is their cost for 4,000 cinder blocks?

2. Bilo needs a tank truck to haul water to construction sites. It considers buying a tank truck, then decides to build one using a 1997 Ford flatbed truck it has out back. The truck cost $38,000 new. A new flatbed truck

will cost $45,000. The book value of the truck is $0. The fair market value of the truck is $2,000. What cost should Bilo assign to the flatbed in connection with the tank truck project?

3. Patrick buys 60,000 cubic yards of gravel in May for $600,000. In May, he sells 40,000 cubic yards at $30 per cubic yard.
   a. What is his cost of gravel in May?
   b. What is his gravel expense in May?
   c. What is his gravel inventory (in dollars) on June 1?

4. Brandon Airships buys components and assembles them into aircraft. Costs include $7,000 per engine, $11,000 per airframe, $4,800 for instrumentation, and miscellaneous components. Certified mechanics cost $30 per hour, and it takes 40 hours to assemble a plane. Variable manufacturing overhead, including electricity and lubricants, is $400 per plane. Rent and other fixed manufacturing overhead is $10,000 per month. Brandon expects to build 48 planes per year. What is the full absorption cost per plane?

5. Charon Books is a publisher with the following cost structure: rolls of paper cost $400 out of which Charon can cut 200 books. Binding and covers cost about $2.00 per book. A printer's wages, tax and workers' compensation costs $150 per day. Such a printer can print about 300 books per day. Ink and shop supplies are about $1 per book. Rent, electricity, and lease payments on printing equipment cost $8,000 per month. Charon prints about 200,000 books per year. What is its full absorption cost per book?

6. Winslow Electronics manufactures electronic motor controls. It has the following cost structure: direct labor is $15 per unit, direct materials are $20 per unit, variable manufacturing overhead is $4 per unit, sales commissions are $10 per unit, fixed manufacturing overhead is $60,000 per year. Winslow expects to manufacture 30,000 units this year. What is their full absorption cost per controller?

7. Winslow Electronics has a beginning inventory of 800 motor controllers at a full absorption cost of $41. Purchases for direct labor are $450,000; for direct materials, $600,000; for variable manufacturing overhead, $120,000; and fixed manufacturing overhead of $60,000 is fully absorbed by 30,000 units. At the end of the year, they have an inventory of 1,100 motor controllers. What is their cost of goods sold?

8. Pennsauken Concrete Beams had a beginning inventory of 20 cast concrete beams at a full absorption cost of $900 per beam. Purchases for direct labor, direct materials, variable and fixed factory overhead were $91,800. Fixed manufacturing overhead was completely absorbed. Ending inventory was 30 cast concrete beams at a full absorption cost of $900 each. What is Pennsauken's cost of goods sold?

9. Brandon Airships costs are $7,000 per engine, $11,000 per airframe, $4,800 for instrumentation and miscellaneous components. Certified mechanics cost $30 per hour, and it takes 40 hours to assemble a plane. Variable manufacturing overhead, including electricity and shop supplies, costs $400 per plane. Brandon has one plane in inventory at the beginning of the year at a full absorption cost of $26,000, and no planes in inventory at year-end. Rent and other fixed manufacturing overhead is $10,000 per month. Brandon expected to build 48 planes per year. However, a delay in shipping engines reduced actual output to 45 planes for the year.
   a. What is the full absorption cost per plane?
   b. What is the amount of unallocated manufacturing overhead, if any?
   c. What is the cost of goods sold?
   d. What is the average cost of a unit sold?

10. Pennsauken Concrete Beams had a beginning inventory of 20 cast concrete beams at a full absorption cost of $1,000 per beam. Purchases for direct labor were $150 per beam, direct materials were $400 per beam, variable manufacturing overhead was $50 per beam, and fixed

manufacturing overhead was $180,000. Pennsauken expected to make 600 beams for the year but only made 540. Ending inventory was 30 cast concrete beams.

a. What is Pennsauken's full absorption cost per beam?

b. Was there any unallocated manufacturing overhead? If so, how much and where would that cost be recorded?

c. What is Pennsauken's cost of goods sold?

d. What is the average cost of a unit sold?

11. Brandon Airships costs are $7,000 per engine, $11,000 per airframe, $4,800 for miscellaneous components. Certified mechanic assembly labor is $1,200. Variable manufacturing overhead, including shop supplies, is $400 per plane. Brandon has one plane in inventory at the beginning of the year at a full absorption cost of $26,000, and two planes in inventory at year-end. Fixed manufacturing overhead is $10,000 per month. It expects to build 48 planes per year. However, because of changes in factory floor layout, Brandon produces 52 planes without increasing fixed manufacturing costs.

a. What is the full absorption cost per plane? Note that if Brandon believed the change in production capacity were permanent, it would want to increase its estimated production capacity from 48 to 52 planes *in subsequent years*. This would lower the fixed manufacturing overhead burden from $2,500 to $2,308 per plane.

b. What is the amount of unallocated manufacturing overhead, if any?

c. What is the cost of goods sold, assuming all 52 planes were sold?

d. What is the average cost of the Airships sold?

12. Pennsauken Concrete had a beginning inventory of 20 concrete beams at a full absorption cost of $1,000 per beam. Purchases for direct labor were $150 per beam, direct materials were $400 per beam, variable manufacturing overhead was $50 per beam, and fixed factory overhead was $180,000. Pennsauken expected to

make 600 beams; however, because of good weather, it
was able to make 650. Ending inventory was 30 beams.
a. What is Pennsauken's full absorption cost per beam?
b. Was there any unallocated manufacturing overhead?
   If so, how much and where would that cost be
   recorded?
c. What is Pennsauken's cost of goods sold?
d. What is the average cost of the beams sold?

13. Washington Equipment Company imports Kubuto
    tractors. Tractors cost $11,000, import duties are $1,650,
    freight in is $1,500. Once they are at the dealers, they
    have to be unpacked and inspected, which takes two
    hours at $30 per hour. What is the cost of each tractor?

14. Brandon Airships costs are $7,000 per engine,
    $11,000 per airframe, $4,800 for instrumentation and
    miscellaneous components. Certified mechanics cost
    $30 per hour, and it takes 40 hours to assemble a plane.
    Variable manufacturing overhead is $400 per plane.
    Brandon has one plane in inventory at the beginning of
    the year at a full absorption cost of $26,000, and two
    planes in inventory at year-end. Fixed manufacturing
    overhead is $10,000 per month. He expects to build 48
    planes per year. However, because of changes in his
    factory floor layout, it produces 52 planes per year
    without increasing fixed manufacturing costs. The price
    of planes is $39,000 each, and sales commissions are 5%.
    What is Brandon's variable cost per plane?

15. Pennsauken Concrete had a beginning inventory of
    20 concrete beams at a full absorption cost of $1,000 per
    beam. Purchases for direct labor were $150 per beam,
    direct materials were $400 per beam, variable
    manufacturing overhead was $50 per beam, and fixed
    factory overhead was $180,000. Sales commission is
    $75 per beam. Pennsauken expected to make 600 beams
    for the year; however, because of good weather, it was
    able to make 650 beams. Inventory was 30 cast concrete
    beams. What is Pennsauken's variable cost per beam?

16. Brandon Airships costs for components is $22,800; direct assembly labor is $1,200; variable manufacturing overhead is $400 per plane; and fixed manufacturing overhead is $10,000 per month. Brandon has one plane in inventory at the beginning of the year at a full absorption cost of $26,000, and two planes in inventory at year-end. Brandon expects to build 48 planes per year. However, it produces 52 planes without increasing fixed manufacturing overhead. Brandon sells his Airships for $39,000 each.
   a. What is Brandon's gross profit per plane?
   b. What is Brandon's contribution margin per plane?

CHAPTER 13 EXERCISES

1. Loren decides to raise her cookie prices to $6 per pound. What is her break-even given variable costs are $2.25 per pound, and fixed costs include cart rent of $800 per month and sales labor costs of $8 per hour for 124 hours per month?

2. Cherry Hill Motor Sports was dismayed when Nissan Corporation discontinued their 300ZX line of sports cars. They approach Nissan with an offer to buy all the tools, dies, patents, and so forth to make 300ZXs. Nissan will continue to manufacture the engines and transmissions. Cherry Hill will subcontract out all other parts and do assembly in a Camden assembly plant. Assuming each 300ZX can be sold for $30,000, variable costs are $22,000 per car, and fixed costs for the plant, and so on are $20,000,000, what is the number of cars Cherry Hill will have to sell to break even?

3. Nissan 300ZX transmissions cost $1,200 each. Cherry Hill buys compatible Mustang Cobra GT transmissions for $700 each. What is the new break-even for Cherry Hill Motor Sport on 300ZX production?

4. Cherry Hill turns to Venture Capitalists to fund startup of 300ZX production. The threshold criteria for this investment is to make $5,000,000 per year profit. Assume Mustang Cobra GT transmissions are going to

be used. What is the break-even number of units needed to meet the Venture Capitalists' investment criteria?

5. Moe, Larry, and Curly decide to open a discount electronics store in the Berlin Mart. They believe that if they limit their margin to 20% on all product lines, they can undercut major chains like Wal-Mart. Their fixed costs are $300,000 per month. What is their break-even in sales dollars?

6. Moe, Larry, and Curly each want to take $10,000 per month out of the business as salary. Using break-even analysis, what would their sales volume have to be to achieve their goal?

7. Curly wants to spend 3% of revenue each month on advertising. Larry doesn't want to raise prices. Nobody wants to take a pay cut. What will their sales volume have to be if 3% of sales is dedicated to advertising, reducing their margin to 17%?

8. Loren has three successful mall carts, each selling cookies in a different mall. Her subcontract bakers are now making about a ton of cookies per month for her. However, she finds the logistics of having many people baking for her, at different locations, is causing both distribution and quality-control problems. She has two alternatives.

   a. A local bakery has just gone out of business, and Loren is considering leasing the facility and bringing all of her bakers together in one place. Pricing tests indicate $5.00 per pound is best. She estimates variable costs will be $2.00 per pound for her cookies, and fixed costs for the three mall stores totals $5,376. Fixed costs for the bakery will be $11,000 per month. What is her break-even?

   b. An alternative is to subcontract with Frank's Bakery, which will charge her $3.25 per pound for cookies, but she knows her quality control and distribution problems will be solved. What is her break-even?

   c. Which of these two alternatives gives Loren a lower break-even?

9. Executive Furniture's marketing department has looked at all its current and potential clients in the Boston–

Washington corridor and assigned expected sales volume and probabilities to each of them. The finance department has used this information to compute the standard deviation of profits, $185,000. The board of directors wants to know what sales forecast would yield a 95% confidence of meeting target profits. Gross margin is 30%, fixed costs are $7 million, and target profits are $3 million.

10. Loren has researched the profitability of other cookie makers and found that the standard deviation of profits is 12%. Loren wants to be somewhat confident, let's say 68% confident, of meeting target profits if she leases and reopens a bakery. Her variable costs per pound of cookies are $2.00, fixed costs for the three mall stores total $5,376, and fixed costs for the bakery will be $11,000 per month. Her target profit is $8,000 per month. What sales volume satisfies all these conditions?

11. Moe, Larry, and Curly want to be 95% confident they can achieve target "profits" of $30,000 per month ($10,000 for each of them) before they invest in a Berlin Mart store. The standard deviation of forecast profits is $20,000. Their margin is 18%; fixed costs are $300,000 per month. What is their break-even in sales dollars?

CHAPTER 14 EXERCISES

1. Jack, a high school teacher, plans to start a lawn care company. He accepts only credit cards. From the time he sends credit card receipts to the bank until money is transferred to his account is about 45 days. Jack pays weekly. Assume his first payroll will be $960. How much cash must he have to cover startup payroll?

2. Collection Services, Inc. just got Biggie Blue Cross as a client. Collection Services has agreed to bill for services on an hourly, rather than its usual contingent, basis. They have hired five new collection agents who will work 30 hours per week at $15 per hour, including employer taxes. Collection services bills and pays weekly. It knows that Biggie Blue Cross pays in 120 days. What is the required cash for collection to take on this new client?

3. Alan Pine, a OrganoGarden franchisee, plans to expand into Voorhees Township this summer. Pine's two major costs are labor, $15 per hour, including taxes, and OrganoGarden liquid spray that costs him $8 per gallon from the franchiser who is located in Pennsauken. The typical garden application takes two hours, and uses four gallons of spray. Clients pay by credit card, Pine doesn't want his crews to have to account for cash or checks, and he doesn't want to have to bill people. His credit card company pays in an average of 45 days. Starting May 1, Alan thinks he can apply OrganoGarden spray to 50 gardens per week. He pays weekly. Crews load up on OrganoGarden spray at the franchiser each morning, so there is no inventory to carry, and the franchiser grants Pine 10 days to pay. What is the total cash required to add Voorhees?

4. Drs. Smith and Jones are officers of Doctor's Medical Service, which has a $150,000 line of credit with Evesham National Bank. Evesham defines borrowing capacity as net tangible assets × 75%. Accounts receivable over 90 days and amounts due from officers and employees are excluded. Given the following asset schedule, (a) what is the borrowing capacity of Doctor's Medical? (b) how much of their line of credit can they draw on?

Cash	$ 2,000
Accounts receivable 0–30 days	$ 60,000
Accounts receivable 31–60 days	$ 40,000
Accounts receivable 61–90 days	$ 20,000
Accounts receivable 91–365 days	$ 95,000
Due from Dr. Smith	$ 35,000
Due from Dr. Jones	$ 25,000
Inventory: medical supplies	$ 6,000
Medical equipment	$ 20,000
Total assets:	$303,000
Accounts payable	$ 40,000
Accrued payroll	$ 10,000
Total liabilities	$ 50,000

5. A collection agency purchases all accounts receivable over 90 days for 30% of their face value, net to Doctor's

Medical Service. Dr. Jones borrows another $5,000 from the practice, reducing cash $5,000 and increasing due from Dr. Jones $5,000. What is their new borrowing capacity?

6. Pesto Bug Strips sell to small mom-and-pop hardware stores that usually pay in 60 to 90 days. Their peak selling season is June and July. They run their factory overtime in April and May. In February, they expect to purchase and install an automatic bug (strip) making machine. Their net, month-to-month cash flow is forecast as follows. How much of their financing should be (a) via line of credit? (b) permanent financing?

January	$ 10,000	July	$ 30,000
February	-$105,000	August	$ 40,000
March	$ 2,000	September	$310,000
April	-$300,000	October	$250,000
May	-$400,000	November	$ 60,000
June	$ 20,000	December	-$ 5,000

7. Argent Manufacturing needs $50,000 to develop a prototype computer controlled valve, and another $250,000 to set up a manufacturing line in its factory. Argent's bank is trying to use the request for an additional $300,000 to impose more onerous conditions on Argent's existing $500,000 line of credit. The president of Argent has asked you whether she can raise the money by laying off workers. She has given you the following information:

ARGENT MANUFACTURING FINANCIALS

Assets		Liabilities	
Cash	$ 10,000	Accrued payroll	$ 150,000
Receivables 0–90 days	$ 2,600,000	Accounts payable	$ 500,000
Receivables 91–365 days	$ 200,000	Line of credit	$ 4,100,000
Inventory	$ 4,600,000	Current portion of loans	$ 250,000
Total current assets	$ 7,410,000	Total current liabilities	$ 5,000,000
Equipment	$ 1,090,000	Bank loans	$ 3,000,000
Plant:	$ 1,500,000	Equity	$ 2,000,000
Total assets	$10,000,000	Total liabilities and equity	$10,000,000

ARGENT MANUFACTURING FINANCIALS

Income Statement

Revenue	$14,000,000	*Operating expenses include
Cost of goods sold	$ 9,800,000	depreciation of $150,000
Gross profit	$ 4,200,000	
Operating expenses*	$ 3,900,000	
Profit before interest and tax	$ 300,000	

Credit terms are 30 days. The average accounts receivable turnover in the industry is 10:1. Collection firms will purchase Argent's accounts receivable without recourse for 25% of their face amount. An aging of inventory based on sales records indicates

Items representing $2,500,000 turn over in 30 days or less. Average turnover 20 days.

Items representing $1,100,000 turn over in 31 to 90 days. Average turnover 65 days.

Items representing $500,000 turn over in 91 to 180 days. Average turnover 120 days.

Items representing $500,000 turn over in more than 181 days. Average turnover 400 days.

(a) How much cash can be raised through better accounts receivable management?

(b) How much cash can be raised through better inventory management?

8. Deptford Heavy Trucks needs $5,000,000 to expand its truck manufacturing facility in Thorofare. A Woodbury factor routinely purchases 91 to 365 day accounts receivable without recourse for 35% of their face value. Deptford's credit terms are 30 days. Average inventory turnover in heavy truck manufacturing is 9:1. How much of that $5,000,000 could be raised by more prudent management of current assets?

DEPTFORD HEAVY TRUCKS FINANCIALS

Assets		Liabilities	
Cash	$ 100,000	Accrued payroll	$ 500,000
Receivables 0–90 days	$ 8,000,000	Accounts payable	$ 1,500,000
Receivables 91–365 days	$ 1,800,000	Current portion of leases	$ 400,000
Receivables > 365 days	$ 200,000	Line of credit	$ 5,100,000
Inventory	$ 7,000,000	Current portion of loans	$ 1,500,000
Total current assets	$17,100,000	Total current liabilities	$ 9,000,000
Equipment	$ 3,900,000	Bank loans	$ 7,000,000
Plant:	$ 4,000,000	Equity	$ 9,000,000
Total assets	$25,000,000	Total liabilities and equity	$25,000,000

Income Statement

Revenue:	$60,000,000	*Operating expenses include
Cost of goods sold	$42,000,000	depreciation of $1,000,000
Gross profit	$18,000,000	
Operating expenses*	$13,000,000	
Profit before interest and tax	$ 5,000,000	

Aged Inventory on an Item-by-Item Basis

Items representing $3,000,000 turn over in 30 days or less. Average turnover 20 days.
Items representing $2,000,000 turn over in 31 to 90 days. Average turnover 65 days.
Items representing $500,000 turn over in 91 to 180 days. Average turnover 120 days.
Items representing $1,500,000 turn over more than 181 days. Average turnover 400 days.

a. How much cash could be raised through better accounts receivable management?

b. How much cash can be raised through better management of inventory?

9. Argent Manufacturing needs to raise $300,000 to finance a new automatic valve prototype and assembly line.

ARGENT MANUFACTURING FINANCIALS

Assets		Liabilities	
Cash	$ 10,000	Accrued payroll	$ 150,000
Receivables 0–90 days	$ 2,600,000	Accounts payable	$ 500,000
Receivables 91–365 days	$ 200,000	Line of credit	$ 4,100,000
Inventory	$ 4,600,000	Current portion of loans	$ 250,000
Total current assets	$ 7,410,000	Total current liabilities	$ 5,000,000
Equipment:	$ 1,090,000	Bank loans	$ 3,000,000
Plant:	$ 1,500,000	Equity	$ 2,000,000
Total assets	$10,000,000	Total liabilities and equity	$10,000,000

Income Statement

Revenue	$14,000,000	*Operating expenses include
Cost of goods sold	$ 9,800,000	depreciation of $150,000
Gross profit	$ 4,200,000	
Operating expenses*	$ 3,900,000	
Profit before interest and tax	$ 300,000	

Argent's beginning and ending inventory were $600,000 and $500,000, respectively. Purchases were $4,800,000.

a. What were the company's payments on accounts payable?

b. What was its average payment per day?

c. What was its accounts payable turnover ratio?

d. On average, how quickly does the company pay its bills (in days)?

e. How much cash could be raised if the company paid its bills four days later on average?

CHAPTER 15 EXERCISES

1. Office Concepts produces movable partitions for offices. It plans to manufacture 10,000 partitions, which it expects to wholesale for $60 each. Variable manufacturing costs are $30 per partition. Variable marketing costs are the sales commission at 6%. Variable administrative costs are

shipping at $7 per unit. Fixed manufacturing costs are
$120,000 for the year. Fixed marketing and administrative
costs are $20,000 and $150,000, respectively. Construct a
planned budget and determine the amount of operating
profit. Assume that 10,200 units were actually produced
and sold. Construct a flexible budget and analyze the
sales volume variances.

	Sales Volume		
	Flexible Budget	Variance	Planned
Budget			
Sales			
Less variable costs			
Manufacturing			
Administrative and marketing			
Contribution margin			
Less fixed costs			
Manufacturing			
Marketing			
Administrative			
Operating profit			

For each of the following variances, indicate whether they
are favorable, F, or unfavorable, U.

a. What is the sales volume variance?

b. What is the variable manufacturing variance?

c. What is the marketing and administration sales
volume variance?

d. What are the fixed cost variances associated with the
sales volume difference?

e. What was the planned operating profit?

f. What was the flexible budget operating profit?

g. What is the operating profit variance?

2. Samantha Corporation plans to make 200 20-Gig disk
drives. The planned, or engineered, price was $300;
budgeted variable manufacturing costs were $180;

commissions were 7%, and fixed manufacturing,
marketing, and administrative costs were $15,000, $1,200,
and $3,000 per week, respectively. Now suppose the
actual price at which each disk drive could be sold was
only $280; variable costs per disk drive were $182; and
actual fixed manufacturing, marketing, and
administrative costs were $17,000, $1,500, and $3,100.
Further, suppose 240 disk drives were actually made and
sold. Complete the actual to flexible budget analysis.

	Actual [1] Budget	Manufacturing Variance	Marketing and Admin. Variance	Price Variance	Flexible [2] Budget
Sales					
Less variable costs					
Manufacturing					
Administrative and marketing					
Contribution margin					
Less fixed costs					
Manufacturing					
Marketing					
Administrative					
Operating profit					

3. Justin Corporation makes toner cartridges for laser
printers and copiers. For the past year, such cartridges
have sold for an average of $35 each; therefore, a price
of $35 is used to budget sales. Commissions are 6%.
Variable manufacturing costs are budgeted at $20 per
cartridge, and variable administrative costs are budgeted
at $2 per cartridge. Fixed manufacturing, marketing,
and administrative costs are budgeted at $6,000, $4,000,
and $3,000, respectively. Justin expected to sell 1,500
cartridges.

Competition in the toner cartridge market is fierce.
Justin actually sold 1,400 cartridges at $33. Variable
manufacturing costs were actually $18, and actual
variable administrative costs were $1 per unit. Fixed

manufacturing, marketing, and administrative costs were $5,500, $4,600, and $2,900, respectively. Use the form on the next page to construct a master budget, and analyze actual to budgeted variances.

CHAPTER 16 EXERCISES

1. Dolly Madison's Fine Furniture wants to make a gross margin of 60% on all their pieces. They recently received a Philadelphia Highboy made by Pennsylvania House. The piece cost $4,000 wholesale. What should its retail price be?

2. Raj Patel purchased a Triple-X gas station. He wants to make a 20% gross margin on all the gas he pumps. He just received a shipment of regular from the Wilson Refinery that cost $.84 per gallon. What should his retail price be to make his gross margin target?

3. Jersey Farm Machinery has designed a light duty tractor for municipal, park, estate, and light construction and light farming work. It is larger than most lawn tractors, yet smaller than most commercial tractors. Research indicates that purchasers of both farm and construction equipment tend to view horsepower as a relevant measure of performance. The light duty tractor has 80 horsepower. The information in Exercise Figure 16–1 Competitive Market Analysis was compiled by Jersey's research department.

   Using horsepower as an indicator of perceived value, and including all four competitors, what should the price be on Jersey's light duty tractor?

EXERCISE FIGURE 16–1

Competitive Market Analysis

Product	Horsepower	Price	Cost/Horsepower
Red Devil Garden Tractor	40	$ 4,600	$115
John Deere Model A Tractor	150	$18,750	$125
Powatan Industrial Tractor	120	$15,600	$130
Kubota Light Tractor	140	$16,800	$120

JUSTIN CORPORATION MASTER BUDGET

	Actual Performance	Manufacturing Variance	Marketing and Admin. Variance	Price Variance	Flexible Budget	Sales Volume Variance	Planned Budget
Sales							
Less variable costs							
Manufacturing							
Marketing							
Administrative	___	___	___	___	___	___	___
Contribution margin							
Less fixed costs							
Manufacturing							
Marketing							
Administrative	___	___	___	___	___	___	___
Operating profit							

4. Woodwind Corporation wants to start making flutes. Market research determines they can sell 6,000 flutes per year if they can price them at $40. Woodwind's gross margin target is 30%. What cost level must the company meet in order to successfully introduce this product?

5. Specialty Lighting Corporation wants to start manufacturing florescent office light fixtures. The market price for such products is well established and marketing indicates they can sell 200,000 units per year at $6 each. Specialty's target profit is 25%. What target cost must the company meet to successfully introduce this product?

6. Home Mart in Dallas, Texas, is across the street from Lumber-Are-Us. Both sell 2 × 4 studs, both price studs at $3.00 each. Last July, Home Mart sold 200,000 2 × 4 studs. This July they decided to cut the price of their studs to $2.50, and they sold 300,000 studs.
   a. What was their stud revenue last July?
   b. What was their stud revenue this July?
   c. Was Home Mart's stud demand elastic? Or inelastic?

7. Mega Mart, Inc., is a nationwide chain of discount stores. They have assembled the data in Exercise Figure 16–2 Mega Mart Analysis of Year to Year Sales Data for their Pea Pod, North Carolina, store. For each item, determine whether the demand is elastic or inelastic.

8. Mopar, a division of General Motors, makes spark plugs. Mopar's variable costs are $.35 each and the

EXERCISE FIGURE 16-2

Mega Mart Analysis of Year to Year Sales Data

	Last Year's Data			This Year's Data		
Item	Units	Price	Revenue	Units	Price	Revenue
a) Lee Jeans	500	$ 33	$16,500	700	$ 29	$20,300
b) No Brand Jeans	1,000	$ 22	$22,000	1,050	$ 19	$19,950
c) T Shirts	3,000	$ 10	$30,000	4,000	$ 9	$36,000
d) MagX TVs—36″	100	$299	$29,900	105	$269	$28,245
e) RCA TVs—36″	90	$329	$29,610	88	$349	$30,712

wholesale market price of its spark plugs is $.50. Under every set of circumstances below, we want to maximize overall corporate profits.

  a. Mopar is *not* operating at capacity. At what price should it sell its spark plugs to other divisions?

  b. Mopar is *not* operating at capacity. If other G.M. divisions can purchase spark plugs for $.45 outside, should they buy Mopar spark plugs or not?

  c. Mopar *is* operating at capacity. If other G.M. divisions want to buy spark plugs from Mopar, what price should Mopar charge?

  d. Mopar *is* operating at capacity. If other G.M. divisions can purchase spark plugs in the market for $.45, should G.M. buy from Mopar or from outside suppliers?

9. Boyle Company makes leather brief cases. Variable costs, including administration and sales commissions, are $36; the full absorption cost of the brief cases is $32. Boyle's target gross margin is 50%. They have national distribution through a number of chain stores. While their factory is at full capacity (8 hours per day, five days per week), they can produce another 500 briefcases per month by increasing their variable costs to $40. A chain store buyer from Argentina offers to purchase 1,000 brief cases for $50 each.

  a. Assuming regular production only, what is Boyle's target price to make their gross margin?

  b. Which are higher, variable costs, if the Argentine order is filled, or full absorption costs?

  c. Does this sale fit one of the three criteria for an opportunistic sale? If so which one?

  d. Should this order be accepted?

10. Tina Louise designs and manufactures business casual women's cloths. She has sold to several national chains, and hopes to sell to many more. Last year she sold 5,000 suits, this year her goal is to sell 8,000. The variable cost of her suits is $66, full absorption cost is $60, and her target gross margin is 50%. A buyer for one of her regular customers offers to purchase an additional 1,000 suits for $70.

a. What is Ms. Louise's target price?
b. Which are higher, variable costs or full absorption costs? And what is the amount?
c. Does this sale fit one of the three criteria for an opportunistic sale? If so which one?
d. Should she accept this order?

CHAPTER 17 EXERCISES

1. Carolina Airlines has provided the following cost information: fuel costs, $30,000,000; interest, $22,000,000; cost of air crews, $24,000,000; cost of gate leases, $7,000,000; cost of ground operations, $8,000,000; in-house ticketing operations, $2,000,000; commissions paid to travel agents and brokers, $6,000,000; depreciation, $6,000,000; other overhead, $8,000,000.
   a. What are Carolina Airlines principal cost drivers?
   b. Is Carolina Airlines' cost structure more sensitive to a 5% increase in fuel prices or a 6% increase in the cost of air crews?

2. Truck Axle Corporation is searching for a cost driver that will help them better understand the cost structure of their company and the cost of specific products. Their Steel Forging Department's budget is $600,000 per year, and they make 10,000 axles using 300,000 pounds of steel and 20,000 labor hours. Compute the Forging Department's cost rate for the following cost drivers:
   a. Pounds of forging
   b. Number of forgings
   c. Hours of forging

3. Sammy Corporation makes power supplies. Some power supplies require one circuit board, some three, and some five. One department assembles printed circuits. The Printed Circuit Assembly Department costs were $750,000 last year, and they assembled 300,000 boards. The Assembly Department used 50,000 hours of direct labor. What cost rate should be used for printed circuit board assembly considering the following cost drivers?

    a. Number of printed circuit boards

    b. Number of assembly hours

4. Pitcarn's Casting Department makes 12,000 pump housings per year using 36,000 pounds of metal and 1,000 hours of direct labor. What rate should be assigned to the following cost drivers?

    a. Pounds of castings

    b. Number of castings

    c. Hours of castings

5. Pitcarn is currently renting a painting booth weekends at Murray's Autobody to paint pump housings. If Pitcarn is trying to figure out which costs to allocate to the painting department, what should they include? Budgets are annual. Assume the company is open 5 days per week, 50 weeks per year, and pays time and a half over 40 hours. The following information is available: one painter working 48 hours per week, straight time rate $10 per hour; one lead painter working 56 hours per week, straight time rate $14 per hour; employer taxes 15%; workers' comp 3.5%; fringe, $160 per worker per month for health insurance. Murray's Autobody rents its shop to Pitcarn for $800 per month; 2,000 gallons of epoxy spray paint at $11 per gallon; and solvents, masks, coveralls, cleanup material, and so on total $15,000. It paints 12,000 pumps per year.

    a. What cost should be allocated to the painting department?

    b. If number of pump housings is the cost driver, what rate per pump housing should be applied?

    c. If Murray's offers to paint the pump housing for $9 per pump housing, should Pitcarn subcontract this work out?

6. During the next 2-week payroll cycle, Burlington Bridge contracts for 9 Union Iron Workers, 40 hours per week, at $25 per hour. Write the journal entry to record the payroll.

7. In the payroll cycle given in Exercise 6, Burlington Bridge applies 200 hours to Hope Creek and 150 hours to Pequad Creek. Write the journal entry to allocate labor to the appropriate WIP accounts.

8. Building on Exercises 6 and 7, write the journal entry to relieve unbilled time from the labor expense account.

9. Hope Creek has a total WIP of $60,000, and Pequad has a WIP of $45,000. Both projects are complete. Write the journal entries to close (bring to zero) the WIP accounts and transfer the labor costs into the cost of goods sold account.

10. If the contracts with Burlington Bridge allowed it to bill Salem and Burlington counties, respectively, for the work on the Hope Creek and Pequad Creek bridges at two times labor cost, what would be the journal entry to reflect the accounts receivable and revenue Burlington should book?

11. American Corporate Radio has two defense contracts underway in the same, 100,000-square-foot building. Each contract is expected to cover its own costs and make a profit. The building costs $1,200,000 per year, including heat, light, insurance, and security. A Navy contract occupies 30,000 square feet. An Air Force contract occupies 70,000 square feet. How should facility costs be allocated?

12. Timber Company can sell logs for $40 per ton, or it can sell 2 × 4s for $0.11 per foot. The company president, a Rutgers MBA and former nuclear power plant engineer, thinks of this as a joint product: sell or process further analysis. Cutting timber and hauling it to their facility costs $30 per ton. Timber Company can get 3,000 feet of 2 × 4s out of a ton of logs. Additional processing, that is, sawing, and so on, costs about $0.06 per foot.
   a. What is the gross margin on unprocessed logs?
   b. What is the gross margin on logs processed into 2 × 4s?
   c. Should Timber Company sell logs or 2 × 4s?

CHAPTER 18 EXERCISES

1. Johnson Engineering just won a software contract with Short Line Railways. The bid contemplates 20,000 hours of programmer time billed at $75 per hour. The project

must be completed in one year. Programmers work 2,000 billable hours per year, which means the project requires 10 full-time programmers. Programmers at this company have been declared nonexempt, which means they must be paid overtime at time and a half. The average programmer's wages are $40 per hour. The company has six programmers on staff for the project.

a. What would be the contribution margin if ten programmers were available (i.e., no overtime paid)?

b. What is the contribution margin assuming six programmers are used full time, and the deficiency is made up through 8,000 hours of overtime?

c. What is the contribution margin on this project if two more programmers are hired?

d. Assume the cost of recruiting and training each new programmer is $15,000. What is the contribution margin on hiring two new programmers after factoring in recruiting and training costs?

2. The Naval Electronics Systems Command awarded a cost plus fixed-fee contract to Curly-Fine Engineering. Curly-Fine's engineers are union and nonexempt. The contract specifies that no overtime premium pay may be charged to the Navy. Engineers are paid a set rate of $36 per hour, including taxes. Tests must be completed in 140 days (20 weeks). The contract calls for 5,000 hours of work. Five engineers are assigned full time. Total payroll costs charged to the work in progress account for engineers are $198,000. How much is the premium pay, and will it have to be backed out of contract costs?

3. Sally's Salads makes prepackaged salads for restaurants. Business is good, and it is hard to find labor. To keep up with demand, Sally runs her 10-man crew 10 hours per day, five days per week. Straight time pay is $10 per hour, including taxes.

a. What is her weekly crew labor cost?

b. How much of this cost is premium pay?

c. How much would profits improve, if at all, if she hired one more person for her crew?

4. Barry Software Consultants hires programmers, on average, for about $750 per week. For the first two weeks, new hires simply follow around more seasoned programmers to get oriented to the business. The following week they are sent to a $1,000 programming school. For the next month (four weeks), they are intensively coached, and on average, produce only about 40% as much as their more seasoned colleagues. Thereafter, they are expected to take on a full workload with minimal supervision. Barry has 60 programmers and an average turnover of 25%. What is his turnover cost, excluding the cost to recruit replacements?

5. The workers' compensation premium for Barkley Software would be $100,000 *at standard rates*. Their claims' history is slightly less than expected for a company of their size and industry. The Compensation Rating and Inspection Bureau has assigned an experience modification factor of 0.991. What is their actual premium?

6. Clevon's is a machine shop that makes parts for high-performance cars. His workers' compensation premium at *standard rates* would be $100,000. His experience modification factor is 1.47. What will Clevon's actual premium be?

7. For years, New Age Thinking Corporation never bothered to challenge unemployment claims. However, in the past year, the director of Human Resources has been keeping detailed records of why people were terminated, and began challenging unemployment claims when she had cause. As a result, New Age's unemployment tax fell from 7.0% to 4.0%. Their taxable payroll has been about $2,000,000 per year.
   a. How much unemployment tax did they pay at the old tax rate?
   b. How much did they pay under the new tax rate?
   c. What was the savings?

Exercise Answers

CHAPTER 1

1. **Modern Medical:** a. COGS, $1.5M; b. Gross profit, $50,000; c. Gross margin, 25%; d. EBT, $50,000; e. Net income, $35,000; f. Profit margin, 1.75%
2. **Modern Medical:** a. Revenue, $2.3M; b. COGS, $1,775,000; c. Gross profit, $525,000; d. Overhead, $450,000; e. EBT, $75,000; f. Taxes, $22,500; g. Net income, $52,500
3. Sybase cash flow: $242,000
4. Wilson cash flow: $110,000
5. a. Accounts receivable, $180,000 use; b. Accounts payable, $25,000 use; c. Accrued payroll, $24,000 source
6. Murray's Boutique Statement of Cash Flows:

ANSWER FIGURE 1-6

Murray's Boutique Statement of Cash Flows

Cash From Operations:	
Net Income	90,000
Depreciation	30,000
Total From Operations	120,000
Changes in Working Capital	
Decrease (Increase) In A/R	−20,000
Decrease (Increase) In Inventory	5,000
Increase (Decrease) in Payables	−60,000
Total From Working Capital	−75,000

ANSWER FIGURE 1-6 (Continued)

Murray's Boutique Statement of Cash Flows

Acquisitions & Divestitures:	
Plant & Equipment Acquired	0
Plant & Equipment Sold	0
Total from Acquisitions & Divest.	0
Financing Activities	
Company Stock Sold (Purchased)	0
Loans Received (Paid)	0
Leases Received (Paid)	0
Total Financing Activity	0
Change In Cash Position	45,000

CHAPTER 2

1. Gray ROA: 10%
2. Wire ROA: 9.3%
3. Gray profit margin: 16.7%
4. Wire profit margin: 9.33%
5. Gray asset turnover: 0.6
6. Wire asset turnover: 1.0
7. a. Gray A/R turnover: 10; b. DSO: 36.5 days
8. a. Wire A/R turnover: 5.45; b. DSO: 67.0 days
9. a. Gray inventory turns: 13.1; b. Days inventory: 27.9
10. a. Wire inventory turns: 8.9; b. Days inventory: 41.0
11. Gray plant turns: 1.14
12. Wire plant turnover: 2.3
13. Gray ROE: 23.3%
14. Wire ROE: 15.7%
15. Gray: a. Income, $4M; b. ROE, 10%; c. ROE, 20.7%
16. Wire: a. Income, $109,500; b. ROE, 7.3%; c. ROE, 7%
17. Gray: Average shares, 900,000; EPS, $3.17
18. Wire: Average shares, 204,110; EPS, $0.49
19. Gray P/E: 9/1, 12.6; 12/1, 17.4
20. Wire P/E: 4/15, 17; 10/31, 25

21. Gray: a. Proper; b. Proper; c. Under; d. Over
22. Wire: a. Under; b. Proper; c. Proper d. Over
23. Gray: Current ratio, 4.61
24. Wire: Current ratio, 1.64
25. Gray: Quick ratio, 4.44
26. Wire: Quick ratio, .98
27. Gray: Cash flow/Current liabilities, 1.74
28. Wire: Cash flow/Current liabilities, .29
29. Gray: Debt/Equity, .85
30. Wire: a. Debt/Equity, 2.98; b. New debt/Equity, 2.52
31. Gray times interest: 4.5
32. Wire times interest: 2.56

CHAPTER 3

1. 90 day T-bill: 4%
2. Minsk bonds: 17%
3. Allegheny DRP: 7%
4. T-note MRP: 2.1%
5. AAA bond: 7.3%
6. C bond: 9.8%
7. Expected rate: 3.5%
8. Commerce rate: 4.6%
9.

ANSWER FIGURE 3-9

Capital Supply Curves for A, B, and C rated companies

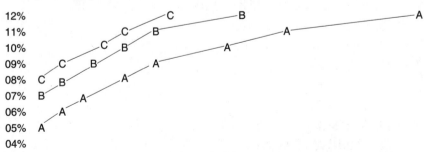

10.

ANSWER FIGURE 3–10

Capital Supply Curve for Foreign Industrial Development Bonds

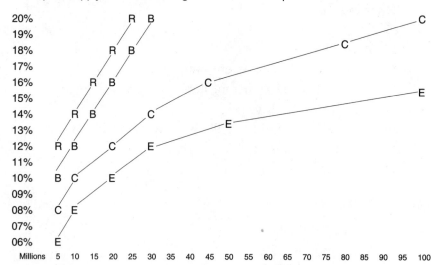

CHAPTER 4

1. Ajax: Ke = 10%, σ = 19%, CoVar = 1.9
2. Xenon: Ke = 13.5%, σ = 7.09%, CoVar = 0.53
3. Ke = 12%, σ = 11.5%, CoVar = .96
4. Wild West: Ke = 37.5%, σ = 73.2%, CoVar = 1.95
5. Lolly: K = 13.8%, σ = 3.3%, CoVar = .24
6. 57.2" to 76.8"
7. Sales forecast @ 95%: 90,100 units.
8. Order 32 or 33 Porsches
9. Steel: 5.0
10. Marla's: 0.5
11. Beta: 1.6
12. Beta: 1.71
13. Kp: 24%
14. Wild West: 28.5%

15. Microsoft: 12.6%
16. Steel: 15.6%

CHAPTER 5

1. CD: $1.276.30
2. Wild West: $126,970
3. CD: $26,878
4. K-9 growth: 32%
5. Master growth: 9%
6. Two-year CD: $5,414.30
7. PV 50–year rate: $5,429.00
8. PV million dollar note: $672,970
9. PV semiannual note: $8,548
10. Fifteen-year IRA: $20,759.40
11. Employer deposits: $3,992.71
12. Truck payments: $697.47
13. Shore house mortgage: $4,935.02
14. Fifteen-year IRA: $20,759.32
15. PV five years of deposits: $3,992.71
16. Eight year retirement plan: $205,902
17. Ten year savings plan: $60,402
18. FVIFA using formula: $60,401.98

CHAPTER 6

1. Minsk bond value: $438,868
2. G.E. bond value: $1,042,657
3. Santa Fe bond value: $86,237.89
4. Wild West Wranglers: a. $2,500; b. 4%; c. 40; d. $70,312; e. 12; f. $107,500 g. $90,607.25
5. Microsoft bond value: $11,164.35
6. Bruno bond yield: 12.7%
7. Wild West Wrangler yield: 14.03%

8. Uganda Railways yield: 16.58%

9. Minsk bond yield: 20.88%

10. Campbell's yield to call: 11.4%

11. Microsoft yield to call: 8.5%

CHAPTER 7

1. Murry's imputed rate: 15%

2. a. Amount financed: $15,996.30; b. Payments: 44; c. Imputed rate: 18.2%; d. 1,024 more cheesesteaks, first year

3. 1950 Leasing Co.: 13.5%

4. New Age: 14%,

5. a. Interest/principal/balance
$242.61/$258.33/$15,737.97
$238.69/$262.25/$15,475.72
$234.72/$266.22/$15,209.53

   b. Booking journal entry

Equipment	$18,000.00
Cash	$ 2,003.70
Leases payable	$15,996.30

   c. First month's payment entry

Interest	$242.61
Leases payable	$258.33
Cash	$500.94

   d. Estimated current leases payable
$3,147.20 = ($258.33 + $262.25 + $266.22) \times 4

CHAPTER 8

1. Tux stock price: $7.73

2. Doctor Exploration price: $51.77

3. Strategic expected return: 23.2%

4. DNA Systems: a. Dividends, $1.00, $2.00, $4.00; b. Pe3,$149.33; c. Price, $103.18

5. Jack's: a. Dividends, $1.20, $1.80, $2.70, $4.05; b. Pe4, $155.25; c. Price, $86.35

CHAPTER 9

1. New bonds: 11.25%
2. Line of credit: 5.7%
3. Kravitz: 8.24%
4. Composite: 9.04%
5. a. 14.4%; b. 13%; c. 13.5%
6. Pinelands: a. 11.02%; b. 10%; c. 13.5%
7. Fractal re-evaluation: 13.02%
8. K-9 WACC: 8.13%
9. Dunn WACC: 7.66%
10. Brooklyn: a. 12.35%; b. 8.63%; c. 12.73%
11. Cinnaminson Soups:

    Accept projects E & C for their returns of 25% and 23% are greater than the cost of capital.

    Project F is rejected under both financing scenarios because above $600,000 the cost of capital jumps to 18% whereas the project will only yield 17%.

    Project B is accepted if the Charleasco option is selected, but rejected if maximum bank financing is used.

    Project A is an alternative to project B which we have already accepted because of its higher rate of return.

    Project D is accepted if the company uses bank financing. Recognize D is an alternative to B. D would be rejected if the financing were via lease because the yield on D is only 13%, whereas the lease costs 14%.

CHAPTER 10

1. Glass Co.: 2.5 years
2. Powdered Metal: 1.833 years
3. Packett Machine Tool: 3.265 years
4. Mega Corporation: 4.565 years
5. Packett NPV: $420,196
6. Mega NPV: $87,436

7. Powdered Metals NPV: $346,656
8. Powdered Metals IRR: 53.5%
9. Packett IRR: 23.7%
10. Powdered Metals IRR: 48%
11. Powdered Metals MIRR: 45.8%
12. Galaxy Paint MIRR: 8.1%

CHAPTER 11

1. Bernard Broadcasting: a. Investments, outflows, $1,220,000; b. Operating cash flows years 1–10, $690,000; c. Terminal cash inflows, $300,000
2. See Answer Figure 11–2: Johnson Telemarketing Capital Budgeting Cash Flows.

CHAPTER 12

1. Bilo cinder blocks: $4,000
2. Bilo flatbed cost: $2,000
3. Patrick: a. Gravel cost, $600,000; b. Gravel expense, $400,000; c. Inventory, $200,000
4. Brandon full absorption cost: $26,900
5. Charon full absorption cost: $5.98
6. Winslow: Full absorption cost, $41; commissions are not included
7. Winslow COGS: $1,217,700
8. Pennsauken COGS: $82,800
9. Brandon Airships: a. Full absorption cost, $26,900; b. Unallocated fixed manufacturing overhead $7,500; c. COGS, $1,236,500; d. Average cost per unit sold: $26,880
10. Pennsauken Concrete Beams: a. Full absorption cost, $900; b. Unallocated fixed manufacturing overhead, $28,800; c. COGS, $479,000; d. Average cost per unit sold, $903.78

ANSWER FIGURE 11-2

Johnson Telemarketing Capital Budgeting Cash Flows

	Year 0	Year 1	Year 2	Year 3	Year 4
Investment Outlays					
1. Building & Land	900,000				
2. Equipment	400,000				
3. Increase in NWC	500,000				
Total Net Investment	1,800,000				
Operating Cash Flows					
1. Switch Revenues		7,000,000	7,000,000	7,000,000	7,000,000
2. Cost of Goods Sold 75% of Sales		5,250,000	5,250,000	5,250,000	5,250,000
3. Selling Costs 5% of Sales		350,000	350,000	350,000	350,000
4. Fixed Costs		150,000	150,000	150,000	150,000
5. Depreciation Building		20,000	20,000	20,000	20,000
6. Depreciation Equipment		100,000	100,000	100,000	100,000
7. Pre-Tax Operating Income		1,130,000	1,130,000	1,130,000	1,130,000
8. Taxes @ 40%		452,000	452,000	452,000	452,000
9. After Tax Income		678,000	678,000	678,000	678,000
10. Add Back Depreciation		120,000	120,000	120,000	120,000
11. Operating Cash Flows		798,000	798,000	798,000	798,000
Terminal Year Cash Flows					
1. Salvage Value of Plant & Equipment					750,000
2. Less Book Value of Plant & Equipment					820,000
3. Gain or Loss On Salvage					−70,000
4. Taxes On Gain Or Loss @ 40%					28,000
5. Plus Cash From Salvage Value Sales					750,000
6. Salvage Cash Net of Tax					778,000
7. Return of NWC					500,000
8. Net Terminal Cash Flows					1,278,000
	Outflow	Inflow	Inflow	Inflow	Inflow
Relevant Cash Flows	1,800,000	798,000	798,000	798,000	2,076,000

11. Brandon: a. Full absorption cost, $26,900; b. Unallocated, $0; c. COGS, $1,361,000; d. Average unit cost sold, $26,686.28

12. Pennsauken: a. Full absorption cost, $900; b. Unallocated, $0; c. COGS, $561,000; d. Average unit cost sold: $876.56

13. Washington Equipment: $14,210

14. Brandon variable costs: $26,350

15. Pennsauken variable costs: $675

16. Brandon: a. Gross profit/plane, $12,100; b. Contribution margin/plane, $13,010

CHAPTER 13

1. Loren raises prices: 478 lb

2. Cherry Hill 300ZX: 2,500 cars

3. 300ZX w/Cobra Trans: 2,353 cars

4. 300ZX w/Venture Cap.: 2,941 cars

5. Moe, Larry, Curly: $1.5 million/month

6. Moe, Larry, Curly w/$30,000 draw/month: $1.65 million/month

7. Moe, Larry, Curly w/advertising: $1.94 million/month

8. a. Loren's own bakery: 5,458 lb; b. Loren at Frank's: 3,072 lb; c. Frank's lower breakeven

9. Executive @ 95% confidence, $33.95 million

10. Loren @ 68% confidence, 8,445 lb/month

11. Moe, Larry, Curly @ 95%, $2.05 million/month

CHAPTER 14

1. Jack's: $6,171

2. Collection: $38,571

3. Pine: $16,843 ($9,643 payroll + $8,000 spray)

4. Doctor's: a. Borrowing capacity $73,500; b. Maximum line draw $73,500

5. Doctor's: After old A/R sale, $168,500

6. Pesto: a. Line of credit financing, $700,000; b. Permanent financing, $105,000

7. Argent: a. $1,250,000 ($50,00 sale of accounts receivable over 90 days + $1,200,000 savings due to increased accounts receivable turnover); b. Inventory savings, $1,000,000

8. Deptford: a. $763,333 ($630,000 sale of accounts receivable over 90 days + $133,333 from improved turnover); b. Inventory savings $2,000,000

9. Argent: a. Payments, $4,900,000; b. Average daily payment, $13,425; c. A/P turnover 8.7; d. Average days 42; e. Additional cash, $40,275

CHAPTER 15

1. a. $12,000; b. $6,000; c. $720 and $1,400; d. None; e. $64,000; f. $67,880; g. $3,880

2. a. $4,560; b. $4,464; c. $1,520; d. $1,416

3. a. $3,350; b. $2,800; c. $3,300; d. $3,828

ANSWER FIGURE 15-1

Office Concepts Flexible Budget

Unit Volume	10,200		10,000
	Flexible Budget	**Variance**	**Planned Budget**
Sales	612,000	12,000	600,000
Less Variable Costs:			
Manufacturing	306,000	6,000 F	300,000
Marketing	36,720	720 F	36,000
Administration	71,400	1,400 F	70,000
Contribution Margin:	197,880	3,880	194,000
Less Fixed Costs:			
Manufacturing	60,000	0	60,000
Marketing	20,000	0	20,000
Administrative	50,000	0	50,000
Operating Profit	67,880	3,880	64,000

ANSWER FIGURE 15-2

Samantha Corporation Weekly Flexible Budget

Units Sold	240 Actual	Manufacturing Variance	Marketing & Admin. Variance	Price Variance	Volume Adj. Flexible Budget	Planned Sales Volume Variance	200 Planned Budget
Sales	67,200			4,800 U	72,000	12,000 F	60,000
Less Variable Costs							
Manufacturing	43,680	480 U			43,200	7,200 U	36,000
Marketing	4,704	0		336 F	5,040	840 U	4,200
Administrative	0	0	0	0	0	0	0
Contribution	18,816	480	0	4,464	23,760	3,960	19,800
Less Fixed Costs							
Manufacturing	13,000	2,000 F			15,000	0	15,000
Marketing	1,300		100 U		1,200	0	1,200
Administrative	3,100		100 U		3,000	0	3,000
Operating Profit	1,416	1,520 F	200 U	4,464 U	4,560	3,960	600

ANSWER FIGURE 15-3

Justin Corporation Monthly Flexible Budget

Units Sold	Actual 1,400	Manufacturing Variance	Marketing & Admin. Variance	Price Variance	Volume Adj. Flexible Budget	Volume Variance	Planned Budget 1,500
						Planned Sales	
Sales	46,200			2,800 U	49,000	3,500 U	52,500
Less Variable Costs							
Manufacturing	25,200	2,800 F			28,000	2,000 F	30,000
Marketing	2,772		168 F		2,940	210 F	3,150
Administrative	1,400		1,400 F		2,800	200 F	3,000
Contribution	16,828	2,800	1,568	2,800	15,260	1,090	16,350
Less Fixed Costs							
Manufacturing	5,500	500 F			6,000		6,000
Marketing	4,600		600 U		4,000		4,000
Administrative	2,900		100 F		3,000		3,000
Operating Profit	3,828	3,300	1,068	2,800	2,260	1,090	3,350

CHAPTER 16

1. Madison: $10,000
2. Patel: $1.05
3. Jersey: $9,800
4. Woodwind: $28
5. Specialty: $4.50
6. Home Mart: a. $60,000; b. $750,000; c. Elastic
7. Mega Mart: a. Elastic; b. Inelastic; c. Elastic; d. Inelastic; e. Inelastic
8. Mopar: a. $.35; b. Mopar; c. $.50; d. Outside
9. Boyle: a. $64; b. Variable $40; c. Not regular customer; d. Yes
10. Louise: a. $120; b. Variable $66; c. No; d. No

CHAPTER 17

1. Carolina: a. Fuel 26.5%, crews 21.2%, and interest 19.5%; b. Fuel
2. Truck: a. $2/lb; b. $60/forging; c. $30/hour
3. Sammy: a. $2.50/board; b. $15/hour
4. Pitcarn: a. $3.83/lb; b. $11.50/casting; c. $23/hour
5. Pitcarn: a. $134,338; b. $11.20/housing; c. Yes

6.	Payroll	$9,000	
	Cash		$9,000
7.	Hope Creek WIP:	$5,000	
	Pequad WIP	$3,750	
	Payroll		$8,750
8.	Unbillable payroll	$250	
	Payroll		$250
9.	Cost of goods sold	$105,000	
	Hope Creek WIP		$60,000
	Pequad WIP		$45,000
10.	A/R Salem County	$120,000	
	A/R Burlington County	$ 90,000	
	Revenue		$210,000

11. American Navy contract, $360k; Air Force contract, $840k
12. Timber gross margins: a. Logs 25%; b. 2 × 4s 36%; c. 2 4s

CHAPTER 18

1. Johnson contribution margins: a. 47%; b. 36%; c. 41%; d. 39%
2. Naval Electronics overtime premium: $18,000
3. Sally: a. $5,500; b. $500; c. $200.75
4. Barry turnover cost: $210,750
5. Barkley WC premium: $99,100
6. Clevon WC premium: $147,000
7. Thinking unemployment: a. $140,000; b. $80,000; c. $60,000

A

Absorption cost, full
cost of goods sold, 190–191, 201–202
inventory, 190–191
for price target, 263–264
of purchased merchandise, 197–198
Accounting principles, generally accepted
(GAAP)
comparability, 16
conservatism, 15
double entry system, 10
entity principle, 15
expenses translated into inventory, 197
managerial accounting versus, 199–201
master budgets, 260
matching principle, 15–16
materiality, 16–17
objectivity, 15
restatements, 133
time periods, specific, 16
Accounting terms
chart of accounts, 14
general ledger, 13
generally accepted accounting
principles (GAAP), 14–17
journal entry, 13–14
trial balance, 14
Accounts payable
customer creditworthiness, measuring,
245–247
master budgeting discrepancies, 260
as a source of cash, 11, 242–245
turnover and days to pay, 26–28,
244–245
Accounts receivable
collection agencies and, 233–235
raising cash from, 235–237
as a source of cash, 11–12, 232–233
turnover, 25–26
as a use of cash, 231–232
Acid test ratio, 43–44
Activity-based costing, 291–293
Adjustments, period-end, 5
Advertising. *See* Operating expenses

Amortization schedules, 96–97, 126
Annual growth rates, 90
Annuity
future value, 87, 98–99
payment years, 94
present value, 98
A priori possibilities, 68–75
Assets
balance sheet, 5–6
capital asset pricing model (CAPM),
84–85, 146–147, 149–151
co-mingling, 15
current, 7–8, 27, 38–39, 217–218, 230
employees, unproductive, 24
equity, 7
line of credit, calculating, 227
marginal cost of capital, 159
portfolio yield, 83–84
return on, 20–22, 32–34, 56
turnover ratio, 23–24

B

Balance sheet
assets, 5–6
equity, 7
income statement, relationship to, 7, 8–10
liabilities, 6
working capital, 7–8
Basic budget, 252–253
Benchmarking, 5, 22, 138, 141
Beta
rate of return, required, 84–85
risk, measuring, 81–83
Bill of materials (BOM) system, 261
Bills, ability to pay
aged accounts receivable, reviewing,
41–42
break-even cash flow, 44–45, 221–222
current and noncurrent assets and
liabilities, 7
customer creditworthiness, evaluating,
26–28, 245–247
Bonds
callable, 104–106, 112–113

Bonds (*Cont.*)
convertible, 36, 106–107
coupon rate, 102, 106, 111
discount rate, 102–104
interest, components of, 52–55, 102–104
interpolation theory, 114–116
rate of return, comparing to cost of capital, 175, 177
required rate of return, 104
supply and demand, interest rates and, 56–65
yield, 107–112, 147, 149–151
Brands
market segmentation, 284
microeconomics pricing theory, 285–286
product selection, new, 309–310
Break-even analysis
cash flow, 44–45, 221–222
described, 205–208
profit, modeling, 208–210
reality testing, 212–213
relevant range, 212
risk and, 213–216
sales volume, 210–212
Budget
basic, 252–253
capital
basic principles, 181–183
cash flow versus, 225
discounted payback method, 168
evaluation methods, 166–167, 178, 179
inflation and price pressure, 185
internal rate of return (IRR), 171–175
interpolation methodology, 177–178
modified internal rate of return (MIRR), 175–177
net present value (NPV), 170–171
phases, 183–185
payback method, 166
replacement equipment, 185
spreadsheet modeling, 185–187
master
described, 251–252
financial statements versus, 259–261
supplemental, 261
Building, opening new
activity-based costing, 293
cash budgeting, 221–226

C
Callable bonds
bond values, 104–106

yield to call, calculating, 112–113
Capital asset pricing model (CAPM)
common equity, 146–147
new common equities, cost of, 149–151
portfolio theory, 84–85
Capital budgeting
basic principles, 181–183
cash flow versus, 225
discounted payback method, 168
evaluation methods, 166–167, 178, 179
inflation and price pressure, 185
internal rate of return (IRR), 171–175
interpolation methodology, 177–178
modified internal rate of return (MIRR), 175–177
net present value (NPV), 170–171
payback method, 166
phases, 183–185
replacement equipment, 185
spreadsheet modeling, 185–187
Capital, cost of
common stock, issuing new, 154–158
cost-free capital, 151
debt, 143–144
decision rules, 160–162
leases, 125–128, 158
marginal cost of capital, 158–160
preferred stock, 144–145
weighted average cost of capital (WACC), 151–154
Capital demand curve, 61–62
Capital gains yield, 132
Capital lease
capitalizing, 125–128
cash flow statement, 13
deposits and prepayments, effect of, 122–125
interest rates, imputed, 120–122
operating versus, 119–120
Capital structure
earnings per share, 34–35
fully diluted earnings per share, 36
price/earnings (P/E) ratio, 37–38
return on assets and return on common shareholder's equity, relation between, 32–34
return on common shareholder's equity (ROCE), 31–32
Capital supply curve, 56–61
CAPM. *See* Capital asset pricing model

Cash
 assets, current, 7–8
 accounts receivable as a source of,
  11–12, 232–233
 demand, inventory and, 238–239
 inventory as source of, 237, 239–240
 profits as source of, 11
Cash budgeting
 described, 218–221
 facility, opening new, 221–226
 line of credit, 226–228
 seasonal cash demand, 228–230
Cash flow
 break-even point after opening new
  facility, 221–222
 discounting for capital projects, 166,
  170–176
 estimating for capital budgeting,
  181–188
 statement of, 10–13
 stock valuation based on, 136–138
Chart of accounts, 14
Clients
 cash budgeting, 218–221
 payroll expense, reallocating, 295
Closing the books, balance sheet and, 5
Coefficient of variation (CoVar), 68, 72
Collection agencies, 233–235
Common stock
 convertible bonds, 106
 cost of new, 145–151
 issuing new, 154–158
 return on, relation to return on assets,
  32–34
Comparability principle, 16
Competition-based pricing, 265–269
Confidence level
 break-even forecasting, 215
 normal distribution curve, 77
Conservatism principle, 15
Constraints, theory of, 300–303
Consumer surplus, 282–283
Contingencies, new facility, 226
Contribution margin
 break-even analysis, 206
 overproduction, effect of, 202
 overtime costs, 314
Convertible bonds
 fully diluted earnings per share, 36
 values, 106–107
Cost
 activity-based, 291–293

basic budgets, 252–253
capital budgets, 181–182
of capital, marginal, 158–160
changes, market-centered pricing
 theory, 266
common equities, 147–148, 151
drivers, 289–291
incremental units, producing, 199–201
job, 293–297
of leased capital, 158
make or buy decisions, 198–199
marginal, 209
market-centered pricing, 265
master budgets, 253–259
opportunistic pricing, 275
overhead allocation, traditional, 298–299
of perfection, 16
pricing theory, 263–265
profit ladder, 303–307
revenue, matching, 15–16
spreadsheet modeling, 185–187
traditional overhead allocation, 298–299
unemployment taxes, 320
Cost accounting, 199–201
Cost drivers, 289–291, 297–299
Cost-free capital, 151
Cost of goods sold
 from company's income statement, 27
 defined, 1, 3
 formula, 28
 gross profit versus contribution, 202
 sales volume break-even, 210
 WIP account data, 295
Coupon rate, bond, 102, 106, 111
Credit
 accounts payable turnover, 26–28, 244–247
 accounts receivable, 230–237
 aged accounts receivable, reviewing,
  41–42
 assets, calculating line of credit, 227
 described, 8, 9
 sales, speed of collection, 25–26
 spread, 60–61
Credit, line of
 cash budgeting, 226–228
 interest coverage ratio, 47
Current assets, 7–8
Current liabilities, 7–8, 217–218, 230
Customers
 accounts receivable, 230–237
 creditworthiness, evaluating, 26–28,
  245–247

Customers (*Cont.*)
  market segmentation, 283–285
  opportunistic pricing, 275–276
  perceptions of value, 281, 282–283
  relationships with, 315

D
Database. *See* General ledger
Data entry errors, 10
Data, historical
  dividend yield, stock value and, 130–131
  revenue and expenses, 15
  weighted average cost of capital
    (WACC), 152
  yield and risk, forecasting, 75–77
Days in inventory (DII), 28–29, 237–238
Days sales outstanding (DSO), 230–231
Days to pay, accounts payable turnover
  and, 26–28
Debit, 8, 9
Debt
  capital, cost of, 143–144
  current liabilities, 7
  equity ratio, cost of financing and, 152,
    154
  return on common shareholder's equity
    (ROCE) and, 34
Decision rules, capital costs, 160–162
Decline phase, product life cycle, 272
Default risk premium (DRP), 52, 54
Demand
  changes, effects on interest rates, 64–65
  curve, shifting, 281
  market segmentation, 283–285
  microeconomics pricing theory, 277
  price elasticity, 270–272
  strategic implications on microeconomic
    pricing theory, 280–281
Deposit, lease, 122–125
Depreciation
  capital budgets, 182, 185–187
  cash flow from operations, 44–45
Derivative, 114–116
Deviation, standard
  defined, 67
  and expected values, making decisions
    with, 77–85
  with historical data, forecasting, 75
  with a priori probabilities, forecasting,
    68, 70, 71

DII. *See* Days in inventory
Discounted payback method, 166, 168–178,
  179
Discounting cash flows, 170–176
Discount rate, 91, 108
Dislocations, 62–63
Dispersion, weighted average measure of,
  70–71
Distribution curve, normal yield and risk,
  77–79
Diversifiable risk, 81
Dividend
  capital, cost of new common equities,
    148–149
  classical stock valuation, 129–132
  common equity, based on, 145–146
  perpetuity, 132–133
  preferred, 31, 33, 34, 144–145
Divisions, transfer pricing, 273–275
Driver, cost, 289–291
DRP. *See* Default risk premium
DSO. *See* Days sales outstanding
Dun & Bradstreet, 4, 22

E
Earnings
  ratio to share price (P/E ratio), 37–38
  restatements, 133
  stock valuation based on, 138–140
  before tax, 4
Earnings before interest and taxes (EBIT)
  defined, 3, 14
  interest coverage ratio, 46–47
  stock value based on, 138–140
Earnings before interest taxes depreciation
  and amortization (EBITDA), 137
Earnings before taxes (EBT), 3, 14
Earnings per share
  capital structure, 34–35
  fully diluted, 36
EBIT. *See* Earnings before interest and
  taxes
EBITDA. *See* Earnings before interest taxes
  depreciation and amortization
EBT. *See* Earnings before taxes
Elasticity, price, 270–272
Engineered cost, 269
Entity principle, 15
Equilibrium, 278–283
Equipment, leasing, 13

Equity
    balance sheet, 7
    debt ratio, cost of financing and, 152,
        154
    liabilities divided by, 45–46
    temporary accounts, 9
Equity risk premium (ERP), 84
Equity, shareholder. See Stocks
ERR. See Exchange rate risk
Errors
    bond market values, 110–111
    percentages, dealing with, 72
Estimates, interest rates components, 53–54
Evaluation methods, capital budgeting,
    166–167
Even payments over time. See Annuity
Exchange rate risk (ERR), 53
Exempt workers, 313
Expectations
    interest rate theory, 54–55
    standard deviations and forecasting,
        77–85
Expenses. See also Overhead
    defined, 2
    employees, unproductive, 24
    historical data, reporting, 15
    inventory versus, 197
    lease, allocating, 96
    operating leases, 119
    payroll, 295, 297–298
    product costing versus, 189–190
    temporary account, 9

F
Facility, opening new
    activity-based costing, 293
    cash budgeting, 221–226
Financial accounting
    full absorption costing, 190–191
    variable costing, 191–193
Financial ratios
    accounts payable turnover and days to
        pay, 26–28
    accounts receivable turnover, 25–26
    asset turnover ratio, 23–24
    inventory turnover and days in
        inventory, 28–29
    plant asset turnover, 29–30
    profit margin, 22–23
    return on assets, 20–22
    revenue per employee, 24–25

Financial statements
    balance sheet, 5–10
    cash flows, statement of, 10–13
    generally accepted accounting
        principles (GAAP), 14–17
    income, 1–5
    master budgets versus, 259–261
    profitability, 201–202
    publicly traded companies, obtaining,
        27
Financing
    leases
        amortization schedules, 96–97, 126
        balance, 6
        capital costs, 158, 159
        capitalizing, 125–128
        cash flow statements, 13
        deposits and prepayments, effect of,
            122–125
        interest rates, imputed, 120–122
        operating versus capital, 119–120
    line of credit, 47, 226–228
    loan amortization schedules, 96–97
    methods, profit margin and, 23
    payments, time value of money, 94–96
    seasonal cash demand, 228
Flexible budget. See Master budget
Flight to safety, 62–63
Flotation costs, 144
Forecasting
    interest rates, 54–55
    yield and risk, 67–86
Full absorption costing, See Absorption
    cost, full
Fully diluted earnings per share, 36
Fund raising, 51
Future value
    of an annuity, 87, 98–99
    mathematical formula, 99–100
    time value of money, 87, 88–89

G
General ledger
    accounts, listing, 14
    allowance for doubtful accounts, 42–43
    defined, 13
Generally accepted accounting principles
    (GAAP)
    comparability, 16
    conservatism, 15
    double entry system, 10

Generally accepted accounting principles
(GAAP) (*Cont.*)
  entity principle, 15
  expenses translated into inventory,
    197
  managerial accounting versus, 199–201
  master budgets, 260
  matching principle, 15–16
  materiality, 16–17
  objectivity, 15
  restatements, 133
  time periods, specific, 16
Gordon model
  company value based on cash flow,
    137
  cost of common equity, 145–146,
    148–149
  expected rate of return of stock, 136
  stock price, expected, 134
Gross margin
  described, 2–3, 4
  news products, selecting, 308, 309
  pricing and, 263, 266
  product costing, 189
Gross profit
  contribution versus, product costing,
    201–202
  defined, 1–2, 4
  new product selection, 308, 309
  pricing theory and, 271–272
Growth phase, product life cycle, 272
Growth rates
  classical stock valuation, 129, 131–132
  constant, computing stock value,
    133–134
  relevant range, planning and
    forecasting, 212

H
Historical data
  dividend yield, stock value and, 130–131
  revenue and expenses, 15
  yield and risk, forecasting, 75–77

I
Imperfect information, pricing theory,
  285–286
Income statement
  balance sheet and, 7, 8–10
  closing the books and, 5
  cost of goods sold, 3
  earnings before tax, 4
  gross margin, 4
  gross profit, 4
  net income, 4
  overhead, 4
  performance standards, 4–5
  taxes, 4
Inelastic demand, 270–271
Inflation, capital budgeting and, 185
Installation, capital budgets, 182
Interest coverage ratio, 47
Interest rates
  annuities, change in, 95
  bond values, discount rate versus,
    102–104
  convertible bonds, 106
  default risk premium (DRP), 52
  discount rate, 91
  estimating, 53–54
  forecasting, 54–55
  growth of sum of money, projecting,
    88–89
  imputed for leases, 120–122, 123
  line of credit, 226
  liquidity premium, 52
  maturity risk premium (MRP), 53
  rate of return, required, 52, 53
  supply and demand, effects of, 56–65
Internal rate of return (IRR), 160, 166,
  171–175, 179
International trade
  exchange rate risk (ERR), 53
  flight to safety, 62–63
Internet shopping, 267
Interpolation
  bond values, 114–116
  capital budgeting evaluation methods,
    177–178
Introduction phase, product life cycle, 272
Inventory
  appropriate levels of, 240–242
  balance sheet transactions, 9–10
  cash demand and, 238–239
  expenses versus, product costing, 197
  factory underutilization, reallocating,
    194
  overproduction, 202, 280
  production targets, exceeding, 195–196
  protecting, 43–44

sales forecasting and, 80
turnover and days in, ratios of, 28–29
working capital, 237–242
Investment
    capital budget format, 183
    portfolio theory, 81–85
    product selection, new, 308
IRR. *See* Internal rate of return

J
Job costing, 293–297
Joint products, 299–300
Journal entry, 8, 13–14

L
Labor costs
    cash budgeting, 218–221
    expense, reallocating to clients, 295
    master budgets, 260
    overhead, allocating, 297–298
    overtime, 313–315
    sales volume, increasing, 219–220
    transforming activities, 291–293
    turnover, 315–316
    unemployment compensation taxes,
        319–320
    workers' compensation, 316–319
Leases
    amortization schedules, 96–97, 126
    balance, 6
    capital costs, 158, 159
    capitalizing, 125–128
    cash flow statements, 13
    deposits and prepayments, effect of,
        122–125
    interest rates, imputed, 120–122
    operating versus capital, 119–120
Ledger
    accounts, listing, 14
    allowance for doubtful accounts, 42–43
    defined, 13
Liabilities
    balance sheet, 6
    current, 7–8, 38, 40
    debt equity ratio, 45–46
Limits, physical, 212
Linear programming, 300
Line of credit
    cash budgeting, 226–228
    interest coverage ratio, 47

Liquidity premium (LP), 52, 54
Loan amortization schedules, 96–97
Loan payments, time value of money,
    94–96
Loss prevention program, 317

M
Make decisions, product costing, 198–199
Management
    measurement of efficient, 20–22,
        32–34, 56
    overtime exemption, 313
Managerial accounting, 199–201
Manufacturing overhead
    constraints, theory of, 300–303
    cost drivers, 289–291, 297–298
    master budget, 257
    unallocated, product costing, 193–196
Marginal cost of capital, 158–160, 177
Margin, gross
    described, 2–3, 4
    new products, selecting, 308, 309
    pricing and, 263, 266
    product costing, 189
Market
    domination, opportunistic pricing, 276
    equity, compared to overall, 146–147
    pricing theory, 265–269
    product life cycle, 272–273
    risk, 81–82
    segmentation, 283–285
Market-clearing price, 278–283
Marketing costs. *See* Operating expenses
Master budget
    described, 251–252
    financial statements versus, 259–261
    supplemental, 261
Matching principle, 15–16
Materiality principle, 16–17
Mathematical formulas
    company value based on cash flow, 137
    cost of common equity, 145–146,
        148–149
    expected rate of return of stock, 136
    future value of an annuity, 99–100
    present value theory, time value of
        money and, 91–92
    stock price, expected, 134
Maturity phase, product life cycle, 272
Maturity risk premium (MRP), 53

Microeconomic pricing theory, 277–286
Modeling
  capital asset pricing model (CAPM), 84–85, 146–147, 149–151
  capital budgeting, 185–187
  cash budget, detailed, 222–224
  internal rate of return calculations, 175
  profit, break-even analysis, 208–210
Modified internal rate of return (MIRR), 166, 175–177, 179
MRP. See Maturity risk premium

N
Name, product. See Brands
Net income, 3. 4
Net present value (NPV), 166, 170–171, 179
Net working capital. See Working capital
New Jersey
  unemployment compensation, 319
  workers' compensation, 317–318
New product selection, 307–309
Nominal accounts, 9
Non-constant growth, computing stock value, 134–135
NPV. See Net present value

O
Objectivity principle, 15
Opening new facility
  activity-based costing, 293
  cash budgeting, 221–226
Operating budget
  described, 251–252
  financial statements versus, 259–261
  supplemental, 261
Operating expenses, 2. See also Overhead
Operating income
  defined, 3, 14
  interest coverage ratio, 46–47
  stock value based on, 138–140
Operating leases, capital versus, 119–120
Opportunistic pricing, 275–277
Opportunity costs, 182
Options, stock, 36
Overhead
  constraints, theory of, 300–303
  cost drivers as allocation method, 297–298
  defined, 3, 4

  incremental cost and, 200
  master budget, 257
  product selection, new, 308
  sales volume break-even, 210–212
  spreadsheet modeling, 185–187
  traditional allocation, 298–299
  unallocated costs, 194
Overproduction, 202
Overtime
  labor costs, 313–315
  workers' compensation costs, 317

P
Packaging, market segmentation, 284
Par value
  bond, 101–102
  stock, 31–32
Payback method, capital budgets, 166–167, 179
Payments
  early, leases, 122–125
  loan amortization, 96–97
Payroll
  cash budgeting, 218–221
  expense, reallocating to clients, 295
  master budgets, 260
  overhead, allocating, 297–298
P/E ratio. See Price/earnings ratio
Percentages, errors dealing with, 72
Perceptions, of value, 281
Performance measurements
  capital structure, 30–38
  financial ratios, 19–30
  risk measurement, 38–47
  standards, 4–5, 22
  weighted average cost of capital (WACC), 152
Period interest rate, 121
Perpetuity stock value, 132–133
Phases, capital budgeting, 183–185
Physical location, market segmentation, 284
Plant asset turnover, 29–30
Portfolio theory
  beta as a measure of risk, 81–82
  capital asset pricing model (CAPM), 84–85
  risk, 82–83
  yield, 83–84
Predicting. See Forecasting

Preferred stock
  capital, cost of, 144–145, 156
  dividends, 31, 33, 34
Prepayment, lease, 122–125
Present value
  of an annuity, 94
  of a bond, 102
  of deposit on a lease, 123
  mathematical formula, 87, 91–92, 98
  tables, 92–94
Present value interest factor (PVIF) table,
  92–94
Price/earnings (P/E) ratio, 37–38
Price equilibrium, 278–283
Price pressure, 185
Prices, setting
  activity-based costing, 292
  consumer surplus, 282–283
  cost-centered, 263–265
  elasticity, 270–272
  engineered cost, 269
  market-centered, 265–269
  master budgets, 253–259
  microeconomics, 277–286
  opportunistic pricing, 275–277
  product costing and, 189, 215
  product life cycle, 272–273
  sales volume and, 209
  transfer pricing, 273–275
Probability
  break-even forecasting, 215
  normal distribution curve, 77
Product
  differentiation, 281–282
  life cycle, 272–273
  market segmentation, 283–285
Product costing
  cost versus expense, 189–190
  expenses verus inventory, 197
  financial accounting, managerial
    accounting versus, 190–193
  gross profit versus contribution,
    201–202
  joint, 299–300
  make or buy decisions, 198–199
  managerial accounting, 199–201
  manufacturing overhead, unallocated,
    193–196
  purchased merchandise, full absorption
    cost, 197–198
  re-engineering, 215

Production overhead
  constraints, theory of, 300–303
  cost drivers, 289–291, 297–298
  master budget, 257
  unallocated, product costing, 193–196
Production targets, exceeding
  gross profit, 202
  manufacturing overhead, unallocated,
    195–196
Professional services, 293–294, 313
Profit
  basic budget variances, 253, 256
  financial ratios, 22–23
  gross
    contribution versus, product
      costing, 201–202
    defined, 1–2, 4
    new product selection, 308, 309
    pricing theory and, 271–272
  modeling, break-even analysis, 205–210
  opportunistic pricing, 275
  pricing theory and, 263–264
  retained earnings, 5, 32
  as a source of cash, 11
  transfer pricing, 273–275
Profit ladder, 303–307
Purchased merchandise, 197–198
Purchases
  computing from financial statements,
    27, 244
  master budgeting discrepancies,
    260–261
PVIF table. *See* Present value interest factor
  table

Q
Quality, brands, 285–286

R
Rate of return
  expected for stock, 136
  internal rate of return (IRR), 160, 166,
    171–175, 179
  modified internal rate of return (MIRR),
    166, 175–177, 179
  required, 53, 84–85, 102, 104
Ratios
  accounts payable turnover and days to
    pay, 26–28

Ratios (*Cont.*)
  accounts receivable turnover, 25–26
  assets turnover, 23–24
  debt to equity, 152, 154
  interest coverage, 46–47
  inventory turnover and days in
    inventory (DII), 28–29
  performance standards, published, 4
  plant asset turnover, 29–30
  price/earnings (P/E), 37–38
  profit margin, 22–23
  return on assets, 20–22
  revenue per employee, 24–25
  working capital, 217–218
Raw materials, purchasing, 240
Reality testing, 212–213
Relevant market, 266–268
Relevant range, break-even analysis, 212
Rent. *See* Overhead
Replacement equipment, 185
Required rate of return, 53, 84–85, 102, 104
Reserves, accounts receivable, 42
Resources, theory of constraints, 300–303
Retained earnings, 32, 145
Return on assets (ROA)
  demand for capital, 56
  financial ratios, 20–22
  return on common shareholder's
    equity, relation between, 32–34
Return on common shareholder's equity
  (ROCE)
  capital structure, 31–32
  increasing through debt, 34
Revenue
  incremental, cost versus, 200
  marginal, 209
  matching to producing costs, 15–16
  per employee ratio, 24–25
  spreadsheet modeling, 185–187
  temporary account, 9
Risk
  aged accounts receivable, reviewing,
    41–42
  break-even analysis and, 213–216
  cash flow from operations versus
    current liabilities, 44–45
  credit analysis, customers, 246–247
  current ratio, 38–41
  doubtful accounts, allowance for, 42–43
  equity capital, cost of, 147
  expansion periods, 225

  long-term measures of liquidity risk,
    45–47
  portfolio yield, 82–84
  quick ratio, 43–44
  ratios, cautions about, 47
Risk-free rate of return, 52, 102
ROA. *See* Return on assets
Robert Morris Associates (RMA), 4, 22
ROCE/ROE. *See* Return on common
  shareholder's equity

S
Salaries. *See* Labor costs
Sales
  credit, collection of, 25–26
  opportunistic pricing, 275–277
  stock valuation based on, 140–141
  yield and risk forecasting with
    statistics, 79–80
Sales commission, 293
Sales costs. *See* Operating expenses
Sales volume
  break-even analysis, 210–212
  labor, adding, 219–220
  master budgets, 254, 258
  product selection, new, 308
  seasonal cash demands, 228–230
Salvage, 183
Scrap, 314
Seasonal cash demand, 228–230
Securities and Exchange Commission, 247
Shares. *See* Stocks
Shipping, 182
Shortages, 279, 280–281
SIC. *See* Standard industry classification code
SKU. *See* Stockkeeping unit
Small businesses, 15
Spread, 60–61
Spreadsheet modeling
  capital budgeting, 185–187
  cash budget, detailed, 222–224
  internal rate of return calculations, 175
Standard deviation
  defined, 67
  and expected values, making decisions
    with, 77–85
  with historical data, forecasting, 75
  with a priori probabilities, forecasting,
    68, 70, 71
Standard industry classification (SIC) code,
  4, 139

Stock at par, 31–32
Stockkeeping unit (SKU), 240–242
Stock, physical. *See* Inventory
Stocks
    balance sheet, 7
    cost of issuing, 145–151
    preferred
        capital, cost of, 144–145, 156
        dividends, 31, 33, 34
    return on common shareholder's equity
        (ROCE), 31–34
    valuing
        capital gains yield, 132
        cash flow, 136–138
        computing, 132–135
        definitions, 130
        dividend yield, 130–131
        earnings, 138–140
        internal rate of return (IRR),
            comparing, 175
        portfolio theory, 81–85
        preferred, cost of, 144–145, 156
        sales, 140–141
        total return, 132
        yield, 136
Store, opening new
    activity-based costing, 293
    cash budgeting, 221–226
Subassemblies, purchasing, 198–199
Subcontractors, 304–305, 307, 314
Substitution effect
    price elasticity, 277
    product differentiation, 281–282
Sunk costs, 181–182
Supplemental budgets, 261
Supply
    changes, effect on interest rates,
        62–64
    microeconomics pricing theory, 278
    strategic implications of,
        microeconomics pricing theory,
        280–281
Surpluses, 278

T
Tables
    future value interest factor (FVIF),
        88–89
    future value interest factor for an
        annuity (FVIFA), 326–327

present value (PV), 92–94
present value interest factor for an
    annuity (PVIFA), 330–331
time value of money, 88
T-account, 294
Taxes
    assets, co-mingling, 15
    capital budgets, 182
    debt capital, real cost and, 143–144, 154
    evaluating companies independent of
        strategy, 14
    income statements, 3, 4
    interest, effect of, 20–21, 23
    preferred dividends, 31
    transfer pricing, 275
    unemployment compensation, 319–320
Temporary accounts, 9
Terminal cash flow, 184
Time periods, specific
    generally accepted accounting
        principles (GAAP), 16
    maturity risk premium (MRP), 53
Times interest earned, 47
Time value of money
    annuities, 94, 98–100
    classes, 87–88
    discounted payback method of capital
        projects, 168–178
    future value, 88–89
    future value of an annuity, 87, 98–99
    loan amortization schedules, 96–97
    loan payments, 94–96
    payback method of capital projects, 167
    present value, 91–92
    present value of an annuity, 94
Total return, stock, 132
Trade, international. *See* International trade
Transfer pricing, 273–275
Treasury bills (T-bills), 51, 52, 53, 54–55,
    102
Trial balance, 14
Turnover cost, labor, 315–316

U
Underutilization, factory, 194
Underwriters, 149–150
Unemployment compensation taxes,
    319–320
U.S. Department of Commerce, 4, 22
U.S. Treasury bills, 51, 52, 53, 54–55, 102

V
Value
    brands, 285–286
    customer perceptions of, 281
    market-centered pricing theory,
        268–269
Value Line, 37
variable costing, 191–193
Volume changes, pricing and, 271–272

W
Warrants, 36
Weighted average cost of capital (WACC),
    143, 151–154
Workers' compensation, 316–319
Working capital
    accounts payable, 242–247
    accounts receivable, 230–237
    balance sheet, 7–8
    common stock, issuing, 154
    described, 182–183, 217–218
    inventory, 237–242

World trade. *See* International trade

Y
Years, annuity payments, 95
Yield
    bond values, 107–113
    forecasting
        with historical data, 75–77
        normal distribution curve and Z
            table, 77–79
        portfolio theory, 80–85
        with a priori (determined in
            advance) possibilities, 68–75
        required rate of return, using, 85
        sales forecasting with statistics,
            79–80
    stock valuation, 136

Z
Z table, 77–79

David E. Vance, MBA, CPA, JD, is an instructor in the MBA program at Rutgers University School of Business, where he teaches graduate and undergraduate courses on topics including managerial accounting, financial management, and financial markets and institutions. He is also director of executive development for the William G. Rohrer Center for Management and Entrepreneurship.